Language, Charisma, and Creativity

Language, Charisma, and Creativity

The Ritual Life of a Religious Movement

Thomas J. Csordas

UNIVERSITY OF CALIFORNIA PRESS

Berkeley / Los Angeles / London

University of California Press
Berkeley and Los Angeles, California

University of California Press
London, England

Copyright © 1997 by The Regents of the University of California

Library of Congress Cataloging-in-Publication Data
Language, charisma, and creativity: the ritual life of a religious
    movement / Thomas J. Csordas.
        p.   cm.
    Includes bibliographical references and index.
    ISBN 0–520–20469–7 (cloth: alk. paper)
    1. Pentecostalism—Catholic Church—History.   2. Pente-
costalism—United States—History.   3. United States—
Church history—20th century.   I. Csordas, Thomas J.
BX2350.57.L35   1996
282'.73'09045—dc20   95–50992
                                                              CIP

Printed in the United States of America

1 2 3 4 5 6 7 8 9

The paper used in this publication meets the minimum requirements
of American National Standard for Information Sciences—Perma-
nence of Paper for Printed Library Materials, ANSI Z39.48–1984 ⊗

For JJ, the most

Contents

Illustrations

A photographic insert appears on pages 97–99.

Tables

Preface

As life moves, persuasion moves with it and indeed helps to move it. More bluntly, whatever God may or may not be—living, dead, or merely ailing—religion is a social institution, worship a social activity, and faith a social force. To trace the pattern of their changes is neither to collect relics of revelation nor to assemble a chronicle of error. It is to write a social history of the imagination.

Clifford Geertz

If the thoughtful attitude toward the place of religion in contemporary life was summed up in the first half of the twentieth century by Sigmund Freud's phrase "the future of an illusion," the corresponding phrase for the second half century has been Peter Berger's "a rumor of angels." Differences among Christians, Jews, Moslems, and Hindus are as salient today as they have ever been, and even the exclusive club of the "world religions" is facing the prospect of admitting the globally dynamic Yoruba religion as a new member. That religious consciousness is not merely persistent but resurgent should be no surprise, for religion has always been one of the defining features of the human world. Just as we have been characterized as *Homo sapiens*, *Homo faber*, *Homo hierarchicus*, *Homo loquax*, or *Homo ludens*, we have also rightly been called *Homo religiosus*.

In the above epigraph Geertz offers a pragmatic program for understanding *Homo religiosus* by identifying religion with persuasion and imagination. Persuasion establishes those perduring moods and motivations that Geertz in his well-known definition of religion has identified so lucidly; imagination refers to the human capacity to constitute and inhabit multiple realities. The trajectory of this book is toward reformulating the general "what" represented in my title by language and creativity into the specific "how" of persuasion and imagination. Across this trajectory charisma is a middle term made necessary by the kind of episode in the social history of the imagination I will examine and made problematic by my particular claim about the way it is a function of language and creativity.

This book addresses language, charisma, and creativity via the empirical example of a contemporary religious movement known as Catholic Pentecostalism, or the Catholic Charismatic Renewal. How do these theoretical issues take into account the significance of a "rumor of angels" in the bosom of what still portrays itself as a secular, scientific society? In this context, to take a close look at a contemporary religious movement such as the Catholic Charismatic Renewal is to embrace one of the primary tasks of anthropology as a scholarly discipline committed to critical thought: to stimulate reflection by making the exotic seem familiar and the familiar appear strange.[1] In an instance like ours, this is more complex than it at first appears. Unlike anthropological studies of distant tribal societies, where the reciprocal movement between familiar and strange ideally occurs simultaneously as a consequence of the ethnographic portrayal of the cultural "other," our task includes showing that people who might be regarded by many as "religious weirdos" are quite like ourselves, and at the same time that people who might be our neighbors in fact inhabit a substantially different phenomenological world. In addition (though it is also increasingly the case of ethnographies in Third World settings), a text such as this is easily available to participants in the religious movement, and for them what is already familiar can be rendered challengingly strange by the relativizing style of ethnographic writing.

Moreover, by a curious twist, this relativizing style renders itself strange (and the ethnographer along with it) when applied to a cultural phenomenon that is so close to home yet so puzzling within the cultural context of academic anthropologists. I am thinking here of the convention in ethnographic prose of describing religious ritual and spiritual phenomena in straightforward declarative language: "The spirit speaks through the medium," or "The deity is propitiated by sacrifice," or again "The deceased becomes an ancestral spirit that is responsible for the well-being of the clan." I have adopted this declarative convention in writing and speaking about Charismatics, with the surprisingly frequent result that I am myself suspected of being a "believer." I am not at all concerned here with the question of whether one can be a believer and still be a good anthropologist. I am concerned instead with an observation that to me is quite ironic: that what is strange in a familiar way (because it is part of one's culture) can render what is familiar (in this case a convention of ethnographic prose) strangely difficult to recognize as such.

The question of whether a religious movement like the Charismatic Renewal is strange or familiar to begin with has a temporal dimension as well. "Conservative Christianity" is a media phenomenon even for those who know little about its specifics. Yet beyond this level of popular cultural representation is a more everyday kind of familiarity. When I first began studying this particular movement in 1973—only six years after its inception—anyone who asked me seriously what I was working on listened to fifteen minutes of background discourse before responding that they'd never heard of such a thing. By the early nineties it was more typical, after mentioning that I had studied the Charismatic Renewal, to get a response like "Oh, my aunt is part of that," or "My mother tried to get me to go to a prayer meeting once."

Finally, the very fact of having been concerned with cultural analysis of the Catholic Charismatic Renewal for twenty years has created the additional consequence of rendering the phenomenon strangely familiar to me, the ethnographer. It is a feature of my intellectual biography, and the ethnographic encounter culminating in the text I present here has inevitably been transposed across a variety of theoretical developments in anthropology during that period. These twenty-odd years span a shift in the very idea of temporality in anthropological work, from an approach that might conceive this period as an example of "long-term field research" (Foster et al. 1979) that deepens and intensifies anthropological knowledge in a cumulative fashion to one that bears the dual injunction to account reflexively for temporality and history in our analytic construction of the ethnographic object and to explicitly recognize the autobiographical element in ethnographic writing (Fabian 1983). Likewise there is a substantial difference among the research agendas summarized by phrases such as religion and social change, movement dynamics, or revitalization movements in the 1960s and early 1970s and those defined by notions of performance theory, interpretation, hermeneutics, and phenomenology from the mid-1970s

through the 1980s. Again, my encounter with this empirical phenomenon spans the period in which the modernization theory dominant
through the early 1970s has been deconstructed by the postmodern
decentering of meaning and the awareness of globalization in the 1980s
and early 1990s. My point here is not to suggest that I am offering a
synthesis of all these approaches, but more modestly to acknowledge
that various insights and passages reflect various periods of my theoretical development as well as of my ethnographic encounter. I would
argue that there is nothing inconsistent in this, any more than it is inconsistent to acknowledge the existence of a postmodern condition of
culture (which I do) while demurring from the impulse to write a
postmodernist ethnographic text (which I also do).

   Given these considerations it is incumbent upon me to specify the
method of my ethnographic investigation over this twenty-year period.
In 1973, having been discouraged by a senior anthropologist from a
plan to study a Native American religious movement, I decided to determine what might be afoot among Euro-American Christians. In a
Christian bookstore I came across an intriguing little book with the apparently oxymoronic title *Catholic Pentecostals,* and soon began a study
of the Catholic Charismatic Renewal in Columbus, Ohio. At the time
in that city there were about half a dozen "prayer groups," most based
in local parishes. I concentrated on the social organization and ritual
life of the largest among them, while attending as well to their differences, the degree of organization by which they were linked to
one another, and their links to the non-Catholic Pentecostal and neo-
Pentecostal communities in the metropolitan area. During this early
period I was aware that these groups were part of a larger "movement" through their circulation of published literature, cassette tapes,
and their own magazines. The importance of the movement as such
was highlighted for me when at the end of this field period I attended
the movement's 1974 "national conference" where I observed twenty-
five thousand people enthusiastically gathered for a large rally in the
football stadium of Notre Dame University.

   Nevertheless, when I began a second period of fieldwork, from
1976 to 1979, for my doctoral dissertation, I returned first to the
group in Columbus. I found that a highly active core group of participants was increasingly attracted to what was already the largest
community within the movement, The Word of God in Ann Arbor,
Michigan. On a visit there with several Charismatic friends from the
Columbus group (who eventually moved to Ann Arbor), one of The

Word of God leaders, called head coordinators, suggested that I should come there—the "center" of the movement—if I wanted to get a full understanding of Charismatic life. Taking advantage of this opportunity meant submitting a proposal to the community's coordinators concerning my interests. One among them was assigned to arrange interview appointments with community members and officials and for me to live for a week in one of the community "households." I was also given access to the community library with its archive of audiotapes of community gatherings and ritual events, from which the bulwark prophecies analyzed in chapter 7 were transcribed.

These experiences led me to problematize anew the sense in which the Catholic Charismatic Renewal could be characterized as a movement. To what extent was it accurate to say that the movement had a center, no center, or multiple centers? Certainly it did not appear to have a single "charismatic leader" as one would expect from the sociological literature deriving from Max Weber. To what extent was it homogeneous as opposed to being separated into regional branches or ideological factions? How could one account for the evident internationalization of the movement as it spread beyond its North American point of origin? What were the scope and nature of this religious phenomenon as an episode in the social history of the imagination?

These questions were evidently not being posed in the small but focused literature that was appearing on the movement, which even when acknowledging the existence of different orientations within it, adopted methods biased toward the perception of homogeneity. These methods were of two types. The first was a statistical homogeneity present in the work of quantitative sociologists who, while selecting groups from different regions or localities, did not distinguish among them (Fichter 1975; Mawn 1975; Bord and Faulkner 1975); this was the homogeneity of the representative sample. The second was a parochial homogeneity present in the work of qualitative anthropologists and sociologists who based their studies on individual groups and communities or on several groups in a particular metropolitan area (Lane 1976, 1978; Hegy 1978; McGuire 1976; Westley 1977; Chagnon 1979; McGuire 1975a, 1982; Neitz 1987); this was the homogeneity of the exemplary community that was also characteristic of my own first study. The Word of God community had also drawn some attention, mostly from the students of the anthropologist Roy Rappaport and the sociologist Max Hirek at the University of Michigan (Harrison 1974a, 1974b, 1975; Keane 1974; and Jeanne Lewis 1995), but primarily as an intentional community in its own right and not with respect to its place within a movement. Something more of an effort to deal with the movement as such in the United States was undertaken by Richard Bord and Joseph Faulkner (1983), who combined a survey study of groups across the country with a closer study of The Word of God community, and Margaret Poloma (1982), whose work begins to capture some of the internal diversity within the movement and devotes much more attention to published sources and documents from the movement than does my ethnographic approach. Thus, with the intent of contributing a more comprehensive perspective from an anthropological standpoint, by the end of this field period I had visited fifteen groups in Ohio, Michigan, Indiana, New York, Pennsylvania, Massachusetts, Rhode Island, Maryland, and North Carolina and gathered additional information about other groups in the United States and abroad. I also subscribed to the newsletters published by the movement's National Service Committee in South Bend, Indiana, and by the International Catholic Charismatic Renewal Office in Rome, Italy (see Csordas 1980, 1983, 1987, 1992 for some of the results from work of this period).

The next period of field research was from 1986 to 1989, when I worked primarily in southeastern New England with a focus on therapeutic process in Charismatic ritual healing (Csordas 1988, 1990a, 1990b, 1993, 1994a). I opened this period with another visit to a national conference, this time in New Orleans and with interdenominational (or ecumenical, as some say) Charismatic participation. Throughout this period I renewed my knowledge of ritual life and the course of the movement during the decade of the 1980s. I revisited several communities from my earlier study, including The Word of God, where I again interviewed leaders and stayed with friends who had been patiently answering my questions since the days they were leaders of the prayer group in Columbus.

The final phase of research was in 1991, when, realizing that The Word of God was well into its second generation, I conceived a study of moral development among community children and adolescents.[2] In the process of arranging for my research assistant to work within the community interviewing teachers, parents, and children, I became aware that major changes in group life had occurred within the past year. We broadened the focus of our work to include these changes and their implications for an understanding of the movement as a whole. This is where my account ends, though it hardly needs saying that we have not had the last word on the Catholic Charismatic Renewal.

It also need not be said that a claim to comprehensiveness with respect either to diversity or to history in a religious phenomenon of the magnitude of the Catholic Charismatic Renewal is eminently futile. There is no disguising the tension between my effort to understand the movement and the need to fall back on more familiar local exemplars such as The Word of God. Methodologically, this tension reflects the struggle of anthropology to move from community-based studies to an understanding of global social and cultural processes. There is another tension inherent in my attempt to spin out the relationship between ritual performance and everyday practice as functions of language, charisma, and creativity. This stems from the methodological difficulty of observing everyday practice in a society such as ours where, in contrast to the anthropologist's traditional "village" research locale, workplaces are dispersed and households are relatively inaccessible to the outsider. This is compounded in tightly structured communities such as The Word of God where access to everyday life is by consent of authorities and is in addition subject to explicit codes of appropriateness vis-à-vis communication with outsiders. In short, the reader will find fewer of the intimate interactional vignettes than is customary in ethnography, since with the diminished opportunity to observe everyday behavior more of the data necessarily consist of interviews and observation of ritual.[3]

In Part One, the first chapter introduces the Charismatic Renewal and surveys its development, first within the Euro-American United States, then cross-culturally and internationally. The account is more descriptive than analytical, and it is intended to convey a sense of the scope and internal diversity of the phenomenon that is the Catholic Charismatic Renewal. Chapter 2 is a more concentrated attempt to place the movement in its cultural historical context given the contemporary postmodern condition of culture, with emphasis on the contemporary nature of rationality, the question of identity as a Charismatic, and the transformation of space and time in Charismatic daily life. I examine the Renewal as a "movement," arguing that this is an obvious but also a problematic theoretical category under which to subsume the phenomenon, and introducing a distinction between religions of peoples and religions of the self.

Part Two presents a thesis ascribing the performative generation of diversity within the movement to a dual process of rhetorical

involution characterized by the ritualization of practice and the radicalization of charisma. This thesis is elaborated through an account of
what is, within the Charismatic world, the largest and most renowned
and at the same time the most controversial of Catholic Charismatic
communities, The Word of God/Sword of the Spirit. Chapter 3 combines a historical sketch of the community's development and an ethnographic sketch of its organization. Chapter 4 examines the dual processes of radicalization of charisma and ritualization of practice within
the community over the course of more than two decades. Special attention is given to gender discipline and the ritual enactment of key
psychocultural themes of spontaneity, intimacy, and control.

Chapter 5 is an interlude between those chapters that problematize
movement and community and those that more explicitly problematize language and creativity. It juxtaposes material from The Word of
God, Melanesian cargo cults, the African Jamaa movement, and the
sixteenth-century movement of Savonarola to point toward a rhetorical theory of charisma grounded in performance. I propose that charisma is a self process the locus of which is not the personality of a
charismatic leader but the rhetorical resources mobilized among participants in ritual performance.

The two chapters of Part Three show how charisma operates as a
collective self process by examining the performance of ritual language.
Chapter 6 demonstrates the creativity of ritual performance, adopting a methodological distinction among event, genre, and act. I describe an intrinsic dialectic between ritual event and everyday life, between genres of ritual language and the motives or terms that are
circulated among participants in performance, and between individual
terms and the metaphors generated from them. Chapter 7 examines
the ritual genre of prophecy, starting with a semiotic analysis of an
important Charismatic prophetic text. This analysis uncovers the rhetorical conditions for the radicalization of charisma that we earlier
encountered in covenant community life at The Word of God. I then
present a phenomenological account of speaking and hearing prophecy and a comparison of prophecy with glossolalia. I suggest that the
existential force of prophecy stems from the sense in which all language can be understood as an aspect of bodily experience, which in
turn proves to be the ground of all experience of force. As a self process, charisma thus appears to be equally a function of textuality and
embodiment.

Chapter 8, a theoretical epilogue written in light of the foregoing discussion of Catholic Charismatic ritual life, foregrounds the anthropological debate about creativity in ritual performance. I examine this issue by comparing the work of Stanley Tambiah and Maurice Bloch, two prominent anthropologists who take contrasting stances on the problem of creativity. The chapter concludes with a summary of how a sacred self is created in practice and performance.

I have been asked on several occasions, including by the scholars who reviewed this book for publication, how the work presented here is related to my earlier volume, *The Sacred Self: A Cultural Phenomenology of Charismatic Healing*. To say that the first book treats the movement's healing system while the present one treats the movement as a whole is accurate, but superficial. Although each volume stands independently, there are between them both elements of a common intellectual agenda and elements of theoretical tension. An initial tension, implicit in the differential focus on "healing" and "movement," is apparent between individual and collective processes, and this tension further implies a distinction between a psychological and a social approach to culture. In principle I mistrust such a distinction, just as I have argued that preobjective bodily experience, the existential ground upon which distinctions between subject and object or mind and body are drawn, is the most productive starting point for cultural analysis (Csordas 1990a, 1994). In this respect I have attempted to use central concepts such as self, habitus, performance, experience, and the sacred consistently across both volumes, in ways that privilege neither an individualist nor a collectivist interpretation.

In other instances, there is a more psychological or sociological emphasis to my use of key terms. In *The Sacred Self*, for example, I discuss imagination predominantly as sensory imagery and secondarily as a feature of a collective habitus, whereas in the present work I have invoked Geertz's notion of a social history of the imagination, though including a description of the individual experience of prophetic imagery. Again, I address the notion of creativity in ritual explicitly here, though in fact it has appeared in other terms in my earlier discussions of therapeutic process, transformation, and healing.

Finally, there are certain themes I take up here that would have been difficult to address in *The Sacred Self*, such as the theory of charisma and the postmodern condition of culture. Conversely, in the earlier work my debt to phenomenology was more evident, as was my effort to problematize the relation between phenomenology and semiotics. Again, in principle I would not align phenomenology exclusively with individual experience and semiotics with collective representation. Maurice Merleau-Ponty (1962), from my standpoint the leading phenomenological theorist, was himself convinced that a phenomenology grounded in embodiment could be the starting point for the broader analysis of culture and history. From the other side, scholars like Gananath Obeyesekere (1981) have pointed us toward personal as well as collective meanings of cultural symbols. Yet despite persistence of the notion of habitus as a nexus of bodily practice and symbolic representation, there is in the present book a relative deemphasis on bodily experience and perception, on the one hand, and greater emphasis on language and everyday practice, on the other. In any case, I have ended with two separate volumes, and the reader of the present one is hardly required to undertake the methodological exercise of integrating their arguments about the Charismatic Renewal or about culture theory.

Acknowledgments

This book has been in the making my entire academic career. As an undergraduate I discovered the existence of the Charismatic Renewal as a cultural and religious phenomenon, and Erika Bourguignon both supported my idea to study the movement and pointed out that I could find Charismatics practicing not far away.

As a graduate student I had the ideal mentors in James Boon and Charles Long, who nurtured my theoretical development in anthropology and history of religions, and for whose loyal support at a difficult moment in my intellectual life I continue to have the deepest gratitude. From Edward Tiryakian I learned more of the sociology of religion, from Weston LaBarre more of psychoanalytic anthropology, from William O'Barr more of sociolinguistics, and from Lawrence Rosen more of symbolic anthropology than I ever could have without their teaching. Roy Rappaport, through a combination of personal warmth and interest in the relation between religion and language, offered both intellectual and moral support during this early work.

A decade later, intellectual and institutional support from Arthur Kleinman, Leon Eisenberg, Byron Good, Mary-Jo DelVecchio Good, Elliot Mishler, and Janis Jenkins sustained me during a second extended period of fieldwork among the Charismatics. Each of these colleagues and mentors has contributed an element of their own inspiration and passion to my work. Graduate students John Garrity, Sue Wasserkrug, and Elisa Gordon helped with various tasks in creating the present volume. At the University of California Press, Stanley

Holwitz, Michelle Nordon, Sheila Berg, and Diana Feinberg transformed the book into a reality.

I am grateful to the many participants in the Catholic Charismatic Renewal who gave their time and thoughtful reflection on their own practices, and trust that in their deep faith they will recognize themselves through the filter of anthropological consciousness. Especially worthy of note are those leaders of The Word of God community who gave me access to community life and supported my work in its various stages, including Bert Ghezzi, Bob Morris, Jim MacFadden, Marty Javornisky, and Phil Tiews.

My greatest debt and most profound thanks are due to Janis Jenkins, whose warmth, energy, and insight are the pillar of my intellectual life and the cornerstone of my existence, and to whom this book is lovingly dedicated.

Some of the material in chapter 1 on the movement's international expansion has previously appeared in "Oxymorons and Short-Circuits in the Re-Enchantment of the World: The Case of the Catholic Charismatic Renewal," *Etnofoor* 8 (1995): 5–26. Elements of the argument in chapter 2 appeared in "Religion and the World System: The Pentecostal Ethic and the Spirit of Monopoly Capital," *Dialectical Anthropology* 17 (1992): 3–24. Portions of chapter 6 on the major genres of ritual language appeared in "Genre, Motive, and Metaphor: Conditions for Creativity in Ritual Language," *Cultural Anthropology* 2 (1987): 445–469. The discussion of glossolalia in chapter 7 is adapted from a similar discussion in "Embodiment as a Paradigm for Anthropology," *Ethos* 18 (1990): 5–47, and parts of chapter 7 on the "bulwark prophecies" appear in "Prophecy and the Performance of Metaphor," *American Anthropologist,* in press. Various stages of the research were supported by a graduate school grant from Duke University; National Institute of Mental Health grant MH40473 on "The Ethnography of Therapeutic Process in Religious Healing"; and a grant from the Armington Research Program on Values in Children of Case Western Reserve University on "The Development of Values in Conservative Christian Children."

PART ONE

Meaning and Movement

1

Building the Kingdom

The Catholic Charismatic Renewal has never had a single identifiable charismatic leader in the Weberian sense, although among the movement elite there exists an informal hierarchy of charismatic renown based on reputation for evangelism, healing, or local community leadership. Neither has the movement had a dramatic history, although there have been apocalyptic moments, periods of internal tension and ideological split, and the occasional intrigue of high Church politics. It is certainly a phenomenon with roots in both Pentecostal and Catholic traditions, as well as a phenomenon with distinct local and global manifestations.[1] To begin, then, we will aim for a sense of the Catholic Charismatic Renewal as a social and cultural phenomenon, a "movement," with the caveat that by the next chapter it will become necessary to problematize the very concept of movement.

Indeed, from the "indigenous" standpoint, Charismatics themselves have occasionally resisted describing the Renewal as a movement. They have often qualified the notion, sometimes emphasizing that theirs is a movement "of the Spirit" in the sense that it is inspired by and belongs to the deity, at other times insisting that it is a "movement" of the Spirit in the sense that what is moving is the Holy Spirit itself. In this latter sense the Renewal is not really a sociocultural phenomenon at all, but strictly a spiritual one. From the standpoint of anthropological theory, in recent years it has become clear that the standard paradigm for understanding social and religious "movements" faces problems in at least three respects: its conception of movements as discrete entities rather than as phenomena characteristic or diagnostic of the cultures in which they are spawned; its ability to account for meaning in addition to causality and social dynamics of movements; and its assumption that the categorical subjects of movements are not necessarily only peoples, populations, or social types but indeterminate selves in a process of reorientation and transformation. We will return to these issues in the next chapter, but to sustain that discussion we must first survey the diversity among manifestations of the Catholic Charismatic Renewal first in its country of origin, the United States, then globally.

The United States

The year commonly accepted as the beginning of the movement is 1967. During a retreat at Duquesne University (the "Duquesne Weekend"), a group of students and young faculty members experienced the spiritual awakening of Baptism in the Holy Spirit through the influence of Protestant Pentecostals. They soon shared their experience with like-minded students at Notre Dame and Michigan State universities. Although on occasion one can hear individuals claim that they individually or with a small prayer group prayed in tongues before or independently of this point, the narrative of origin among this relatively young, well-educated, and all-male group is standard. It has consistently been recounted as a kind of just-so story in greater or lesser detail by virtually all social science authors who have addressed the movement (Fichter 1975; Mawn 1975; K. McGuire 1976; M. McGuire 1982; Neitz 1987; Bord and Faulkner 1983; Poloma 1982), while for some among the movement's adherents it has attained the status of an origin myth. The new "Catholic Pentecostals" claimed to offer a unique spiritual experience to individuals and promised a dramatic renewal of Church life based on a born-again spirituality of "personal relationship" with Jesus and direct access to divine power and inspiration through a variety of "spiritual gifts," or "charisms." The movement attracted a strong following among relatively well educated, middle-class suburban Catholics (Mawn 1975; Fichter 1975; McGuire 1982; Neitz 1987; Poloma 1982). Since its inception it has spread throughout the world wherever there are Catholics.

In the United States, development of the Catholic Charismatic Renewal can be roughly divided into stages:

1) Prior to 1967 Catholics who underwent the Pentecostal experience of Baptism in the Holy Spirit often were persuaded by their Protestant mentors that Catholicism and Pentecostalism were incompatible, and frequently left the Catholic church.

2) From 1967 to 1970 Catholic Pentecostalism was a collection of small, personalistic prayer groups emphasizing spontaneity in worship and interpersonal relations, loosely organized via networks of personal contacts, and not fully differentiated from other associations such as the Cursillo movement. Protestant Pentecostals and nondenominational neo-Pentecostals remained a strong influence.

3) From 1970 to 1975 the renamed Catholic Charismatic Renewal underwent rapid institutionalization and consolidation of a lifestyle including collective living in "covenant communities," distinctive forms of ritual, and a specialized language of religious experience. Prayer groups and covenant communities were often composed of both Catholic and Protestant members, though the leadership was predominantly Catholic.

4) From 1975 to the end of the decade the movement entered an apocalyptic phase, based on prophetic revelation that "hard times" were imminent for Christians. Many covenant communities saw their form of life as essential for coping with the coming trials, and a split occurred in the leadership between those who held that the prayer group is a separate type of Charismatic organization with its own role and those who held that it was an initial stage in a necessary development toward a full-scale covenant community.[2] In general, leaders attempted both to influence the direction of the Catholic church and to maintain an ecumenical outlook, while the Charismatic Renewal progressively attained international scope.

5) The 1980s brought recognition by movement leaders that its growth in the U.S. had dramatically decreased. They also saw an increasingly clear divergence between Charismatics gathered into tightly structured intentional communities who wanted to preserve the earlier sense of apocalyptic mission and those who remained active in less overtly communitarian parochial prayer groups. A second split occurred, this time among covenant communities themselves, over issues of government and authority, as well as over relations to the larger movement and the Church as a whole. By the mid-1980s both streams of the movement had initiated evangelization efforts directed as much at their less committed or

flagging Charismatic brethren as at the unconverted.[3] Also in the 1980s, a new wave of Protestant influence was introduced with the rising popularity of so-called Third Wave Pentecostal evangelists.

6) By the late 1980s and early 1990s some among the communitarians considered themselves a distinct movement. Among the parochially oriented stream, Catholic identity became heightened as fewer groups cultivated combined Protestant and Catholic "ecumenical" memberships and as the Church took a more active supervisory role. Meanwhile, boundaries between Charismatics and conventional Catholics became more ambiguous, as many who no longer attended regular prayer meetings remained active in their parishes and as many Catholics with no other Charismatic involvement became attracted to large public healing services conducted by Charismatics.

From its earliest days the movement began to develop a sophisticated organizational structure to coordinate activities such as regional, national, and international gatherings and to publish books, magazines, and cassette tapes of devotional and instructional material. The twelve-member National Service Committee has coordinated activities in the United States since 1970, based at first in South Bend under the sponsorship of the People of Praise covenant community, then moving in 1990 to a new "Chariscenter" headquarters near Washington, D.C.[4] The National Service Committee's work is supplemented by the National Advisory Committee, constituted of well over a hundred members chosen by geographic region. The International Communications Office began in 1975 at Ann Arbor under the sponsorship of The Word of God covenant community, moving eventually to Brussels and then to Rome as the movement sought to establish its presence at the center of the Catholic world.[5] Higher education is available at the Charismatic-dominated Franciscan College of Steubenville in Ohio.

Most American Catholic dioceses have appointed an individual, almost always a Charismatic, to serve as liaison to the local bishop, and the liaisons themselves meet periodically. The institution of diocesan liaison is instrumental in preserving cordial relations between the movement and the Church hierarchy, wherein there are perhaps only twenty bishops who affiliate with the movement. The National Conference of Catholic Bishops also has an ad hoc committee on the Charismatic Renewal, with one of its members serving as liaison to the movement. Official joint statements by the bishops comprising the national hierarchies of various countries, including the United States, have been released periodically. Such statements typically adopt a cautiously supportive tone, urging participants to continue "renewing" Church life while warning them against theological and behavioral "excess."

From the early 1970s the most influential and highest-ranking cleric openly affiliated with the Renewal was the conservative Belgian cardinal Leon Joseph Suenens, who following an incognito reconnaissance visit established relations with The Word of God community and subsequently became Rome's episcopal adviser to the movement.[6] With Suenens's retirement and the declining fortunes of The Word of God vis-à-vis the Church in the 1980s, the most influential cleric became Bishop Paul Cordes, vice president of the Pontifical Council for the Laity and Rome's new episcopal adviser to the movement. At the center, Pope Paul VI took note of the movement's existence as early as 1971 and publicly addressed its 1975 international conference in Rome. Pope John Paul II (1992) has continued to be generally supportive, apparently tolerating the movement's relatively radical theology for the sake of encouraging its markedly conservative politics, its militant activism for "traditional" values and against women's rights to contraception and abortion, and its encouragement of individual spirituality and contribution to parish activities and finances.[7]

The division into covenant communities and parochial prayer groups has been the most evident feature of internal diversity among American Charismatics. By far the majority of active participants are involved in prayer groups whose members assemble weekly for collective prayer but do not maintain intensive commitments to their group and sometimes participate in several groups simultaneously or serially. At the opposite pole are the intensely committed and hierarchically structured intentional communities organized around the provisions of a solemn written agreement, or "covenant."

Several dimensions of variation in group organization are related to this primary one between prayer group and covenant community. The smallest prayer groups may have only a few adult members, whereas until 1990 the largest among covenant communities numbered 1,500 adults and another 1,500 children. An intermediate-size prayer group (from about 40 to 200) will likely include a "core group" of members who want both greater commitment and a greater sense of intimacy and common purpose with others. Such a group is typically led by a "pastoral team" of several members. It also exhibits a division of ritual labor into "ministries" with functions such as leadership, teaching, music, healing, or provision to participants of movement literature. Leadership in some groups is primarily in the hands of lay people; in others it is deferred to priests and nuns and may be open to both men and women or restricted based on the fundamentalist principle of "male headship."

Charismatic groups may be based at a parish (though they often attract transparochial participation), a school, or a private home. Group membership may be either predominantly Catholic or "ecumenical," drawn from a variety of mainstream Protestant denominations. Although in general over time the proportion of Protestants appears to have declined somewhat, the degree of ecumenical participation also appears to vary by region, with Charismatics in the Northeast from the beginning having tended to form predominantly Catholic groups and those in the Midwest inclined toward ecumenical participation.[8] Denominational religious obligations in ecumenical groups typically take on the character of private devotion separate from community life, whereas predominantly Catholic groups integrate liturgy and sometimes Marian devotion into their ritual life. Nevertheless, the movement as a whole has consistently been in contact with Protestant Pentecostals (e.g., Assemblies of God) and nondenominational neo-Pentecostals, periodically adopting and adapting their ritual practices. Some groups are more charismatic in the sense of the frequency with which participants exercise "spiritual gifts" such as glossolalia, healing, or prophecy, whereas others never incorporate these characteristic features of ritual life.[9] Among more highly developed groups, ritual specialization in one or more of these charisms is sometimes found: it is said by some both that each individual is granted a charism to be used for the benefit of collective life and that each community is granted a distinctive charism that will complement the charisms of other communities within the Charismatic "Kingdom of God."

While all Catholic Charismatics share the communitarian ideal, it has been a point of debate within the movement whether everyone can or even should belong to a full-scale community. In such communities, each member must go through an initiation and indoctrination process lasting as long as two years. This "underway" process culminates in a ceremony of formal commitment to the provisions of the covenant. These provisions vary from one community to another and give it greater or lesser claim over the time and resources of the member. The particular focus here on covenant communities is warranted both because they have most fully elaborated the ritual life of the movement and because even among them there is an identifiable range of cultural diversity. We begin with brief characterizations of four exemplary communities. All four originated in the movement's early years, 1968–1969, and not only represent alternative communitarian models but reflect the regional diversity of North American Catholic culture as well. The first two are independent freestanding communities and will be treated only briefly. The next two are the centers of translocal communities or networks of allied communities, and their story is critical to understanding the central role of covenant communities within the movement as a whole.

A Benedictine abbey in Pecos, New Mexico, under Abbot David Geraets, has become a leading center of Charismatic teaching on spiritual growth and ritual healing, a kind of Catholic Charismatic Esalen. The community's influence is quite broad, since in addition to sponsoring popular on-site retreats, it operates one of two Catholic Charismatic publishing houses, Dove Publications. Although permanent membership is only about forty, structure as a conventional religious order allows virtually full-time participation in religious activities. Community structure and discipline are determined by Benedictine principles, except for the innovation of organizing as a "double community" that includes both men and women.[10] Community life and ritual healing are self-characterized as a "holistic" synthesis of Benedictine rule, Charismatic spiritual gifts, and depth psychology. The latter influence is prominent in defining the Pecos community in relation to other Catholic Charismatic communities in at least two ways. It defines relations between men and women as a "balancing and heightening of masculine-feminine consciousness" in an approach explicitly derived from Carl Jung. This is in sharp contrast to those covenant communities that promulgate "male headship," the ultimate authority of men over women based on a fundamentalist interpretation of Christian Scripture. The Pecos community also broadens the practice of ritual healing to include a range of elements of eclectic and holistic psychotherapies. This places its style of ritual healing at the "psychological" end of a continuum whose other pole is a "faith" orientation that purports to rely on the direct intervention of divine power.

Saint Patrick's in Providence, Rhode Island, began like many other Charismatic parish prayer groups, but under the founding leadership of Catholic priests John Randall and Raymond Kelley it had by 1974 transformed its base of operations into a "Charismatic parish."[11] The two priests were assigned to a decaying inner-city parish, and more than fifty families in the community eventually sold their suburban homes and relocated in the neighborhood surrounding the church. The principal structural innovations were the sharing of authority among a pastoral team that included lay members, the adoption of collective living in "households," and the transformation of the parochial school into a Charismatic school staffed by community members and requiring all students and their parents to undergo the initiatory Life in the Spirit Seminar. Community members explicitly chose the parish model on the example (and under the guidance) of the Episcopalian Charismatic Church of the Redeemer in Houston, in contrast to the model of lay leadership, multidenominational membership, and independence of parish structure contemporaneously being developed by midwestern Catholic covenant communities. Due in part to the effort of maintaining a parish the membership of which never truly coincided with that of the community itself, as well as to the proportions of the task that included revitalizing a neighborhood and parish already in serious decline, this community had by the middle 1980s declined in vitality and visibility within the movement, though a core of original members maintains an active Charismatic community presence.

The two leading communities of the Midwest developed side by side, and for some time considered themselves to be closely allied sister communities. The People of Praise in South Bend was led by Kevin Ranaghan and Paul DeCelles, and The Word of God in Ann Arbor was headed by Steven Clark and Ralph Martin. All were among the group from Duquesne and Notre Dame that initiated the synthesis of Catholicism and Pentecostalism. All took the opportunity to turn the newly discovered experience and ritual forms into tools for the building of "community." Both groups underwent rapid early growth by recruitment from major universities, and between them they provided many of the resources for institutional development within the movement. The South Bend community remains the headquarters of the Charismatic Renewal Services and publishes the Charismatic magazine *New Heaven, New Earth*, until 1990 was the headquarters of the National Service Committee and its National Advisory Committee, and has been the force behind the movement's annual national conferences. The Ann Arbor community remains instrumental in publishing the movement magazine *New Covenant* and in operating the influential Servant Publications for books, founded the movement's International Communications Office, and for years was the leading force in training for national and international movement leaders.

The history of relations between these communities is essential to an understanding of the communitarian ideal among Charismatics. The critical period was the first half of the 1970s, when covenant communities and the Charismatic Renewal as a whole underwent their most rapid expansion. Movement participation in the United States was estimated at 200,000 in 1972 and 670,000 by 1976 (*World Christian Encyclopedia* 1982), and in the same period the membership of The Word of God community grew from 213 to 1,243. A symbolic event of critical import to the movement's future course occurred with a decision in 1975 to hold the annual Charismatic conference, until then hosted by the People of Praise on the campus of Notre Dame University, at the center of the Catholic world in Rome. During the conference the pope formally addressed the movement. Charismatic liturgy including prayer in tongues was conducted in Saint Peter's Basilica, and in this symbolically charged setting, "prophecy" was uttered.[12]

We will examine prophecy as a performative genre of ritual language in chapters 6 and 7. In the present context, I am concerned with the impact of the prophecies delivered at Saint Peter's, which were uttered principally by prophets from The Word of God community. Understood as messages from the deity spoken through a divinely granted charism, they warned of impending times of difficulty and trials for the Church. They stated that God's church and people would be different and that "buildings that are now standing will not be standing. Supports that are there for my people now will not be there." They declared that those who heard this divine word would be prepared by the deity for a "time of darkness coming upon the world," but also for a "time of glory for the church and people of God." An inclination to take these words literally and with urgency was reinforced by the Charismatic delegation from Lebanon, whose country had just entered the throes of its enduring civil war, and where indeed buildings that had been standing were already no longer standing. Members of the Beirut community returned to Ann Arbor and remained affiliated with The Word of God. The immediacy of their plight lent a sense of urgency to continued prophecies in the late 1970s. This sense of urgency was maintained in the 1980s by the affiliation to The Word of God of a community of conservative Nicaraguan Charismatics troubled by Sandinista attempts to create a new society in that country.

Until the Rome conference, prophecy had been understood by Charismatics as utterance intended for the edification of their own groups, or of individuals within the groups. Now for the first time, reinforced by the powerful symbolic setting of their utterance, these words were deemed to be a direct message from God to the public at large. The

"Rome prophecies," as they began to be known, were widely disseminated through *New Covenant* and widely discussed in Charismatic gatherings and conferences. Charismatics began to see fulfillment of the prophecies in the fuel shortages of the late 1970s, in disastrous mud slides in California, and in the blizzards of 1977 and 1978 in the Northeast. Beyond the signs included in natural disasters and in the perceived moral decline of American society, however, the prophecies were construed to indicate that the Catholic church was in peril. There was not only the long-observed decline in religious vocations, and the perceived retreat of Catholicism before Protestantism in the third world, but also a compromise with secular values and a consequent decline in moral authority that made the Church ill equipped for the coming "hard times." These concerns appeared to be referents of the Rome prophecies' warning, "Supports that are there for my people now will not be there."

While some movement leaders had from the outset in the late 1960s expressed the goal of *renewing* the entire Church, and thus eventually becoming indistinguishable from the Church itself, the logic of the prophecies appeared to be that the role of the Charismatic Renewal was actually to *protect* the Church. Thus it was an ideal not only for Catholics to become Charismatic but also for Charismatics to band together into covenant communities and covenant communities into larger networks, for these were thought to be structures in which the faithful could best gird themselves for the impending battle with the forces of darkness. To be sure, not all Charismatics and not all covenant communities adhered to this philosophy, and a formal split between moderates and radical communitarians occurred at the movement's 1977 national conference in Kansas City. The difference was summarized polemically by a female Catholic theologian who was a disaffected early participant in the community at Notre Dame. Shortly after the Rome prophecies she published a book critically distinguishing "Type I" (world-renouncing, authoritarian, and patriarchal) and "Type II" (accommodating, liberal, and egalitarian) charismatics (Ford 1976). Meanwhile, in distinction to the radical vision offered in publications and teaching disseminated by the People of Praise and The Word of God, a more moderated "Type II" voice appeared with the introduction in 1975 of the periodical *Catholic Charismatic*, based at the freestanding Children of Joy covenant community founded by Fr. Joseph Lange, O.S.F.S., in Allentown, Pennsylvania. Without the compelling centripetal impulse of the prophetic vision, however, both the new publication and the community that supported it were short-lived. In contrast, the most dramatic instance of community consolidation came in 1977 when more than a hundred members of San Francisco's St. John the Baptist community moved en masse to join the People of Praise in South Bend (see Lane 1978).

In this charged atmosphere, the radical formulation of the Rome prophecies marked the years between 1975 and 1980 as a phase that was the closest the Catholic Charismatic Renewal has been to a position of apocalyptic millennialism. Even prior to these developments, however, The Word of God and the People of Praise had for some time taken the lead in plans to formalize ties among covenant communities. The principle was that, just as in a single community each member is thought to be granted a spiritual gift or charism that contributes to the collective life of the community as a "body" or a "people," so each community had a particular gift or mission. Taken together, they could thus form a "community of communities," a divinely constituted "people" ultimately combining to build the Kingdom of God. The Rome prophecies increased the urgency of this plan, and in 1976 the Association of Communities was formed.

By 1980–1981, however, the two leading communities themselves acknowledged irreconcilable differences. A three-way split occurred in the network, with some communities following The Word of God, some following the People of Praise, and yet others following the Community of God's Delight from Dallas and their close allies in Emmanuel Covenant Community of Brisbane, Australia. The original association had included seven communities at the "council" or oversight level, and another thirty were involved to lesser degrees. Following their parting of ways, The Word of God founded the Federation of Communities, the People of Praise went on to develop the Fellowship of Communities, and the Community of God's Delight went on with Emmanuel to develop the International Brotherhood of Communities.[13] Under the leadership of The Word of God, the federation in 1982 became a single supercommunity, renaming itself the Sword of the Spirit. By 1988 the Sword of the Spirit included forty-five branches and associated communities, twenty-two of which were in the United States.[14] The six main communities within the fellowship, all in the United States, eventually came to consider themselves branches of the People of Praise but maintained a semiautonomous confederal relationship.[15] The even more loosely structured brotherhood increasingly cultivated its Catholic identity and relation to the Church. In 1990 the ecumenical brotherhood was succeeded by the Catholic Fraternity of Charismatic Covenant Communities and Fellowships, with three founding communities from the United States, six from Australia and New Zealand, and four from other countries. In 1994, four more communities were advanced from underway to full membership in the fraternity. For the most part the three networks parted ways and remained essentially out of contact throughout the 1980s. Crudely speaking, the Sword of the Spirit went increasingly its own way, the People of Praise consolidated its links to the larger Charismatic Renewal, and the brotherhood communities consolidated their relationships with their local bishops.[16]

At about this time The Word of God/Sword of the Spirit had applied for canonical recognition of the geographically dispersed Catholics among its multidenominational membership as an international association of Catholics. Given the political organization of the Church, this would have required either that the local branches of the community be under more direct control of local bishops or that Steven Clark, the community's paramount leader, be granted a status similar to the head of a religious order, equivalent to a bishop. The application was not approved. Now in the wake of the split among communities, the Vatican apparently decided to take a more active role in supervising the movement. The pope assigned Bishop Cordes, the episcopal adviser to the movement who replaced The Word of God's now retired ally Cardinal Suenens, to visit and assess the range of groups, communities, and structures within the Charismatic Renewal. After visits in two consecutive years in the mid-1980s, he invited the brotherhood communities to apply for canonical recognition. Reorganized as a fraternity excluding Protestant communities and individuals who had been members of the brotherhood, this network was granted status by the pope as a "private association of the Christian faithful of pontifical right." Following exclusion of the Sword of the Spirit from a status its leaders appeared to regard as essential to their role as vanguard of Church renewal, this ecclesiastical recognition was an explicit statement of Vatican preference for one of several extant models of covenant community networks.

Let us dwell for a moment on the differences among these communities with respect to structure, "vision" or goals, and practice. This will serve the purpose of summarizing the nuances of covenant community values, as well as the kind of issues that led to the historical split among the groups. In thus setting the stage for the later extended discussion of The Word of God, we will also guard against representing that one community as in all ways typical of the movement as a whole.

We will do well to begin by noting a demographic difference among the communities. That The Word of God was centered around the public University of Michigan reinforced its tendency toward an ecumenical or multidenominational membership, whereas the People of Praise connection with Notre Dame University reinforced the predominance of Catholics. In comparison to both, the Community of God's Delight was not closely affiliated with a university. From the beginning its members were somewhat older than those in the two leading communities—indeed, one of the personal dramas of the movement is that Bobbie Cavnar, head coordinator of the Dallas community, is the father of James Cavnar, one of the four founders of The Word of God—and its membership remained relatively stable from the early 1970s. While the Community of God's Delight also originally cultivated multidenominational membership (a community leader estimated that originally Catholics comprised 50 to 70 percent of the membership), with its increasing push toward a Catholic identity many Protestants moved away from the covenant community and back to local congregations. At the end of the 1980s membership in the Community of God's Delight was 95 to 98 percent Catholic, the People of Praise was 92 percent Catholic, and The Word of God was 65 percent Catholic.

Much of the difference that led to the split, however, has to do with the exercise of authority a) among related communities, b) in relation to the Church, c) among individuals within communities, and d) by means of prophecy. The Word of God's idea was that the association would be a single supercommunity under a single translocal government. This became the case in the Sword of the Spirit, where, for example, community leaders can be assigned to move from one branch to another to oversee or train members. The People of Praise preferred a confederation of semiautonomous communities, though as noted their constituent groups have come to regard themselves also as a single community. The Community of God's Delight and its brotherhood rejected any translocal authority, emphasizing that each member community "submit to the authority of" or "be in communion with" its local Catholic bishop. These differences in turn directly affect relations with the Catholic church. Indeed, that the Sword of the Spirit has a translocal government and that in principle this government is multidenominational rather than strictly Catholic has been one source of tension between it and the Church.

The leading covenant communities are all hierarchically structured under elders, or "coordinators." Decisions are made by consensus among coordinators as they jointly "listen for what the Lord might be saying in a particular area." Final judgments are made by an overall coordinator or head coordinator, but there is variation among communities as to whether this role is one of ultimate authority or one of "tiebreaker" in the absence of consensus. In the model originated by The Word of God and the People of Praise, the general membership traditionally had input by solicitation from the coordinators in a "community consultation" about a specific major issue, but coordinators were not obliged to take these opinions into account. Coordinators were appointed by other co-ordinators, with the founders of each community remaining in authority insofar as they were the original coordinators. In the period following their divergence, the People of Praise instituted a modified form of election for its coordinators, described as midway between the community consultation and simple election. Nominations are solicited from full or "covenanted" members within each community subdivision. These members pick three people, from whom one is selected by the overall coordinator. The Word of God retained the older system of coordinator self-selection, adhering to the commonly heard dictum that "the Kingdom of God is not a democracy," or in the words attributed to Overall Coordinator Steven Clark, "Democracy is not a scriptural concept." In these communities the job of coordinator is a highly demanding full-time position. In the Community of God's Delight, by contrast, coordinators have jobs outside the community, which itself maintains only two full-time employees.

The exercise of prophecy is another key difference in the organization of authority among the communities. While all Charismatics recognize prophecy as one of the spiritual gifts or charisms, there is a significant difference both in the formal recognition of gifted individuals and in prophecy's authoritative role as directly inspired divine utterance. For some people, prophecy is an occasional and momentary gift; others are individually recognized as being gifted on a regular basis; some communities have an organized "word gifts" group composed of confirmed prophets who together "listen to the Lord" in order to "discern his word for the group." The Word of God developed prophecy into an institution, with the formal office of Prophet held by a man consecrated by the community as a specially gifted channel of divine communication to the community. He oversees not only a word gifts group within the community but also a translocal "prophet's guild" that originated in the early 1980s. The People of Praise has a word gifts group but no formal office of community prophet. The Community of God's Delight has no organized word gifts group, and the community elder who oversees this aspect of ritual life is charged not with prophesying but with "discerning" the prophecies of others who wish to share them in group settings.

All of the communities take prophecy quite seriously in that their leaders consider the meaning of prophetic messages in their deliberations concerning group life and publish certain of them in community newsletters. The structural differences, however, highlight the different degrees to which prophecy penetrates the various aspects of collective life as a medium of charismatic authority. Whether prophecies can be prepared in advance or are required to be spontaneous, whether there is a regular flow of prophetic inspiration from members to coordinators, whether prophecy is a feature of interpersonal as well as collective discourse, are related differences in practice deeply embedded in the habitus of each community. Again, we can here only point to these differences in preparation for a more thorough examination of one community, and again note that the institutionalization of prophecy as direct and authoritative communication from the deity is another dimension of tension between the Sword of the Spirit and those covenant communities intent on demonstrating their submission to the sole authority of the Catholic church.

I will briefly touch on four more specific differences in the organization of authority among the leading communities, including denominational structure, education of children, pastoral supervision of adults, and gender role prescriptions. First, The Word of God in 1979 created four "fellowships" internal to the community, partially collapsing denominational distinctions while maintaining differentiation among Roman Catholic, Reformed, Lutheran, and Free Church members.[17] Meanwhile, all members of the People of Praise and the Community of God's Delight remained simultaneously members of local parishes, in effect limiting the pastoral authority of their communities.

Second, all three communities have schools for their children, with differences reflecting the degree of world renunciation cultivated in community life. In both The Word of God and the People of Praise, classes are segregated by sex; during the 1980s students at The Word of God school were also required to walk on opposite sides of a yellow line that extended the length of the corridors. Both are oriented toward Charismatic Christian education, though they differ in the importance they place on inculcation of Charismatic values at an early age: The Word of God school includes grades 4 through 9 while the People of Praise teach grades 7 through 12. In addition, The Word of God school restricts enrollment to children of community members, whereas the People of Praise school is also open to noncommunity children. Likewise, The Word of God curriculum was relatively more "scripture oriented," whereas the People of Praise included the thought of "worldly" thinkers such as Socrates, Mortimer Adler, and Jacques Maritain. The Community of God's Delight's preschool adopted the Montessori method, and its classes through grade 12 are run by a Catholic religious order, the Sisters of Our Lady of Charity.

Third, all three communities formalized the practice of headship or pastoral leadership, in which individual members are supervised in their daily lives by a person regarded as more "spiritually mature." From the perspective of most observers, this is one of the most controversial aspects of covenant community practice, for it has to do with the critical theme of relinquishing personal control ("submission to authority") as a requirement of commitment to a covenant. I will discuss headship at greater length in a subsequent chapter, and here note only that the People of Praise have appeared interested in portraying themselves as somewhat less authoritarian in this regard than their counterparts in The Word of God. Yet the difference between the two communities appears exceedingly subtle and was indeed described by them as similar to the difference between regional accents by speakers of the same language.[18] The Community of God's Delight originally followed The Word of God model of headship but later instituted a substantial revision at the level of community coordinator. Concluding that authority over community activities should be distinct from authority over personal lives, a second coordinator was appointed for each geographic district within the community. One has responsibility for community activities such as "sharing groups," "service ministries," and collective gatherings; the other is devoted to pastoral care, with a reformulation of headship using the teachings of the Church on Catholic "spiritual direction."

Fourth, in all three communities the highest office that can be held by a woman is "handmaid," the responsibilities of which are to "teach women on womanly affairs, give advice, help in troubled situations," and lead specialized women's activities. The chief handmaid was always under the authority of a male coordinator in The Word of God; in the Community of God's Delight the handmaids meet with the group of coordinators once a month. Practices defining "men's and women's roles" in "scriptural" terms were of concern to both The Word of God and the People of Praise, though the latter regarded themselves as taking a more "flexible" position.[19] Both communities hold that a man not only is head of the household but must also be the "spiritual head" or "pastoral leader" of his wife, while his own "head" is another man. Domestic division of labor along culturally "traditional" lines was explicitly held to be an essential part of Christian life.[20] The Community of God's Delight in principle professes more moderation, with male headship in the family residing in the role of tiebreaker in decisions between two otherwise equal spouses. Again, both The Word of God and the People of Praise prescribed gender-appropriate dress, prohibiting "androgyny" in clothing. Within The Word of God this principle led, for example, to public disapproval of community handmaids wearing slacks instead of dresses. Leaders of the People of Praise, on hearing of this practice in the mid-1980s, decided that their former partners were being overly rigid. Finally, the People of Praise claimed to encourage female higher education and employment, whereas The Word of God remained somewhat ambivalent about these issues.

Although many of these differences among communities appear quite nuanced and even trivial, they are precise inscriptions in practice of what I will describe below as a rhetorical involution that determines the incremental radicalization of charisma and ritualization of life. The qualitative dimension of their differences in "vision" and "mission" can be summarized as a greater pessimism on the part of The Word of God about developments in the contemporary world, the Catholic church, and the Charismatic Renewal. The Word of God saw the Charismatic Renewal as ideally evolving into a tightly knit network of communities that could protect the weakened Church against impending hard times, basing their approach directly on Christian Scripture and literal interpretation of prophecies such as the Rome prophecies. On opting out of this vision, the People of Praise reformulated its approach to the surrounding world as a "Christian humanism" grounded in the Second Vatican Council's "Pastoral Constitution on the Church in the Modern World." In the words of one of their coordinators, they decided that the motivation for what they wanted to do had to be "love of God and neighbor" rather than the call to "gather the wagons in a circle." Whereas The Word of God mobilized to "stem the tide of evil" they discerned to be flowing over the earth, their former partners concluded that this was an "exaggeration."[21]

By the late 1980s, many adherents of the Rome prophecies in the Charismatic Renewal regarded most of its elements as already fulfilled, save for an impending "wave of evangelism such as the world has never known." Anticipating this wave of evangelism, some began to reconceive the threat to the Church not so much as from the outside as from inside: they warned of the possibility of collapse when, in its perceived weakened condition, the Church was flooded with the expected rush of new converts. This retrenched position was not only less dramatic but also offered a wide range of potential explanations should the predicted wave of evangelism fail to materialize. For many it also made reintegration into Catholicism easier. Meanwhile, The Word of God and the Sword of the Spirit network of communities itself underwent schism, moving increasingly away from the center of the movement and, according to some critics, increasingly distant from the Catholic church. We will take up the story of this third split in the movement in Part Two.

The International Scene

Ethnographic and social science literature on the international expansion of the Catholic Charismatic Renewal is sparse. In general, the literature on the movement in North America (see the preface above) tends to emphasize issues of community and personal religious experience, that on the movement in Latin America is slanted toward its role as a conservative political force in opposition to liberation theology, and that on Europe, Africa, and Asia highlights practices of ritual healing within the movement. What follows is a tour of those locales for which some documentation on the movement is available, beginning with distinct national and ethnic communities within the United States.

NORTH AMERICA AND EUROPE

In the United States, by 1992 the movement's National Service Committee included "ethnic representatives" for Filipino, Korean,[22] and Portuguese Catholic Charismatics. Semiautonomous service committees had also been created for Hispanic and Haitian Charismatics. Here I will elaborate briefly only Hispanic participation in movement events, which was reported beginning in 1976 with the continental conference that included Spanish résumés and one Spanish-language workshop. Hispanic leaders in the United States met for the first time in 1977. In 1982 the movement's National Service Committee added a Hispanic member and allocated funds to support Missiones Hispanas, an arm of The Word of God community active both in Latin America and among domestic Hispanic groups. In 1988 Hispanic Charismatics from the United States were officially represented for the first time at the eleventh conference of Catholic Charismatic leaders from throughout Latin America, and in 1991 a separate Hispanic National Service Committee was established with a structure parallel to the already extant committee.

Although the movement is developed among Mexican, Cuban, and Puerto Rican Hispanics, I will mention only the Puerto Rican case based on research I conducted in New England during the late 1980s.[23] The movement was introduced to the island in 1971 by Redemptorist missionaries from the mainland, then reintroduced to the mainland by members of their community invited to stage a retreat at a Puerto Rican parish in Boston. One intent of my interviews was to elicit leaders' perceptions of differences between Puerto Rican and Anglo-American Charismatics with respect to healing (see Csordas 1994a). Two issues emerged. First, Charismatic leaders suggested that healing was more "liberating" for Puerto Ricans. This was in part because they reportedly experienced "deeper hurts" with respect to poor self-image as a result of colonial exploitation. They were also prone to exaggerated guilt and *remordamiento* (remorse) arising from intense moralism and to harboring emotional pain that turns to hatred when it is left unexpressed out of respect for parents. Finally, they were felt to bear an ingrained fear of the dark, of curses, and of spirits. Second, Puerto Rican Charismatics appeared to place greater emphasis on family and interpersonal relations. This was said to be evident in the practice of home visits by the healing team, in which neighbors and relatives were expressly included. It was also evident in the practice of "deliverance" from evil spirits insofar as the common afflicting spirits appeared to reflect cultural differences (for Anglos, spirits with an ego locus such as Depression, Bitterness, Resentment, Fear, Self-Destruction; for Puerto Ricans, spirits with an interpersonal locus such as Hatred, Disobedience, Envy, Respect, Slander, Criticism, Robbery, Violence, Rejection of God, Impurities, Masturbation, and Homosexuality). There also appeared to be a difference in the cultural understanding of why people are vulnerable to affliction by evil spirits: for Anglos, emotional trauma is often regarded as the developmental occasion in which the demon gains entrée; for Puerto Ricans, trauma was acknowledged but not typically connected with evil spirits.

The latter difference may be accounted for by the fact that for Puerto Rican Charismatics the most prominent source of evil spirits is the competing religious practice of Espiritismo (see Garrison 1977; Harwood 1977; Koss-Chioino 1992). When Hispanic Charismatics say that the Renewal is "very effective against spirits," they tend to have in mind the spirits of the deceased encountered in spiritism, African spirits, curses, and the evil eye. (Similarly, Haitian Charismatics often reinterpret the deities of *voudou* as demonic spirits.) My interviews suggested two general points: (1) Espiritismo is condemned as demonic deception insofar as an evil spirit is thought to be imitating the voice of a dead person, in that spiritist writings use Christian Scripture but admix folk belief and pagan ritual, and in that the devil has the power to heal as part of his repertoire of deceptive tactics; (2) Espiritismo is said to be characterized by negativity and is "not liberating" because it deals only with hate and revenge while also deceiving people and taking their money.

The movement has also in a limited way penetrated indigenous peoples such as the Navajo, where it began in the early 1970s in the Fort Defiance area and in the 1980s spread to the community of Tohatchi. One Charismatic healer, a Navajo nun, exemplifies the heteroglossia that renders notions such as syncretism obsolete in the postmodern condition of culture (see chapter 2 below). She regards herself as equally at home in traditional Navajo ritual, the practices of the Native American Church with its sacramental peyote, and in Christianity. Indeed, she planned to use the honorarium she received from our project to help finance a traditional Blessingway ceremony for herself, since her limited stipend as a religious sister made it difficult for her to afford the services of a medicine man. She identified fundamentalist Christian, Charismatic Christian, and New Age spiritualities as among those she could relate to. She was formally trained as a Catholic spiritual director at Loyola University and underwent a nine-month course in San Francisco related to the recovery movement and healing the inner child. She refers to traditional and Native American Church observance as part of her "prayer life," a term common among Charismatics. She also uses the same term, "prayer meetings," for both Native American Church and Charismatic services and defines the former as a spiritual way of life instead of as a church, so that like her Charismatic participation it does not conflict with her membership in the Catholic church.

Her account of becoming a healer is virtually identical to that of other Charismatics I have heard, with one symbolic and one ethnopsychological twist. She says that at a Charismatic conference three people asked her for healing prayer, which she politely obliged but which made her uncomfortable, so that she "disappeared." The next year at the conference seven people asked for prayer, and again she obliged but "disappeared" afterward. Then at another event she asked for a blessing from a Catholic Indian known for presenting an eagle feather to the pope. He not only blessed her but also presented her with an eagle feather, which she at first protested she had not earned, but accepted as a responsibility on his insistence. At the next summer's conference she prayed for people who came steadily from ten o'clock in the evening until two o'clock in the morning. She now feels challenged to live a life of purification. Briefly, the ethnopsychological twist is the description of demurral from the calling as "disappearing," evocative of the Navajo tendency to self-effacement in certain social situations. The symbolic twist is the eagle feather as emblem of a Charismatic healing ministry. For this healer, the idea of "picking up the feather" leads to analogy between priest or healer and those traditional ceremonial clowns who in their capacity as protectors of ritual dancers must have a familiarity with evil, which she notes extends among the neighboring Pueblos to the point of acting out the perversities of the people.

Three studies document the movement in Quebec based on material from the 1970s (Reny and Rouleau 1978; Chagnon 1979; Zylberberg and Montminy 1980). They agree in dating the movement's advent to 1971, when one Father Regimbal returned from a Charismatic experience in Arizona to stage a retreat in the provincial town of Granby. Paul Reny and Jean Paul Rouleau (1978: 131–132) observe a rapid growth from its inception to fifty prayer groups in 1973, four hundred by 1974, and seven hundred (with an estimated membership of 60,000) by 1977 (cf. the more conservative estimate of 301 prayer groups in 1975 and 550 by 1979 by Zylberberg and Montminy [1980]). Participants were predominantly middle-class women of "mature age," but notably in comparison with the United States nearly 25 percent of members were men and women in religious orders, especially nuns; Jacques Zylberberg and Jean-Paul Montminy (1980: 139) concur that there are two "hard-core" elements of adherents, one composed of lower-middle-class, middle-aged provincial women and another composed of clerics shifting from a sacerdotal to a prophetic mode of attaining ecclesiastical prestige.

Zylberberg and Montminy (1980) attempt to place the movement in macrosocial context in relation to the dynamic of state, capital, and religion in Quebec. In a society historically characterized by clerical domination and a provincial state, they identify the movement as an ostensibly apolitical attempt to break the stalemate between future-oriented Catholic social activists and tradition-oriented Catholic conservatives. While 70 percent of Charismatics voted in elections, only 12.4 percent chose the nationalist *Parti Quebecois*, and only six percent reported participation in any overtly political group. The authors interpret the nationalists as representing a state nationalism and organizational modernism that are not merely rejected but are symbolically opaque for Charismatics, with an emphasis on French monolingualism symbolically contradicted by the universal spiritual language of speaking in tongues. This is the case even though within the movement itself certain frustrations experienced by francophone participants in a bilingual Canadian Charismatic conference in 1973 led them to stage a separate francophone conference the following year (Reny and Rouleau 1978: 131). Support for the Liberal political party is by default and habit, resulting in adherence to the status quo. The priest/anthropologist Roland Chagnon (1979: 101, 140) likewise understands the movement's social impact as a reinforcement and enlargement of the base of the social status quo in the face of both the broad cultural malaise of the 1960s and the specific social conditions of Catholicism in Quebec. These conditions include the erosion of the traditional view of life with its emphasis on religion and the clergy, rural life, and the importance of a simple communitarian life, all said to have resulted in a crisis of identity for many individuals.

Following Charles Glock and Rodney Stark (1965), Chagnon distinguishes among religious experience that is *confirmative* of the existence of God, that which is *correlative* insofar as it is a reciprocal sense of divine presence and divine attention to the person, that which is *ecstatic* and combines the preceding two types with enhanced intensity, and that which is *revelational* or *mystical* insofar as the deity makes the person a confidant in an atmosphere of emotional serenity. Sixteen of twenty cases Chagnon documents are of the correlative type, none is confirmative, one is ecstatic, and three are mystical, and he concludes that what is characteristic of Charismatic experience is an "affective encounter with God" (1979: 82), a displacement of the sacred from the figure of a severe and distant God to that of a "God of love" (1979: 84), and in contrast to an emphasis on world transformation a distinct penchant "to remake the self, to reconstitute it in profundity" (1979: 91).[24] Finally, Chagnon summarizes Charismatic spirituality as characterized by the cultivation of the senses of interior peace and divine presence, affective encounter with both God and others, and participation in divine power through abandonment of the self to God (1979: 171–178). The other commentators draw the consequences of this kind of spirituality: given both an experiential interior and a social interior constituted by the prayer group and its relations to the ecclesiastical community, there is an attitude toward external society characterized by the goal of "enlargement of interiority until it encompasses the exterior" (Reny and Rouleau 1978: 130), or in which "the exterior world has to be absorbed by the interior world" (Zylberberg and Montminy 1980: 143).

All three accounts take pains to account for the movement's significance with the sociopolitical and culture historical specificity of Catholicism in Quebec, warning against too close homology with the movement in the United States. It may be that the role of the clergy and of middle-aged women (more likely only the former) has been greater in Quebec, and that the movement in Quebec was co-opted by the hierarchy and declining in rate of growth somewhat sooner than in the United States. Nevertheless, Reny and Rouleau's (1978) comparison of the Charismatics with Catholic left-wing social activists ("les socio-politiques") corresponds closely with McGuire's (1974) similar comparison in the United States. The apolitical orientation and the cultivation of an interiority that presumes social transformation will occur as a consequence of self-transformation are also similar to those observed in the United States (Fichter 1975; McGuire 1982; Neitz 1987).

Catholic Charismatics in France acknowledge borrowing the movement from the United States. At the same time they point out the anomaly that for the first time in history a movement within Catholicism has come to them from across the Atlantic, and suggest that to the extent that French Charismatics find their identity to be national and ecclesial, American influence declines (Hébrard 1987: 245). The date of origin can be traced to 1971 when two Catholics among two hundred Protestants attended the first interconfessional Charismatic convention sponsored by a Charismatic element of the Reformed Church, L'Union de Prière de Charmes. By the third such event in 1973 there were two hundred Catholics alongside two hundred Protestants, and after that Catholics became dominant, with a movement and momentum of their own. By 1974 covenant communities had formed at Lyons, Grenoble, Montpellier, Cordes (mostly university towns), and Paris and began sponsoring their own assemblies (Hébrard 1987: 283).

The diversity among French covenant communities parallels that in the United States, and I will mention only two of the most prominent. Emmanuel community began in 1972 among a group associated with a Catholic school of oratory in Paris, when a young couple just returned from the United States gave a powerful testimony about their experience with the Charismatic Renewal. In a year the group had grown from five to five hundred and took Emmanuel as its name, and the first collective household began in 1974. In 1976 thirty members visited covenant communities in the United States and in 1977, formally became a covenant community themselves. In 1986 Emmanuel had three thousand members distributed throughout Paris and the provinces, six other European countries, and four African countries. The orienting theme of community activities is evangelization: at the core of their organization is the Fraternity of Jesus, a missionary group comprising both lay and religious, and to which one must be initiated in order to take a leadership position in the community. Their outreach extends to multiple segments of the population, and like The Word of God in the United States they are a media force, publishing the periodicals *Il Est Vivant* and *Psychologie et Foi* and operating a book and tape distribution service. As of 1986, a community-based foundation for international spiritual, social, and economic aid (FIDESCO) was functioning in seventeen dioceses in Africa, Latin America, and Asia (Hébrard 1987: 57–70). As a conservative force favored by the Church hierarchy Emmanuel was recognized in 1986 as a Private Association of the Faithful by the French Cardinal Lustiger. In 1990 it became a foundation member, along with the Community of God's Delight of Dallas, U.S.A., and the Emmanuel Covenant Community of Brisbane, Australia, of the new Catholic Fraternity of Charismatic Covenant Communities under the auspices of the Pontifical Council for the Laity. In 1992 Emmanuel community was recognized as a Universal Association of the Faithful of the Pontifical Rite by the Vatican.

The Lion of Judah and Sacrificial Lamb was founded at the tourist town of Cordes-sur-Ciel and exemplifies the postmodern melding of cultural genres. It is based at a monastery but in a tourist town, its members pursue professional careers but adopt a contemplative Carmelite spirituality, it emphasizes chastity while including married couples and their children, and it was founded by Protestants but is now thoroughly Catholic—with the addition of Hebrew Sabbath observances. Like the French Emmanuel community and the American Sword of the Spirit, it has spread its branches well beyond its origin, into twenty-five French dioceses and seventeen foreign countries. In 1991 the community changed its name to Community of the Beatitudes on the grounds that the Lion of Judah was an unacceptable symbol in some of the countries in which its members have moved. The community is particularly renowned for its healing ministry, based at its Château Saint Luc staffed by sixteen residents, its clinic staffed by physicians and psychologists who "discern" as well as diagnose their patients, a group charged with visiting the sick, and the group Mère de Miséricorde that takes in women who have had or who have contemplated having abortions (see Csordas 1996). Their yearly gatherings held since 1983 produce videotapes of notable healings, and in 1987 the community organized a widely popular pilgrimage to Lourdes. At Saturday public healing services during retreats, participants regularly "rest in the spirit" (Hébrard 1987: 71–91).

The core of healing practice is "psychospiritual accompaniment," in effect two weeks of around-the-clock attention that allows, claim its practitioners, such innovations as decreasing a patient's dosage of neuroleptic medication to a minimum. Giordana Charuty (1987) has produced a vivid description of Charismatic healing in France and Italy that conforms in most respects to its practice in the United States (see Csordas 1983, 1988, 1990b, 1994a; McGuire 1982, 1983, 1988). She identifies the "healing of memories" as the guarantor of transformation in psychospiritual accompaniment. Community healers and therapists for whom Carl Rogers and Carl Jung are de rigueur also practice the revelatory charisms of prophecy, discernment, and word of knowledge, all the while condemning practices such as yoga and transcendental meditation as demonic. Charuty quite rightly identifies the therapeutic of a triple anamnesis: psychological through review of biographical memory, initiative through recovery of the emotional fundamentals of early religious experiences, and mythic through directing the person into the imaginal realm of early Christianity. In language directly relevant to what I will refer to below as religions of the self, she points to the centrality of "symbolic manipulations put in place to produce an acculturation to Christianity anchored in exaltation and the socialization of individual unhappiness" (1987: 463).[25]

The Charismatic Renewal was introduced to Italy by foreigners in 1971. Here as in France, growth of the movement was reported to be dramatic following its first international conference in Rome in 1975. By the time of the first national leaders' conference in 1977, the movement had an estimated active membership of seven thousand throughout the country. The second national conference was held in 1979 at Rimini, as a challenge to present "Christian witness in an almost entirely Marxist environment" (*ICO Newsletter,* May–June 1979). The pope addressed gatherings of an estimated fifteen thousand Italian Charismatics in 1980 and again in 1986, and by 1988 the eleventh national conference at Rimini drew an estimated forty thousand participants. Enzo

Pace (1978) describes the movement in the region of Veneto as having two distinct manifestations: the Rinnovamento nello Spirito, or Spiritual Renewal, affiliated with the international Charismatic Renewal, which was initiated locally at Padua in 1972 and which is composed of both prayer groups and communities; and the Charismatic movement founded in Italy in 1967 by Franca Cornado, which was introduced into Veneto in the 1970s and whose adherents are primarily conservative elderly and middle-aged persons oriented toward the experience and documentation of manifestations of spiritual charisms. The latter is more explicitly politically conservative and pre-Vatican in its Catholic orientation; the former distinguishes itself from the political sphere by emphasizing the spiritual values of quotidian life, personal relations, and community, rejecting the close link between the "personal" and the "political" favored by left-leaning social activists.[26]

Discussion of the movement in Europe would not be complete without reference to what was perhaps the most prominent religious event of the last two decades, the apparition in 1981 of the Virgin Mary to several children in the Croatian village of Medjugorje. Quickly approaching the stature of Fatima, Lourdes, and Guadalupe, Medjugorje attracted an estimated ten million Catholic pilgrims by 1986 (Bax 1987: 29). Although the role of the Franciscans has been noted in transforming Medjugorje into a prominent site of pilgrimage and spiritual tourism (Bax 1990; Vukonic 1992)—to the point where some cynics reportedly began to refer to the apparition as "Our Lady of Foreign Currency"— the importance of Charismatics is less well known. During my research in the 1980s one prominent New England healer suspended her ministry to lead groups of pilgrims to the site. Worldwide pilgrimage coordination was based at the Franciscan College of Steubenville in Ohio, which is the Charismatic institution of higher learning under the presidency of Fr. Michael Scanlon, a prominent movement leader. It is probably safe to say that had the Charismatics not been primed for an episode of world reenchantment of this sort, the global phenomenon at Medjugorje would likely not have blossomed.

SOUTH AMERICA, AFRICA, AND ASIA

Evidence suggests that the typical pattern for the movement's introduction in a third world region is as follows: a missionary priest visits the United States, is exposed to Baptism of the Holy Spirit, organizes a prayer group on his return, and subsequently calls on outside help for doctrinal instruction, healing services, or administration of the Life in the Spirit Seminar (a widespread initiation rite that provides both indoctrination and a controlled setting for the Baptism of the Holy Spirit). In some cases, such as that documented by Johannes Fabian (1991) in Zaire, there may be a preexisting network of non-Charismatic prayer groups that is subsequently co-opted into the international movement. Perhaps a dozen major figures regularly make excursions to movement outposts (non-Catholic evangelists are sometimes called on). There is an apparent tendency for groups to maintain relations with the individual or group responsible for initial instruction and organizational assistance. Such relations of moral dependency may be more than superficially analogous to those in the political-economic sphere between a "metropole" in a dominant region and specific locales in a dependent "periphery." However, regional integration on a continental basis has been ongoing for some time, in Latin America since the early 1970s through the Encuentros Carismatico Catolico Latino Americano (ECCLA), in Asia beginning with the 1980 Asian Leaders' Conference that attracted representatives from fifteen countries, and in Africa with the Pan-African Congress first held at the end of the 1980s and planned to take place every four years since 1992.

In Mexico the initiation of Catholic Pentecostalism is attributed to the American Missionaries of the Holy Spirit. In 1971 Mexico City had one prayer group of forty members; by 1975 it was estimated that more than ten thousand Mexicans had become involved in the movement. As described by a Charismatic priest (Talavera 1976), a Mexico City group based at the Archdiocesan Social Secretariat began the first move to incorporate the "very poor" in Ciudad del Lago, a squatter settlement adjacent to the city's airport. Population growth in this area had been extremely rapid: from 1960 to 1970 the municipality directly east of the airport grew from sixty thousand to six hundred thousand (Cornelius 1973). The Social Secretariat group established a satellite prayer group at Ciudad del Lago in 1972, two years after the settlement appeared, with a resident factory worker as leader.

The Pentecostal experience was credited with significant motivational change in members of both parent and satellite groups. The middle-class organizers began to conceive their task as "conversion to Christ" instead of as "concern for the poor." By the priest's account, squatters began to abandon an individualistic materialism that emulates the middle class for an increasing communitarianism and pride of status. The new group developed communal patterns of authority and decision making and established patterns of labor exchange. A women's group began to knit and sell clothing as the basis for a common fund for emergencies, loans to needy members, and wholesale group food purchasing. Families took turns preparing a communal Sunday meal.

In addition to their emphasis on conversion, the middle-class group provided legal advice, architectural planning, and financing, which assisted the squatters in gaining legal title to land in Ciudad del Lago. They proposed to build individual family dwellings but decided against individual ownership of lots. The combination of religious motivation and middle-class patronage also affected the squatters' attitudes toward civil authority. Whenever police came to search for illegal building materials, or lawyers came talking of eviction, the people began to greet them with hospitality instead of anger and fear. Whereas their communications with authorities had been characterized by submission and flattery, they began to demand recognition as rights-bearing citizens. The prayer group successfully resisted a government resettlement plan that would have separated its members in different quarters of the city (Talavera 1976).

A similar situation arose among squatters near the municipal dump in the border city of Juarez, which by 1969 had a total of thirty-eight squatter settlements (Ugalde 1974). Several local social workers were converted to Catholic Pentecostalism and in 1972 established liaisons with a middle-class Catholic Pentecostal group across the border in El Paso, Texas, which was interested in helping "the poorest people they knew." Working together, they facilitated reconciliation between two factions of *peperiadores* (scavengers) at the dump, who subsequently organized their trash industry into a profit-sharing cooperative. Following a 1975 crisis in which the dump manager refused to pay for sorted and collected trash, the governor ceded the dump's management and income to its residents. Critical to this enterprise was assistance from middle-class Charismatics in the form of administrative work, identification of markets, and research on importation procedures (Talavera 1976).

In Chile, Catholic Pentecostalism was introduced in 1972 by Maryknoll and Holy Cross missionaries from the United States. Movement sources report that middle-class groups account for about a third of the total number of prayer groups and two-thirds of the groups are located in poor neighborhoods. Although specific data are not available, it may be surmised that similar liaisons have developed between Charismatics across class lines. A movement leader (Aldunate 1975) describes a

Charismatic retreat among the Mapuche Indians of Chile that was organized on the analogy of the traditional Mapuche fertility rite, or *nil-
latun* (Faron 1964). The retreat included participation of the female ritual specialist, or *machi,* whose traditional function includes dispersion of
evil spirits, healing, and the utterance of unintelligible inspired messages, functions that directly correspond to Pentecostal deliverance, faith
healing, and prophecy in tongues. Indeed, Protestant Pentecostal congregations in this region feature female prophets who speak in tongues
and healers (Lalive d'Epinay 1969: 200–203), but within a ritual organization that is separate and exclusive while remaining formally analogous to the indigenous model. Catholic Pentecostalism in this instance
assimilates the indigenous model directly, converting Mapuche culture as
well as Mapuches themselves and thus creating a single ritual totality, a
single horizon of possibilities for sacred reality (see Csordas 1980b).

In Brazil, Catholic Pentecostalism is described by Pedro A. Ribeiro de
Oliveira (1978) as found almost exclusively among the middle and up-
per middle classes, "gens des couches aisées." Certainly the topography
of religious participation in Brazil is complicated by the diversity of options, including Afro-Brazilian and spiritualist groups. If Ribeiro de Oliveira's report is correct, however, Brazilian Charismatics come from a
generally higher-class background, with greater prior involvement in
Catholic organizations. To a degree much greater even than in the United
States, they may be wary of the "lower-class" associations of faith healing practices and threatened by the powerful presence of Protestant
Pentecostalism as a religious option. Such insularity appears atypical in
Latin America, and it is likely that the survey method overlooked the
kind of liaisons with the disenfranchised undertaken by the Brazilian
Catholic Pentecostal community Esperança e Vida in the rehabilitation
of drug addicts (ICCRO 1987). By 1992 the movement's international
office reported two million Catholic Charismatics in Brazil (for additional discussion of the movement in Latin America, see Csordas 1980,
1992).

The origin and context of Charismatic Christianity in Nigeria is discussed by Matthews A. Ojo (1988), who observes that the movement
originated in the early 1970s among college students and university
graduates of various denominations. As in many third world settings a
primary emphasis is divine healing, but in addition there is much attention to *restitution* "for one's past sins, mistakes, and every sort of un-
christian act" (1988: 184), reflecting aspects of the traditional Yoruba
concern for purification. Restitution often takes the form of returning

stolen articles, which Ojo interprets as a reaction against the quest for material wealth following the Nigerian oil boom of the 1970s, and which is being duplicated during the mid-1990s among students at American Christian colleges in a wave of public confessionals quite likely in reaction against the quest for wealth during the "yuppie me generation" of the 1980s (Associated Press 1995). Restitution applied to marriage assumes the greed of a polygynous man who makes amends by divorcing all but his first wife (Ojo 1988: 184–185).

Among Catholics, by 1976 the movement's first national leadership conference in Benin City attracted 110 participants with official support from the local bishop. In 1983 the National Advisory Council was formed to oversee movement activities. Francis MacNutt, the first and most widely known among American Catholic Charismatic healers, recounts a Charismatic retreat in Nigeria in which traditional deities were cast out or "delivered" as occult spirits, including the following case of a man in Benin City:

An outstanding Catholic Layman, he was a convert who had been brought up in the old religion. He discovered as a child that after certain practices of dedication his toes were affected by a divining spirit. If the day of his plans were to be propitious, one toe would pinch him; if they were to be unlucky, a different toe would pinch. Consequently, he came to plan his life around these omens, which he said always came true, even if he tried to disregard them. When he desired to pray out loud at our retreat, however, his unpropitious toe began to act up; at this point, he decided that these strange manifestations must be from an evil spirit and had to be renounced. (MacNutt 1975: 9)

This incident is a variant of the time-honored Catholic strategy of ritual incorporation of indigenous practices based on acceptance of their existential reality but negation of their spiritual value, condemning them as inspired by the demonic forces of Satan.

This pattern recurs in especially vivid form in Zambia. Here the movement had two beginnings: one in the early 1970s led by Irish missionary priests (ter Haar 1987) and one in 1976 led by Archbishop Emmanuel Milingo of Lusaka, who in that year established a relationship with The Word of God community and founded his own Divine Providence community, after having quite independently begun to practice faith healing in 1973 (Milingo 1984). In 1979 the archbishop was a prominent participant in a Charismatic pilgrimage to Lourdes. By the early 1980s there was irreconcilable tension between the missionary-led and Milingo wings of the movement, with the latter prevailing and the archbishop being recalled to Rome in 1983.

The archbishop's case is remarkable for two reasons. First, it shows a simultaneous "indigenization" of Charismatic ritual healing and a "Charismatization" of a distinctly African form of Christian healing. As described in his own writings, Milingo's (1984) services included typical elements of Charismatic ritual such as resting in the Spirit, speaking in tongues, naming evil spirits after problematic emotions or behaviors, calling out evil spirits to identify them, recognizing problems caused by ancestral spirits, calling on angels and saints for spiritual protection, anointing of supplicants by lay assistants, and in general a distinction among three types of healing termed physical healing, inner healing, and deliverance. However, within his cultural context God took on material as well as paternal features, and Jesus was reinterpreted as an intercessor of a kind similar to traditional ancestors except in that rather than an ancestor for a single family he was a universal ancestor for all. Moreover, Milingo distinctly recognized and addressed his practice to *mashawe,* a form of spirit affliction recognized in the traditional cultures of Zambia. He made a critical distinction between orderly, intentional liturgical dances appealing to ancestral spirits for protection and disorderly, spirit-controlled dances in what he called the satanically inspired "Church of the Spirits" (Milingo 1984: 32–33). As in traditional culture, but also like many other Catholic Charismatics, he acknowledged that family ancestors could cause affliction, but he also recognized evil spirits that sometimes "take noble names, such as those of famous men. . . . Thus they want to be honored" (1984: 119). Finally, he distinguished between witches, figures from traditional culture who he defined as having given themselves over completely to Satan, and the possessed, who retain sufficient free will to seek help for their condition. To date, this sketchy outline is as far as ethnological scholarship can go in documenting the adaptation and transformation of the Charismatic healing system to a culture different from the Euro-American one in which it originated.

The second remarkable feature of Milingo's case is that within a decade his healing ministry had created such controversy that he was recalled to Rome.[27] There he was detained and interrogated. In a deal with the Vatican, he eventually relinquished his ecclesiastical post, in return for which he was granted an appointment as special delegate to the Pontifical Commission for Migration and Tourism, with the freedom to travel (except to Zambia), and was reassured by the pope that his healing ministry would be "safeguarded" (Milingo 1984: 137). Gerrie ter Haar (1987) plausibly suggests that three lines of political cleavage converged to determine this event. First was the cleavage between Milingo and Rome over the extent and legitimacy of the Africanization of Catholicism. Second was that between Milingo as a popular and charismatic figure and the other Zambian bishops as a bloc representing the ecclesiastical status quo. Third was the cleavage between the missionary-led wing of the Zambian Charismatic Renewal whose approach revolved around prayer groups and cultivation of the Baptism in the Holy Spirit and Milingo's version of the Renewal oriented toward healing in large events, personal encounters, or communal settings. Ironically, given that the overt goal of his recall was in part to protect Zambian Catholics from what must have appeared to Church officials as a kind of neopaganism, Milingo has subsequently become immensely popular as a healer among Italian Charismatics (Rev. Kenneth Metz, pers. comm.). With established followings in ten Italian cities, and already a figure on national television, in 1987 he moved his public healing service from the church of Argentini of Rome to a large room in the Ergife Hotel. Once again in 1989 his controversial ministry was temporarily suspended by the Church and later renewed outside Rome in Velletri (Lanternari 1994). He moved to a new diocese yet again in the early 1990s, and in 1994 the bishop's conference in Tuscany issued a pastoral note on demonology and witchcraft quite likely targeted at Milingo's ministry.

Vittorio Lanternari has written on the Italian adventure of Milingo since 1983. He describes the effect as a "religious short-circuit" between Africa and Europe, and in a surprisingly postmodern image, as the replacement of metaphysical mythology by science fiction mythology (1987, 1994). Lanternari is intent, however, on demonstrating the African provenance of many of Milingo's ideas on witchcraft and sorcery and its homology with folk Italian notions about witchcraft, sorcery, evil eye, and occult powers (see also Charuty 1987: 454), rather than the way it articulates with the Charismatic Renewal. He also makes the observation that devotees in both Rome and Lusaka share the same behavioral manifestations of demonic crisis but attributes this directly to what he describes as Milingo's techniques of instigating then calming these crises by evoking emotional contagion and dependency. Even if relevant, such contagion is no more unique to African Charismatic prophets than to American Protestant Charismatic healers from Derek Prince and Don Basham in the 1960s to John Wimber in the 1980s. (At the same time Lanternari appears to acknowledge that some of the similarity may be due to social milieus that in either the Italian or the African setting create "the sense of bewilderment and impotence in confrontations with common disorder.") Again, what Lanternari refers to as the indiscriminate intertwining of exorcistic and medical-charismatic models of healing may be no more than recognition of the Catholic Charismatic genres of deliverance and physical healing (Csordas 1994a). A generally negative attitude is revealed in the author's accusation that patients in crisis are mocked with such statements as "These are not human beings," which a more generous critic might interpret as referring to the afflicting demons rather than the afflicted persons. However, what in the end Lanternari describes as most typically African is perhaps also most typically postmodern: linking illness not with the more (or biological) but with the domain of impurity, danger, contamination, and pollution. For in then looping back to link illness and evil through multiple entities like Satan, witches, malign spirits, vices, and disgraceful behavior, Archbishop Milingo contributes to a decentering of meaning that cannot but take place in a global movement whose key symbol is, after all, the verbal multiplicity of speaking in tongues.

For Zaire, Fabian (1991, 1994) has discussed the Charismatic Renewal's existence in an urban milieu alongside the Catholic Jamaa movement, the African Bapostolo movement, and traditional African mediumship. On Fabian's account, prayer groups in Lubumbashi appear to have been founded by several local women around 1973. These women in turn cultivated the involvement of several indigenous Catholic clergymen in the role of healer. Only subsequently, largely through the policy of the local archbishop, did these groups come under the influence of the international movement represented by several Jesuit missionary priests and by visits from internationally known figures including (probably in the mid-1970s) Archbishop Milingo from Zambia.

Roughly similar to the distinction noted above for Italy and Zambia, Fabian observes two loosely related types of groups, designating them as *charismatiques* and *renouveau*. The former draw membership from both the middle class and the working poor and are organized into prayer groups based on exercise of the Pentecostal charisms by a core group assembled around a principal leader, with a wider circle of participants who seek to benefit from the charisms around them. The latter consist largely of young, educated adults, are not organized around a single leader, and tend to deemphasize use of the charisms while making group prayer their principal activity. Healers typically take seriously traditional problems caused by sorcery (*fetichisme*), the use of magical objects for protection (*dawa*, or *bwanga*), and spirit affliction (*bulozi*), though preoccupation with spirit possession and witchcraft appears to be greatest in groups with only indirect connections to the international movement. Occasionally politically powerful individuals resort to the Charismatics to escape the escalating necessity of invoking increasingly powerful and dangerous traditional means of spiritual protection. In spirit affliction, the causal agents often appear not to be demonic spirits but those of persons, living or dead and frequently relatives of the afflicted, who are identified and name themselves through the voice of the patient.

Fabian notes several intriguing links between the Jamaa and the Charismatic Renewal. Like Milingo later in Zambia, the Belgian founder of the Jamaa, Fr. Placide Tempels, was recalled from Africa in part for his indigenizing moves, but quite notably had as a protector the Belgian Cardinal Suenens who later emerged as the highest-ranking Church official within the Charismatic Renewal. However, Tempels consistently suppressed Pentecostal manifestations such as glossolalia that probably occurred under the influence of the contemporaneous Protestant Pentecostal Bapostolo movement. Nevertheless, by the 1970s the new Charismatic groups were drawing their leaders and followers from among the ranks of the Jamaa, resulting in the melding of Jamaa ideas and modes of discursive practice with those of the Charismatics. Fabian contrasts the optimism, humanism, and universalism of the early Jamaa with the inward-looking ritualization of personal problems and interpersonal relations characteristic of Charismatics. Along with this, he draws a contrast between the language-centeredness of Jamaa with respect to its oral initiatory practices and the Zairean Charismatics' emphasis on inspired reading of Scripture and their relatively elaborated ritualization of practice. As a note for comparative research, language-centeredness was also characteristic of Catholic Charismatics in the United States at least through the 1970s (Csordas 1987, 1996), but with relatively less emphasis on teaching than on prophecy, a genre of ritual language that from Fabian's account appears to be little elaborated among contemporary Charismatics in Zaire.

Fabian suggests that a feature of social differentiation between the two movements may be that whereas the Jamaa promotes and even requires that its members be married couples, Charismatic groups do not prohibit participation by unmarried youth, adolescents, and divorced people. A second feature is that whereas the followers of Placide Tempels were predominantly workers, the Charismatic Renewal strongly appeals to the growing professional class. This is in part related to what Fabian sees as a general embourgeoisement of Zairean society, but must be seen in the context of the postmodern condition in its Zairean manifestation. For what finally strikes one in Fabian's account is the current state of diversification within Jamaa, the overall proliferation of religious alternatives in the cultural milieu, and the dispersal of charismatic (in the Weberian sense) authority through society. Moreover, access to power is enacted in terms of ingesting and incorporating powerful substances rather than by occupying a territory or imposing order, such that "power is here tied to concrete embodiments rather than to abstract structures" (Fabian 1994: 271). Fabian suggests that this "expresses a cultural preference for a kind of anarchy . . . that encourage[s] the ardent pursuit of power, as well as the proliferation of its embodiments" (1994: 272). In line with the analysis I am developing here, this preexisting local cultural preference takes on particular significance as it is highlighted or comes to the fore in the context of the global hypertrophy of semiosis characteristic of the postmodern condition.

Crossing now to Asia, the Charismatic movement was introduced to Indonesia by Protestants. Indeed, an inspirational book popular among American Catholic Charismatics in the early 1970s was *Like a Mighty Wind* by the Indonesian Protestant neo-Pentecostal Mel Tari. As of 1976 it was still reported that Jakarta prayer groups tended to be half Catholic, an ecumenical mix common in the Midwest of North America but apparently in few other regions. It was said that the movement had made such an impact among Christians in Indonesia that the principal distinction was no longer between Protestants and Catholics but between "those who clap in Church and those who don't," referring to the ebullient style of Charismatic worship (Shelly Errington, pers. comm.).

According to S. E. Ackerman (1981), in neighboring Malaysia the Renewal began in the early 1970s through the activities of a French missionary priest who had become involved in the movement and began to exercise charismatic healing in conjunction with his official status as a diocesan exorcist in Kuala Lumpur. His lay assistant exorcists were active in establishing other Charismatic groups and stimulating growth of the Renewal in the area. Ackerman describes Catholic Pentecostalism in Malaysia as an idiom of spiritual power that replaces those used by traditional mediums and folk healers as a means for dealing with evil spirits and other supernatural forces while at the same time being "derived from concepts of power embedded in popular supernaturalism" (1981: 94). Ackerman describes the experience of an individual who, following episodes of hallucination and uncontrollable violence that he attributed to the effects of sorcery, sought treatment from a *bomoh* (shaman). Having experienced a cure the man began a process of initiation as a shaman himself, only to reject the opportunity in exchange for a parallel role in the "deliverance ministry" among Catholic Charismatics on the grounds that as a traditional practitioner he would be feared and loathed while as a Charismatic healer he would be respected. Ackerman describes spirit possession cases as exceedingly frequent among Malaysian Charismatics, requiring a great deal of lay assistance that innovatively provides opportunities for lay leadership, thus redefining the relationship between laity and clergy. However, there are indications in Ackerman's account that the surge of popularity of deliverance declined somewhat when ministers backed off from an overwhelming demand, and it would be worth investigating whether this corresponds to the surge and decline of deliverance in the United States at roughly the same period in the late 1970s and early 1980s. By 1992 the movement's national convention, with the local archbishop in attendance, attracted over two thousand participants from Malaysia, Brunei, Myanmar, Indonesia, and Singapore, and a covenant community called Light of God was active in the Malaysian city of Taiping.

The Catholic Charismatic Renewal began in Japan in 1972 when Canadian missionaries at a Tokyo parish began a prayer group following a Holy Spirit Seminar conducted by a visiting ecumenical team from Canada and the United States. Members of this group played a large role in spreading the movement. In 1975 the first national leadership conference was held, with roughly half of the participants missionaries from French-, Spanish-, and English-speaking countries. By 1995 there were some seventy-five prayer groups from Hokkaido to Okinawa with a total participation of approximately one thousand (Mathy 1992). Ikegami Yoshimasa (1993), writing on a Protestant Charismatic church in Okinawa, emphasizes both the continuity and competition between them and traditional *yuta* (shamans) with respect to exorcism of demonic spirits. He suggests that although in comparison to the rationalizing and promodern "new religions" of the 1950s and 1960s the Charismatics count among the magical-spiritualistic "new new religions" that participate in the reenchantment of the world, in comparison to traditional shamanism they favor an individualism compatible with modern society rather than the yuta's fatalistic orientation toward life. Further research could examine whether this relation holds among Catholic Charismatics in Okinawa and elsewhere in Japan.

Conclusion

Our global survey of the Charismatic Renewal is only a glimpse at the scope and diversity of the movement. Certainly the phenomenon offers a rare opportunity for ethnological analysis, for although there have been attempts to compare different religious movements or different forms of ritual healing, there has never been a comparison of cultural variants of what is ostensibly the *same* movement or form of healing on a scale more manageable than that, say, of a comparison between "European Catholicism" and "African Catholicism." In this respect the current chapter stands as the barest of outlines and an exhortation to comparative research.

The survey also allows us, or more accurately requires us, to identify multiple dimensions of social analysis relevant to the course of the movement's development across different national and cultural contexts. Within the movement these dimensions sketch the analytic space between radical and moderate visions of community, between parochial and covenant community standpoints, between emphasis on mass manifestations of healing charisms and on collective prayer and worship, between the routinization of charisma and the continued impetus for charismatic renewal. Within the Catholic church they sketch the space between Charismatics and movements espousing social activism, between laity and clergy, between movement and hierarchy. In society at large they outline interaction between the movement as an element of Christian neoconservatism and trends of secular society and culture, between microsocial and macrosocial analysis with respect to interpersonal interaction and institutional constraint, between personal and political with respect to issues of power and experience, between local and global with respect to cultural process and relations of dependency, between premodern and postmodern with respect to the structure of meaning and authority.

Certainly the tensions, dynamics, and consequences within each of these dimensions could be drawn out in greater detail and analyzed as symptomatic of the contemporary condition of culture. For economy of argument, however, I will collapse these issues into a single question. In this respect the global survey will constitute the backdrop against which, in the next chapter, we will consider the empirical and theoretical consequences of what it means to characterize the Charismatic Renewal in its local and global manifestations as a "movement" in the postmodern condition of culture.

2

Religion in the Postmodern Condition

In early March 1973, I made arrangements to attend my first Catholic Pentecostal prayer meeting. I was especially anxious to hear speaking in tongues and was reflecting on the latest anthropological accounts that identified such "ecstatic speech" as a phenomenon of altered states of consciousness.[1] I rode from campus to the suburban midwestern church where the weekly meeting of the Christ the King prayer group took place with a male medical student and a female undergraduate who were group members. On the way, the medical student suggested prayers as a way to prepare spiritually for the meeting. I was in the back seat of the car as both people in front devoutly spoke in tongues. Theories of trance and altered states of consciousness completely preoccupied my thoughts as we approached a red traffic light. I wondered whether someone in trance could stop in time, and why my first empirical evidence on the topic had to be acquired with such apparent risk. Nothing happened. I had no sense even that the driver's reaction time was slowed. Yet that initial encounter was a critical moment in the development of questions that were to guide my research on this religious phenomenon.

It became increasingly evident that the significant questions were not about psychological states, or even about characteristics of people who were attracted to a movement that included speaking in tongues. Instead, I became concerned with the meaning of such ritual utterance across the shifting states and settings of a daily life transformed by experience of the sacred, that primordial sense of otherness the capacity for which defines us as *Homo religiosus* (Eliade 1958; van der Leeuw 1938). More precisely, I became concerned with the creative processes by which this sense of otherness was mobilized to transform daily life in the first place. Charismatics aspire to a culturally coherent world of ritual, experience, language, value, interaction, and presupposition. It is not a world into which they were born but one which is an ongoing collective project, synthesized over a period of some thirty years. The process of this synthesis is a cultural one, of rhetoric and self-persuasion, enacted both in ritual performance and in everyday social practice. Its modus operandi is not one of conversion in the usual sense from nonbeliever to believer (see Harding 1987; Stromberg 1993) but of cultural creation that forges a sacred self. This sacred self, transcending the standpoint of individual experience, exists insofar as it participates in what I take to be the sine qua non of culture: a world that is taken for granted in a deep sense and a life conditioned to be lived in terms of that world.

Yet as a student of the anthropology of religion, from the time of my first encounter the expression "Catholic Pentecostalism" struck me as a perfect oxymoron. Far from designating a reality that could be deeply taken for granted, it suggested the blend of what I assumed were two incompatible versions of Christianity. The "postmodern" was not yet current as an analytic category that could subsume such an apparent cultural anomaly. There was at the time only a limited repertoire of anthropological and sociological concepts to describe what I was observing. Thus Catholic Pentecostalism was a "revitalization movement" that aimed at breathing new life into a tired cultural tradition, in this case Roman Catholicism. The mix of Catholicism and Pentecostalism was a kind of "syncretism," the fusion and mutual reinterpretation of formerly alien cultural traditions. The growing complexity of symbolic, behavioral, and organizational forms within the movement was an example of "intracultural variation" within a "religious subculture" or "part-society." In the two ensuing decades, interpretation and hermeneutics, a revived concern with cultural criticism in an interdisciplinary cultural studies, and the reformulation of anthropology in poststructuralist and postmodern terms have rendered these concepts entirely problematic. In this view revitalization can be transformation and movement can be dispersal; syncretism erroneously presupposes discrete forms that are subsequently mixed; intracultural variation becomes multiculturalism; and subcultures are fragments in a cultural pastiche (see Lyotard 1984; Baudrillard 1983; Featherstone 1991; Tyler 1987; Marcus and Fisher 1986; Sangren 1988; Strathern 1987).

Karla Poewe has argued specifically that Charismatic Christianity as a whole, both Protestant and Catholic, is a postmodern phenomenon particularly in its interpretation of experience, the universe, and history in terms of metonymic signs that directly manifest and point to the creative activity of the Creator rather than in terms of metaphor (1989: 367; see also Roelofs 1994). My argument is that the Catholic movement is not accurately described as a postmodern cultural phenomenon because of marked impulses toward traditionalism and centralism (see Cohen 1986, 1993; Hébrard 1987). Nevertheless, it does exist within a postmodern condition of culture. Specifically, there are three features of this postmodern condition that I have found valuable in understanding the Charismatic movement: the dissociation of symbols from their referents in such a way as to facilitate a free play of signifiers over the cultural landscape; the decentering of authority in meaning, discourse, and social form; and the globalization of culture associated with consumerism and the information revolution.[2] In the remainder of this chapter I will examine this thesis, bringing to bear critical conceptions of movement, identity, self, performance, practice, and habitus.

Movement: The Conventional Problematic

Let us first review some of the more conventional formulations by which one might account for the phenomenon of the Catholic Charismatic Renewal, then turn to a more critical problematization. In one sense the synthesis in the United States of Catholicism and Pentecostalism, the latter of which has been described by Martin Marty (1976) as the only real indigenous form of Christianity in that country, is a culmination of the "Americanization" of Catholicism begun with the proletarianization of Catholic European peasants who came as strangers and immigrants to the cities of an already established nation (McAvoy 1969).[3] This blending of forms might also be situated in the context of the Catholic movement of "modernism" over the past century and a half, including features such as liturgical reform, ecumenism, revitalization of biblical scholarship, a more responsible role for the laity, collegiality in Church government, and the engagement of the Church in the "external world" (O'Dea 1968).

In addition, the moment in which the movement originated coincided with the beginning of the "post-Tridentine" epoch of Catholic history, the Second Vatican Council of 1962–1965 marking the end of a regime of doctrine and practice that had lasted four hundred years since the Council of Trent in 1545–1563. Changes instituted in the immediate post-Vatican period created the conditions of possibility for the Charismatic Renewal in several respects. The council's position on the theoretical possibility of charisms[4] opened the way for the adoption of the Pentecostal spiritual gifts in their already extant ritual forms. Reinterpretation of the sacraments, wherein penance or confession became the sacrament of reconciliation (rather than of guilt) and extreme unction or the last anointing became the sacrament of the sick (rather than of the dying) opened the way for Charismatic faith healing. Changes in liturgical form such as turning the altar to face the congregation and adopting vernacular language opened the way for paraliturgical innovation such as the Charismatic prayer meeting. The new biblicism has been taken up wholeheartedly by Charismatics, sometimes to the point of fundamentalism, and the movement is a stronghold of lay initiative and ecumenism.

These changes coincided with the culmination of the post–World War II era in the cultural ferment of the 1960s. Its racial strife, the morally devastating Indo-Chinese War, and mass college enrollments of the baby boom generation spawned movements of black power, feminism, and eventually the New Age. Catholics had a variety of options ranging from the Christian Family movement, Marriage Encounter, the Cursillo, the Christian Worker movement, and the "underground church"[5] to discussion and encounter groups, home masses with avant-garde liturgies, and the political thought of liberation theology. Many of these were characterized by motives of community and renewal, and the catalyst of Pentecostalism added a totalizing enthusiasm and experience of the sacred, precipitating a new movement out of post-Vatican II Catholicism.

To suggest that the Charismatic Renewal is a "crisis cult" (La Barre 1970) that developed in response to cultural malaise within the Church and within society at large does not, however, account either for its success or for why some people and not others become Charismatics. Neither does it account for the movement's dramatic international expansion across a multiplicity of local cultural settings. When we turn to the question of whether individual participation was precipitated by a discrete personal crisis of faith or meaning or by a traumatic life event, the results are mixed.[6] While some American participants acknowledge joining in the wake of an intense personal crisis or conversion experience, others regard it as a perfectly natural step to have taken at a particular moment in their lives. While it is acknowledged that the movement attracts "needy" and "wounded" people, it also attracts the well adjusted who regard it as their responsibility to care for and "minister to" the troubled. Even as a response to crisis, the intensity with which someone embraces the movement may be rather subdued, as in the case of one North American Charismatic who stated matter-of-factly that she had been suffering from postpartum depression following the birth of her second child, that attending the Catholic Charismatic prayer meeting "seemed to help," and that consequently she and her husband decided to continue their participation.

Alongside crises in meaning and traumatic events we must also consider, at least within North American culture, the role of expectable crises of psychosexual development. Two suggestive facts are that the Charismatic Renewal originated among graduate students and young university faculty and that Benedict Mawn's (1975) data from the early years of the movements reveal that 40 percent of Charismatics were between the ages of twenty and thirty-four. We can hypothesize, then, that the movement's interpersonal and ritual style owes a great deal to a cohort of people who were at the developmental stage, following Erik Erikson, defined by the ego conflict of "intimacy versus isolation." In this period a person must "face the fear of ego loss in situations which call for self-abandon: in the solidarity of close affiliation, in orgasms and sexual unions, in close friendships and in physical combat, in experiences of inspiration by teachers and of intuition from the recesses of the self" (Erikson 1963: 264). With the synthesis of Catholicism and Pentecostalism, the developmental need for the "solidarity of close affiliations" became realized in the Charismatic ritual forms of personal relationship with the deity, collective prayer, and communal life. Coming to grips with "intuitions from the recesses of the self" took the public form of divinely inspired prophetic utterance and the private forms of "inner healing" from emotional disability and "leadings from the Lord" through prayer and inspiration.[7]

While this formulation might be appealing, it will not do to characterize the movement by too much youthful vitality, for since 1967 it has undergone a demographic transition. Aside from the smaller covenant or intentional community segment, Charismatics themselves have not only aged but have also attracted increasingly older members, such that the modal age of participants is at present probably in the fifties. The Charismatic Renewal is no longer the vanguard movement it conceived itself to be in its first phases. It has a stable bureaucratic organization, and by the late 1980s it had participated in a Vatican conference on an equal footing with Catholic organizations such as Opus Dei, Marriage Encounter, and the Cursillo. In this sense it has become one among other conservative movements in global Catholicism, as well as in contemporary North America (see Smidt 1988), while in another sense it has fulfilled a goal of merging back into the mainstream Church with renewed spirituality, since many former Charismatics remain active in parochial affairs. By 1990 the Catholic Charismatic Renewal was composed of some five thousand prayer groups in the United States and an unspecified number internationally, various diocesan renewal centers and independent covenant communities, three more or less tightly structured covenant community networks (two of these being transnational in scope), and an international office based in Rome with links to the hierarchy as well as to national service committees around the globe. Despite diversity and even disagreement, participants continue to recognize not only that they have common roots in the Catholic Charismatic Renewal but also that they are part of the larger Pentecostal world.[8]

This leads us to another question central to the conventional problematic, what constitutes an identity as a Catholic Charismatic? This question can be taken in two senses: that of social identity reflected by the statement "I am a Charismatic" and that of personal identity constituted by what it means to be Charismatic. Parallel to the reserve noted at the beginning of chapter 1 about calling the Charismatic Renewal a "movement," especially in the early years some participants would reject the label "Charismatic" because it appeared to violate their sense of spontaneity. They would say that they could not *be* Charismatics because it was "not an organization but a movement of the Spirit." As the movement progressed, some would refuse the label because it might "appear elitist" within the Church, or alienate other Catholics who had come to regard Charismatics as religious weirdos.

Nevertheless, there are various resources that allow us to assess the number of individuals claiming identity as Charismatics. Table 1 shows an estimate of the relative numbers of classical and neo-Pentecostals (see chapter 1, note 1, for the distinction) as of 1980. These figures, however, do not reflect the dramatic growth of Pentecostalism in the past fifteen years. By the end of the 1980s George Gallup and Jim Castelli (1989: 126) estimated that there were 14,117,000 Protestant and 2,500,000 Catholic Pentecostals or Charismatics in the United States. The theologian Harvey Cox (1995; xv) cited a worldwide membership

Table 1. *Adult Pentecostals and Neo-Pentecostals, 1980*

Classical Pentecostal denominations		2,766,337
Neo-Pentecostals in other denominations		
Mainline Protestant neo-Pentecostals (Baptist, Lutheran, Methodist, Presbyterian, Reformed)	700,000	
Black neo-Pentecostals	350,000	
Orthodox neo-Pentecostals	10,000	
Anglican neo-Pentecostals	100,000	
Catholic neo-Pentecostals	1,000,000	
		2,160,000
Total		4,926,337

SOURCE: *World Christian Encyclopedia* 1982.

of 410,000,000 just in the formal Pentecostal churches alone, with an annual growth rate of 20,000,000 per year.

A critical point in the movement leadership's own assessment of the numbers of Catholic Charismatics, evident in the discrepant figures for that year and for 1987 in table 2, occurred about 1980. The smaller figures represent the leadership's perception of decline in active participation; the larger figures reported by outside observers most likely include three categories in addition to currently active participants: those who were once but were no longer active, those who were only periodically or occasionally active, and those only peripherally exposed to Charismatic activities.

Of the first category, those who had "gone on to other things" and no longer actively participated might or might not still consider themselves to be Charismatic, and might or might not continue to speak in tongues in private. Regarding the second category, there is evidence that Catholic Charismatics are more likely to be occasional participants than their Protestant counterparts. Although Gallup and Castelli's (1989: 126–127) survey found that 15 percent of Charismatics/Pentecostals are Catholic, only 11 percent of those who attend regularly are Catholic. Table 3 shows an estimate of regular active participation in the United States drawn from the movement's own irregularly published directory of prayer groups. These figures are only indicative, however, in that it is impossible to determine from the average reported attendance the size of the stable core of those who participate every week and those who attend

Table 2. *Adult Participation in the Catholic Charismatic Renewal, U.S.A.*

1967	——
1972	200,000
1974	500,000
1976	670,000
1980	1,000,000
	200,000 *
1987	2,500,000 **
	160,000 ***

SOURCES: *World Christian Encyclopedia* 1982.
* *NCO Newsletter* 1980, 1981
** Gallup and Castelli 1989
*** National Communication Office 1987

Table 3. *Average Prayer Group Attendance*

Year	Number of Groups	Group Average Attendance	Total Average Attendance
1975	2,183	51.5	115,283
1983	4,004	35.8	156,864
1986	4,814	17.8	120,762
1990	4,700	30.6	143,755
1992	5,141	27.7	142,504

SOURCE: Charismatic Renewal Services, prayer group directories.

occasionally and in that the directories appear to exclude most of the movement's covenant communities, although at a generous estimate these account for no more than five thousand to seven thousand additional adults. Finally, much of the peripheral exposure of the third category undoubtedly took place in healing services led by Charismatics, which became frequent after 1975 and which by the late 1980s were quite popular among Catholics across the country. Many who attended these services did not consider themselves Charismatics and may not even have been aware that they were participating in a Charismatic activity.[9] Indeed, among all those who attend Charismatic/Pentecostal services or prayer meetings, Catholics are the most likely (33%) to have

Table 4. *Roman Catholics with Some Exposure to the Movement*

United States	1980	8,000,000
United States	1980	6,000,000–7,000,000 *
United States	1987	10,000,000 **
International	1987	20,000,000 **

SOURCES: *World Christian Encyclopedia* 1982.
* *NCO Newsletter* 1980, 1981
** National Communication Office 1987

attended only once (Gallup and Castelli 1989: 127). It is this level of participation that is reflected in the inflated estimates in table 4.

Given the variations both in willingness to claim Charismatic identity and in degrees of participation, there is yet a way to identify Charismatics by their engagement in a coherent body of key ritual practices. Using data from our late 1980s survey of participants in New England Catholic Charismatic healing services, we adopted attendance at prayer meetings and speaking in tongues as two practices suggested by ethnographic experience as valid criteria of Charismatic identity. We categorized frequency of attendance into weekly and less than weekly (including never) and frequency of speaking in tongues into often and never. The analysis showed that healing service participants clustered predominantly into two large groups, one identifiable as Charismatics who attended prayer meetings and spoke in tongues and one identifiable as non-Charismatics who rarely if ever attended prayer meetings and never spoke in tongues (table 5). When we then compared these categories with respect to whether people had ever experienced divine healing and how often they had undergone the experience of resting in the Spirit,[10] analysis showed that those people we classed as Charismatics were significantly more likely to respond affirmatively.[11] In other words, those people had in fact engaged in Charismatic ritual practices (typically involving laying on of hands) leading to experiences of healing and resting in the Spirit.

These analyses show in statistical form what can also be observed ethnographically, namely, that Charismatics participate in a coherent system of ritual performance. The importance of such performance for defining Charismatic identity is evident in situations where a Catholic prayer group may already exist but defines itself as non-Charismatic or pre-Charismatic. In her study of a Catholic prayer group's efforts to "become" Charismatic, Frances R. Westley (1977) shows that speaking

Table 5. *Consistency of Charismatic Practice among Healing
Service Participants*

Frequency of Prayer Meeting Attendance	Frequency of Speaking in Tongues	
	Often	*Never*
Weekly	144 (30.6%)	84 (17.8%)
< Weekly	79 (16.8%)	164 (34.8%)

NOTE: The chi-square value with 1 degree of freedom was 44.32, and the statistical probability of these results occurring was .00. The proportions of active Charismatic and non-Charismatic are virtually identical across genders. Of 587 participants in five healing services who responded to our questionnaire, 108 failed to complete one or both of the items in this analysis, leaving an effective *n* of 479.

in tongues alone is not a necessary and sufficient criterion of being Charismatic. Instead, the performative ritual genre of "sharing" (see chapter 6) the intimacy of one's life experiences and thoughts "was not only seen as an important part of becoming a charismatic, it was at times expressed as the essence of charisma. . . . [I]ndividual members saw the moment that they began sharing as the moment of their rebirth," and members stated that until they began sharing their prayer group was not a Charismatic group (Westley 1977: 929).[12] What is critical here, and what will become clear as the discussion proceeds, is that sharing is not a casual form of interaction but a named genre of ritual language. Correspondingly, the badge of identity is best described not as individual behavior but as the collective performance of self in ritual terms.

However, personal identity as a Catholic Charismatic is not merely a function of experiencing the Pentecostal Baptism in the Holy Spirit, of being healed, or of participating in prayer groups or communities. Despite the currency of the notion of being born again, Charismatics are more likely to say that religious experience allows them to discover their "real self" than to claim that they have been given a "new self." This is identity in the sense of coming to know "who I am in Christ." It is where collective life and ritual healing converge as self-transformative dimensions of Charismatic life. This convergence is essential and accounts for why Charismatics typically say that everyone is in need of healing and that spiritual growth is a process of healing. It has been observed in one way or another by previous commentators on Catholic Pentecostalism. Meredith McGuire (1982) treats community life and ritual healing in separate sections of her monograph while giving equal treatment to both. Charuty (1987), writing on Catholic Charismatics in France and Italy, views the experience of conversion through Baptism in the Holy Spirit as strictly analogous to that of healing through the practices of healing of memories. Neither is it accidental that my own treatment of the phenomenon appears in parallel monographs or that the notion of self is critical to the theoretical underpinnings of both.[13]

Movement: The Critical Problematic

To conclude simply that the Charismatic Renewal has passed through the process described by Max Weber (1947, 1958) as the "routinization of charisma" or completed Anthony F. C. Wallace's (1957) life cycle of a "revitalization movement" would not be entirely accurate. Neither would it address the questions we have set for ourselves about religion as a form of human creativity and its role in the life of culture and the performance of self in the postmodern condition. Accordingly I must make good on the promise to adopt a critical attitude toward my use of the term "movement" in a way that shows why what is to come is necessary. Traditional anthropology often assumed that a movement can be treated as a bounded unit of analysis, a kind of "tribe" or "subculture," in spite of the fact that movements are invariably reactions to or attempts to alter conditions in their cultural milieu. Ralph Nicholas (1973) compared this conception of movements with Alfred Kroeber's description of peasant societies as "part-societies with part-cultures" but remained within the standard paradigm in wondering whether such units of analysis were "representative" of anything larger than themselves. Such a position fails to recognize either that the issues raised by a movement are coterminous with themes of the culture in which it occurs or that the course of the movement is itself bound up with the interaction of its participants with the society through which they are "moving." This point is underscored in the observation made by Fabian (1971) that in the Catholic Jamaa movement in Zaire there were few visible social activities, and none of the ritual paraphernalia, insignia, biblical attire, or communal buildings typical of many African religious movements. Faced with this lack of overt boundaries, he concluded that a movement could neither be taken for granted nor postulated theoretically as a discrete entity.

The Charismatic Renewal and the neo-Pentecostal movement of which it is a part are themselves significant in problematizing the notion of a movement as a social entity. First, while charismatic leadership was always a principal concern of research on religious movements, the standard paradigm cannot account for the observation first made by Luther Gerlach and Virginia Hine (1970) that Pentecostalism has a "reticulate and acephalous" organization. In other words, it is characterized by more or less closely interacting networks of groups and has no single recognizable leader. Second, while a major achievement of the standard paradigm was an explanation of religious movements as reactions to deprivation, or the perception of deprivation relative to more privileged groups, it was inadequate to deal with the fact that many Charismatics and neo-Pentecostals are relatively affluent and have relatively stable lifestyles.

Beyond the issue of boundedness, the very concept of movement is in fact highly metaphorical. James Fernandez (1979) identifies three kinds of movement implicit in this metaphor: analytic movement that creates abstract dimensions of scientific thought; moral movement or the change in qualitative states through the use of metaphors themselves; and architectonic movement or the change in qualitative state achieved by the movement of bodies through culturally structured space. He implies that the creativity inherent in moral and architectonic movement is missed by studies of religious movements that are primarily descriptive or concerned with questions of causality. The latter in particular tend to regard "movement" as something that happens to people rather than something they accomplish, and is often concerned primarily with the discovery of mechanisms that could explain its existence. Thus the dominant questions have been those of movement dynamics: what caused the movement, what was the role of charismatic (in the sense elaborated by Weber) leaders, what were the mechanisms of recruitment and indoctrination, and what were the typical stages in the life cycle or natural history of movements. These are by no means invalid questions, but a different sense of what a movement must be begins to emerge with the shift from concern with the social *mechanisms* that account for it to the phenomenon as a formulation of *meaning* in its cultural milieu.

A third issue relevant to rethinking the concept of movement is that the standard paradigm was developed in large part to account for movements occurring in situations of culture contact and colonial domination. Virtually all were what we can refer to as *religions of peoples*. Though they were typically described as requiring personal transformation and cultivation of a "new man," the ultimate subject of their spirituality is an ethnic or political collectivity. The classic examples are Melanesian cargo cults, the American Indian Ghost Dance, peyote religion, Handsome Lake religion, the African Watchtower movement, and Zulu Zionism. This paradigm might appear to apply to a movement like the Charismatic Renewal that includes a ritual self-definition as a "people" of God and a goal of "revitalizing" the Catholic church. However, early attempts to apply the classic explanation of relative deprivation in the face of an apparent lack of oppression led to such strained suggestions as that Catholic Charismatics suffered from "affective deprivation" (McGuire 1976) or "transcendency deprivation" (Mawn 1975). In contrast to the religions of peoples, there is another and heretofore virtually unrecognized category of religious movement that we may refer to as *religions of the self*. These occur under somewhat different conditions, and whatever social or political change they desire is expected to be a side effect of their ultimate goal of subjective transformation. They include the Indian Radhakrishna bhajanas, the Javanese aliran kebatinan mystical sects, Japanese "new religions," African Aladura churches, perhaps some early European heretical movements and more recent enthusiastic movements in the eighteenth and nineteenth centuries, and certainly the American New Age movement. Among these religions of the self, I would argue that the Charismatic Renewal's desire to become a "community" and a "people" does not qualify it as a religion of a people but instead idealizes a kind of self characteristic of what Ferdinand Tönnies long ago labeled "gemeinschaft" (personalistic, sociocentric community) in distinction to the autonomous self of "gesellschaft" (impersonal, egocentric society).

These three issues—conceiving a movement as an entity, facing the problem of meaning, and accounting for religions of the self—intersect with the features of the postmodern condition of culture identified earlier. Specifically, a movement can hardly exist as a bounded social and cultural entity in a milieu constituted by unbounded and free-floating signifiers. The source of meaning can hardly be secure given the decentering of authority in meaning, discourse, and social form. Not only the self, but a particular form of self, takes precedence over peoples under the condition of globalization of consumer culture.

Placing the notion of movement in this critical light has the immediate advantage of allowing the original designation of Catholic Pentecostalism to appear not as an isolated oxymoron or cultural anomaly but as an example of the breakdown of boundaries between symbolic forms whose referents are no longer stable. A similar point can be made in response to Lanternari's (1987) characterization of the appeal of former

Zambian Archbishop Milingo's healing ministry to Italian Charismatics as a "short-circuit" between African and European forms of spirituality: there is less, not more, anomaly in the Milingo case if it is acknowledged that the contemporary situation is best represented not as a
modernist circuit diagram but as a postmodern montage of transposable
spiritualities.

Moreover, not only does the movement merge Pentecostalism and
Catholicism, it participates to varying degrees and with varying degrees
of self-acknowledgment in other contemporary cultural trends—certainly with religious neoconservatism in its advocacy of "traditional"
gender roles and its opposition to abortion rights, but also with the
New Age in its emphasis on personal growth, community, healing energy, the Sufi Enneagram (a technique of personality evaluation), and
the integration by some faith healers of techniques like "therapeutic
touch" with Pentecostal "laying on of hands." Hollywood movies like
The Exorcist series are of immediate concern, and are condemned not
as sensationalist superstition but as sensationalist exaggeration of real,
sober spiritual warfare against the demonic legions of Satan; and there
are real "Ghostbusters" who do not regard their work as amusing. The
influence of popular psychology is present in the appeal to Charismatics
of "twelve-step" programs and of concepts of the psychosomatic, addic-
tion, codependency, "adult children" of alcoholic parents, and the "inner child" buried in a person's psyche. Charismatics cite research findings
that stress may be implicated in certain types of arthritis to support their
conception that faith healing works not directly on the physical affliction
but by removing the emotional stress that causes it. Evil spirits are sometimes described in psychological terms as "autonomous complexes."
Healers cite Jung on the shadow, on the importance of spirituality, and
on the healing power of imagery processes. The experience of resting in
the Spirit, a sacred swoon in which one is overcome by the power of
God, is at once described in terms of Teresa of Avila's exposition of
three types of ecstasy and compared to Abraham Maslow's eleven criteria of peak experience.[14]

In the background is the constant drone of speaking in tongues, a
form of sacred utterance lacking any semantic component and hence
the ideal typical case of free-floating signifiers. Indeed, glossolalia was
an early image of the postmodern semiotic deluge in the fiction of
Thomas Pynchon (Lhamon 1976), and it is relevant to my argument
both as a ritual practice and as a linguistic phenomenon. As a ritual practice, with the advent of the neo-Pentecostal movement, it became de-

tached from its evident sociological moorings. No longer merely an ecstatic manifestation of spirituality characteristic of a bounded lower-class
segment of society, it moved out of small Pentecostal churches and became routinely available across Christian denominations, and out of the
back woods and inner cities to become routinely available in suburban
living rooms and college campuses. As a linguistic phenomenon, the issue is more complex, for Charismatic glossolalia is less an instance of the
free play of signifiers than it is a problematization and commentary on
the second characteristic of the postmodern condition, the decentering
of meaning. First, while speaking in tongues emphasizes the detachment
of linguistic utterance from its semantic moorings, it at the same time
emphasizes utterance as a bodily act, a giving voice. Second, glossolalia may occur either in the highly centered, authoritative genre of prophecy, an inspired message from God, or in the form of prayer that demo-
cratically (narcissistically?) expresses the private intention of the speaker.
Third, as prayer, while in principle it may mean everything and nothing,
it is frequently assigned the unitary meaning of expressing "praise" to
the deity. Fourth, while it allows for infinite improvisation, in practice
this is frequently repetition of a limited repertoire of phrases, and different sets of glossolalic phrases are sometimes recognized as distinct
"prayer languages," of which an individual may be "gifted" with more
than one.[15] Finally, as a simulacrum of language in the sense described by
Jean Baudrillard (1983) as characteristic of postmodern American culture, it is precisely a phenomenon that problematizes expressive authenticity by becoming more true and more profoundly meaningful than
natural language.[16]

The problematization of a center for Charismatics takes place in sociological terms as well. One of the earliest accounts of Protestant neo-
Pentecostalism is famous for describing the social organization of the
phenomenon as "acephalous and reticulate" (Gerlach and Hine 1970).
At the time this struck many observers as an anomaly among religious
movements—an anomaly on the same order as the apparent oxymoron
of Catholic Pentecostalism—since such movements are typically assumed
to be led by a single Weberian charismatic leader. The Roman Catholic
version of neo-Pentecostalism, given its cultural context in a postmodern condition and its institutional context within one of the most tena-
cious of premodern institutions, has undergone a series of revealing and
sometimes painful recenterings. As we have seen, while it began as a
loose collection of prayer groups, it soon established a centralized bu-
reaucracy around its National Service Committee. Moreover, it has from

the outset been characterized by tension between local prayer groups and tightly organized communities that claimed a central, vanguard role in the movement. Finally, as the movement proliferated internationally in what was at least initially a grassroots, reticulate manner, its coordinating office moved from the control of a North American community in Ann Arbor to Brussels under the dual auspices of the Word of God community and Cardinal Suenens and finally to the ultimate center of Rome and beyond the control of the original covenant community leadership. The Word of God neither moved to the center as the leading force behind the international office nor received legitimacy from the center as an international covenant community, losing out in the latter respect to the Catholic Fraternity of Charismatic Covenant Communities and Fellowships, but instead became the center of its own international network of covenant communities (the Sword of the Spirit), only to once again undergo a decentering when it split into two factions in 1991 (see chapter 3).

The international proliferation of the movement introduces the third element of the postmodern condition, the globalization of popular culture. This overlaps with the problem of centering in two ways. First, glossolalia is again the key image of universal communication, each individual in a "personal" relationship with the deity, regardless of whether the phonologist can identify regional "dialects" of speaking in tongues. Second, there is no consensus over whether the movement spread initially from a North American center, and later from its official center in Rome, or whether separate local movements eventually became co-opted by the Charismatic Renewal and hence tied to its social center and ideological agenda. As I noted above, it appears typical for the movement to have been introduced into third world nations by a missionary priest who became involved during a visit to the United States, organized a prayer group on his return, and subsequently called for outside help with doctrinal instruction and other assistance, eventually setting up a national service committee tied to the movement's international office in Rome. However, Setha Low (pers. comm.) has suggested for Costa Rica and Johannes Fabian (1991) has documented for Zaire that non-Charismatic Catholic prayer groups began independently and were subsequently co-opted into the international movement. In Zambia, the movement had two origins, one with missionary priests and one with former Archbishop Milingo (1984). In Italy independent groups appear to have existed outside formal movement sanction (Pace 1978).

Let us take the argument one step farther, and for the sake of future analysis distinguish among three complementary positions that can be identified by the phrases "world system," "local and global dialectic," and "postmodern condition" (see also Csordas 1992). From the generalized *world system* position (Wallerstein 1977; Chirot and Hall 1982), the need to account for a phenomenon such as the Charismatic Renewal suggests adding an explicit ideological/religious dimension to the notion of a global social system (see also Csordas 1992; Robertson and Chirico 1985; Robertson 1992; Friedman 1994; Wuthnow 1980). Specifically, it would appear that the increasing articulation of the world social system generates an ideological impulse toward formulations of universal culture such as this movement. However, to the extent that world systems theory is concerned with the social relation of dependency between center and periphery, there is a tendency to neglect a process identified by a second position, the cultural dialectic between *local and global* processes (Fabian 1991; Poewe 1989, 1994). There is doubtless more than meets the eye, for example, in Charismatics' acknowledgment that everywhere in the world they "do the same things" in the practice of ritual healing but that there are some "very different manifestations" (Rev. Kenneth Metz, pers. comm.). The case of Archbishop Milingo is perhaps the most vivid example of local-global interaction, insofar as the resumption of his healing work in Italy with substantial impact on Charismatics there somewhat ironically expanded the global influence of a centrally repressed local "ministry."

These considerations lead back to the third position, that of the *postmodern condition*. Rather than presuming that the disjunctive features of the "postmodern" are incompatible with the integrative implications of a world "system," could it not be that postmodernism is a label that usefully describes the cultural structure associated with such a global political-economic system? I do not believe that this suggestion requires reducing the principles of either position to those of the other. Consider Mike Featherstone's argument that under contemporary conditions "the sacred is able to sustain itself outside of organized religion within consumer culture" (1991: 126). If this means that consumer culture and its spectacles relocate and diffuse the sacred into culture at large, it would seem to be a postmodernist version of Robert Bellah's (1970; Bellah and Hammond 1980) civil religion thesis. In fact, Charismatic religion *as religion* is highly adaptable to postmodern forms, as Susan Harding (1988) has shown in her examination of the world of televangelism.

Furthermore, the notion of a postmodern condition does not imply that modern meanings are superseded by postmodern ones, but that in becoming decentered they are resituated such that their authoritativeness is altered with respect to competing or divergent meanings, thus constituting the multiplicity and relativity much touted as characteristic of the postmodern. For example, and specifically with respect to the Charismatic Renewal, Martine Cohen (1993) has compared two French covenant communities, arguing that one conforms to the ethos of advanced, postindustrial capitalism (particularly in that it melds the notions of salvation and self-realization) while the other conforms to the ethos of paternalistic capitalism (in its mode of embracing hierarchical order).

At the same time, as literature on Catholic Pentecostalism in different cultural settings begins to allow the kind of international sketch I presented in the preceding chapter, it is apparent that the movement embodies the dialectic between local and global processes as much or more so than earlier forms of classical Pentecostalism. In what Featherstone (1991) has called the postmodern "globalization of diversity," the cultural other ceases to be exotic as cultures stand face-to-face and natives talk back. Where otherness among humans becomes mundane and taken for granted, the Charismatic formulation of a universal culture in the sense posited by world systems theory reasserts the sacred other as a kind of cultural counterweight. It offers a distinct metalanguage for the heteroglossic simultaneity that exists due to the "overproduction of signs and loss of referents" in global consumer culture (Featherstone 1991). It is the language of charisma and community, but most critically it is the language of absolute otherness. After all, there is no more characteristically postmodern phenomenon than speaking in tongues—which means nothing, but which everyone can understand.

Clearly no definitive conclusions can yet be drawn from such an outline. It can be said, however, that the multiple reinterpretations, reflections, backwashes, anchorings, hybridizations, and discontinuities of the Charismatic Renewal in its global manifestations is an ideal showplace of the postmodern condition of culture. Further, it can be argued that globalization is not isomorphic with Westernization. Consider the example of Satan, the West's great subsuming symbol of the spiritual domain, portrayed by Miguel Asturias in his remarkable novel *Mulata* as the colonial master of all dark forces. A conventional approach to colonialism or cultural imperialism would see in Satan a homogenizing function and a reduction of moral indeterminacy to moral dualism. The postmodern hypothesis would call attention instead to the entropic destabilizing of key symbols such as that of Satan, with the consequence of semiotic decentering and fragmentation. To borrow from the Bible, with a nod to Alexander Leighton, an underlyingly unitary Satan can no longer announce "My name is legion," but a dissolved and suspended Satan must be recognized whose "essence is legion." The leaders of the movement at its international office in Rome have a vested interest in uniformity and orthodoxy. Yet the tension between local and global, uniformity and multiplicity, is being worked through every day among participants in this proliferating social phenomenon. Global culture is not homogeneous, nor are its dynamics determined by homogeneous processes.

Reason and Religion

Not the least significant feature of its existence in a postmodern condition of culture is the style in which Catholic Charismatics integrate science and religion (see also Poewe 1994). If the interaction between medical and religious sensibilities is vivid in the French healing community discussed in the preceding chapter, an even more striking example is the Charismatic medical and scientific examination of the Marian apparitions at Medjugorje. Going well beyond the practice of Catholic authorities who attempt clinical verification of miracle healing at Lourdes, a Charismatic theologian and his surgeon colleague conducted a series of electroencephalogram, electro-oculogram, heart rhythm, and blood pressure tests of the visionary youths (Laurentin and Joyeux 1987). Their purpose was in part to inquire into the normal or pathological character of the experiences, but also to examine the physiological correlates of ecstatic/mystical states. Their striking photographs of pious youth with heads crowned by a halo of electrodes emphasize the postmodern juxtaposition of science and the sacred. In yet another of Medjugorje's postmodern juxtapositions, while international Charismatic pilgrims were praying for healing in their way, Mart Bax (1992) reports, traditional peasant women were being terrorized by devils and evil spirits. The women complained of experiencing mental and physical ailments, and there was a growing incidence of accidents, deaths, and domestic mishaps. According to Bax, on being dismissed as hysterical by the priest they approached for exorcism, they went to "wise old women" instead for advice on illness "of the head" and "of the heart" and for exorcism, amulets, and protective herbs.

Meanwhile, in the United States, a priest whose followers typically experience the sacred swoon of resting in the Spirit (see Csordas 1994a) was eager to conduct electrocardiogram measurements to demonstrate not only the reality but also the beneficial nature of the phenomenon. Medical school researchers declined to collaborate on the grounds that there were too many variables involved. Again, a Catholic physician extrapolating from the pathophysiology of a rare neurological condition published an article attributing the common experience of warmth while laying on hands to divine activation of the parasympathetic nervous system, causing increased blood flow to the afflicted body part of the patient and often as well to the hand of the healer. Finally, a team of Charismatic healers documented on film an attempt in a Catholic hospital to clinically validate the effects on illness and injury of prayer with laying on of hands.

Despite the apparent incongruity of these juxtapositions, careful consideration of their underlying cultural logic suggests caution about what is implied by terms such as "modern" and "postmodern." Those who conducted the tests at Medjugorje were not looking for a natural *cause* except to rule out pathology, and still less were they looking for physiological *explanation* of the phenomenon. They did not interpret sensory disengagement and spontaneous behavioral coordination among the visionaries as evidence of hypnotic dissociation and suggestion, but as ecstatic concentration on a spiritual object, and they supported this interpretation with EEG results that provided neither pathological nor somehow "special" data but showed "normal" wakefulness and attentiveness. Thus scientific data are used to determine psychophysical *correlates* of mystical experience, or to establish *evidence* for whether the cause is divine. In the case of the physician explaining warmth during laying on of hands, parasympathetic activity describes not a *cause* but a *mechanism,* or at most a proximate cause of the phenomenon. The ultimate cause is again presumed to be divine action. Scientific reason is not denied but is used only to understand the mode of divine action and not for purposes of explanation: for the faithful, science addresses the how but not the why of phenomena.

This observation about science and religion recalls the well-known argument by Robin Horton (1970) analogizing traditional African religion and European science. The analogy is appealing in that both are male-dominated institutions for the control of privileged knowledge, but Horton's concern with comparing the modes of thought characteristic of those institutions ultimately becomes strained. At one point he develops a distinction between common sense and theoretical reasoning by evoking the example of the industrial chemist who simultaneously entertains understandings both of the domestic use of common table salt and of its chemical properties as defined by atomic theory. He then argues that a similar distinction between common sense and theoretical knowledge exists within African traditional thought (1970: 141). What is missing from Horton's example is that the Western industrial chemist might also entertain a *religious* use of salt. Such a use is exemplified in the Charismatic practice of sprinkling blessed salt through a house to protect it from malevolent spiritual influence, or on the occasion of a ritual prayer for casting out evil spirits. To argue that this is an isolated case of which Horton could justifiably remain unaware is unacceptable given the long use of sacramental blessed salt in Catholic ritual. The contemporary Charismatic practice is itself a popularization or laicization of what was formerly an esoteric prerogative of a male-dominated institution for the control of ritual knowledge. This third understanding of salt suggests a weakness of Horton's analogy and makes us wonder what would have been the result if he had compared Western religious thinking with African religious thought.

Let us pursue this question—what is known in anthropology as the "rationality" question or the question of the apparent irrationality of "primitive" thought—with a consideration of Edward Evans-Pritchard's (1976) discussion of how misfortune is accounted for among the Azande. Evans-Pritchard gives the example of an expert woodcarver who typically explained cracks in the bowls and stools he made by the action of witchcraft perpetrated by jealous and spiteful neighbors. When the anthropologist replied that those neighbors appeared well disposed toward the craftsman, the latter held up a cracked utensil as concrete evidence, excluding the priority of natural or coincidental reasons. A more famous example cited by Evans-Pritchard is the occasional collapse of an Azande granary, resulting in the injury of a person resting in its shade. The people typically acknowledge that the granary actually collapsed because its supports were eaten away by termites and that the person sitting there at that moment was there to seek shelter from the midday sun. However, by referring to the action of witchcraft, they are also able to account for why what we would regard as coincidental events occurred at precisely that time and place.

Compare these Azande examples with the report by a Charismatic couple that soon after they began attending prayer meetings their five-year-old began waking up at night screaming and crying because of nightmares. Two electroencephalograph tests at local hospitals concluded that there were no neurological abnormalities, but that the child was a sleepwalker. The episode ended after six months. What made it the relevant content of a religious narrative was that the parents did not stop attending prayer meetings even though the incident was the kind of thing "that happens so you'll stop going." If pressed, these parents might acknowledge that the child may have been reacting to their unaccustomed absence from home at night. However, the coincidence is explained by *demonic harassment*, the attempt by Satan to interfere with the parents' exposure to God through Charismatic activities. Such harassment is frequently reported by people involved in healing or evangelization, consistent with the cultural assumption that Satan has a great deal at stake in disrupting such work of God. Other examples, cited by a husband and wife who worked as a team in ritual healing, included a garbage disposal that turned on and off by itself at the time when they were first becoming deeply involved in the practice of healing, glass in front of their fireplace cracking during the summer when there was no fire, the battery on the husband's fishing boat going dead the day after a session of ritual healing, and damage to the woodwork in their house by a squirrel that had entered through the chimney while they were out of state conducting a session for casting out evil spirits. While proximal causes may be acknowledged (faulty switch, humidity, infrequent use of the battery, greater likelihood of entry by animals when the occupants are away), the ultimate cause linking apparently coincidental events is demonic harassment.

The equivalence between witchcraft among the Azande and demonic harassment among Charismatics subsists primarily in the mode of reasoning and not in the cultural content. Specifically, Azande witchcraft is unequivocally an interpersonal affair, whether or not a direct accusation is ever made. Demonic harassment among North American Charismatics, however, is an affair of the self, for if the misfortune is attributed to a spiritual entity, no occasion for social conflict can ensue. Although there are exceptions, the existential significance of the adverse event for Charismatics typically has to do with one's ability to fulfill a religious goal and not with any impediment to social life imposed by jealous neighbors or enemies. A second cultural difference is relevant to Horton's (1970) argument that science and religion differ as systems of thought because science is logically *open* to alternatives whereas traditional religious thought is *closed* due to isolation and its consequent lack of pluralistic lines of reasoning. As we have already seen, Charismatic thinking is neither isolated nor closed even to scientific reasoning itself. It is precisely this openness that situates the Charismatic Renewal within the postmodern condition. One must not only account for the relation between common sense and science, or between common sense and religion, but must also include the relation in Charismatic thought between religion and science. Being able to identify the openness that blurs and crosses boundaries among these modes is a distinct methodological contribution of invoking the postmodern—the condition of culture conditions the phenomenon. Interpretation thus eludes the methodological traps of labeling it a "subculture," treating it as a kind of "tribe," or construing it as the religion of a "people," all of which isolate it from a cultural milieu in which its participants are themselves significant actors. It frees us to examine precisely the manner in which those actors creatively constitute existential boundedness, meaning, and self in the postmodern milieu.

Self, Habitus, and the Daily Life of Charismatics

I have suggested above and in previous writing (Csordas 1994a) that through ritual performance and everyday social practice a Charismatic sacred self comes to inhabit a deeply taken for granted cultural world. In light of the discussion of religion in the postmodern condition of culture, it will not do to construe the notion of a sacred self as favoring the individual standpoint over the collective, emphasizing psychological process over social practice, or theoretically privileging self over world as the locus of analysis. Just as earlier I identified a tension between local and global in terms of otherness, the notion of a sacred self summarizes a tension in the Charismatic phenomenon between premodern and postmodern at the critical cultural nodes of boundedness, meaning, and authority. In comparison to religions of peoples, such a religion of the self is a creature of modernity; and to the extent that its participants must come to terms with contemporary trends toward the fragmentation and commodification of self, it must adapt to the condition of postmodernity. However, given the traditional Christian conception of the sacred that includes a discrete and bounded personal identity, a unitary and explicit meaning to life in terms of salvation, and a centered patriarchal authority, an appeal to the sacred is a turning toward premodernity. In the end, the uneasy juxtaposition of premodern and postmodern images, as in the media marvel at Medjugorje, is itself symptomatic of the postmodern condition of culture.

I have chosen the term "self" from among a large set of related and near-synonymous terms[17] both because it is compatible with the goals of our study and because it most accurately reflects the core existential concerns expressed in the movement we are studying. Indeed, commentators on the Charismatic Renewal such as McGuire (1982) have acknowledged this concern. Chagnon (1979: 91) argues that a principal aim of the movement is "to remake the self, to reconstitute it in profundity." Mary Jo Neitz (1987) devotes a chapter to comparing the Renewal with the "personal growth movement" with respect to the theme of self-awareness. Especially because the larger contemporary culture and popular discourse are preoccupied with matters of self, however, we must take care to distinguish our theoretical notion of self from any of these.[18] In my work on Charismatic healing (Csordas 1994a) I formulated a working definition of self intended to be sufficiently general for application across cultures, avoiding intellectual commitment to cultural presuppositions of substance, entity, or Cartesian autonomy of consciousness as a priori defining features. Instead, I take self to be an indeterminate capacity to engage or become oriented in the world, characterized by effort and reflexivity. Self processes are orientational processes in which aspects of the world are thematized, with the result that the self can be objectified as a person with a cultural identity or set of identities.

This formulation owes much to the work of A. Irving Hallowell (1955, 1960), the first anthropologist to move toward a phenomenological theory of the self. Hallowell defined the self as self-awareness, the recognition of oneself as an "object in a world of objects." His concern with the cultural context of self processes is summarized in the term "behavioral environment," borrowed from the Gestalt psychology of Kurt Koffka. Hallowell's protophenomenological approach accounts for an essential feature of this behavioral environment, namely, that it includes not only natural objects but also "culturally reified objects," especially supernatural beings and the practices associated with them. The concept thus did more than place the individual in culture, linking behavior to the objective world, but also linked perceptual processes with social constraints and cultural meanings. Accordingly, the focus of Hallowell's formulation was "orientation" with respect to self, objects, space and time, motivation, and norms, and this is what I mean by orientation in the world.

The Charismatic sacred self is objectified and represented as a particular kind of person with a specific identity in relation to other sacred selves. However, precisely because persons are representations or objectifications, the cultural world may be inhabited by a variety of types of persons other than human persons. Among the Ojibwa, for example, Hallowell (1960) showed that persons are any phenomenologically real beings that inhabit the cultural world and with which human beings presumably may come into interaction. A similar situation holds among Charismatics, for whom the domain of person includes not only human beings both adult and child but first of all God. The Charismatic deity is really three persons, each with a character corresponding to one of the three parts of the tripartite human person. Thus Father, Son, and Holy Spirit correspond with mind, body, and spirit, and implicitly each divine person is most congenial with its matched subfield within the human person.[19] Also considered persons in this sense are deceased human spirits, and at the opposite end of the life course, human embryos and fetuses. Relative to societies in which they are actively propitiated, ancestral spirits are largely neglected, except insofar as they are occasionally held to be the cause of some affliction. Unborn spirits are, however, a cause célèbre that lead Charismatics to intense political involvement in the North American cultural debate about abortion (see Csordas 1996).

Evil spirits or demons also populate the Charismatic behavioral environment, though Charismatics would doubtless prefer not to grant them the "dignity" of being persons and instead use a term like "intelligent entities." One healer was on such disrespectfully familiar terms with her adversary (ultimately Satan, despite the multiplicity of individual demons under his dominion) that she referred to him as "the Old Boy" and "the creep." Other spiritual persons are of decreasing salience for interaction with humans. The importance of the Virgin Mary is proportionally less in "ecumenical" groups where Catholic devotees demur out of politeness to Protestants, whose traditional culture excludes defining Mary as a person who interacts with humans. Saints are not prominent actors even in predominantly Catholic groups, in this case not out of deference to Protestants but largely because they become relatively superfluous as intermediaries in a religion that cultivates direct person-to-person interaction with the deity. Michael the Archangel is invoked as a protector against evil spirits or as a reinforcement in episodes of "spiritual warfare" against them, but angels as a class of spiritual person are typically absent from the Charismatic world, appearing but rarely in healing or prophetic imagery.

A behavioral environment is composed not only of culturally constituted types of persons and entities *toward which* the self becomes oriented but also of psychocultural themes *in terms of which* the self becomes oriented. These are themes in the broad sense introduced by Morris Opler (1945) to describe global preoccupations of a culture, but in the phenomenological sense they are also issues thematized or made salient in the orienting processes of self-objectification. Three such themes present in the cultural world of contemporary North America are of preeminent importance in this discussion of the Catholic Charismatic sacred self. *Spontaneity* is sought after in American culture both as a personal trait and as a feature of interpersonal relations. The kind of person who initiates or at least participates in "impromptu gatherings" or events is valued (Varenne 1986), and the notion that mental health is related to the "spontaneity of the self" is found in some versions of professional psychological theory (Greenberg and Mitchell 1983: 200). Charismatics, reacting to the ritualistic Catholicism in which many were raised, are highly motivated by the ideal of spontaneity in spiritual experience as well as interpersonal interaction. The theme of *control* is likewise prominent in the cultural psychology of Americans. Robert Crawford (1984), for example, has analyzed the American concept of health as a symbol that condenses metaphors of self-control and release from pressures. Charismatics thematize both positive and negative aspects of control. On the one hand, they learn not only that they should "surrender" themselves to the will of God but also that overwhelming situations can be "given to the Lord." On the other hand, the influence of evil spirits is suspected precisely when negative behaviors or emotions are out of control. Finally, *intimacy* is the primary cultural ideal for relations between spouses, summarized in the notions of romantic love and close communication (Bellah et al. 1985; Levine 1991). When an American refers to a group of friends or co-workers as like a family, the connotation is more likely to be that members are intimate and so close that one can tell them anything than that they are loyal solely because a social relationship exists. Charismatic self processes of intimacy are found in the genre of ritual language known as "sharing," in their motive toward community, in the body technique of laying on of hands, and especially in the form of intimate relationship cultivated by a private "prayer life" with a divinity conceived explicitly as a "personal God." These themes appear repeatedly in performance and practice among Charismatics.[20] They are critical features of the cultural world in which the indeterminate self becomes sacred insofar as it comes to be oriented in the world, and to define what it means to be human, in terms of the wholly other than human (Otto 1927; van der Leeuw 1938; Eliade 1958).

While Hallowell's conceptualization of the self in its behavioral environment is valuable for its emphasis on orientation, in itself it does not go far enough for my purposes, and to take my argument further I will now expand on some earlier reflections about why this is so (Csordas 1994a: 5–6). Although for Hallowell the self is always already in the world in that it is constituted by orientational processes, his emphasis on reflective self-awareness as the defining abstract feature of self leaves it as a discrete entity, a kind of Cartesian mind in contrast to the indeterminate capacity for orientation by which I define it above. In defining the self as the product of a reflexive mood, he could not take full cognizance of the constant reconstitution of the self, including the possibilities not only for creative change in some societies but also for varying degrees of self-objectification cross-culturally. Moreover, relative to the early interactionist sociologist like George Herbert Mead and Charles Horton Cooley (his near-contemporaries), Hallowell excluded the essential presence of other selves from his outline of elements in terms of which the self was oriented. There is a discrete individual self and its "behavior," distinct from though oriented within an "environment."

We can at least in part circumvent the potential solipsism in this conception of self by translating Hallowell's notions of behavior and environment into the more contemporary language of "practice" within a "habitus." We owe this language in large part to Pierre Bourdieu (1977: 72), who defines habitus as a system of perduring dispositions that constitutes the unconscious, collectively inculcated principle for the generation and structuring of both practices and representations. For our purposes, this language offers an important element of theoretical balance: the notion of practice "socializes" that of behavior by introducing the connotation of shared and culturally prescribed routine, and the notion of habitus "psychologizes" that of environment by defining its constitution in terms of dispositions. Collapsing the dichotomy between psychological and social corrects for a Cartesian understanding of self and allows for our conception of self as indeterminate capacity for orientation. In so doing it also begins to account for the susceptibility to processes of commodification and fragmentation characteristic of self in the postmodern condition, as well as for the possibility of transformation and reorientation in ritual performance.

Indeed, there is a stream of research that has emphasized the constitution and reconstitution of self in ritual performance (e.g., Kapferer 1979c; Schieffelin 1985; Roseman 1990; Csordas 1990a, 1994a; Laderman and Roseman 1996). Performance is typically a collective undertaking—and more formalized than everyday social life. There is a danger in confining analysis of self process to events of ritual performance, however. Just as there is an unacceptable theoretical gap between self and environment in Hallowell's conception, there is a gap in the conceptualization of ritual performance between event and self-transformation. In some performance theory that gap remains invisible due to what Bourdieu (1977: 81–82) refers to as the "occasionalist illusion" that presumes the meaning of an event to be exhausted by what goes on within the boundaries of that event. This leads to a predicament quite different from Hallowell's, but just as problematic. Whereas for Hallowell the definition of self was pinned to an a priori reflexivity, performance risks a definition of self pinned to a posteriori objectification. Focusing solely on the formal representations of ritual performance could easily lead us back to a conception of self as a kind of entity, objectified or represented. For these reasons, I will insist as much as possible on the permeability of boundaries between ritual events and everyday life, indeed looking for the meaning of those events in life beyond the events themselves. Stated in other words, my analysis will show the creation of meaning to be a function of the continuity between performance and everyday practice. To observe self processes, or processes of self-objectification, is then not only to observe a striving for a sense of entity through performance but also to examine a series of shifting orientations among performance, experience, habitus, and everyday practice.

There is an interpretive advantage to bridging the conceptual gap between self and environment with the notion of habitus and to filling the conceptual gap between event and transformation with practices of everyday life. In the case of the Charismatic Renewal, that interpretive advantage is to facilitate conceptualization of how performance transforms conventional dispositions that constitute interpersonal, domestic, civic, and geographic spaces. It is also to allow conceptualization of how performance transforms time, both in the sense of altering the sense of duration and in terms of establishing sequences of ritual events. Much of the subsequent discussion will be dedicated to showing how these performative transformations come about. To conclude this chapter, it will suffice to summarize these elements of space and time in the Charismatic habitus.

Transformation of interpersonal space. In the foreground of this category is the classic body technique of laying on of hands while praying. While often physically experienced as a transfer of divine power, laying on of hands also condenses a series of symbolic meanings. It imitates the divine healing touch of Jesus portrayed in the Bible; it enacts the solidarity of the Christian community, especially when a group lays hands simultaneously on a person; and it achieves intimacy insofar as touch breaks the culturally constructed interpersonal barrier constituted by an ethnopsychological notion of the individual as a discrete, independent entity.[21] Thoughtful Charismatic leaders acknowledge, however, potential negative consequences of this overcoming of interpersonal boundaries. This is evident in the occasional report of someone being overwhelmed and "smothered" by an overzealous group attempting to lay on hands. The possibility of inappropriate eroticization is recognized in the dictum that participants should be wary of one-on-one healing sessions between members of the opposite sex.[22]

One of the most obvious features of a Charismatic prayer meeting to anyone attending for the first time is the use of an embrace in greeting. The "holy hug" as a ritual greeting originated as a bodily expression of both spontaneity and intimacy, in contrast to the culturally typical handshake or verbal greeting alone. Parallel to the hug of greeting, the characteristic Charismatic prayer posture of hands open palm up was a bodily expression of "openness" and "receptivity," in contrast to the traditional prayer posture with hands closed palms together. As the movement has developed it has become more frequent to observe, in addition to the palms-up posture, a palms-out posture with a hand or both hands raised above one's head, as if laying hands on the situation being prayed about, directing the force of prayer outward (see pl. 5).

These gestural practices are the primary means by which Charismatics modify interpersonal space. Clothing plays a comparatively small role in the Charismatic presentation of self. Ritual assistants in healing services, and members of some covenant communities, sometimes wear an additional identifying item of ritual garb over their regular clothes (see pls. 1–4). Such ritual clothing is not an element of everyday practice but is worn only in settings of ritual performance. In some covenant communities, a particularly bland style of dress characterized by gender-differentiated standards of appropriateness has come to predominate. A final way in which interpersonal space is transformed is that people who become Charismatic frequently report shifting their loyalties and social activities away from previous friends and acquaintances and toward other Charismatics. This at times includes weakened ties between younger Charismatics and their parents, but also between older Charismatics and their adult children.

Transformation of domestic space. Well beyond the traditional crucifix on the wall, or the statue of the Virgin in the yard, religious objects are common in the domestic decor of Charismatics. The simplest Christian religious representation—say, a pillow embroidered with the slogan "Jesus is Lord"—is perceived as having some spiritual value. Especially in the 1970s, Charismatic households were often draped with colorful wall banners bearing religious slogans. An affectively consequential transformation of domestic space was effected by a Charismatic couple who replaced the photographs of their non-Charismatic adult children with images of saints—a change perceived by the children as a gesture of rejection. In another case, a healer having difficulties with the sometimes trying work of praying for others was, in a moment of prayerful frustration, graced with the appearance in her yard of a kind of bird that she had never seen in that area. Taking this as a sign from God that she should continue her work, she adopted the bird as a personal totem. Gradually her home became filled with representations of the creature, both collected by her and given as gifts by other Charismatics.

The architectural configuration of domestic space may also be transformed, as some Charismatics set aside or even build an additional room to serve as a prayer room. Domestic units can also be constituted as Charismatic households. Especially common in the 1970s in covenant communities as elaborations of communal intimacy, such households might be composed of two nuclear families along with one or more unmarried adults, or of a group of same-sex unmarried adults.

Domestic space is also transformed by a series of Charismatic ritual techniques for protection from demonic influences. Prominent among these is use of the traditional Catholic sacramentals holy water and blessed salt, which may be sprinkled about the house to repel evil spirits. The practice of "calling down the blood" involves symbolically, and sometimes in visualization, "covering" the premises with the blood shed by the crucified Jesus. The spiritual power of the divine blood is held to be not only redemptive but protective as well, and in this ritual technique it forms a kind of curtain, barrier, or coating against malign influence. Finally, angels and archangels are sometimes invoked to surround the house with their protective presence.

Transformation of civic space. This dimension is most strikingly evident in events in which spiritual influences are projected into public spaces. In one such case, a well-known healer noted that a quarry near his home was frequently used by local youth for activities he found objectionable, such as nude swimming, sex, and consumption of alcohol and drugs. Presuming either that such activities attracted evil spirits or that the youth were attracted to the locale and to their activities by resident demons, he proceeded to pray for "deliverance," to cast out the spirits from the quarry. In another such event, a Charismatic gathering was held in the public library of a city where fourteen violent deaths had occurred among teenagers in a one-month period. Participants conducted a mass, along with prayers for casting out evil spirits named Suicide, Violence, and Death from the library, city hall, and other civic locations. Again, a Protestant Pentecostal evangelist visiting a large Catholic Charismatic community discerned a spirit named Unbelief hovering over the university town where the community is located, and cast it out.[23]

A subtler transformation of civic space took place in a covenant community where local neighborhood districts instituted as a pastoral structure became superimposed on and overlapped with the boundaries of other culturally defined units such as school districts, precincts, parishes, and dioceses. One can imaginatively grasp this transformation as the creation of a city within a city, or as the superimposition of a sacred city on a secular one. In another covenant community, a controversy over civic space arose when neighbors complained to the authorities that Charismatic multifamily households violated local zoning regulations.

Transformation of geographic space. Charismatics have renewed interest in pilgrimage to traditional sacred sites of Catholicism such as Rome, Jerusalem, or Lourdes, and as I have noted are among the most enthusiastic visitors to the site of the contemporary Marian apparitions at Medjugorje. The Charismatic map of the United States is also transformed, with "destination cities" for travelers not traditional vacation attractions like New York City or San Francisco but centers of Charismatic activity like Ann Arbor or Pecos. Accompanying this transformation of geographic and global space is a transformed conception of natural processes. This conception was articulated by a prominent

Charismatic leader speaking to ten thousand people at the movement's national conference, during the peak of apocalyptic fervor and divine empowerment in 1976.

When we're dealing with nature, because man's supposed to have a loving domination over nature, what we do is command and give orders for the rain to stop, or the storm to cease, or for the rain to begin again in time of drought. That's a command or *order* we can give when God says [indicates to us] that this is what he wants.[24]

No metaphor is intended in this passage, which claims for contemporary ritual healing prayer the capacity to repeat the miracles attributed to Jesus, including those in which he commanded the forces of nature. The Charismatic transformation I am describing is thus not only a transformation in the sense of place but also in the mode of inhabiting natural space.

Transformation of time. Charismatics typically cultivate a "personal prayer life," which ideally includes time set aside for prayer every day. Other routines involving the organization of time include periodic events such as weekly prayer meetings, periodic seminars and courses, retreats, workshops, "days of renewal," and annual regional or national conferences. Some covenant communities have a more elaborated ritual calendar of periodic gatherings culminating in an annual community anniversary celebration and ceremony of "public commitment" to the community. It is not only the organization of time that is transformed, however, but also the experience of its duration. Whether in personal prayer or in a prayer meeting, the temporal aspect of glossolalia is virtually one of pure duration, since it is speech with no semantic dimension, no argument or conclusion. The common experience of resting in the Spirit while overcome with divine power (see note 10 and Csordas 1994a) is also a suspension of the temporal flow of daily life. Finally, the inevitable ambiguity of personal affairs is addressed by cultivating a specific disposition for patience referred to colloquially as "waiting on the Lord" and based on the notion that if one prayerfully "submits" or "surrenders" difficult decisions or situations to the divine will, the appropriate course of action will eventually become clear.

A related alteration of temporality can be observed in the Charismatic housewife who in exhaustion declares, "I cannot do this housework, Lord, you'll have to do it for me." This is quite distinct from a more conventional supplication such as "Lord, give me strength," and its motivation is likewise distinct from that of an agent forcing herself to do the work "for her husband and children" or even "for the Lord." Neither is it interpretively adequate to conclude simply that the house-wife succeeds in her task by going into "trance," even though in the narrowest sense she may in fact do so, praying in tongues all the while. This is because, along with the experience of time passing tolerably, we are faced with reorientation in her experience of *effort,* which was iden-tified above as an essential characteristic of self (see also Csordas 1994a). In the woman's abdication to the deity of her struggle for control in her daily environment, we also have a vivid enactment of key psychocultural themes I have identified. Control over the very source of effort, and hence an essential self process, is displaced. The existential meaning of having the intimately personal Lord do the work must then be under-stood in terms of how the themes of intimacy and control, even of one's ability to act, are integrated among the above aspects of a pragmatically orchestrated Charismatic habitus.

The ritual transformation of dispositions related to temporality must be distinguished from the alternation between mundane and sacred time that takes place in rituals of the fixed, liturgical type. As Rappaport (1992) has observed, such rituals are invariant and precoded for the performers. Insofar as Charismatics increasingly have rediscovered and cultivated a Catholic sacramental spirituality, they participate in this al-ternation that is intrinsic to the temporal structure created by a liturgi-cal order. However, the kind of ritual transformation I am pointing to is more like what Rappaport gets at in discussing rituals that occur so frequently that

the liturgical order attempts, as it were, not only to regulate daily behavior, but to penetrate to the motivational bases of that behavior. . . . High frequency . . . may be instrumental in rooting whatever dicta are encoded in the ritual so con-tinually and routinely in everyday life that they seem to be natural, or at least of "second nature," rather than merely moral. To abandon them, if this is the case, would be painfully self-alienating. (1992: 18)

Rappaport's language of penetrating the motivational bases of be-havior, creating a second nature grounded in sacred dicta, and risking profound self-alienation if such dicta are abandoned describes precisely what is at issue in the performative transformation of habitus. It is hardly an accident that the Orthodox Jews whose attempts through frequent rituals and observances of the Halakah to "bring the divine into this world" and those cloistered communities of religious specialists who try through both long and frequent rituals to "spend their lives part-way to heaven" are examples cited by Rappaport (1992: 19) that have also appealed to Catholic Charismatics, especially those in covenant communities. Phenomenologically it is moot whether the alternation between sacred and mundane time is still experienced, whether it becomes extinguished, or whether it becomes so rapid as to be imperceptible. The coordinated dispositions of the habitus that generates practices and representations are altered, and therefore, as in the example of the housewife and her experience of effort, mundane time itself is fundamentally altered.

The dispositions toward space I have summarized for the Charismatic habitus are ways of inhabiting space, ways of projecting oneself into the world, taking it up and making it a sacralized human space. The dispositions toward time are particular ways of being in time, organizing it and experiencing it as duration. As we shall see, the movement from an everyday habitus to a distinctively Charismatic habitus has been the function of what we can call the ritualization of life, a process on whose horizon lies the potential for a radicalization of charisma. Let us now begin to take a closer look at the social setting in which the above elements of habitus are most elaborated and integrated into a collective form of life, the Charismatic covenant community.

PART TWO

Habitus and Practice

3

A Communitarian Ideal

The impulse toward community has characterized the Catholic Charismatic Renewal from its outset. Charismatics invoke the communalism of the "early Church" and the symbolism of the Church as a "mystical body" (O'Neill 1985) as grounds for their efforts. They cite the ascetic movement of the fourth century, the mendicant movement of the thirteenth century, and the communitarian religious orders such as Benedictine, Franciscan, and Jesuit (Clark 1976; O'Connor 1971).[1] Contemporary Charismatic covenant communities fall under the sociological category of "intentional" communities and can be placed in historical context alongside a variety of communitarian developments in North America, especially those that emerged from the cultural ferment of the 1960s (Holloway 1966; Zablocki 1971, 1980; Kanter 1972; Fitzgerald 1986; Carter 1990). The more tightly structured among these communities approach what Lewis Coser (1974) has labeled "greedy institutions" that encompass all dimensions of members' lives. More precisely, although members often work in conventional jobs and live in neighborhoods among non-Charismatics, in these groups the nature of such outside relationships and the kind and degree of contact with the "world" of secular society—attendance at movies, teenage dating—is circumscribed by community teaching. Insofar as they are successfully constituted in the community's terms, that is, in self-declared opposition to the broader North American culture, even outside relationships are drawn into the totalized behavioral environment of covenant community life.

Indeed, the discipline cultivated in Charismatic communities is characterized by an enduring tension between what Weber (1963) called world-rejecting asceticism and inner-worldly asceticism.[2] Condemnation and retreat from the world while accepting a mission to transform the world is a variant of the paradoxical Christian injunction to be "in the world but not of it." This injunction takes on a distinctive configuration in the middle-class American society of most Catholic Charismatics, and as we have seen creates lines of differentiation within the movement itself. Radical communitarians come to speak patronizingly about their fellow Catholic Charismatics adrift "out there in prayer group land" and closely allied covenant communities split over the degree to which their ideals are threatened by the world. Indeed, for some the focus of evangelistic effort appears to have shifted from the spiritual "renewal" of Catholics at large to the rank and file of supposedly inadequately prepared Catholic Charismatics themselves.

The idea that I want to play out over the following chapters is that the differentiation of "visions" of the Renewal, ranging across the spectrum of prayer groups and covenant communities I described in chapter 1, can be described as the result of a *rhetorical involution*. By this I mean an increasing intensity and complexity, generated in ritual performance and in everyday life, in the meanings attributed to basic themes, principles, and motives of group life and in the implications for action of these themes, principles, and motives. Understanding this rhetorical involution will be the key to understanding charisma as a self process among Charismatics. As a preliminary example, consider how the North American psychocultural themes of spontaneity, intimacy, and control identified above are taken up into the transformed Charismatic habitus. For Charismatics, *spontaneity* appears to mean the ready availability of others for face-to-face (or telephone) interaction, the knowledge that there are people one can call on freely at any time. In addition, Charismatic communities are understood to have developed from what was seen as the celebratory spontaneity of the prayer meeting, and thus ideally provide the permanent setting for the experience of divinely inspired spontaneity. The problem of *control* appears to include the fear of being unable to fulfill one's responsibilities because life situations are beyond one's control or unable to maintain the effort of attempting to control one's circumstances. The results of surrendering control to God are made concrete in the commitment of one's affairs to the life of a community of like-minded persons within which a member finds both active support and explicit direction. *Intimacy* is elaborated in part by the cultivated sharing of spiritual experience and life concerns as principal foci of face-to-face interaction. In another sense, there also exists a generalized intimacy based on common commitment to the divinely appointed mission that Charismatic communities see as part of the reason for their existence. Finally, there is ideally a concrete intimacy in marriages between community members, nurtured not only by shared belief, lifestyle, experience, and commitment but in some cases by a community-mediated courtship process and arranged betrothal.

The diversity among Catholic Charismatic communities can be understood in part as the result of local variations on these themes as they are woven into the habitus as dispositions created in practice and performance. The intensity and complexity that define what I am calling rhetorical involution are results of the specificity with which these themes are elaborated in collective life. There is another involutional rhetorical dynamic that comes into play, however, which is that collective elaborations of each theme appear in varying degrees to generate and embrace their opposites. Thus spontaneity itself becomes ritualized and conventionalized. The hug as a spontaneous gesture of intimacy in greeting becomes a ritual alternative to the handshake. Spontaneous expression of praise to the divinity becomes conventionalized in form. Likewise, the surrender of control to divine will may result in an increasingly standardized and controlled style of life including tightly scheduled daily activities and restrictions in choice of clothing. Finally, intimacy may generate authority, as mutual concern and support becomes commitment to abide by canons of collective life promulgated by a leadership that represents the intimate fatherly concern of a paternalistic deity.

Without getting too far ahead of my argument, I want to formalize the dimensions of complexity and intensity as a dual process, which I will call the ritualization of practice and the radicalization of charisma. In the next chapter I will show in detail how this dual process characterizes the development of The Word of God/Sword of the Spirit, the Charismatic community in which these processes have been carried to the greatest lengths and hence are most clearly describable. To do so, however, we must become familiar in greater detail with the history and organization of the community. Accordingly, the remainder of this chapter is an ethnographic sketch that will provide the context for the more process-oriented discussion in chapter 4.

I, and those who are with me, call
you The Word of God

Recall that The Word of God originated in 1967 when Steven Clark and Ralph Martin, who had begun their partnership at Notre Dame University through activity in the Cursillo movement and who had undergone the Pentecostal Baptism in the Holy Spirit during a weekend retreat with the original Catholic group from Duquesne University, were invited to work at the student parish of the University of Michigan. With two comrades they held their first prayer meetings in a rented apartment, a site that remains a landmark on a Charismatic tour of Ann Arbor. Within a year they had recruited additional members from the local university and from Notre Dame and as was typical for rapidly expanding prayer groups at the time, added a second smaller weekly meeting for the core group. As in most Charistmatic prayer groups, core group participants defined themselves as those who were more committed and who wanted to maintain a setting of spontaneity and intimacy free from the need to "serve" or integrate newcomers. A formal initiation process originated when one bedroom was set aside for an explanation session and another for laying on hands in prayer for Baptism in the Holy Spirit. By 1969 the initiation was formulated by Martin into the Life in the Spirit Seminars, which incorporated the basic Pentecostal religious experience, teaching about Christian life, and integration into the group.

The idea of a covenant that would bind members together was put forward in a community conference that year. The conference also established a council of twenty, centered around the community's founders, with vaguely defined leadership responsibilities. A dimension was added to the group's ritual life with the visit of Don Basham and Derek Prince, leaders of the nondenominational neo-Pentecostal Christian Growth Ministries of Fort Lauderdale. They instructed the community on the disruptive effects of evil spirits on interpersonal relationships and on "God's work" and taught the practice of deliverance from evil spirits. During a prayer session that became known as Deliverance Monday the two preachers cast out demons, which exited their hosts in a paroxysm of screaming, crying, and coughing. The reported effect for those who were not frightened away was freedom from "relationship problems" and a "bottled up" feeling, in a situation in which the intensity of interpersonal relationships was already having a transformative effect on participants' mode of dealing with the world and each other. Other early covenant communities were also discovering deliverance at this time, and it frequently became a required experience for people entering community life.

At a second community conference in 1970, the name "The Word of God" was formally adopted, based on prophetic messages uttered by group leaders. In addition, the leaders put forward a conception of covenant as a formal written commitment among members. Understood to be desired and sanctioned by the deity, it would be publicly accepted by each member in a solemn ceremony. The covenant has four elements: all must attend community assemblies, all must contribute some service to the welfare of community members, all must respect the community order (i.e., the accepted way of doing things and the accepted pattern of authority), and all must support the community financially by tithe. At the conference Clark and Martin outlined their plan for restructuring the group to facilitate community growth. The Life in the Spirit Seminar was subsequently revised to emphasize community living, and members were required to take or retake an additional twelve-week Foundations in Christian Living course. Prospective members could make a preliminary or underway commitment, but only after completing all the courses and being invited by community leaders could they make a "full commitment" to the covenant. "Growth groups," small-scale spiritual development groups that were characteristic of Charismatic prayer groups from the movement's beginning, were reorganized on geographic lines within subcommunities.

The functions of community leaders were categorized by specialty, including charismatic gifts such as prophecy, services in support of the community, and offices such as elder. Those specializing in service received the title "Servant" if male or "Handmaid" if female. The former were charged largely with administrative responsibilities, while the latter's functions included limited pastoral responsibility for other women. Invoking biblical justification for a principle of "male headship," women were excluded from the position of community elder. To eliminate the possibility that outsiders would interpret their actions as aimed at starting a new church, Clark proposed the term "coordinators" instead of elders for those male leaders who, with increased authority under the covenant, would replace the loosely structured council. Martin and Clark became overall coordinators with authority over the others. The local bishop received a proposal outlining this "pastoral experiment."

The authority of the coordinators was consolidated during 1971–1972, as was the structure of the community and its self-conception as a "people." A series of "teachings" on the theme of "repentance" sobered members' attitudes toward their collective project. The coordinators' decision that it was within their power to expel a woman accused of "false prophecy and unrepentant homosexuality" highlighted both their increasing authority and the existence of boundaries between the community and the outside world. The generality of the covenant allowed coordinators gradually to appropriate authority over more aspects of members' lives, and they regarded it as part of their divine mission under the covenant to do so. A decision-making process emerged based on consensus among coordinators as to "what the Lord was telling them" through discussion, prayer, and prophecy, with the ultimate authority residing in Steven Clark.

Input from the community at large was formalized via "community consultations." These were called for by the coordinators when major changes were under consideration, such as adoption of the covenant or formation of the Sword of the Spirit. Five such consultations were held between 1968 and 1990. Each lasted for several weeks or months, during which members "prayed about" the matter and communicated insights, opinions, or prophecies to the coordinators. In less focused periods, the coordinators expected a general flow of "prophecy mail" from members. The content of prophecy mail was understood as the outcome of members' personal efforts to "listen to the Lord" and receive prophetic inspiration that would propose, comment on, or confirm ideas and trends in group life. Along with these changes, a strict notion of "community order" evolved. This order was exercised in 1975 when a man was excluded from the community after taking his complaints about the hierarchical/authoritarian (and decreasingly "spontaneous") direction of group development directly to the local bishop, rather than through "proper channels," namely, the coordinators themselves.

The consolidation of coordinators' authority in 1971–1972 placed them at the apex of four distinguishable hierarchical systems, based on living situation, personal headship, prophecy, and community service.

The cornerstone of the living situation hierarchy was the "household," organized on a model adopted from the Episcopalian Charismatic Church of the Redeemer in Houston. The household ideally consisted of one or more married couples, their children, and one or more unmarried people. The primacy of intimacy as a goal is evident in the possibility for individuals who did not share a common domicile still to be members of a "nonresidential household." Following the principle of male headship, the eldest married man was pastoral head of his household. As the community grew into as many as fourteen geographic "districts," each household head was made subordinate to one of several "district heads," who were in turn responsible to a "district coordinator." In 1972, a year after the institution of households, coordinators assumed authority for assigning people to households. In 1976 three higher-level "head coordinators" were ceremonially consecrated to oversee communitywide affairs, with Steven Clark remaining as overall head coordinator, a structure that with minor variations remained in effect until 1990.

The "personal head" is similar to a spiritual adviser, except that he is not necessarily ordained and that "full headship" (required of those publicly committed to the community covenant) entails obedience to the head in matters related to morality, spirituality, and community order.[3] Although formally distinct from the headship of living situations, the same persons often function as heads in a variety of contexts. Furthermore, a household head was often the personal head of most members of that household, and a husband was always personal head of his wife. The coordinators' heads were the head coordinators, who in turn were each other's heads in a tight circular relationship.

In a culture that emphasizes the value of individual autonomy, headship was perhaps the most controversial of covenant community practices, from the perspective of both outsiders and other Charismatics. At the same time, the cultural logic in defense of headship was implicitly framed in terms of the psychocultural themes I have identified as central to Charismatic self process. With respect to control, members were quick to argue that only the most advanced and committed were "under obedience" to their heads. For average members, it was said that heads typically gave advice rather than orders, although given the divinely sanctioned nature of the relationship, such advice had an implicitly coercive overtone. This potential for coercion was dealt with not only by invoking benevolence and attributing divine guidance to the head but especially by appealing to the theme of intimacy. People would describe their relationship as one of deep "sharing" and say "My head really knows me." Finally, the theme of spontaneity was relevant in that although most members typically met with their heads by appointment, there was a sense that they were always available when needed.

Prophecy was originally uttered within and outside of prayer meetings by anyone who felt inspired, but in 1971 a "word gifts group" composed of those recognized for exercising this charism began to meet regularly. As the community grew in size, public prophecy began to be restricted to members of this group, and a hierarchy of prophets emerged, including both men and women. In 1975 the office of prophet was created within the community and one of the head coordinators, Bruce Yocum, was consecrated as its holder. Under his direction, members of the word gifts group cultivated their capacity to listen to the Lord and took responsibility for distilling and screening the divine word as it came to the coordinators from the collectivity in the form of prophecy mail. In addition, prophecy at community gatherings came to be dominated by this group, and regular members wishing to prophesy would have to clear their message before uttering it to the assembly. This development shows clear compromise between themes of control and spontaneity: although universal access to spontaneous divine inspiration was preserved in prophecy mail and in public gatherings (as well as in smaller service groups, families, and interpersonal relationships), it was subject to control by being filtered through the word gifts group and the community prophet.

While all Charismatic prayer groups have a variety of "ministries" in which members can participate, the requirement of covenanted members to contribute some service to community life led to development of multiple "services." By 1972 an anthropology dissertation on the community recorded forty-four formal services such as evangelization, child care, music, pastoral leadership, healing, initiations, guest reception, or "works of mercy" (Keane 1974: 98–99). These services generated their own hierarchy of headship, again with its apex among the community coordinators.

In 1972 the conservative Belgian Cardinal Suenens paid an incognito visit to The Word of God, subsequently announcing his endorsement of the group and encouraging its members to expand the international horizons of their work. The other principal development in 1972 was the founding of a "brotherhood" of men under Clark and Yocum. These men dedicated themselves to greater discipline and asceticism in service to the community. Living communally in the state of "single for the Lord," or celibate bachelorhood, they became the shock troops of the international expansion encouraged by Suenens. Christened the Servants of the Word, the brotherhood held a ceremonial public commitment for its members in 1974. A "sisterhood" of women living single for the Lord called the Servants of God's Love was not established until 1976, and remains less developed than the parallel brotherhood.

In 1974 a series of teachings by the coordinators reemphasized the principle of male headship in outlining acceptable gender roles. The office of handmaid was discontinued, perhaps because its holders expected more pastoral responsibility than the coordinators were prepared to grant. The office of handmaid was reinstituted only some years later, after the community's conservative and male-dominated definition of gender roles was firmly entrenched. Also in 1974, the ritual practice of "loud praise" was borrowed from the covenant community in Dallas, transforming collective prayer of praise to the deity from quiet speaking or singing in tongues to loud vocalization and hand clapping. A second visit by the ministers who had in 1969 introduced the practice of deliverance from evil spirits prepared community members to be transformed by divine power through prayer and revelation.

Events accelerated dramatically in 1975. A more apocalyptic tone characterized prophecies and coordinators' teachings. The coordinators decided that the community must become reoriented to a worldwide sense of mission. To emphasize the importance of this mission, each publicly committed member was required to retake the advanced initiation seminars and make a formal recommitment to the covenant. Adapting a practice that Martin had observed in a French covenant community, at the recommitment ceremony each male member was vested with a mantle of white Irish linen, and each female with a veil of white Belgian linen (see photo insert following this chapter). These were to be worn at community gatherings as a symbol that members belonged to a "people" with a divine commission. Internal resistance to adoption of ritual clothing, to the increased demand for commitment of time and finances, and to the additional increase in coordinators' authority led to the first major crisis in the community. For the first time, there was a substantial loss of members—or "pruning" in the biblical metaphor of the faithful—as some declined to make the recommitment and others were excluded from it by the coordinators. Extracommunity developments were highlighted by three events: the annual community conference, which was held jointly with the People of Praise in anticipation of a coming merger; the establishment of the movement's International Communication Office by Ralph Martin and Cardinal Suenens in Brussels; and the utterance of the Rome prophecies at the movement's international conference.

In 1976 the two goals of establishing an Association of Communities and establishing an international evangelistic "outreach" based in Belgium were finally realized. Community coordinators promulgated a series of teachings on "getting free from the world." Community ritual life was augmented by household "Sabbath ceremonies" adapted from the Jewish seder by a born-again Jewish member. Teachings the following year elaborated community standards of "honor and respect" for one another, between people of different ages and genders, for coordinators and others in positions of authority, and for God. Solemn respect for God was emphasized in ritual life by the new practice of prostration, lying prone or kneeling with one's face to the floor in deeply silent prayer that came to alternate with periods of loud praise. Honor and respect for others was ritualized by the adoption of foot washing, and children began to be taught not to address adults by their first names.

The trend toward world renunciation gained momentum when the public prayer meeting, a feature of the group's ritual throughout its ten-year career, was restricted to members and their guests or prospective members and rechristened a general community gathering. Members were to further simplify their lifestyles, use less meat in their diets, and contribute more to the financial support of the community's mission. In 1979 the community instituted four denominational "fellowships," each with its own chaplain to provide liturgy and church services for members from the Catholic, Free Church, Reformed, and Lutheran traditions. A majority of members, representing approximately twenty denominations, withdrew from local congregations into the community fellowships. This move caused some controversy in the broader Ann Arbor Christian community, given that they took both their volunteer energies and the half of their tithe that they had been contributing to their churches. Also in 1979, a rural district of the community was established on a 260-acre farm purchased by The Word of God.

In spite of the latter development, the community's distinctive style of world renunciation has consistently entailed economic self-sufficiency and sharing of personal resources, rather than withdrawal to rural poverty. Members who own businesses such as a computer firm and a grocery store often employ other members. Members recognize that skilled and white-collar work outside the community both strengthen its financial position and provide opportunities for recruitment. The world renunciation that characterizes this "college-educated community of yuppies," as one of its officials described it, is of a kind that is financially sound.

Yet world renunciation it is. This was nowhere more evident than in the efforts by coordinators to endow their people with a distinct and disciplined culture adequate to the community's perceived mission, by instituting an intensive series of teachings in 1980–1981. Known as the Training Course, the teachings were based on a massive tome by Steven Clark entitled *Man and Woman in Christ* (1980). Clark's course made minutely explicit prescriptions for proper comportment, gender-appropriate dress, child-rearing practices, and the domestic division of labor. In addition, it identified global trends presumed to threaten the community mission of building the Kingdom of God—Islam, communism, feminism, and gay rights. With knowledge of its contents withheld from the majority of publicly committed members, the Training Course was initially given only to coordinators and district heads and their families. This strategy for the first time created explicit recognition of the existence of a true elite within the community—and stirrings of apprehension about the coordinators' motives for secrecy. The greatest immediate repercussion of the new formulations was not discontent within the community, however, but the already described split from the People of Praise and the breakup of the Association of Communities, whose members were unwilling to follow the "vision" and "mission" of The Word of God.

Retreat from the "ways of the world" continued in 1982 with the founding of a community school encompassing grades 4 through 9, judged to be the most formative years for community children's morality and spirituality. Partly because many families now had young children, multiple-resident households became less pragmatic and began to be replaced by nuclear family dwellings organized into "household clusters." Meanwhile, The Word of God's distinct vision was promulgated to the broader Catholic Charismatic Renewal through the series of FIRE rallies (see chap. 1 n. 3) conducted independently of the national movement organization, in which the People of Praise remained prominent. Most important, leaders reconstituted around themselves a new network of like-minded communities and formally inaugurated the super-community the Sword of the Spirit. Member communities came under the jurisdiction of a translocal governing council with Steven Clark at its apex, and the communities' word gifts groups became a single translocal "prophecy guild" under the headship of Bruce Yocum. In the following year, the Servants of the Word brotherhood built the International Brotherhood Center as their global headquarters in Ann Arbor. The brotherhood zealously assumed the bulk of training and cultivating those affiliated groups who aspired to become full Sword of the Spirit branches.

Both external and internal difficulties arose in 1985–1986. Externally, an episode occurred that marked the moment of greatest tension between the Catholic church hierarchy and the Charismatic Renewal in the nearly twenty years of the movement's history. The episode concerned, not Pentecostal ritual practices such as speaking in tongues, faith healing, casting out of evil spirits, or resting in the Spirit, but ecclesiastical jurisdiction over communities bound by covenant to the authority of the Sword of the Spirit. Branches in Akron, Miami, Steubenville, and Newark all encountered difficulties with the bishops in their local dioceses, but it was the latter that drew the broadest attention. The episode originated with the aforementioned creation within The Word of God of denominational fellowships equivalent to parishes but entirely contained within the covenant community. The Catholic fellowship was approved by the local bishop in the Ann Arbor case, and with the formation of the Sword of the Spirit as a single international community its governing council petitioned the Pontifical Council for the Laity in Rome for official recognition of such "fellowships" for Roman Catholics within covenant communities. Since in effect this was a request for creation of an entirely new ecclesiastical category, the Church moved slowly in its deliberations on the petition, and in the meantime each Sword of the Spirit branch had to request independent approval from its own local bishop.

When in 1985 the People of Hope branch submitted the statutes for their Catholic fellowship for approval to the bishop of Newark, they were rejected. Prominent among the reasons were irreconcilability between "submission" to any transdiocesan authority and the expectation of a bishop for authority over all Catholics within the geographic territory of his diocese. Also of concern was the ambiguous meaning of a "covenant" between Catholic and non-Catholic members of a community. The People of Hope appealed to Rome, which deferred to its yet incomplete consideration of the overall Sword of the Spirit petition. In the process the Newark bishop resigned, but a new bishop adopted essentially the same position, and the situation remained in a stalemate. Ten years earlier Clark (1976) had written that based on the precedent of "renewal communities" in earlier centuries of Church history, a covenant community challenged by a local bishop should consider moving to a more receptive diocese. However, the eventual possibility of a favorable outcome, combined with the practical dilemma of disposing substantial community property and moving more than a hundred adults, militated against this solution.[4] The People of Hope partially acquiesced, formally withdrawing from the Sword of the Spirit while continuing to send its coordinators as observers to meetings of the supercommunity's leadership.[5]

Internally, tensions provoked by implementation of the Training Course mounted. The intensity of behavioral restrictions created family tensions, particularly in two respects. First was the increasingly specific prescription of male headship and gender discipline. Second was the requirement on parents to supervise community children and teenagers, who were expected to refrain from worldly activities such as attending dances, listening to rock and roll music, or wearing blue jeans. The result was an exodus of community members comparable to that during the recommitment of 1975. One community district whose coordinator was especially strict in implementing Training Course teachings lost not only rank-and-file members but also the majority of its district heads. Ultimately even one of The Word of God's longtime head coordinators resigned and left the community. Circumstances were such that for the first time coordinators publicly "repented" for the secrecy and speed at which they had implemented the Training Course, though notably not for any of its contents or intended goals. In an effort to protect the community's reputation, Martin also held a meeting for "reconciliation" with former community members and formally repudiated what had become a de facto practice of shunning those who had renounced their public commitment.

However, the crisis over the Training Course had left a mood of self-assessment about the community's effort to create a culture for itself as a people. The interpersonal demands created by household clusters proved unworkable, and a return was made to small interpersonal groups, now segregated by gender, as the principal mechanism of intimacy. Certain elements of community practice perceived as isolating it and inhibiting its growth began to be modified. There were no longer community-sponsored block parties with evangelistic intent. Opposition to women working outside the home and to marriages outside the community began to ease somewhat. The term "head" was replaced (in official terminology if not in popular usage) by "pastoral leader" or "longterm elder." The stated reason for this change was the archaism of "headship," and, in the words of one head coordinator, its connotation to outsiders of "more substantial directive authority than we see in pastoral relationships." The physical aspect of the domestic environment was also moderated, with the decline of inscribed wall banners and the reintroduction of televisions, stereos, and videotape players, even if used only for religiously acceptable programming.

Coincident with the reaction to the Training Course, however, these years also saw the infusion of new energy into the ritual life of the community. As Derek Prince and Robert Mumford had done earlier in the community's history, around 1985 Protestant evangelist and healer John Wimber visited The Word of God, bringing the practice of "power evangelism."[6] Wimberite prayer encourages manifestations of divine power in the form of "signs and wonders" such as healing, spontaneous waves of laughter or sobbing that spread through an assembly, and the falling in a sacred swoon known as resting in the Spirit. Wimber's emphasis on participants' laying on of hands for each other initiated a renewed interest in healing prayer among the community rank and file. This enthusiasm extended beyond already typical practices of informal healing prayer in households, within the personal headship relation, or by district heads and coordinators visiting the sick in their biblically defined role of community elders. Advocacy for making spiritual gifts of power more accessible to the rank and file also played a part in the initiation in 1986 of Charismatic prayer meetings for children at some Sword of the Spirit branches. Perhaps encouraged by the Wimberite influence, and acting on a longtime awareness that their retreat from the world to consolidate a Charismatic culture would make them less accessible to the general public and slow their rate of growth, the coordinators in 1987 also once again began to hold an open prayer meeting.[7] A new experiment was inaugurated in 1989 as several members of The Word of God relocated to Colorado to live alongside members of John Wimber's Vineyard Ministries, developing an order of life synthesized from covenant community pastoral forms and power evangelism forms of access to divinity.

By 1990 The Word of God branch of the Sword of the Spirit included fifteen hundred adults and an equivalent number of children, first among equals within the Sword of the Spirit and a powerful voice within Charismatic Christianity (see tables 6–8). In 1990, however, enduring tension within the international leadership of the Sword of the Spirit surfaced over, in the words of one community official, "differing visions of community structure and differences between strong, zealous personalities." Ralph Martin and Steven Clark represented the two factions, with Martin proposing that those communities who wanted more local autonomy but who wanted to remain within the supercommunity be allowed to assume a new status of "allied" communities. Through the traditional means of a "community consultation," the plan was submitted to The Word of God members, who reportedly had little forewarning that a serious rift had developed within the community elite. The majority of members and coordinators agreed on the move to allied status. However, Clark's brotherhood, the Servants of the Word, announced that they were an autonomous body not bound by

Table 6. *Demographic Change in The Word of God: Age*

Age	1968 %	N	1969 %	N	1972 %	N	Age	1976 %	N	1982 %	N
							0–4			51*	433
							5–9			26*	221
							10–14			16*	147
14–17	—	—	1	1	1	3	15–17			7*	43
18–19	36	15	22	23	29	59	18–20	12	154	0.3	5
20–24	55	23	50	51	53	112	21–25	42	521	13	185
25–29	5	2	4	4	10	24	26–30	24	294	32	447
30–39	2	1	10	10	3	7	31–40	13	162		
							31–35			27	380
							36–40			11	148
40–49	2	1	11	12	1	2	41–50	4	52	5	77
50–79	—	—	2	2	3	6	51–60	2.3	9	2	35
							61–70	1.7	9	1	19
							71 and above	0.6	3	0.7	8
							Not known	2	20	0.6	6
Total	100	42	100	103	100	213		100	1,243	100	1,387

*Percentage is that of all children in the community.

SOURCE: Figures for 1968, 1969, and 1972 are drawn from Keane 1974. Figures for 1976 and 1982 are from internal surveys by The Word of God, graciously made available by head coordinators.

Table 7. *Demographic Change in The Word of God: Gender*

Sex	1968 %	N	1969 %	N	1972 %	N	1976 %	N	1982 %	N	1989 %	N
Male	48	20	42	45	50	106	46	568	49	686	49	750
Female	52	22	58	62	50	107	54	675	51	701	51	776
Total	100	44	100	107	100	213	100	1,243	100	1,387	100	1,526

SOURCE: Figures for 1968, 1969, and 1972 are drawn from Keane 1974. Figures for 1976, 1982, and 1989 are from internal surveys by The Word of God, graciously made available by head coordinators.

Table 8. *Demographic Change in The Word of God: Marital Status*

Marital Status	1969		1972		1976		1982	
	%	N	%	N	%	N	%	N
Married	13	14	19	39	38	476	60	838
Single	87	92	81	171	58	721	37	513
Divorced	—	—	—	—	2	26	1.4	22
Separated	—	—	—	—	1	11	0.6	6
Widowed	—	—	—	—	1	9	0.8	8
Total	100	106	100	210	100	1,243	100	1,387

SOURCE: Figures for 1969 and 1972 are drawn from Keane 1974. Figures for 1976 and 1982 are from internal surveys by The Word of God, graciously made available by head coordinators.

the community decision and that they would remain within the Sword of the Spirit. Several of the coordinators and a core of rank and file rallied around them and reconstituted as a new branch of the Sword of the Spirit. A schism had occurred.[8]

In 1991, of the presplit membership of approximately 1,500 adults, the Sword of the Spirit branch claimed 230 members. The Word of God claimed somewhere between 600 and 800. Perhaps reflecting the family tension over personal conduct associated with the Sword of the Spirit Training Course, it appeared that families with older children tended to remain in The Word of God and those with younger or grown children constituted the bulk of the new Sword of the Spirit branch. It also appeared that the diminished Word of God membership was roughly evenly divided among Protestant and Catholic (see table 9 for presplit proportions). The smaller Sword of the Spirit appeared to become predominantly Catholic in reaction to a perception of inordinate Protestant influence in The Word of God.[9] Rank-and-file Catholics from both communities continued to attend the denominational Christ the King fellowship, which as a result of the schism had been removed by the local bishop from within the community and declared to be a kind of nongeographic floating parish under direct diocesan jurisdiction. Perhaps 150 former community members chose to remain active in the fellowship without allegiance to either The Word of God or the Sword of the Spirit. From all indications the remaining four hundred to five hundred members, disaffected and disillusioned, terminated participation in any community-related activity.

Table 9. *Demographic Change in The Word of God: Denomination*

Denomination	1969 %	1969 N	1972 %	1972 N	1976 %	1976 N	1982 %	1982 N	1987 %	1987 N
Catholic	79	84	61	129	58.5	727	64.0	888	64.1	1,003
Non-Catholic	21	22	39	82						
Lutheran	—	—	—	—	7.0	87	6.0	85	7.1	111
Presbyterian	—	—	—	—	6.4	79	4.0	57	5.9	93
Methodist	—	—	—	—	5.9	73	4.0	60	3.0	47
Baptist	—	—	—	—	3.6	45	2.0	31	1.7	26
Unaffiliated	—	—	—	—	3.1	39	3.5	54	—	—
Free Church	—	—	—	—	—	—	3.0	40	6.6	104
Episcopalian	—	—	—	—	3.0	37	3.0	36	2.0	31
Reformed	—	—	—	—	.5	7	1.0	16	.6	9
Christian Reformed	—	—	—	—	.5	7	.5	8	1.0	16
Assembly of God	—	—	—	—	.7	9	.5	8	.4	7
Jewish	—	—	—	—	.5	7	.5	5	.5	8
Pentecostal	—	—	—	—	.6	8	.5	6	.3	4
Orthodox	—	—	—	—	.4	5	—	—	.3	5
United Church of Christ	—	—	—	—	.5	6	.5	5	.1	1
Congregational	—	—	—	—	.3	4	.5	6	.1	2
Quaker	—	—	—	—	.1	2	.1	2	.1	1
Other	—	—	—	—	1.0	14	—	1	1.3	19
Unknown	—	—	—	—	7.2	90	5.0	68	5.0	78

SOURCE: Figures for 1969 and 1972 are drawn from Keane 1974. Figures for 1976, 1982, and 1987 are from internal surveys by The Word of God, graciously made available by head coordinators.

Several issues underlie the overt split in the Sword of the Spirit over local autonomy versus centralized government. Most appeared to be a legacy of the crisis over the Training Course. The stance of Martin and The Word of God leadership was to "repent" for elitism and arrogance relative to other Christians. They also "repented" for internal abuses of authority in enforcing practices that, because of their rigor and the difficulty of conforming to them, led to unhealthy feelings of inadequacy among members. The stance of Clark and the Sword of the Spirit was that they would remain faithful to the original divinely inspired community "vision," adhering to the substance of the Training Course while continuing to admit that it was awkwardly implemented. They see themselves as maintaining the structure of a covenant community, including headship, and The Word of God as retreating to the status of a sophisticated prayer group.

The Wimberite influence also proved to be a point of controversy. From the perspective of many members, this influence marked a kind of spiritual renewal within the community. However, Clark's faction construed the embrace of Wimber's power evangelism by Martin and Head Coordinator James McFadden as an abandonment of Catholicism. McFadden's collaboration with the Wimberites in founding a sub-community of The Word of God in Colorado was seen as an abandonment of the covenant community model in favor of Wimber's Vineyard congregations.[10]

A third issue is the recent popularity among rank-and-file members of twelve-step support groups based on the model of Alcoholics Anonymous and related "codependency" theory. Community interest in these groups coincided with their popularity in the broader North American society during the 1980s.[11] The Sword of the Spirit perceived them precisely as alien influences, incompatible with the pastoral structure of the covenant community and potentially creating "confusion" by offering support based on competing principles. Indeed, another branch of the Sword of the Spirit explicitly declared that anyone who joins such a group cannot be in the community. The Word of God saw the popularity of support groups as a sign of inadequacy and need for reform in their own structure of interpersonal support. They speculated that perhaps members were seeking support from tensions generated by community life itself, or that perhaps their mode of life attracted (or at least keeps) the kind of people who are in need of such support. In fact, twelve-step groups are by definition "anonymous," and may thus constitute not only a search for additional support but also reaction against the intense communitarian elaboration of the psychocultural theme of intimacy.

In 1992 The Word of God, while remaining an allied member of the Sword of the Spirit, adopted a dramatic set of reforms. Moreover, rather than use the old community consultation format, these changes were instituted as a result of direct democratic vote. The sweeping changes can be divided into categories of community life and membership, leadership, and symbols of groups identity. I will summarize the changes in each category.

First, in an effort to restore mature responsibility for personal decision making to members, the community abolished the institution of pastoral leadership (headship), long a cornerstone of group organization. The system of "pastoral care" was to be replaced by one of "fraternal support." The Training Course was officially "set aside" as an "ill-advised venture" with much associated "bad fruit." Although its fundamental values were reaffirmed, members were advised to judge for themselves which elements to keep and which to reject. Even beyond this, the long series of initiation/indoctrination courses that prepared people for "public commitment" as full community members was to be modified and streamlined. The community in effect repudiated Steven Clark's formulation of group life by abandoning the key Living in Christian Community course, codified in Clark's book *Patterns of Christian Community* (1984). In the new model, the basic Life in the Spirit Seminar was to be followed only by a course on the Charismatic spiritual gifts and a course on community membership. Members voted to decrease the demands on the amount of participation and activity required of them. Leaders were to retain the ability to terminate members for denial of "Christian truth" or offense against "Christian righteousness," but termination for inadequate participation was reserved to a board the majority of which was to be rank-and-file members.

In the domain of leadership, it was voted that the current coordinators resign in favor of a newly constituted leadership team of five to eight members. This team would be chosen, advised, and overseen by a council of twenty-five members elected by the general membership. A proposal granting the "senior leader" of the leadership team a veto over team decisions was explicitly defeated in the vote. The most momentous change, however, was that women were to be included as voting members of both the leadership team and the council (six women were subsequently chosen as council members). A male was still to be the senior leader of the leadership team, of the council, and of small-scale support groups ("men's and women's" groups or "growth" groups), "as a way of expressing the leadership of men seen in the New Testament." Nevertheless, the importance of the change was evidenced in the inclusion of a vote about whether to delay inclusion of women as leaders, pending a ruling by the international governing council of the Sword of the Spirit as to whether the proposal would undermine the allied status of The

Word of God. The membership voted not to wait. In the words of one male leader, the consensus was that "in this time and place, it's appropriate to have women as leaders." The time and place, it will be noted, coincided with the confrontation in American society between Anita Hill and Clarence Thomas over the latter's Supreme Court nomination and with the confrontation between Desiree Washington and Mike Tyson over the latter's rape of the former, events that led to the emergence of the political scene of many prominent women as candidates for national office in the 1992 election.

The most profound change in symbols of community identity was abandonment of mantles and veils, which had been worn as a sign of public commitment. These items of ritual garb, which had distinguished members from outsiders and different classes of members within the community, were to be turned in "so that they can be disposed of respectfully." In addition, the members voted to consider whether to keep, modify, or drop the formal community covenant. Until such a decision was made, new members were given the option of committing to "simple membership" rather than "full commitment." Finally, members voted to consider changing the community name from "The Word of God" to something like "The Word of God Community." These latter two issues can be understood only by recalling that both the covenant and the community name were understood to have been bestowed directly by the deity and were therefore considered essential to the community's divine mission and its identity as a "people of God." To consider becoming merely a community *named* The Word of God, rather than continuing to *be* The Word of God, was anything but mere semantics.

What the possibility of a change in name indicated, along with the other changes in 1992, was the reversal of the rhetorical involution to which I referred earlier in this chapter. For years the community had avoided the process identified by Weber as the routinization of charisma with an ever-escalating rhetoric embedded in practice and performance. The schism in The Word of God was a kind of apocalyptic break, a crisis of the sacred self in which Clark's faction remained on the tightening spiral of charisma while for Martin's faction the tightening discipline, authority, and apocalyptic tension snapped like an overwound watch spring. In the next chapter we will examine the rhetorical process leading up to this apocalyptic break, filling in our ethnographic/historical sketch with a detailed account of the radicalization of charisma and the ritualization of practice.

Plate 1. *Community gathering of The Word of God in 1987. Participants are arranged in concentric circles, with the central circle visible in the top center of the image. The disposition of bodies in space retains the original emphasis in Charismatic prayer meetings on the intimacy of face-to-face interaction among participants seated in a circle. The addition of concentric circles as gatherings grew in size, with community leaders occupying the central one, did not replace the original sense of intimacy but added that of the center as locus of authority toward which participants were oriented. Bentley Historical Library, University of Michigan, Peter Yates photograph.*

Plate 2. *Head coordinator Ralph Martin addresses the community gathering from the center of the circle. Bentley Historical Library, University of Michigan, Peter Yates photograph.*

Plate 3. *Publicly committed women at the community gathering wearing veils of Belgian linen. Bentley Historical Library, University of Michigan, Peter Yates photograph.*

Plate 4. *Publicly committed men at the community gathering wearing mantles of Irish linen. Following the community schism in the early 1990s, use of mantles and veils was discontinued by The Word of God faction on the grounds that it had contributed to exaggerated exclusivity, isolation, and elitism. It was re-tained as a symbol of commitment by the Sword of the Spirit faction. Bentley Historical Library, University of Michigan, Peter Yates photograph.*

Plate 5. *Community members engaged in loud praise, 1990. Courtesy of Philip Tiews, The Word of God.*

4

Ritualization and Radicalization

I have suggested that the Charismatic transformation of self and habitus can be described in terms of a rhetorical involution composed of the dual ritualization of practice and radicalization of charisma. My preliminary example was how psychocultural themes are taken up into ritual life. Working with our example of The Word of God through twenty-five years of its history, we must now take the next step and identify the rhetorical principles that have become involuted. Specifically, the principle that becomes involuted in the ritualization of practice is that God is constituting the members of the community as a people and that as a people they should be actively concerned with developing a distinct culture. The notion of a culture is explicit—and is indeed the way community leaders related to my interest in them as a cultural anthropologist. The principle that becomes involuted in the radicalization of charisma is that there is increasingly more at stake in the expanding threat posed by "the world, the flesh, and the devil," a threat that demands increasingly greater commitment that will be rewarded by increasing access to divine power. In the rhetorical deployment of these principles it is evident that ritualization and radicalization are really two dimensions of the same process, insofar as successive ritualizations went hand in hand with rhetorical escalations that not only proclaimed their beneficiality but also asserted their necessity.

Weber (1947: 370–371) argued that a decisive motive underlying the routinization of charisma is always the striving for security and the most fundamental problem is transition to a form of administration adapted to everyday conditions. By contrast, ritualization of practice sacralizes everyday conditions and radicalization of charisma suspends security in favor of a grander striving. It is not so much that life becomes extraordinary but that the ordinary is revved up in anticipation of the divine kingdom, power, and glory. Again, most discussion of the routinization of charisma has taken place on the level of organization and movement dynamics. By contrast, the radicalization of charisma becomes analytically accessible on the level of self process, understood as an incremental advance into an imaginative terrain. Ritualization is the complementary consolidation of features in this imaginative terrain by incorporating them into a habitus, endowing the self with dispositions in the sense that it becomes "disposed" within a previously alien but now familiar terrain.

In his study of the Northern African Kabyle people, Bourdieu argues that

one of the effects of the ritualization of practices is precisely that of assigning them a time—i.e., a moment, a tempo, and a duration—which is relatively independent of external necessities, those of climate, technique, or economy, thereby conferring on them the sort of arbitrary necessity which specifically defines cultural arbitrariness. (1977: 163)

In this passage, Bourdieu is discussing an ethnic "people" in the strict sense, among whom practices were in fact ritualized long ago. He can thus refer to the "effects" of ritualization, but the actual process of ritualization is inaccessible to examination. This inaccessibility also makes it difficult for him to distinguish the sacred in ritualized practices from the purely conventional in habitualized practices. This question is very much at issue in Bourdieu's work on the Kabyle, whose practices presumably are invested with an aura of the sacred. Examining the development over time of a group like The Word of God allows us to see not only the "arbitrary" that persists, and not only the sense of "necessity" that for the Kabyle is shrouded in customary time, but also the way in which Bourdieu's apparent oxymoron "arbitrary necessity" makes sense.

The rhetorical conditions of possibility for this dual process in The Word of God were, first, prophecies in which the deity appeared to call for completely open-ended commitment, with the promise of incremental revelation and preparation for fulfillment of the divine plan. Second, from the time of its adoption, commitment to the covenant was defined as commitment to the life of the community and not to specific ritual or organizational forms. On the one hand, this gave the appearance of preserving spontaneity and avoiding "legalism"; on the other, it gave coordinators a free hand in determining group organization. The most compelling single item of evidence for existence of the routinization/ radicalization process is the acknowledgment by community leaders that successive prophecies and innovations were repeatedly regarded at first as either poetic hyperbole or just plain crazy, but that the more such divine promises come true, or perhaps are made true by actions of the faithful, the more willing they are to believe even larger promises.[1]

I will describe the dual process of radicalization and ritualization within four dimensions of group life. First, time is sacralized as the community's history is transformed into a mythical charter that plots the creation of the sacred self by its incorporation into a sacred people charged with a divine mission. Second, in the domain of worship, or ritual in the strict sense, we trace an involution and escalation in the meaning and experience of spontaneity and divinity. Third, the domestic sphere becomes increasingly elaborated as the space of intimacy and the arena of gender discipline. Fourth, the organization of personal conduct epitomized by the practices of initiation, headship, and courtship is a highly specific involution and interplay between interpersonal intimacy and control.

Time, Myth, and Identity

The transformation of time in The Word of God took place both with respect to historical time, as the contemporary history of the community was assimilated to "salvation history," and with respect to cyclical time, in the evolution of an annual calendar of ritual events. The creation of mythic time in both respects is closely bound up with development of the notion of a sacred covenant. Prior to 1970 "covenant" was a term that, while prominent in everyday interaction, had not become the central principle for organizing practices. One informant recalled that covenant was virtually synonymous with "agreement," such that covenants were made constantly on any subject. It was common, for example, to make a covenant to meet someone for lunch at a particular time, and individual collective households sometimes were organized around periodically renewed covenants among their residents. By 1970 covenant had become transformed into a synonym of "commitment." On being defined as a formal document adopted in a solemn ceremony, it became not only a covenant among members but also a covenant with God. The commitment progressively became construed as commitment to a global mission, and this was rhetorically articulated in the "recommitment" of 1975. With the covenant and the people it created redefined by this "making oneself available" for a God-given mission, the rhetorical escalation of the Training Course that would complete the transformation of a people into an army of God became possible. Both the recommitment and the Training Course were sufficiently demanding redefinitions of self and collective identity that significant numbers were unwilling to tread farther into the imaginative terrain they illuminated and toward the horizon of existential engagement they outlined. By performative means that we will examine below in Part Three, the notions of covenant, people, and mission were imbued with a sense of participation in both mythic reality and cosmic time. Insofar as I have defined self process as orientational in nature, their rhetorical function was thus to orient members not only in terms of commitment but also in terms of temporality.

This transformation was also advanced by the way the community "received" its name. Catholic Charismatic groups are typically named either after the place where they meet (a group that meets at Saint James Church will be called Saint James Prayer Group) or by the inspired predication of a particular collective religious identity onto the group (examples are The Word of God, the People of Praise, the Work of Christ). Only in the latter type is there a rhetorical transformation of collective identity, but it is critical that the transformation is not an automatic result of the sign-function or metaphoric predication. The phenomenological component defined by recognizing that the name is willed by God, which in the Charismatic world implies becoming convinced that the name is necessary, contributes something essential to the collective self process. Consider the following description of the naming of a (no longer existing) Catholic Charismatic community:

Our group has a lot of intellectual skeptics (I'm one of them) who thought this whole idea of community names was too much like college fraternities to be taken seriously. Well, about sixty of us went to the 1971 Notre Dame Charismatic Conference; and when we were praying together, there was a prophecy that we were the Lord's "children of joy." It just so happened that one of the group had already written that on his name tag. We got a little excited about the coincidence, but we really didn't want a name so we waited a little longer to discern what the Lord had in mind. At our next prayer meeting, a seminarian who wasn't at Notre Dame and who had not been around for about two months also prophesied that we were the "children of joy." That was even more interesting, but still not convincing. Finally a priest who likewise hadn't been around for months prophesied that we were to be the Children of Joy. At last we decided that maybe the Lord wanted to give us a name, no matter how dubious we were about it. (Lange and Cushing 1974: 145)

Such a name thus defines not only collective identity but also collective essence as prescribed and bestowed by the deity.

At The Word of God, practical considerations provided the first impetus to naming the group, which others referred to as "the Pentecostals at Saint Mary's," and which referred to itself as "the Ann Arbor community." The campus Newman Center[2] was about to publish a booklet listing parish activities, and adoption of some descriptive tag seemed in order. A meeting was called, and several suggestions for names were presented, with the Word of God entered "at the last minute" by a member who found it when inspired to turn to a particular page of the Bible. At the meeting's end two prophecies were uttered. The first said, "You are my people. I formed you—you are mine, therefore you shall be called by my name." The second said that the group was taking the idea of a name too lightly.

Not only did the community's name become, through the performance of ritual language, charged with more than pragmatic significance, but the name was declared *already to exist* in the mind of God, to be revealed through inspiration to those who "sought" it. The decisive prophecy was uttered at a second meeting.

Listen to me, listen carefully to me, so that you can believe the promises I make to you. The promises which I make to you are far beyond your comprehension. Listen to me so that you can believe them. My promises are certain. I and those who are with me call you the word of God, because you are my word now to the whole face of the earth. I have called you and I have created you not for your own sake but for my sake, and for the sake of all those whom I would gather to myself. I am going to give you my Spirit in a way in which I have never given my Spirit to any people. I am going to make you my people in a way in which I have never before made any people my people. I am going to pour out on you a spirit of power, and of grandeur, and of glory, so that all who see you will know that I am God and that I am among you. Therefore this is my word to you: You have been first in all of my thoughts. Have I been first in all of your thoughts? I have in every way come to you. Have you in every way come to me? I have poured myself out to you and given myself to *you* without reserve. Have you given yourselves entirely to me? Seek me. I have already sought you. Look to me. Make me first in your lives. I have become your God and I have made you my people. Look to me. Seek me.

In this text the bestowal of a sacred name is couched in the language of open-ended commitment (and hence one-sided domination) to which

I alluded above. Divine promises are beyond comprehension, a global mission is foreshadowed, and the community is implicitly compared with the biblical Israelites as a chosen people. The deity, in the infinity and omnipotence of his thought, giving, and seeking, demands an equivalent response from his mortal listeners.

The naming of Charismatic groups in this way is not merely the choice of a likely metaphor. It is the profound alteration of the very significance of a name, such that it can give form to an "inchoate we" (Fernandez 1974). Collective symbolic action elevates the name from merely practical to fully sacred significance by declaring that it was the deity's idea to name the group. This is more than a rhetorical trick or mystification; it is a creative reorientation of a group's attention to their collective world. Names are thought to express something essential about the community. With respect to the movement as a whole, they identify the particular charism possessed by each community as distinct from other communities, constituting a kind of totemic system by means of which communities are both linked and differentiated. Thus the childlike simplicity cultivated by a community called the Children of Joy contrasts with the evangelistic aggressiveness of The Word of God. With respect to the internal activities of a group, its name defines the nature of collective life, or the mission of the community.

In addition to the open-endedness of prophetic language and commitment to a covenant, then, the metaphoric potential of a community's name must be added to the rhetorical conditions of possibility for the dual process I am describing. A community in which the sacred self is constituted as the Word of God may tread on imaginative terrain into which the Children of Joy or the Bride of Christ, or even the people of Praise, may not venture. This potential is evident in the series of related images in which The Word of God presented itself to itself over the years. At first an exemplary "shining white cross," it came to be self-described as a "fiery brand," an "army," and a "bulwark" to protect a Church besieged by tides or social currents that assault Christian values. The most telling exploitation of rhetorical potential came with the taking up in 1982 of the militant biblical injunction to be armed with "the word of God which is the sword of the spirit." The essence of the community was transformed with its name as it became a branch of the Sword of the Spirit. A name given by God, so the community's written account of its own naming states, is not meant for mere identification, for "in naming us, God has not only given us a phrase by which men will know us, but he has *established* once and for all what our role and purpose is to be in his plan for the universe."[3]

The place of the community in historical and mythical time is elegantly, and somewhat startlingly, displayed in the following text. It is a call-and-response litany adapted from the Jewish seder and uttered at the community's annual anniversary celebration.

O God our father, if you had only made us in your image . . .

    (Response: . . . that would have been enough for us.)

If you had only walked with us in the garden . . .

If you had only promised to redeem us after we fell from your grace . . .

If you had only showed yourself to our father Abraham . . .

If you had only made a covenant with us . . .

If you had only made us strong in Egypt and not given us Moses to lead us . . .

If you had only given us Moses to lead us, and not brought us through the Red Sea . . .

If you had only brought us through the Red Sea, and not fed us in the desert . . .

If you had only fed us in the desert, and not made a covenant with us at Sinai . . .

If you had only given us the covenant, and not brought us into the promised land . . .

If you had only brought us into the promised land, and not given us the prophets . . .

If you had only sent us the prophets, and not given us your word in the scriptures . . .

If you had only given us your word in the scriptures, and not sent us your word in the flesh, Jesus the Lord of Glory . . .

If you had only given us Jesus, and not given him up to death for our salvation . . .

If you had only brought us to life in the death of Jesus, and not given us the Holy Spirit . . .

If you had only given us the Holy Spirit, and not left us the gospels . . .

If you had only taught us about the Baptism in the Holy Spirit, and not brought us to Ann Arbor . . .

If you had only brought us to Ann Arbor, and not given us the Thursday night [prayer] meetings . . .

If you had only given us the Thursday night meetings, and not added to our number day by day . . .

If you had only added to our number, and not given us the gifts of the Holy Spirit [charisms] . . .

If you had only given us the gifts, and not taught us how to pray together in unity and power . . .

If you had only brought us together to pray, and not spoken to us about being a people . . .

If you had only taught us to be a people, and not spoken to us about a covenant . . .

If you had only made a covenant with us, and not shown us how to live together in households . . .

If you had only taught us how to live together in households, and not spoken to us about sharing our resources . . .

If you had only taught us to share our goods with one another, and had not given us wisdom about family life . . .

If you had only given us wisdom about family life, and not baptized our children in the Holy Spirit . . .

If you had only baptized our children in the Holy Spirit, and not spoken to us about being your servants in the whole world . . .

O Lord you've done so much. And you haven't stopped there, you've continued to do more and more.

This collective prayer[4] achieves the rhetorical and mythopoetic task of situating the community in the flow of "salvation history." The abrupt yet seamless transition from mythical to contemporary events assimilates the community to ancient Israel, identifying it as a New Testament chosen people. Not only is the pattern of life sacralized by making it, ex post facto, an act or initiative of God, but successive developments are characterized as unexpected, *spontaneous* surfeits of divine beneficence. The anniversary celebration from which the text is drawn is also an occasion for recitation of the group's history as a kind of mythical charter.[5] A narrated slide show of the community's "early days" shows its "four founders" as blue-jeaned hippies, in sharp contrast to their present business-suited demeanor. Although on the surface this is an endearing retrospective with the ostensive message "We head coordinators have had our ups and downs and are really not much different from you," the narrative dramatizes their current distance from the rank and file with the rhetorical subtext "Look at the amazing thing God has made of us from such humble beginnings."

The anniversary celebration itself belongs to a ritualization of cyclical time that began with the original weekly prayer meeting, mentioned in the litany as the Thursday night meeting. Originally set for that night because it fit the schedules of all the original members, it came to be endowed with a surplus of meaning and regarded as a gift from the deity, a kind of extra Sabbath. Likewise, the second weekly meeting for the inner circle of committed members began on Monday, but was eventually changed to Sunday, the actual Christian Sabbath. By the late 1970s an implicit annual cycle was in place, with a national Charismatic conference in the summer, a community conference early in the fall, the anniversary celebration coinciding with Thanksgiving, and the ceremony for public commitment of new full members shortly before Christmas. In the field at the time, I asked whether the emerging "people" was cultivating a ritual calendar such as was familiar among many peoples studied by anthropologists. A coordinator responded that no such cycle was explicitly recognized, but soon thereafter it was reported that talk was afoot about declaring a "season of celebration" that would roughly coincide with the Christmas season and extend from the community anniversary to the public commitment. Acknowledging that my own presence may have stimulated an ethnographic development, I would emphasize instead the eagerness of The Word of God for any innovation that would support its aspiration to a "culture" of its own.

Worship and Embodied Charisma

To speak of ritual or worship in the strict sense may be somewhat misleading, since the comprehensive ritualization I am outlining eventually leaves no room for distinction between sacred and secular action even in everyday life. By the same token, it is not always relevant to distinguish between everyday practice and formal performance. Nevertheless, it is possible to demonstrate that as charisma became radicalized, practices of collective and individual worship increasingly became techniques of the body in the sense defined by Marcel Mauss (1950). In the language of textuality, we might say that charisma was inscribed in the body through discipline of the body at prayer. In the language of embodiment, we might say that the charismatic self process was generated by bodily experience. For either articulation (see also Csordas 1994b), it is accurate to say that the inculcation of dispositions within a ritual habitus corresponded to the disposition of bodies in space.

Let us begin with the following two ethnographic observations. First, the dominant purposes of Charismatic prayer, whether in glossolalia or in the vernacular, are praise of the deity and petition for divine intercession. Praise is understood to be a spontaneous expression of exuberance about an all-good and glorious deity. Petition is directed toward a deity understood as paternally and intimately responsive to and concerned for the well-being of his creatures. Second, the palms-up prayer posture and the laying on of hands are universal techniques of the body in Charismatic prayer. While outsiders most often associate laying on of hands with prayer for healing, it can be used in any situation in which a person is being prayed for or "prayed over," including consecration of prayer group leaders or coordinators. As I mentioned above, the palms-up posture has been supplemented by a variant in which hands are raised with palms facing outward, a posture that appears to assertively direct the power of prayer outward rather than inward toward the supplicant (see pl. 5). A shift from spontaneity to convention in use of the prayer posture can be observed in The Word of God when it was taught to children, who were sometimes reprimanded for not raising their hands in prayer during community gatherings.

The Word of God's first major radicalization in the domain of worship came with the introduction of loud praise. The principle behind loud praise is that collective praise for God is more "edifying and expressive of real feeling" the louder it is. Worshipers should thus attempt to "raise the roof" with loud vocalization and hand clapping. In this practice, Charismatics have rediscovered a virtually universal connection between sound and spirituality first formulated by Rodney Needham (1972). Needham's thesis would have us focus not on the general clamor of loud praise but on its percussive element, the expression of praise by tumultuous clapping or applause. He argues that "practically everywhere it is found that percussion is resorted to in order to communicate with the other world," specifically in rites of passage from one social status or condition to another (1972: 395–396), such that the impact of percussion in effect impels persons across the boundaries of social categories.

If we were to apply this interpretation to The Word of God, we might say that loud praise effects a transition from a collectivity of selves to a single people. However, the differences between our case and Needham's discussion must be pointed out and must suggest modification of his position in certain respects. For Needham, the onset of percussion marks a transition from everyday silence to sacred sound, whereas in our case the onset of percussion marks the *escalation* of sacred sound. In addition, whereas in Needham's example the transition takes place once and for all within a single ritual event, in The Word of God the transition is an *ongoing* one, sustained by the practice of percussive praise as a regular feature of collective ritual. Finally, whereas Needham was preoccupied with an apparent incompatibility between the affective impact of percussion and the logical structure of category change, we must emphasize the unity of affect and cognition in the percussive generation of a *phenomenological* shift for participants. That is, loud praise not only moves people across category boundaries, it also helps to create those very categories.

Putting these three points together, we are able to be quite specific in elaborating Needham's point that what is at issue in ritual percussion is "aurally generated emotion." In our case, percussion must be considered as an accompaniment to vocalization in two respects: first, insofar as applause is a form of praise; and second, insofar as the aural is the privileged sensory modality for transmission of the divinely inspired "word." An escalation of volume is then quite literally an escalation of enthusiasm. My own impression on hearing loud praise continue uninterrupted for a period of minutes was that the louder the collective clamor becomes, the more it appears to have a life of its own. It is an unmistakably Durkheimian occurrence, in which the reality of the collectivity becomes more vivid than the reality of its individual members. The sense of spontaneous outpouring that characterizes quiet collective prayer of praise is transformed to one of self-sustaining transport, and hierophany occurs. The ritual practice is a vehicle of radicalization, upon which people enter an imaginative terrain as a divinely constituted people and advance toward the horizon of a divine plan for their lives.

The phenomenological immediacy of this effect is enhanced by the fact that loud praise is a technique of the body. It is thus existentially engaging insofar as it requires that *effort* that we have seen as essential to a definition of self grounded in embodiment. Needham is correct in observing that sound has "not only aesthetic but bodily effects," but he conceives these effects in terms of sensory reception (representation) rather than of physical production (bodily experience). Just as the phenomenological effect of speaking in tongues is as much in the vocal gesture of the speaker as it is in audition of the syllables produced (Csordas 1990a), the effect of loud praise has its locus in the physical engagement of the body in the act of worship. In this connection, the Charismatics' own phrase "raising the roof" should be understood as an image of strenuous effort (see Knauft 1979).

The bodily effect in question comes not only from the vibrations of sound but also from the motion and from the heat and redness generated in one's hands as they repeatedly strike one another. Adding to this dimension of bodily engagement, along with loud praise, members began to gingerly jump or hop in place while praying, both in solitary devotion and in collective worship. The result was a virtually calisthenic spirituality of corporal commitment, and furthermore one that explicitly reinforced the social principle of male headship with a cultural celebration of masculine energy. The masculinization of practice that characterizes covenant community gender discipline will be more apparent in our consideration of domestic life and personal conduct. In the case of loud praise, the *kind* of bodily engagement required was designed to aid the recruitment of men by offering an alternative to the female-dominated spirituality of Charismatic prayer groups that was perceived as too introspective and emotional.[6] According to one Sword of the Spirit coordinator, "You had to be manly to do what we were trying to do," and "grunting, lifting heavy objects, and spittin' was the thing to do" for covenant community men, so that one did not have to "feel like you had to be a sissy to be holy." Members entered the imaginative terrain with their bodies as well as their minds.

The next step toward radicalization was made the following year with the "recommitment" and adoption of mantles and veils to be worn as symbols of public commitment during community gatherings. Members reflected that this was not the first occasion in which an idea that at first appeared "crazy" came to be accepted and cherished as a symbol of a covenant with God. It was, however, the most controversial, both because of the new requirements that went along with recommitment and because overt ritual adornment of the body was felt by some to be a potentially elitist and even odd practice. Familiar enough to students of ethnology, such ritual garb is incongruous in the cultural context of middle-class North America. Some objected that the practice was too radical for sensible people and that its adoption would make members appear foolish, alienating outsiders. When the community prophet, Bruce Yocum, then uttered a prophecy declaring that the wearing of mantles and veils was the will of God, for the first time some objected that this was an unfair coercive use of ritual language, since it is unthinkable to contradict a word spoken directly by God. Divinely construed authority prevailed, and a practice began which reinforced both the sense of the community as a people and the growing trend to become "free from the world."

In 1977, along with the series of "teachings on honor and respect," kneeling, prostration, and foot washing were added to the repertoire of ritual techniques of the body. Although Catholics are accustomed to kneeling at prescribed times in liturgy, prostration is a much more thorough and much less familiar engagement of the body. Moreover, these practices offered a new venue for interplay between spontaneity and control in ritual. Members could be requested to prostrate themselves at any time during a collective gathering (or choose to do so if in solitary prayer) and be commanded at any time to kneel to "receive" the divine word in prophecy. Foot washing is customary in certain Christian sects such as the Mennonites, but is again a radical innovation among middle-class Catholics.[7] Thus, in the context of The Word of God development, these innovations fit the pattern of radicalization of charisma through ritualization of bodily practice.

The final major development came with the adoption around 1985 of a Wimberite spirituality of signs and wonders. These include waves of spontaneous laughter or sobbing that spread through an assembly, waves of power visible as trembling or vibration in the hands of individual participants, spontaneous healing, and resting in the Spirit as a person falls under the influence of divine power and presence.[8] Resting in the Spirit is of particular interest in this respect, for while it had already been popular in the broader Catholic Charismatic Renewal for some ten years, it had never been prominent among covenant communities. Only within the complex of Wimberite practices of divine empowerment did it become widely accepted in the Sword of the Spirit. Some light is thrown on this change by recalling that it occurred precisely at a time when the Sword of the Spirit's influence in the Charismatic Renewal was somewhat in eclipse, when it was beleaguered by the ecclesiastical difficulties of its People of Hope branch, and when it was living through the internal repercussions of the Training Course. The innovation appeared to diffuse the experience of divine empowerment throughout the community, and some coordinators sensitive to their own reputation for authoritarianism were quick to emphasize that the discovery of Wimber's approach was a "grassroots movement" in the community not initiated by themselves. The direction of spiritual experience toward ritual healing and corporeal manifestations appeared to reinforce a relative turning inward. In general, a more devotional turn was evident, and even the tempo of the typical repertoire of Charismatic songs was observably slower. This shift is not incidentally related to bodily engagement, since its effect appeared not only to enhance a sense of duration and solemnity but also to endow the vocalization of song with a sense of physical deliberation and ponderousness.

Along with these changes, leaders acknowledged a swing of the pendulum away from urgent and aggressive masculinity, an orientation that had militated against devotional and passive practices such as resting in the Spirit. This gendered definition of the collective self had been evident in the contrast between covenant communities and the larger movement composed of Charismatic prayer groups, which were understood to practice a more "feminized" spirituality. Evangelization of fellow Charismatics by means of the FIRE rallies, and the notion that covenant communities were exemplary models, a vanguard of the movement, and protectors of the church, conformed to the cultural principle of male headship. Stated in more theoretical language, the Sword of the Spirit's claim to leadership among Charismatics had been predicated on an implicit structural opposition between dominant male and submissive female. The mode of bodily engagement invoked by Wimberite practices points to the increasing tension that characterized collective gender identity in the post–Training Course period. That is, although it was clearly an upsurge of empowerment, it was in a form that was relatively altered from the established notion of empowerment as aggressive masculinity.

Whatever their gender symbolism, introduction of the Wimberite practices continued the trend toward progressive engagement of the body. We can understand how this constituted a radicalization of spontaneity by contrasting the spontaneity of Wimberite signs and wonders with that characteristic of the long-accepted practice of collective singing in tongues. During prayer in tongues one member of the assembly will begin a glossolalic chant, or in a large gathering instrumentalists may provide a suggestive tonality. Participants will gradually take up the chant, blending and harmonizing improvisation around the initial tone. The result is a swelling of glossolalic song that gradually subsides again into the accustomed babble of glossolalic prayer. A sense of spontaneity is derived both from the collective taking up of the chant and from the improvised vocalization around the initial tonality. However, this is an intentionally coordinated spontaneity, much like that observable in the "wave" of spectators in an American sports arena who serially stand, raise their arms high, and sit, usually (for some reason doubtless grounded in their habitus) in a clockwise direction around the arena. By contrast, in the signs and wonders phenomenon there is, first, a variety of possible responses with no established order or precedence. Second, these responses are generally understood to be inherently more "somatic" than is singing or speaking in tongues—*and therefore more inherently spontaneous* than any form of speech. Thus even when a wave of laughter begins with a single person and spreads, the spread can be perceived only as spiritual contagion and not as intentional uptake, for an "authentic" laugh can *only* be spontaneous. In this case, spontaneity is doubly and necessarily a criterion of authenticity, since the laughter is understood to be divinely inspired and not the result of a human stimulus such as a joke. As with all the developments we have examined in this section, the sense of charismatic empowerment grows with the embodied advance into imaginative terrain.

Domestic Life

In the domestic domain ritualization occurred in two ways. First, practices were not only incorporated into habitual behavior, they were elevated beyond habit by being invested with the sacred. Second, ritual in the strict sense (e.g., prophecy or healing) was extended beyond the boundaries of ritual events, eventually permeating everyday life. The principal arena for ritualization of domestic life was the living situation. Most Charismatic prayer groups and early covenant communities included "growth groups" of seldom more than ten people who would meet weekly for prayer, Bible reading, discussion about life problems, and support in their process of "spiritual growth." These were the loci of interpersonal intimacy, and precursors of the community residential household. That households were the direct successors to these groups as more permanent settings for intimacy is demonstrated by the existence of the intermediate and curiously named "nonresidential households," which were in effect formalizations of the growth groups. Residential households were intended to provide both intimacy and a supportive environment for the "Christian life." In addition, unmarried youths were expected to learn from the household head and his wife as role models for "mature" Christian family life. The largest residential households at The Word of God numbered as many as twenty. Such large groupings were quickly found to be unwieldy, however, and were abandoned.

The evolution of living situations illustrates what Bourdieu (1977) refers to as "regulated improvisation" within a habitus, in this case the generation of alternatives with respect to the disposition of bodies in domestic space. Members repeatedly affirmed that "nothing is set in stone in The Word of God." This referred in part to the flux and diversity in living situations, as coordinators shifted personnel and experimented with different household compositions.[9] It also referred to the fact that each district or subcommunity has a slightly different pattern of organization worked out by its coordinator and district heads. Coordinated within a totality of tacit understandings and explicit principles, the generation of domestic alternatives gave members the vivid impression of spontaneity and thus enacted a critical psychocultural theme for the Charismatic self. This is also in conformity with the open-ended commitment discussed above, in which members were reminded that their commitment is to the covenant rather than to specific forms.

By the mid-1970s, of 1,243 members, 600 were living in apartments or single-family dwellings. Most of these participated in nonresidential households under the headship of a man who was typically also the head of his own residential household. "Dorm households" composed of students at the two local universities accounted for another 157 members. "Christian living situations" composed of unmarried men or women under the headship of one of the residents or a "more mature" outside person accounted for 165 members. Residential households accounted for 314 community members, and of these 140 lived in the most "committed" of living situations, the "common offering household." Members of common offering households owned no personal property. They gave all their earnings to the household head, who tithed the community on behalf of the household, paid for food and household maintenance, and distributed personal allowances to residents.

Let us take a closer look at the ritualization of domestic life in a common offering household in which I was permitted to live for a week in 1976. The household consisted of a married couple, their infant child, and eight single men and women. All were in their mid-twenties. The house itself appeared in most respects to be a typical small-city or suburban dwelling, with the major exception that one room was designated a prayer room to which residents could retreat for undisturbed devotion. Banners with slogans such as "Jesus Is Lord" or "Praise Him in All Things" were hung in the prayer room and dining room, and every room had a crucifix or devotional picture on the wall. As was the case with most community households, a television was kept in a closet and brought out only when a morally acceptable program (such as a sporting event) was to be watched. The household was designated a "service household," because aside from the household head, who was looking for employment as a banker, others worked for the community itself (in Charismatic Renewal Services, *New Covenant* magazine, or at The Word of God community offices). The head's wife was a community handmaid, another resident headed the Works of Mercy (charity) service group, and another worked in the Initiations (seminars for prospective members) service group. Two household residents were themselves heads of all male or female Christian living situations.

The daily routine began at ten minutes before seven, when everyone woke or was awakened with a knock on his or her door. Breakfast began promptly at seven. Cooking was done by the housewife, as was most housework, although the household head occasionally delegated other women residents to help her. All meals were taken collectively, beginning with prayers and ending with a religious song. At breakfast everyone reported how they felt that day, and whether they were in need of special prayer because of being tired. Only one person was permitted to speak at a time, with the stated purpose that everyone's words would be attended to and recognized as worthwhile by all. Guests were received for dinner one night per week, and one night was free for eating outside the household. Once a week the heads of Christian living situations were dismissed to eat with their charges. At the time, some households were transforming Sunday meals into a Sabbath ceremony with prayers adapted from the Jewish seder.

Between meals each person pursued his or her occupation. Collective household prayers were held each evening. Saturday evenings were set aside for nuclear family activities and independent activities by unmarried residents. An essential part of everyone's day was a period of private personal prayer in the prayer room. In addition, each member had a chart describing a weekly schedule, devised in consultation with his or her personal head. This schedule included weekly community gatherings on Sunday and Thursday nights, service to the community, and meetings with heads or with those over whom one had headship responsibility. The most active and committed members had little personal interaction with non-Charismatics and hence little activity that did not presuppose and reinforce Charismatic forms of experience and discourse.

This ritualization of time and space in households is far easier to describe than is the ritualization of conduct and interaction in the casual interactions of daily life. Household members in passing may pause to pray for deliverance from an evil spirit of Anger that began harassing one of them after an unpleasant incident at work in the secular world. One person may utter a few words of prophetic encouragement and reassurance to a fellow household member who expressed unusual fatigue at that morning's breakfast. A housewife pursuing her daily tasks may break out in a few bars, not of a "top 40" song, but of one from the community's Charismatic repertoire. These vignettes are no more than clues to, paraphrasing Alfred Schutz (1970), the sedimentation of ritual knowledge in the covenant community life-world. They color the interactive dimension of the everyday behavioral environment with the themes and motives of ritual reality.

On the more easily observable level of lifestyle, the cultural contrast between conventional and Charismatic households was not lost on non-Charismatic neighbors. In particular, the composition of community households led to protests against zoning violations in neighborhoods restricted to single-family dwellings. In 1975 The Word of God appropriated money for legal defense of a household faced with litigation on these grounds, and a similar situation arose at the People of Praise. There in South Bend a public hearing was held to discuss an ordinance the purpose of which was to prevent college students and hippies from invading suburban neighborhoods. Since this would directly affect them, People of Praise members presented a case for their own respectability and the sufficiency of their property upkeep. The hostile reaction by other citizens surprised them and served to reinforce a sense of persecution at a time when a principal message of prophecy and teaching was already to "get free from the world."

The radicalization promulgated in the Training Course at the beginning of the 1980s also included a reorganization of living situations, with the institution of household clusters. This innovation was in one sense a retreat from the single large household. It had a pragmatic side, since as the membership aged there were fewer unmarried people to be assigned to households, and as nuclear families grew, parents found it increasingly difficult to both care for children and maintain large domestic groupings. While there remained a few households of single men or women, and situations in which a single man or woman lived with a married couple to prepare for their own married life in the community, clusters were to be composed of nuclear families living adjacently. Geographic proximity had for some years been recognized as a goal for members of covenant communities, but The Word of God/Sword of the Spirit now began an ambitious disposition of members in what was anticipated to be a permanent space of interdomestic intimacy.

The stated ideal of intracluster relations was free ongoing social involvement, mutual aid in sickness and with child care, collective recreation for children, and reinforcing faith and Christian/community ideals as a group of people whose lives would be substantially intertwined. Men were expected to exercise self-regulating social control in the form of "fraternal correction" and encouragement of one another. Equivalent sororal relations were, however, discouraged by a gender ideology that explicitly subordinated women to men. Mutual encouragement and support were expected, but mutual social control among women was restricted to "light correction." One coordinator explained the cultural logic of this discrepancy as follows: "The men are responsible for their wives, so that some part of what is transacted among men doesn't get transacted among the women." In other words, men were responsible for themselves and their fellowmen, but women were responsible *to* their husbands.

The expected benefit of combining proximity with intimacy in clusters was predicated on the expectation that members would be "mature Christians" who could take a great deal of "pastoral responsibility" for one another, thereby reducing the "burden" on district heads and coordinators. In addition, members of a cluster were expected to share resources in a way reminiscent of the common offering household. The "vision" for transformation of domestic space extended to the idea of building interconnected houses. Problems quickly arose, however. Clusters were formed by assignment, based on questionnaires soliciting members' preference for living under particular district heads and coordinators. This frequently resulted in clusters with significant personal incompatibilities, not only of temperament but also of age and financial means. What I referred to above as regulated improvisation was put to the test as clusters were reshuffled: one person reported being in three "long-term" clusters within two years. The most serious difficulties arose when nuclear families, having purchased neighboring homes, found themselves unable to get along. One cluster of four families built four adjacent homes in the $200,000 to $300,000 price range, only to have their cluster disband (to their good fortune they remained on neighborly terms).

Of the few clusters that survived when I visited The Word of God/Sword of the Spirit in 1987, one included a couple who had been my friends and informants since 1973 and who had been among the community elite who first took the Training Course. They were invited to be in a cluster with three other families, so they put their house on the market and moved from the community district in neighboring Ypsilanti to Ann Arbor. The cluster built two new houses and helped them buy since they were not in a financial position to build. When the sale of their old house fell through, the men in their cluster chipped in, and for five years they were able either to make double house payments or rent it to others. Eventually, one of the original four families decided to leave the cluster, in part because they felt that they would fit better in a community district where there were more older children like their own. They sold the house they had built to another community family. The cluster's final composition was attained when two other community families who lived in the same neighborhood subsequently joined.

My friends described the financial generosity of their cluster not only with the example of how they were helped to support the expense of their former house but also in terms of everyday affairs. When one man was out of work, a cluster woman who buys food in bulk observed that since her bins were always full, it seemed silly for the other family to go to a store and pay. "Fill your bins from mine," she said. Cluster women reported they had a close working relationship even though they saw themselves as "very different from one another, and would never be together based only on what they have in common. One likes to can vegetables and be a homemaker, while others wouldn't dream of it; one is very athletic (aerobics), while the biggest exercise for others is chasing children around." Similar differences were perceived among cluster men, with the implicit assumption that since they would never be drawn together by natural compatibility, their intimate ongoing relationship was divinely ordained. Particularly in comparison to other clusters, they saw their cluster's success as "God's blessing." However, they also attributed their cluster's longevity to bonds established during the period of my friends' real estate troubles, to the fact that all the couples were more or less in the same age cohort, and to the presence from the outset of "a lot of combined pastoral wisdom" among the men.

By the end of the 1980s, the general failure of geographic clusters led to the development of men's and women's groups as the principal extrafamily structure of intimacy and social control. The groups are addressed in part to the culturally defined needs of men to experience "brotherly" ties and of women to experience "sisterly" ties, both of which are perceived to be weak in secular society. Community thinking on the role of these groups was expressed by a community head coordinator in 1987:

[They are] meant to counteract spouses being everything to one another and men having no male associates. Some men tend to be on the passive feminized side and [in men's groups] they get a good dose of influence from other men who are more established in their masculinity—[that's] of significant help. A lot of women in society today are pretty edgy about relating to other women, some kind of competitiveness or withdrawal or something—I don't understand the ins and outs of it completely. So we felt people often need help in learning to relate in a trusting way to other woman sisters. The second objective was, particularly for the men, that you can more decisively pastor them as a group of men separately [from women]. You know, you don't want to give some guy hell for some of his sins with five other guys' wives there in a group, or something like that, so just practically you can do a different kind of pastoring in that situation.

A given men's group is not necessarily paralleled by a women's group composed of their spouses.

When there's the right group of men it's not guaranteed that their wives will be the right group. . . . It seems to be a characteristic of human nature that you can get most any group of guys to do pretty well together, but that's not true for most any group of women, I think maybe because women are more sensitive and personalized or something, but the guys, you know, maybe they talk about baseball instead of their personal lives (chuckle). . . . I don't know, there's some reason that men can just accommodate one another better than women. So getting a good fit for a group of women is more of a challenge, we find. . . . That is, some of the women's needs you'd think of as being met through their husbands, where there isn't a counterpart in the life of the men within the group, so the men would probably meet more one another's needs in a certain sense, particularly in respect to direction, and correction, and encouragement.

These remarks clearly exhibit a gender ideology in which women need to be controlled and in which women's "needs" are expected to be met by their husbands, while husbands' needs cannot be completely fulfilled by their wives. Thus, in addition to being a domain in which regulated improvisation maintains the appearance of spontaneity, the extrafamily groups can be understood as additional arenas in which the themes of intimacy and control are played out in the idiom of patriarchal gender discipline. Specifically, intimacy and control are redistributed across cultural boundaries between the private and public domains. To understand this critical observation, three points must be made.

First, we must conceptualize cultural definitions of public and private with respect to the relation both between household and community and between household and the broader middle-class North American cultural milieu—the world, in Charismatic ritual language. The former of these relations is symbolically articulated in the representation of the community as a distinct people. If in microcosm the community is a people, then what is public is what occurs among this people. The mystification in this cultural definition is evident in the practice of referring to the community's initiation ceremony as a public commitment, when from a broader perspective it is in fact a private ritual for members only.

The latter relation is not symbolic, but is the material articulation between community households composed of wage earners and the public at large. Despite their rhetoric of world renunciation and their apparent social isolation in some respects, community members participate in an economic arena and inhabit a civic space with which they are oppositionally engaged.

Second, gender discipline is nowhere else in this conservative movement elaborated as explicitly as in covenant communities like The Word of God/Sword of the Spirit. I have already noted the community's explicit antagonism to feminism, classed as one of the four major threats posed by the world. In the symbolic redistribution of intimacy and control across boundaries between public and private we can perceive that the rhetorical underpinnings of gender discipline go beyond the contemporary clash between feminist and patriarchal values. Gender difference is a prime example of what Mary Douglas (1973) has called a "natural symbol" that can be taken up to articulate social categories. Specifically, with regard to gender symbolism in the domain of religion, Caroline Walker Bynum (1986a) has noted that it is profoundly polysemic and can be about values other than gender. For The Word of God/Sword of the Spirit, gender is both an issue in its own right and a rhetorically efficacious symbol that articulates a broader agenda. In its own right, for example, leaders of the community once observed that the Bible declared we are all "sons of God." They magnanimously concluded that women, too, must then be considered "sons of God"—but not sons who could serve as community leaders.[10] The broader agenda articulated by the symbolism of gender includes emphasis on discipline, authority, hierarchy, natural/divine law, conformity, sexual morality, primacy of loyalty to the collective project over loyalty to a spouse, and the regulation of psychological dependence between spouses.

Third, the distribution of intimacy and control between public (civic) and private (domestic) space must be understood in the context of the historical development of those spaces.[11] This is especially the case since the rhetorics of "traditional Christian" and even "early Christian" values are invoked in covenant community thinking. Bryan Turner formulates this development as follows:

The division between female passion and male reason is thus the cultural source of patriarchy. While patriarchy exists independently of the capitalist mode of production, being a specific distribution of power, capitalist society has articulated this division by providing a spatial distribution of reason and desire between the public and private realm, institutionalized by the divorce between the family and the economy. (1984: 37)

The "arbitrary necessity" required for the ritualization in contemporary society of archaic affective distinctions between male and female is evident in the rationale for male headship given by a Word of God/Sword of the Spirit woman who, years before, had been joint leader with her husband of a prayer group in another city. She abdicated the position and accepted male headship, she said, because when problems arose she found herself getting more upset and emotional than her husband and because she found that men became uncomfortable and resistant when faced with leadership by a woman. The cultural arbitrariness of the principle is evident in its contradiction with the often articulated notion that Charismatic spirituality is a "religion of the heart, not of the head," a principle that, based on the same cultural logic, would appear to favor female headship (or perhaps heartship).

According to the historical interpretation put forward by Turner, the superimposition of capitalism on patriarchalism displaced economic productivity from the domestic unit and left it primarily as a space of intimacy. In the covenant community intimacy is expanded *beyond* the nuclear family, either by expanding the size of households or later by linking domestic units in clusters or men's and women's groups. Conversely, control is expanded *within* the domestic unit with the adoption by the husband of a ritualized role as head of the household, personal head of his wife, and executor of varying degrees of behavioral austerity at the behest of the community and its covenant. This redistribution of "passions" and "reasons" can be further specified, borrowing Turner's (1984: 38) terms, as a partial transfer of gemeinschaft, affectivity, and particularity from the private domain to the public domain of the entire "people," with a reciprocal transfer of masculinity, formality, specificity, asceticism, and productivity from the public to the domestic sphere.

The element of this transformation that requires elaboration beyond what I have already said is the recasting of the covenant community household in the image of the preindustrial unit of production. This is achieved first through gender discipline, which reached its most radicalized form in the sexual division of labor implemented through the Training Course. The course taught that husbands were to perform all yardwork and household tasks regarding the care of animals (the latter an echo of Old Testament pastoralism even if it was a question only of house pets) and were to teach their sons manly activities such as hunting and fishing. Wives were to do all housecleaning, cooking, dishwashing, and child care and were to teach their daughters feminine activities such as cooking and sewing. A man at home alone with an infant was instructed to call on another community woman if the child required a change of diapers. Pregnant women were assigned other experienced women as coaches in labor and delivery; although the husband was to be the general overseer, he was excluded from the actual birth. These prescriptions gave behavioral substance to the community's longtime masculine motto "Seize the territory" and its feminine equivalent "Make a place." The patriarchal disposition that accompanied and justified the inculcation of pseudo-preindustrial gender discipline was expressed by community men, not in terms of their power, but in terms of the demands placed on them: "I'm taking care of my family much better than before. I have so many more responsibilities, believe me it's not easy."

In addition, the community household became a productive unit within the religiously constituted people in the sense that the tithe in fact produced the community's subsistence. In this age when even the *New York Times* can refer to "money and other commodities,"[12] it requires no greater symbolic imagination to understand the wages generated by household heads as the community's principal commodity than it does for members to understand themselves as a "people." However, the entire effect is illusory in the broader social context beyond the community. In this broader context, members' productive activities appear in a distinctly postmodern way, embodying, if anything, a transition from the work discipline of industrial capitalism to that of corporate multinationalism rather than a return to the work discipline of a preindustrial pastoral people. Members are not trained as herdsmen but as teachers, physicians, engineers, and accountants. The Sword of the Spirit is a multinational concern in which families as well as individuals experience mobility among branches, and whose resources are arrayed against competing global ideologies. Indeed, the apparent success of men's and women's groups in contrast to both extended residential households and household clusters may be related to their organizational affinity to corporate work groups and task forces free from the necessity to accommodate shared residence or spouse relationships.[13] None of this is to say that The Word of God/Sword of the Spirit members live an entirely illusory existence, for community members themselves would not be surprised at being compared to a multinational corporation. Our emphasis must be on the phenomenological effort and consequences of sustaining the collective sacred self of a preindustrial people in a post-industrial world. This leads to a consideration of the ritualization of personal conduct.

Personal Conduct

Let us begin with an ethnographic fact that in my view illustrates virtually all the issues with which we have been concerned thus far. It is the transformation of the Charismatic practice of greeting by embrace, the holy hug that from the very beginning of the movement was important as a spontaneous gesture of intimacy and thus instantiated important psychocultural themes in a specific technique of the body. By the middle to late 1970s at The Word of God, the direct face-to-face embrace had been partially replaced by a side-to-side embrace with each person putting an arm over the other's shoulder. In self-observation, and not without humor, community members noticed the evolution in their own behavior and began to distinguish between "full front forward" and "sidearm swipe" types of embrace. I have no reason to believe that this change was promulgated by the teaching of coordinators, and it appears to mark the emergence of what Bourdieu (1977), in a characteristic oxymoron, refers to as a "spontaneous disposition" within the habitus.

To understand this change as a product of ritualization and radicalization, we must distinguish at least three relevant conditions. First is that of economy of motion, really an issue of convenience and habit, as with continued daily interaction with other community members the meaning of the gesture came to be conveyed by an abbreviated motion that required less time and effort. Second is the trend toward masculinization, which at least in North America is reinforced by a conventional bodily technique that consists in two men slinging their arms over each other's shoulders as opposed to joining in an affectionate hug. Third, and standing as a radicalization of the psychocultural theme of control, the face-to-face embrace has an erotic potential that was increasingly problematized along with the radicalization of gender discipline. As the community became ever more mobilized against "worldly and fleshly" trends, the holy hug became an occasion of temptation to sin. Its place within the habitus became modified, no longer being a disposition only of spontaneity and intimacy but of control as well.

Within this intensely intimate interpersonal context, the first major ritual innovation was the 1969 introduction by visiting Protestant evangelists of deliverance from evil spirits. As is typical in the Protestant style of deliverance, the expulsion of demons took place through pronounced somatic reactions in the forms of screaming, writhing, coughing, weeping, and vomiting. At first an explicitly cathartic release of interpersonal tension among members, deliverance became ritualized as part of the community's initiation process. The radicalization in this case was not defined by an increase in somatic manifestations, for in fact prayer for deliverance became increasingly tame. Instead, group initiation was radicalized insofar as, to the simple rite of instruction and laying on of hands for Baptism in the Holy Spirit, there was now added a rite of purification in which inductees were purged of satanic contamination.

Also from an early date, the ritualization of personal conduct extended to practices of everyday speech, with teachings on "speech and wrongdoing" included in the initiation seminars attended by every member. Thus someone who does wrong should never say "I'm sorry," a phrase that constitutes a one-sided gesture, but should say "Will you forgive me?" to obtain a response and establish a relationship with the offended person. Speech should always "lead our listeners to love and respect those we are speaking about," and the proper mode of reprimand or correction was to "speak the truth in love." Nothing leading to mistrust or conflict, or reflecting on another's righteousness or competence should be said, with complaints addressed only to the person responsible or to that person's head. Even worse is "speaking against," defined as negative or hostile criticism of another person, family, household, or community. Care was taken to specify that it is not speaking against to report wrongdoing to a head, to ask a mature person how to deal with wrongdoing, or for a head to explain at a community gathering that a person is being disciplined or has become unwelcome at such gatherings.

It is said that these restrictions should not prevent one from speaking about good things or even misfortunes that befall others, unless such utterance could cast another in a negative light. People should be open about sharing their problems but should not pass on to others knowledge thus gained. They should say nothing about courtship matters (e.g., "John likes Mary") until an announcement has been made about a relationship, for this is unacceptable "gossip." Although it is acceptable to request or instruct someone not to relate certain information to others, no one should ask for or make a *promise* of confidentiality, since a potential gossip should not have been trusted in the first place and since in some cases one may have a responsibility to reveal something once one knows about it. People should not reprove others for actions they did not witness, or evaluate activities in which they were not involved, or look into another's affairs unless they are that person's head. Problems in a work or service group should not be mentioned outside that group, and problems in the community should not be mentioned to outsiders. No one should listen to either speaking against or gossip, and necessary complaints or criticisms should never be expressed in a "negative spirit."

As has been observed in the domain of worship, the ritualization of personal conduct progressed from such predominantly linguistic to increasingly somatic behaviors. The notion that gentlemanly respect for women should be part of a Charismatic culture led to ritualization of men rising when a woman enters a room, which elsewhere in North America has become an optional gesture of politeness used by both genders. While conservatism in dress was increasingly the norm, and it was common especially for children to wear used clothing from the community storeroom, dress was formally thematized as an aspect of gender discipline in the Training Course. Androgynous and unisex dress was forbidden, and clothing had to be "identifiably feminine or masculine." Teenage and adult women should not wear blue jeans, and pantsuits as opposed to skirts or dresses were frowned on for community handmaids. Men should avoid certain colors, patterns, fabrics, and jewelry: as one informant put it, "Pink flowered shirts were out for men."

The principal device for ritualization of conduct was personal headship (pastoral leadership). Only members of the Servants of the Word and community leaders at the rank of district head and higher were bound by full-scale "obedience" to headship. Other publicly committed members were in a relationship of "submission." In the words of a community head coordinator, a person in submission is

committed to receiving the advice of the pastoral leader [head] but not bound by obedience to act on it except in matters of serious sin. Finances is an example where we'd give direction if a person needed it, and the person, unless it's a matter of sin, could choose not to follow our advice. Refusal might not be greeted with wild acclaim, but they could refuse and it wouldn't be unrighteous. If it's gross negligence of their family, that's different.

Headship incorporates an essential psychocultural theme in its premise that spiritual growth is predicated on the kind of control and order introduced into personal life by submission to the advice of an elder. Of equal importance is the appeal to intimacy that is used to justify submission to the authority of headship by those subject to it. Members typically say that they do not fear loss of personal control in subordinating themselves to a head precisely because the relationship itself is predicated on intimacy: "My head really knows me, and therefore would never advise me in a certain way unless he was really convinced it was best for me."

An example of how headship works can be drawn from the ritualization of courtship practices that occurred during the mid-1970s. Covenant communities tend to be endogamous, and matches are sometimes arranged by community leaders, recently even between members of different Sword of the Spirit branches. If an unmarried man is interested in a particular woman, he may on his own initiative suggest to his head that their living situation and hers plan a joint social activity. This practice is explicitly directed at allowing the two to meet without the social pressure and emotional trauma that members feel is often generated by the North American custom of the "date." It is presumed that if the prospective couple do not "hit it off," no one else will know about it, and hence no one will be embarrassed. If the couple gets along they enter a "dating relationship," a period of getting acquainted that should last no longer than a few months, so that neither party is "led on" into expecting greater commitment. The couple then decides, in consultation with their personal heads, whether to enter a "serious relationship" entailing a commitment to seriously consider marriage. A couple that progresses to the stage of "engagement" is understood already to have made a commitment, and an engagement should not be broken without good reason. Weddings are regarded as community events, the couple entering not only a commitment to each other but a phase of commitment to the community anticipating the founding of a nuclear family.[14] These practices can be understood as a feature of gender discipline directly addressed to the control of sexuality and its associated emotions, as well as to the reproduction of a new generation of community members.

Child-rearing practices and the personal conduct of children were also subject to ritualization, both in the home and in the community school that was founded in 1982. Children four years of age and older also learn by attending prayer meetings with their parents, who encourage them to participate and explain the proceedings in terms such as "This is what God is telling you," "This is what the words of the song mean,"

"That was a prophecy," and so on. The story is told of a toddler who was learning to ask forgiveness instead of saying he was sorry. He became angry while alone in the bathroom and violently slammed the lid of the toilet. From the next room he was then heard to say, "Will you forgive me, Mr. Toilet?" After a moment's pause the verbal formula was completed as, in a deep voice, the child said, "I forgive you, Tommy." Thus the child was able to identify a morally inappropriate reaction on his own part and employ the ritual remedy before he was able to discriminate between sentient beings and inanimate objects.

The incorporation of community values in play (the ritualization of play) is illustrated in the following examples. One community woman described a typical situation in which a group of little girls imitating adults would be competing "to be the mommy." A woman caretaker suggests that "they all be mommies, like the women's group," and the girls restructure their play to have tea together and care for their doll babies. Some girls have been observed to refer to their play group as a "girl's group." Another example illustrates the inculcation of social boundaries between community children and outsiders. A former neighbor of a community household observed that noncommunity children were unable to get along in play with young Charismatics engaged in building a snow fortress, because they were unprepared to understand the play in terms of the biblical scenario of the walls of Jericho.

Community children were deeply affected by the Training Course, which specified respectful terms of address for adults instead of first names, rising or explicitly greeting their father when he returned home from a day's work, avoidance of "worldly" influences such as rock music, and restrictions on clothing such as blue jeans. According to some, the overprotective strictness of Training Course requirements led to an exacerbation of North American "teen rebellion" and attendant problems associated with drugs, sex, and rock and roll. These developments were apparently central to the reevaluation of community structures and the split between The Word of God and the Sword of the Spirit. By the early 1990s there was a substantial degree of uncertainty over whether the "people" they had created could or should be perpetuated into a second generation.[15]

The radicalization of control over personal conduct has without doubt progressed farthest within Steven Clark's elite brotherhood, the Servants of the Word. Young men who aspire to the brotherhood have already been instilled, through seminars leading to their public commitment, with a Pauline idealization of celibacy, or "living single for the

Lord." One young man, concerned about whether one could "be on fire for the Lord" when faced by the demands of caring for a family and for the "spiritual development of his wife," abandoned his desire for celibacy only when a trusted older man prophesied that he should marry instead. Those who complete the lengthy trial period are initiated in a special commitment ceremony to which noncommunity family members may be invited as to an ordination. Brothers adopt not only celibacy but other aspects of asceticism as well. They frequently sleep on the floor instead of in beds, and own no personal property—it is said that each owns only a few shirts and pairs of trousers. Working full time in service to their religious goals, they rely on financial support from the community and on solicitations from family and friends.

Servants of the Word typically travel in pairs on the model of the biblical disciples of early Christianity. This appears to be the case even when brothers visit their families outside the community, suggesting that constant companionship is also a protection from doubts likely to be planted by relatives concerned about the young men's abandonment of independent lives and careers to the total commitment demanded by the brotherhood. Vows of lifelong obedience to the leaders of the brotherhood and of willingness to be martyred in pursuit of their mission require that members be prepared for assignment to any Sword of the Spirit branch or affiliate in the world, as well as for even life-threatening adversity. Although entire community families may occasionally be assigned to live in a developing branch for a period, the unmarried brothers are organized into ongoing "outreach teams," a permanent "mobile field force" for the growth of the Sword of the Spirit.

Little else is known about the inner workings of the brotherhood, but one practice is ethnologically relevant to the present argument. This is the chewing of tobacco, an act that within the behavioral environment of the brotherhood takes on a meaning beyond that which it possesses in the broader contemporary culture. Tobacco was traditionally in widespread use among American Indian tribes for both secular and religious purposes—as medicine, as a marker of ceremonial solemnity, and as a psychotropic that assisted shamans to enter the altered state of consciousness in which they could contact their spirit helpers (Driver 1969; La Barre 1970). In contrast, in contemporary North America chewing tobacco establishes an ethos of rugged masculinity (most evident in its prevalence among professional baseball players). The popularity of tobacco chewing among the Servants of the Word lies between these types of use epitomizing the blurred boundary between ritual performance and habitual practice in the Charismatic world. Although there is no evidence that the brothers intentionally seek an altered state of consciousness, the ethos of masculinity itself possesses a ritual significance defined by divinely sanctioned male headship, gender discipline, and the requirement of male toughness for building the Kingdom of God in a climate of spiritual warfare. As the elite advance guard of this enterprise, the brothers are thus not Bible-reading nerds but tobacco-chewing soldiers of Christ. They are the ones committed, should it be called for, to the most radicalized engagement of the charismatic body, subjection to martyrdom.

This is indeed how they are seen in the community. The purpose of the Training Course was to get the rest of the community "up to speed" not only for the collective mission but with the vanguard Servants of the Word. The repudiation of the Training Course by The Word of God was a repudiation of the radicalization of charisma and ritualization of life, processes whose locus had become the Servants of the Word. It was in this context that the brotherhood declared itself independent and formed the nucleus of the schismatic Sword of the Spirit branch.

Conclusion

At a much higher level of ritualization and radicalization, the issues that led to The Word of God/Sword of the Spirit schism in part reiterated those that split the prayer groups from the covenant communities in 1977, and The Word of God from the People of Praise in 1981. This suggests an enduring consistency of themes that, as we will see in Part Three, is grounded in an authoritative system of ritual language. It also suggests two apparently contradictory conclusions about ritualization and radicalization as dominant collective self processes. On the one hand, they can generate a kind of centrifugal force that results in the spinoff of those unwilling to follow the tightening spiral of charisma. On the other hand, they can be interrupted at different points by moments of self-reflection. The apparent contradiction is reconciled by a disjunction in attribution, for while radicalization is experienced as an inherently *sacred* process, retreat from radicalization is based on attribution of *human* error. In The Word of God/Sword of the Spirit schism, the "true," that is, divine, source of charisma was never questioned by either party. It is this fact that leads us to theoretical consideration of the nature of the "charisma" that drives these processes.

Interlude

5

Toward a Rhetorical Theory of Charisma

To consolidate our analysis of charisma as a kind of self process, we must enter the debate on the locus and mode of operation of charismatic action. Recalling that Weber transformed a theological concept into a sociological one, we must emphasize that Charismatic Christians themselves virtually never use the nominal "charisma." Neither do they typically use the nominal "grace," which is readily available in the Catholic theological lexicon. Instead, they refer to discrete "charisms," "spiritual gifts," or "gifts of the Holy Spirit" through which human beings experience or are the instruments of divine "power." The Charismatic gift is essentially separable from the person who exercises it. Its purpose is the "upbuilding of the community," and successful community life requires a sufficient "charismatic density" of people exercising such gifts. In principle spiritual gifts are available to all Charismatics, and this precludes their exclusive adherence to a single individual. Gifts may also be taken away by their divine giver at any time, in effect a recognition that they may vanish for a variety of reasons ranging from failure of nerve to withdrawal of legitimating group consensus.

Whereas Catholic Charismatics have used the theological concept to undergird a system of ritual practice, Weber took that same concept and transformed it into a tool of sociological theory.

The term "charisma" will be applied to a certain quality of an individual personality by virtue of which he is set apart from ordinary men and treated as endowed with supernatural, superhuman, or at least specifically exceptional powers or qualities. These as such are not accessible to the ordinary person, but are regarded as of divine origin or as exemplary, and on the basis of them the individual concerned is treated as a leader. . . . It is recognition on the part of those subject to authority which is decisive for the validity of charisma. This is freely given and guaranteed by what is held to be a "sign" or proof, originally always a miracle. . . . But where charisma is genuine, it is not this which is the basis of the claim to legitimacy. This basis lies rather in the conception that it is the *duty* of those who have been called to a charismatic mission to recognize its quality and to act accordingly. Psychologically this "recognition" is a matter of complete personal devotion to the possessor of the quality, arising out of enthusiasm, or of despair and hope. (1947: 358–359)

Group solidarity under charismatic authority is "based on an emotional form of communal relationship," with no formal officials or hierarchy beneath the leader and no discrete spheres of authority or competence. Pure Weberian charismatic authority is "outside the realm of everyday routine and the profane sphere," foreign to all rules and foreign to everyday economic considerations of making a living. Charisma has the potential to bring about "a radical alteration of the central system of attitudes and directions of action with a completely new orientation of all attitudes toward the different problems and structures of the 'world'" (Weber 1947: 363).

In addressing the question of whether the Charismatic Renewal conforms to the sociological model of a charismatic movement, several points must be kept in mind. First, Weber presents us with an ideal type of charismatic authority that is likely to be mixed with other types. He points out that the "Roman conception of office" led to the formalization of a hierarchy in the Occidental earlier than in the Oriental Christian church (Weber 1947: 370). This fact is relevant to the development of a hierarchy of offices such as coordinator and prophet in a Roman Catholic Charismatic community like The Word of God even prior to the crisis of succession that for Weber typically precipitates the routinization of charisma. Second, Weber (1963: 2) assimilated charisma not only to the Christian notion of grace but also to the ethnological repertoire of terms for spiritual power including *mana, orenda,* and *maga.* Thus he meant it to be a generalized umbrella term under which it is appropriate to include our Charismatics' experience of the power of the Holy Spirit. Third, the concept of charisma exists today in a variety of popular and scholarly forms, many of which focus almost exclusively on the character of the "charismatic leader." It should then reward us to take a brief excursion through some theoretical statements that may allow us greater precision in a concept of charisma.

Fourth, and most important for our purposes, the ethos of the Charismatic Renewal corresponds in quality to those "milder forms of euphoria" associated with "prophets of ethical salvation." Here Weber explicitly anticipates the analysis of charisma in terms of transformation of
self and habitus, suggesting that what these religions created instead of
acute charismatic spiritual intoxication was a "milder but more permanent habitus, and moreover one that was consciously possessed" (1963:
158). Variously stated by Weber, the goal is "the incarnation within man
of a supernatural being," "self-deification," or "spiritual suffusion" by
the deity, and the method is "to eliminate from his everyday life whatever
was not godlike," where "the primary ungodlike factors were actually
the average habitus of the human body and the everyday world" (1963:
158–159).

The Locus of Charisma

In following Weber's insight it will be useful to distinguish among the object of charisma, its source, and its locus. I have already identified the object of charisma as the self and its orientational
being-in-the-world. The attitudinal transformation and transformation
of habitus referred to by Weber constitute a fundamental shift in the
way people inhabit the cultural world, such that the world itself is altered. The source of charisma is a problem that Tambiah (1984) accuses
Weber of having neglected. Tambiah sees the source of charisma to lie
in transcendental, that is, extraworldly, claims that along with the "internal ordering and boundaries" of a cultural world define varying conceptions of charisma in different religions (1984: 325). Thus for Christianity the transcendental source of charisma is the deity's gift of grace,
while for Buddhism it is disciplined attainment of the norm encoded in
the Dhamma (1984: 330). This is indeed important for comparative
purposes, but what Tambiah does not acknowledge is that for Weber to
make a statement about the source of charisma was doubtless also to
make a theological commitment. That Christian charisma originates in
a gift of grace from the deity is thus an ethnographic but not a theoretical statement about the source of charisma, unless Tambiah is in fact
claiming that charisma is an ontological entity, substance, quality, or energy. I think this is the problem Weber sought to avoid by adopting a
"value-free" stance.

However, if we cannot address the source of charisma, we can address its locus. Here we face a formidable task, largely due to the tenacity of Weber's apparent claim that charisma is a "quality" of the leader's "personality." My postulate is this: to say that charisma is *perceived* as residing in an individual personality is data; to accept this as an *empirical* phenomenon is an instance of misplaced concreteness. It should make all the difference in the world to refer to the "quality of an individual" as distinct from a "quality imputed to an individual," and the fact that Weber said the former has caused endless trouble for the theory of charisma. Charisma is reified both in the popular imagination and in social science, for both share a pronounced ethnopsychological proclivity to explain phenomena in terms of personality attributions (Jenkins 1991).

Let us begin with theories that concentrate on the charismatic leader. According to Thomas Dow,

In Weber's original formulation, charismatic authority is said to exist when an individual's claim to "specific gifts of body and mind" is acknowledged by others as a valid basis for their participation in an extraordinary program of action. . . . The courage the follower requires to abandon himself . . . is provided by identification with the charismatic leader in that the leader, on the basis of his apparent gifts of body and mind, his heroism, is perceived as a model of both release itself and the apparent power that makes release possible. . . . [T]he follower is moved to "complete personal devotion" because he sees in the leader, forces that exist within himself, forces that are being freed from the restraint of convention by the being and action of the leader. Accordingly, the follower obtains freedom from the commonplace, the ordinary, the recurrent by surrendering to both the initiatives of the leader and the emotional centers of his own being. (1978: 83–84)

Dow argues that Weber linked ecstasy with charisma as a destructive subjective condition and defines the essence of charisma as Dionysian, a state of total release. He emphasizes charisma's irrationality and irresponsibility, proposing Joseph Conrad's Kurtz as the archetype of charismatic abandon. While the leader is in some respects exemplary, while his gifts may be only "apparent," and while the locus of charisma is traced in part to the emotional constitution of the follower, the choice of Kurtz as an archetype definitively locates charisma in the "destructive subjective condition" of the leader's personality. Weber himself, while noting the transitory nature and lack of meaningful content that made ecstatic charisma apt to have little impact on everyday behavior, argued that milder forms of euphoria compatible with ethical prophecy could lead to a more enduring charismatic condition. Emphasis on "charismatic abandon" pre-supposes a social matrix reduced to a powerful leader and a faceless mass of followers. This both reifies charisma and defines it as only the crudest of self processes. Such a formulation has the character, not of an analytic ideal type, but of an ideological argument against charisma.

Ann Ruth Willner likewise appears to accept the existence of charisma as a personal quality:

Insofar as charisma can be seen as a quality of an individual, it lies in his capacity to project successfully an image of himself as an extraordinary leader. This is the sense in which Weber's phrase "a certain quality of an individual personality" should, in my opinion, be interpreted. The questions of what components can contribute to this capacity to project, what images can be projected, and what means can be used to project them form the bounds of this study. (1968: 4)

Here charisma remains overtly a quality, and its locus the personality of the individual leader, but Willner directs her inquiry to the images and means by which charisma is projected toward a group of followers who must recognize that leader. She qualifies her point further by suggesting that the locus of charisma is not so much in the leader's personality as in the perceptions of his followers (1968: 6; 1984: 15). She also points out that definitions of leadership roles as well as of what counts as an extraordinary quality vary across cultures (1968: 74; 1984: 15).

Likewise Bellah, while declaring that "charisma is primarily a quality of the individual," immediately goes on to state that

charisma is a relational concept, that is, it comes into existence only when it is recognized by a group. It links deeper levels of psychic organization, within the charismatic individual and in the members of the group who recognize him, with the social process and particularly with the possibility of radical discontinu-ities in social development. (1970: 7–8)

In this view charisma is not merely *legitimated* in the recognition of followers, as it was for Weber; it is only the followers' recognition that brings charisma into existence in the first place. Weston La Barre goes even further, arguing that "the 'supernatural' gift is no more than the messiah's phatic prescience of the people's needs. His communication is not new information on the structure of the world, but only of new inner structuring in people's culture-personality" (1970: 360).

Edward Shils makes a subtle but decisive contribution, beginning by reminding us that the quality labeled charisma may be attributed to other than human beings:

Charisma, then, is the quality which is imputed to persons, actions, roles, institutions, symbols, and material objects because of their presumed connection with "ultimate," "fundamental," "vital," order-determining power. (1975: 127)

Charismatic quality is attributed to expansive personalities who establish their ascendancy over other human beings by their commanding forcefulness or by an exemplary inner state which is expressed in a bearing of serenity. (1975: 129)

Here Shils is arguing that the locus of charisma may be in acts, images, social relations, and objects as well as in persons who use or act in terms of them. He is somewhat equivocal about the nature of charisma as a quality, implying that it exists only insofar as it is "imputed" or "attributed" to the entities he lists, even when the entity is an "expansive personality." This in turn suggests once again that the locus of charisma is in a relation. It is not only a relation between leader and followers, because charisma may reside elsewhere than in the person of the leader. Neither is it a passive relation of mere recognition, but an active one of attribution and imputation of charisma.

Shils grounds the possibility of this attribution in the connection of charisma-bearing entities with ultimate, order-determining power. A similar theme is elaborated by Clifford Geertz as the "connection between the symbolic value individuals possess and their relation to the active centers of the social order. . . . It is involvement, even oppositional involvement, with such arenas and with the momentous events that occur in them that confers charisma" (1977: 151). While specifically referring to kingship in Elizabethan England and Madjapahit Java, Geertz's analysis is relevant also to the Catholic Charismatic Renewal as a religious movement. While Tambiah (1984) might interpret Shils's remark about order-determining power to refer to the transcendental sources of charisma, the Charismatic Renewal derives its charisma not from a *gratuitous* divine gift but from a *motivated* gift intended for the "renewal" of the order-determining power of the Church. The Church is conceived precisely as an active center of the social order. Moreover, as we have seen, the radicalization of charisma in The Word of God is precisely a radicalization of the sense of mission in relation to the Church.

Weber saw that charisma was separable from persons insofar as it could inhere in objects or in offices.[1] However, insofar as it is separable and transferable, charisma usually appears as a substance or energy and is thus entified as much as or even more than when conceived as a personal quality. In fact, objectification or institutionalization is for Weber a "depersonalization" that presumes a personal locus to begin with. Our intent is instead to denominalize or deentify charisma, and at the same time to decenter it from the personality of the leader. The value of such an undertaking was already recognized by Johannes Fabian, who argued that

Weber's aim was *not* to do the impossible, that is, to formulate a sociological theory of charisma as a purely personal "mystical" quality. His influential if fragmented writings on charisma may at times encourage such a view but he should not be held responsible for the kind of pop sociology the term charisma seems to inspire today. Weber's thought about charisma was embedded in two larger pursuits: a) a general theory of types of authority which was developed on the basis of b) an even wider search for the relationships between rational and irrational forces in society. (1979a: 18)

Fabian is arguing here that understanding the basis for charismatic authority must come before understanding charismatic leadership and the relevance of leaders' personal qualities. His point about the relationship between rational and irrational forces raises the question of persuasion and motivation, or what authoritatively moves people to act. The response to this question by Fabian and a small group of like-minded others at the end of the 1970s was to reconceive movements as discourse and performance. This was perhaps the most significant theoretical contribution to the study of religious movements since Wallace (1957) coined the concept of revitalization movement, for it identifies the locus of charisma, and hence the social reality of movements, in terms of social action and cultural meaning rather than in terms of social relationship or personality characteristic. In the emphasis on discourse and performance we find a theoretical link between notions of spiritual power and political power (see Fogelson and Adams 1980) and a starting point for a rhetorical theory of charisma (Fabian 1974, 1979c; Csordas 1979).

In summary, thus far we have seen that charisma may be said to have its locus in the personality or qualities of the leader, in the relationship between leader and followers, in the cultural media by means of which it is expressed, in the symbolic resources drawn on for its formulation, or in the relation of its possessors to the centers of social order. Could it not be that just as Edward Sapir (1961) argued that the true locus of culture is in the interactions of specific individuals and the meanings they abstract from those interactions, so the locus of charisma is *among* participants in a religious movement? Could not charisma be a product of the rhetorical apparatus in use of which leader and follower alike convince themselves that the world is constituted in a certain way?

These considerations lead directly to the question of how the theoretical concept contributes to understanding the Catholic Charismatic

Renewal. McGuire (1982: 44) argues that the Renewal is not a charismatic movement at all if charisma is defined as a kind of authoritative social interaction between leader and followers, since it is mostly a movement of religious virtuosi. To salvage the concept's relevance, she attempts to redefine a leaderless charisma in a Durkheimian mode as "the empowerment of individuals drawing on the collective force of the group" (1982: 45). She also favorably cites Benjamin Zablocki's definition of charisma as "a collective state resulting from an objective pattern of relationships in a specific collectivity that allows the selves of the participants to be fully or partially absorbed into a collective self" (1982: 46; Zablocki 1980: 10). In contrast, R. Stephen Warner (1988), in a case study of the related Protestant evangelical/neo-Pentecostal/Charismatic movement, avoids the notion of charisma entirely. Instead, he finds it useful to follow the sociologist Francesco Alberoni in emphasizing the interplay between groups in a "nascent" state and those in an "institutional" state, a distinction analogous to that made by Victor Turner (1969, 1974) between communitas and structure. To be sure, an approach that highlights oscillation between these poles is apt given that what is being "renewed" in the Charismatic Renewal is an institutional church.[2]

However, both McGuire and Warner thus answer the question of the locus of charismatic authority by shifting it from the leader or from the leader-follower relationship to the Durkheimian collectivity. For Warner charisma is subordinated to nascence, effervescence, or liminality, while for McGuire both the rank-and-file participant and the occasional charismatic figure or "star" are subordinated to the collective force of the group. Although these moves certainly have merit (see Handelman 1985; Tiryakian 1995), we do not need to follow their Durkheimian trajectory to turn to theoretical advantage the apparent uniqueness of a movement with no single dominant leader, with a variety of collective and communal tendencies distributed across an international terrain, with a strong bureaucratic streak, and cast as much in terms of ethical salvation as of millennialism. If anything, studying such a movement should allow us to isolate the theoretical common denominator for charisma across cultural settings and historical examples. In short, if we adopt the premise that the locus of charisma is in the interaction of specific individuals, and if Fabian (1979a) is correct in arguing that religious movements are discourse, then charisma is rhetoric.[3] It is a particular mode of interpersonal efficacy: not a quality, but a collective, performative, intersubjective self process.

Profiles of Charismatic Action

To argue that charisma is rhetoric allows both the possibility that particular individuals may have degrees of rhetorical skill that make them appear to be possessors of a mystical quality and the possibility that certain persons may have charisma attributed to them or be elevated to charismatic status through the influence on them of others' rhetoric. The Catholic Charismatic Renewal is an apt arena for this study, in part because as a form of Pentecostalism it partakes of the "reticulate and acephalous" organization described by Gerlach and Hine (1970) and in part because as a form of Catholicism an allegiance to the pope as bearer of institutional charisma tends to preclude allegiance to a single "charismatic" leader. Yet while there is no such individual, there is a class of individuals who fit the description of charisma bearers, some with international reputations and others known regionally or within particular communities. Most prominent is a cohort of healing evangelists such as Francis MacNutt, Barbara Shlemon, the Rev. Ralph DiOrio, the Rev. Emmanuel Milingo, and the brothers Dennis and Matthew Linn, S.J. Charisma on a more modest local scale is exemplified by other clerics and lay people such as the priest whose consistent use of sacramental blessed salt earned him the nickname "Father Morton," or one reputed for his "gift of praise," a talent for orchestrating spontaneous vocal prayer in prayer meetings.

Movement leaders exhort participants to concentrate on the divine source of these gifts rather than on the personalities of individuals who exercise them, people referred to in the movement's pastoral slang as "charismatic stars." Nevertheless, these stars are often attributed some of the characteristics, and acquire some of the devotion, traditionally associated with charismatic leaders. Critical for our purposes is that charisma originates in a mobilization of communal symbolic resources that are realized in a mode of discourse or performed in a genre of ritual language within particular social settings. The following vignette illustrates what I mean. Two "charismatic stars" were present in an assembly. Through the act of laying on of hands by one of them, everyone present was "slain in the Spirit" and fell to the floor in a sacred swoon— everyone, that is, *except* the other "star." He offered the appropriately humble explanation that his own weakness prevented him from experiencing the divine power through his colleague, perhaps an implicit confession of arrogant confidence in the strength of his own personality confronted by a potential rival. Other healers have explained the same phenomenon by saying that they become so filled with divine power themselves that the wave of power that rushes into others and causes them to swoon has relatively less effect. In rhetorical terms, we might say instead that it is the accustomed role as a persuader—the one who stays on his feet during collective performances—that inures them to the rhetorical force of a colleague's prayer.

A second example is even more clear-cut. Several members of a community renowned as a center of prophecy, but who themselves had no experience as prophets, were prevailed on to join the group of prophets at another community they were visiting. In this instance it was the rhetorical weight of the visitors' home community, The Word of God—in Geertz's (1977: 151) terms an "active center of the social order" within the movement—that allowed, in fact required, them temporarily to fill the role of charisma-bearing prophets. Their ability to do so and be recognized as effective depended in turn on the existence of a shared set of rules and expectations for the ritual performance of prophecy, rules and expectations that establish the form of the utterance and the relation between performer and audience.

Let us now turn to an example by means of which we might test our effort to detach charisma from the locus of the leader's personality. The example returns us to The Word of God/Sword of the Spirit and its leaders, Steven Clark and Ralph Martin. Especially in its first decade, the community was a remarkably active center of the social order, disseminating movement literature and teaching, drawing in pilgrims for workshops and exposure to an exemplary lifestyle, and recruiting members not only from local parishes and colleges but also from cities at often considerable distances. As its founders and paramount leaders, Martin and Clark conform to the historical pattern of a charismatic pair; they are the Moses and Aaron, Luther and Melanchthon, Hiawatha and Dekanawida of the covenant community movement. Martin is noted for his outgoing personality and his eloquence as a visionary orator, Clark for his reserved personal manner and the expression in profound writing of direct insight into "God's plan for the world." Moreover, prior to their split they formed the polar anchor of exemplary lifestyle in the community. Martin is the model of family life—the scion of a large Catholic family, he has six children of his own and two sisters married to other community leaders. An outspoken campus atheist at Notre Dame, he experienced a Charismatic conversion under the influence of Clark. Clark himself is the model of ascetic commitment. The only child of a

Jewish mother and a nonbelieving father, he converted to Catholicism of his own accord. He has gathered around himself the tightly disciplined, celibate brotherhood of the Servants of the Word.

Clark's ambiguous personal background, his ascetic lifestyle, and his status of outsider turned convert suggest the makings of a Weberian charismatic leader. Willner (1968: 51, 62) cites heterogeneity of background and exposure to a variety of social environments as frequent attributes of the charismatic figure, along with vitality, inexhaustible energy, little need for sleep, imperturbability under stress, the capacity to project a powerful intellect, and sexual appeal. Indeed, it is said that while away in Europe for a year Clark led members of the brotherhood on a hike up a mountain "without getting tired." It is not incidental to our argument that his reputation was thus enhanced while he was away from the community: his absence as a social actor facilitated his treatment as an object of symbolic discourse. Clark is known as an indefatigable worker, such that it was major news in the late 1970s when his fellow coordinators insisted that he spend a year away from his duties because he was exhausted. Members' conversation about his exhaustion emphasized, not Clark's human susceptibility, but the enormity of his devotion to the divine work. Clark is also reported to be a powerful intellect with "an IQ of 180," a particularly striking boast in face of the movement's promotion of a religion "of the heart, not of the head."

To pursue their Charismatic mission, both leaders relinquished graduate fellowships in philosophy, Clark a Rhodes scholarship to study Wittgenstein, Martin a Fulbright to study Nietzsche. It is again of relevance to my argument that the rhetorical resources provided in their earlier studies very likely influence the shape, tone, and effectiveness of their contribution. Moreover, the tones of a distinctly postmodern form of charisma become audible as we hear echoes of Wittgensteinian "forms of life" in the ritualization of linguistic practice that requires "asking forgiveness" and prohibits "speaking against," and echoes of a Nietzschean "superchristian" in the urgent implementation of the Training Course and the passionate appeal of the FIRE rallies.

With Clark and Martin we can also observe the personal devotion that Weber marked as typically inspired by charismatic leaders. This is best expressed in the words of a coordinator of a Sword of the Spirit community in the late 1980s:

What makes the two of them so special? The same thing that makes the pope so special I guess, and Mother Teresa. They've given it all. If you check their personal life, their personal life backs up everything they have to say. . . . Neither one of them clings to poverty, but Steve and all the men [in the brotherhood] only have so many shirts, so many pants—that's their lifestyle, and that's the way Steve looks every day of his life, and there's no "Let's take a trip to the Bahamas for fun." If he goes to the Bahamas he works. . . . Ralph lives a modest life, and he could be a multimillionaire at this point. You get a man like that who has the potential to do anything he wants and gives all his time and energy to two things—building up the body of Christ and his own family. He's a very good family man, he really works at being a good father and husband. You have to admire him, you have to be willing to follow someone like that, because there are not many kinks in the armor. I'm sure they've been angry once or twice in their life (chuckles), they've even had [*sic*] a cussword, but not much more [in terms of sin]. That's why I'd follow them anywhere—their life backs up their story. It's not theory, it's practice.

The charismatic status and achievements of these men as chosen instruments of God are placed in counterpoint by the narrative and slide show of their "early days" as college students, which is presented at the community anniversary celebration and which was described in chapter 4 as a kind of mythical charter for The Word of God.

Their status is placed in negative counterpoint by an anecdote circulated among alienated former members concerning these same "early days." The story goes that at the prayer meetings the "four founders,"[4] unlike the rest of the participants, always knew in advance "what was going to happen." To understand this it must be noted that in Charismatic daily speech things are said to "happen" in a way that implicitly indicates their divine spontaneity. Thus "what is going to happen" contrasts with "what we are going to do." Prior to the prayer meetings the four founders would meet among themselves, and "Ralph and Steve" would tell the others what was going to happen. Before that, Ralph and Steve would meet, and Steve would tell Ralph what was going to happen. Even before that, Steve and God would meet, and Steve would tell God what was going to happen.

Given the evidence, can we argue that the Sword of the Spirit is not a product of Martin's and Clark's "charismatic personalities"? Certainly they have personalities that can be described as forceful. But our argument that charisma is a rhetorical self process instead of a quality, trait, or substance means that the leader's personality too is taken up in that process. In The Word of God, with increasing size and structure the paramount leaders became simultaneously less accessible to the rank and file and more imbued with a charisma of office that compounded their apparent personal charisma. This shift was enhanced as spiritual gifts became increasingly the prerogative of ritual specialists, so that charisma even in the strictly theological sense became concentrated at the pinnacle of community structure. In addition, the figure of the leaders was incorporated into the body of symbolic discourse generated by the community, ranging from the ritually celebrated historical narrative to the sarcastic anecdote of disaffected members. To summarize, not only does the leader as performer contribute to and mold discourse, and not only do attributions and perceptions of him change with changes in social position among members, but the leader himself becomes a topic for performances that transform him into a symbolic object, the bearer of charisma.

The best example I can offer is an incident that occurred shortly after Steven Clark's return to The Word of God after a year's absence for outreach work in Europe. On being presented to the community's general gathering, he received a standing ovation that lasted several minutes. To understand the rhetorical edge of this response, we must recall the introduction two years earlier of loud praise in community worship. This radicalization opened a kind of semiotic gap between the conventional meaning of applause as praise of a person and its ritual meaning as praise to the divinity. It was the rhetorical condition of possibility for a range of mutually resonant meanings:

1) praise of the leader in recognition of his achievements;
2) praise of the divinity because the beloved brother and leader has returned;
3) praise of the leader in acknowledgment of his status as messenger and servant of the divinity; and
4) praise of the leader and divinity identified as one.

The semiotic possibilities in this event are indisputable. Its rhetorical import lies precisely in its ambiguity. Its phenomenological consequences for leader and followers alike remain unspecified but pregnant. What is critical to the analysis here is that the locus of charisma is in the performance of the ritual gesture: the applause of loud praise does not "legitimate" charisma, but creates it. More precisely, there is no nominal charisma, only charismatic action, and that is a rhetorical process.

Notes for a Comparative Theory

Unsatisfied that my reader is convinced, I will offer three brief examples to suggest that even the charisma of the most archetypal charismatic leaders is the product of persuasive performance. For the

New Guinea Kanakas of Kenelm Burridge's classic study of cargo cults, the social order had been decentered by the evolution of an unstable triangular relation among the colonial administration, Christian missionaries, and the Kanakas themselves (1960: 275). Faced with the dominating presence of the whites, the Kanakas could respond by ignoring them, rejecting them, capitulating, or compromising with the "moral European" conceived in mythical terms as an elder brother. Burridge sees "cargo" as a symbol of synthesis and compromise between alien forms of life, and charismatic action by cult participants as the creation of a new moral universe and a "new man" to inhabit it. Such a task is essentially rhetorical, to persuade Kanakas out of guilt and inferiority by reaffirming the preeminence of their ancestors and to persuade whites to behave as moral Europeans by appealing to the moral equality of "brotherhood."

Burridge's discussion of four charismatic figures suggests a way to understand that the locus of this essentially creative charisma is in collective performance rather than in the personal magnetism of the leader. Mambu and Yali were prophets whose messages precipitated the formation of actual cults. Irakaku was a business leader whose commercial success and solid community ties established his position as one who could deliver cargo, a potential charismatic cult leader without a prophetic message. The nameless "youth from Pariakenam" had a message that was received with spontaneous enthusiasm, but whose adherents were almost immediately overtaken by disillusionment. What places these persons in the same category is the rhetorical condition of possibility for their emergence as charismatic figures, the shared repertoire of symbolic resources contained in their "myth-dream": "a body of notions derived from a variety of sources such as rumours, personal experiences, desires, conflicts, and ideas about the total environment which find expression in myths, dreams, popular stories, and anecdotes" (Burridge 1960: 27). Circulation of these items constitutes the cutting edge of persuasiveness and creativity in charismatic action. For Burridge the condition of creativity is the organic, dialectical relation between the charismatic figure and the myth-dream. The prophet's role is to "refertilize," "energize," and "feed" the myth-dream, yet at the same time the prophet himself is "swallowed by" the myth-dream of which he is the personification, ceasing to be an actor and becoming a creature of discourse.

Burridge states the case quite strongly that "charismatic articulation" not only creates a "new man" in a new moral synthesis but also creates the charismatic figure himself: "He himself has something. He must have. But on the whole circumstances, the men about him, rumours, and the community which gives the rumours validity, actually create him" (1960: 256).[5] The key rhetorical device of the myths, dreams, and rituals that surround the charismatic figure is that, in contrast to the exuberant mode and setting of traditional stories, they are performed in a style that is sober, quiet, and ominous.

In traditional culture the genre of dream narration was the vehicle for interpreting affairs and developing programs of action in consultation with the ancestors who were thought to dwell in the people's subconscious being. In the cargo movement "cult dreams" became programs for collective action instituted through Yali's "dream men," the Weberian administrative staff who served as coordinators of the collective vision. Rituals—communal meals and dances—achieved their rhetorical purpose by placing unaccustomed emphasis on the individual, then immediately emphasizing the individual's relation to the community. To the communal dance was added the innovation of successive solo performances during which, as in many such movements, the dancer is prone to trance and the production of unintelligible utterance. The locus of charisma is thus in its collective articulation.

Charismatic articulation attempts to translate the myth-dream into principles or objectives which are capable, not merely of being apprehended, but comprehended by the community. Then the community can act on them. And it is at this point, when the myth-dream is being externalized—pulled out of the being of each individual and out of the community in which each individual participates—that trances, hysteria, fits, and the like occur. (Burridge 1960: 249)

In the same way we can understand the spontaneous individual or collective signs and wonders in a covenant community assembly as rhetorical articulations of the Charismatic vision. The locus of charisma is, in Burridge's word, its articulation, and its object is the "new man" of a new moral synthesis. In line with our distinction between religions of peoples and religions of the self, the critical difference between the cargo cult and the Charismatic Renewal is that in the former the image of the new man mediates the political relation between peoples and is a reformulation of collective identity, whereas in the latter the image of the person born again mediates the constitution of the self in relation to the possibility of community and is a reformulation of personal identity.

Let us turn to an even more challenging example of a leader who at first glance appears to exude charisma as a personal quality, the fifteenth-century Italian priest Girolamo Savonarola. In a study little known by anthropologists, Richard Sennett points out that as a Dominican preaching friar Savonarola was "led into the paths of oratory as a religious

duty" (1975: 172), such that the basis of his achievements was a cultivated talent as a public speaker. Sennett argues that the basis of his appeal
was neither that he offered a worldview people could not find elsewhere
nor that because they were living in a passive, tired society they longed
for a vital leader. Instead, it rested in the performative efficacy of what he
said: "Savonarola's appeal can be summed up as the legitimation of religious action in the world, unbeholden to secular law, expressed through
theatrical acts" (Sennett 1975: 174). Through dramatic gesture and spectacle, Savonarola transformed life into theater, succeeding in moving the
stage from the pulpit to civic life, justifying religious action that was independent of the law and hence potentially amoral.

The importance of the charismatic figure is undeniable, but in relation
to the populace he was as performer to audience. He "inspired them to
theater; were he not there, or were he unable to demonstrate his grace,
then the members of the crowd would be like actors with lines to read on
a stage without lights" (Sennett 1975: 178). Yet the rhetoric of performance both created Savonarola and was his undoing. It was spectacle
that temporarily saved him when challenged by the authorities, as he
"created a scene" by drawing a magic circle around himself that others
feared to cross. However, the logic of the charismatic spectacle also required him to submit to trial by fire even when his opponents backed
out. This he was loath to do, and his followers' hunger for spectacle remained unsatisfied until he was able to survive two and a half hours of
degradation before he was finally burned. His followers were "not fickle,
not tired; they wanted charismatic experience, they had an unbroken
appetite for it. But in breaking the illusion of Savonarola's power, they
broke their own" (Sennett 1975: 179).

Sennett seems to be arguing that as a gesture unconstrained by law,
charisma generates freedom but that the idiom of localizing charisma in
the leader's personality betrays that freedom. As theater, charisma is a
radical playing with reality that succeeds in objectifying the law as a target for critique. Removing these bounds, however, requires the presence of a stabilizing force, and hence the creation of a charismatic leader:
"in the terror of play, adults must have some reassurance that they will
not destroy themselves by being free. Some one person will have to appear to have acquired a power unlike the power of mankind in general;
his character will embody the very idea of having transcended the law,
and will reassure them that in becoming free and pure they will not suddenly be empty or weak" (Sennett 1975: 180). Weber suggested that
the only way out of this dilemma was a rationalization in which "instead

of recognition being treated as a consequence of [charismatic] legitimacy, it is treated as the basis of legitimacy" (1947: 386). For Weber this is the invention of democracy, but it is important for our argument that such a shift in recognition does not decisively exclude it from charismatic rhetoric. Weber's insistence that the basis of all authority is *belief* (1947: 382) prevented him from seeing that it can also be based on commitment.[6] This is the case for Catholic Charismatics, who, faced with doubt about the reality of prophecy as a divine gift, resolve the dilemma by "making a decision" that prophetic utterance conveys the word and will of the deity.

Our final example is from Fabian's (1974) account of the contemporary lay Roman Catholic Jamaa movement of Zaire, founded by the Belgian priest Placide Tempels. The rhetorical locus of charisma is yet more evident in this than in the other movements we have considered, as it is dispersed among members in accordance with their command over three specific genres of ritual language. *Mafundisho,* or public instruction, combines the charisma of ritual performance with a kind of charisma of office.

Prominent speakers are, in fact, also carriers of authority, although it must be understood that the legitimation of their power is based on rhetorical influence and a position as interpreters and manipulators of ideology, and this is only one aspect of authority. More important are criteria derived from the high positions of these leaders in lineages of spiritual filiation that are established through initiation. (Fabian 1974: 256)

Mashawao is a kind of ritual counseling, the rhetoric of which is based on the use of formulas addressing a conventional series of problem domains such as marital discord, magical protection, and ancestor worship and other forms of traditional, non-Christian religion. Finally, *mawazo* is a private discourse or testimony—public testimony and glossolalia are specifically excluded—used in situations of initiation or prophecy among members, and often including accounts of dreams. Fabian suggests that these dream interpretations may evolve into "one of the few explicit prerogatives of Jamaa leaders," yet they are not so much authoritative utterances as ones that tend "to express discontent, claims to leadership, and often attempts at reformulating doctrine and changing ritual procedures" (1974: 260). In addition, dream interpretation is inherently a social task, situating the locus of charisma in the interaction among members rather than in either solitary brooding or the consultation of ritual specialists frequent in traditional society (Fabian 1966: 557).

The rhetoric of ritual language is, again, also the means by which the charismatic figure is imbued with his charisma. Just as we saw in the case of Steven Clark, Fabian (1971) describes the enhancement of the charisma of Father Tempels in his absence. This took place through discourse *among* movement participants following Tempels's return to Europe, not through concrete words and deeds of his own. But being a creature of rhetoric can also mean being trapped in rhetoric. Just as Burridge described Mambu and Yali as being "swallowed by the myth-dream" and Sennett described Savonarola and his followers as victims to the "terror of play," Fabian (1979b) sees Tempels and participants of the Jamaa as trapped by the "terror of the text." The erstwhile liberating message becomes a fatal logic as the prophetic discourse of mawazo becomes habit and "ritualistic pedantry." I would not argue that this process is inevitable, that a charismatic message cannot be renewed or integrated into a stable but open form of life. I would, however, argue that the radicalization of charisma we observed in The Word of God/Sword of the Spirit was precisely an attempt to outrun the fatal logic, an attempt impelled by the same rhetorical dynamic.

The apocalyptic break between The Word of God and the Sword of the Spirit was precisely a rhetorical break. It is of particular interest that there appeared to be no war of words between prophets of the two factions, each claiming the loyalty of members based on the charismatic quality of its leader, or of its leader's access to authentic divine vision. While there was much talk of "differing visions," there was an overall decline in prophetic utterance. This bespeaks a tacit agreement that if prophecy is the message of the deity, to risk inconsistency and competition among prophetic messages is to risk the sacred validity of prophecy itself. The result was to protect prophecy itself as a rhetorical locus of charismatic legitimacy.

Charisma and Self

If it is granted that charisma is a rhetorical process, we must still add a few words about how it is explicitly a process of the self for the majority of adherents. Charles Lindholm (1990) shows that many contemporary theories of charisma are predicated on an existential tension between self-loss and independent identity. This tension is typically formulated in either-or terms and with an ethnopsychological

bias in favor of the integral, bounded self. Is the self "lost" when subordinated to a collectivity defined as a "people" under Charismatic covenant community authority? Lindholm (1990) observes that charismatic
groups nearly universally undermine dyadic bonds between individuals
and subordinate them to group loyalty. To the extent that this is the
case in the covenant community, it would appear to promote "self-loss"
and perhaps devotion to an individual charismatic leader. It would appear, in addition, to contradict the cultural value of intimacy between
integral selves. Indeed, dating and courtship relations, arranged marriages, and the idea of marrying for the building of the community conform to this pattern. So does the imbalance institutionalized by male
headship within the family, which places the burden of final responsibility on a husband, makes him responsible to God and the community
for the "spiritual welfare" of his spouse, and sets up "honor and respect"
as behavioral ideals alongside intimacy. Men's and women's groups not
only supersede dimensions of intimacy between husband and wife but
even replace some of the intimate functions of one to one "personal
headship."

We are led to somewhat different conclusions if we follow a rhetorical rather than a personality-based theory of charisma and a definition
of self as an indeterminate capacity for orientation in the world rather
than as an integral entity that can be lost and found. Rhetoric moves
and persuades, and tracing its phenomenological consequences allows
us to perceive not gross abolition but a shift in orientation with respect
to intimacy as a theme within a cultural configuration. Courtship practices are in part intended to protect the self against a perceived vulnera-
bility to intimacy. Male headship is seen as the introduction of intimacy
with the divinity into the relation between spouses, as well as having the
pragmatic intent of promoting harmony by precluding the possibility of
serious arguments. Men's and women's groups extend the capacity for
intimacy beyond the dyadic bond to an experience of "brotherhood and
sisterhood" that ultimately includes the entire community. The rhetorical impetus for this cultural transformation of self is, as Weber noted, a
sense of duty to a charismatic mission. It is an error, however, to assume
that this sense of duty is inspired only by devotion to a leader. Just as are
the qualities of the charismatic figure himself, both duty and devotion
are functions of the rhetorical process and its inherent dynamic.

While we may not agree with the values on which it is predicated, the
Charismatic transformation of the North American self and habitus are
world creating. Yet any effort to alter the self is equally as likely to be

defensive as it is creative, and thus we consider the hypothesis of Irvine Schiffer (1973) that charisma is a defense against, indeed is the antithesis of, the uncanny. The uncanny is formally represented in the Charismatic ritual system as the "occult" and "demonic" against which Christians are embattled in "spiritual warfare." In the sense introduced by Freud, experience of the uncanny is a reminder of the inexorability of death. Schiffer's analysis is directed toward explaining attachment to a charismatic leader in terms of psychoanalytically formulated developmental crises of the individual. This approach can loosely be applied to the three psychocultural themes we have seen to be elaborated in Charismatic life. I do not think it is necessary to extend his argument about recapitulation of infantile symbiosis with mother to the thematization of intimacy among Catholic Charismatics, but it is reasonable to regard the elaboration of intimacy in the communitarian ideal as a defense against the uncanny. Likewise, Schiffer's notion that the will, as the seat of an "illusory self-control," is a defense mechanism threatened by the uncanny corresponds with the thematization of control in charismatic self process. Finally, the spontaneity of charismatic action is thematized precisely as divinely inspired vitality of a kind that for Schiffer counteracts the ominous message of the uncanny.[7]

A more penetrating analysis is offered by Richard M. Zaner (1981), who shows the uncanny to be grounded in our very embodiment. The inescapableness of our embodied nature and the limitations it imposes contribute to the feeling that our bodies are in a sense "other" than ourselves. Our intimacy with our own bodies also implicates us in whatever happens to them, and realization that we are thus "susceptible to what can happen to material things in general" corresponds to experiencing the "chill" of mortality. In addition, our bodies are always "hidden presences" to us, both insofar as autonomic processes typically go on outside of awareness and in that these goings-on establish conditions to which we must adapt: we cannot be at our place of employment without first getting in the car or bus that will get us there. Our bodies are thus alien presences to us at the same time as they are compellingly ours, and just as the paradoxical nature of embodiment led Bourdieu to coin essential oxymorons, so Zaner calls the body intimately alien and strangely mine:

My body is at once familiar and strange, intimate and alien: *"mine" most of all yet "other" most of all*, the ground for both subjective inwardness and objective outwardness. Whatever I want, wish, or plan for, I irrevocably "grow older," "become tired," "feel ill," "am energetic." . . . [T]he basis for *the otherness* (and thereby the otherness of everything else) *of the embodying organism is its having a life of its own,* even when the person is most "at home" or "at one" with it. . . . The otherness of my own body thus suffuses its sense of intimacy. (1981: 54–55; emphasis in original)

The experience of the uncanny is thus grounded not in an abstract recognition of mortality but in the concreteness of everyday embodied existence. Insofar as charisma is the antithesis of the uncanny, it is a struggle to reconcile this inevitable paradox of embodiment. Here finally we can understand why the radicalization of charisma is also a progressive engagement of the body. It is an attempt to co-opt the uncanny by uncovering the body's hidden presence through loud praise and calisthenic spirituality, clothing the alien presence in ritual garb, and finally enlisting the body's own otherness in the spontaneously coordinated manifestations of signs and wonders.

The dual process of rhetorical involution, characterized by the ritualization of practice and the radicalization of charisma, was essential to the cultural transformation of self and habitus according to the communitarian ideal we have been studying. This process is implicitly available to all Catholic Charismatic groups, though it is elaborated to a greater or lesser degree depending on situational exigencies and individual initiative within particular communities. The theologian may argue that the *source* of charisma is divinity, while the humanist may trace it to the human spirit. I have argued neither, pointing instead to the *locus* of charisma in rhetoric, that is, in the persuasive means by which a vision is articulated. The personality of charismatic leaders and the propensities of their followers are relevant insofar as leaders command necessary skills of rhetorical performance and followers the capacity to act as engaged audience. Accordingly, we must now show how charisma operates as a collectively articulated self process by examining the very rhetorical apparatus that is its condition of possibility. This we will find in the movement's system of ritual performance.

PART THREE

Metaphor and Performance

6

Ritual Language
Speaking the Kingdom

If charisma is a rhetorical process that transforms self and habitus, and if the locus of charisma is in the language and performance of religious ritual,[1] a central hermeneutic task must be to determine the way language and performance achieve their transformative effect. Can the characteristic persuasiveness, the metaphorical vividness, and the evocation of the sacred in ritual language justifiably be said to be creative, orienting the self toward new patterns of engagement and experience? Or, on the contrary, is such language primarily the servant of a linguistic and cultural status quo, lacking the creative potential inherent in the language of poetry or even in everyday speech? In the remainder of this book I choose to argue for the creativity of ritual language as a self process. To do so effectively, however, my argument must meet two criteria: (1) to demonstrate precisely how that creation is achieved by identifying the conditions under which creativity is possible and the processes through which it works; and (2) to demonstrate that something in particular is created, whether it be a new meaning, a new state of mind, a new way of understanding the world, a new community, or a new social order.

Within the repertoire of Charismatic ritual elements, let us first clearly distinguish among ritual objects, gestures, somatic manifestations, and language. Ritual objects are limited to traditional Catholic sacramentals (blessed oil, salt, or water), the occasional use of candles, the decoration of homes with pictures or banners, and the rare use of ritual clothing.

Ritual gestures are limited to the customary prayer posture and the laying on of hands, and more rarely to the hopping, kneeling, and prostration found in the calisthenic spirituality of The Word of God. Somatic manifestations include resting in the Spirit and other signs and
wonders as well as physical sensations or images taken as instances of
revelation, or "words of knowledge." Ritual language includes a system
of genres and a specialized vocabulary.

Catholic Charismatic ritual performance is characterized by a marked
linguisticality, in that most of what goes on is verbal. In this sense it is a
religion of "the word." Catholic Charismatic ritual is not based on the
recitation of written texts (except when a passage from the Bible is read
during a gathering) or a preestablished liturgy (except when a prayer
meeting is integrated into a "Charismatic mass") but is predominantly
oral. Bound by the mortar of oral performance, ritual events become
the building blocks of Charismatic life. However, this occurs in a manner distinct from that found in societies typically treated in the anthropological literature. Anthropological accounts of traditional societies customarily treat ritual as a window on the nature of society, as events that
throw light on underlying cultural and structural patterns: *society creates ritual as a self-affirmation*. In a movement like Catholic Pentecostalism, this relation between society and ritual is inverted. Ritual events
like prayer meetings are both historically and structurally prior to the
generation of distinctive patterns of thought, behavior, and social organization. The events provide the earliest models for the organization of
aspects of community life that subsequently transcend the boundaries of
the events: *ritual creates society as a self-affirmation*. We must accordingly undertake a hermeneutic of the rhetorical conditions that define
the creativity of oral performance in Catholic Charismatic ritual.

A Synthetic Theory of Performance

There are three relevant schools of thought on performance in anthropology, each of which approaches the problem from a
slightly different angle, and which taken together constitute an adequate
theory of performance. These are the cultural performance approach of
interpretive anthropology (Singer 1958, 1972; Peacock 1968; Geertz
1973; Grimes 1976; Kapferer 1979a, 1983; Laderman 1991; Schieffelin 1985; Fernandez 1986; Manning 1983; Roseman 1991; Csordas

1994; Laderman and Roseman 1996); the performance-centered approach from sociolinguistics and folklore (Abrahams 1968, 1972; Gossen 1972, 1974; Hymes 1975; Bauman 1975; Jansen 1975; Fabian 1974, 1979b; Goldstein and Ben-Amos 1975; Samarin 1976; Csordas 1987; Bauman and Briggs 1990), and the performative utterance approach borrowed from the philosophy of language (Austin 1975; Searle 1969, 1979; Finnegan 1969; Bloch 1974, 1986; Tambiah 1985; Rappaport 1979; Ray 1973; Gill 1977). All share a hermeneutic sense of the importance of context but complement one another in that the first formulates performance as event, the second as genre, and the third as act. I shall briefly elaborate each of these approaches.

In Milton Singer's formulation, cultural performances as events are elements of tradition on the "cultural level of analysis" and ways in which

content is organized and transmitted on specific occasions through specific media. . . . [A performance] has a definitely limited time span, a beginning, and an end, an organized program of activity, a set of performers, an audience, and a place and occasion of performance. (1958: 194)

Analysis of cultural performances runs in terms of constituent factors such as cultural institutions, cultural specialists, and cultural media, which in part, at least, are amenable to the direct observation of the field worker. (1972: 78)

For Singer, performances are "the most concrete observable units" of culture, from which progressive analytic abstraction can lead to the structure of kinds of performances and thence through examination of linkages among these structures to constructs of cultural structure or value system (1972: 64).

Whereas classical anthropological theories typically limited the scope of ritual efficacy to its exemplary or legitimating functions, in this view performance has a creative dimension aptly summarized by Geertz.

[Performance, by] ordering [important themes of social life] into an encompassing structure, presents them in such a way as to throw into relief a particular view of their essential nature. It puts a construction on them, makes them, to those historically positioned to appreciate the construction, meaningful—visible, tangible, graspable—real in an ideational sense. (1973: 443–444)

My argument is that performance makes key psychocultural themes real not only in an ideational sense but also in a phenomenological sense. This is consistent with the notion that cultural performance has a power to transform both experience and social relations. Singer recognizes that it is not through evocation of emotion that performance acts, but by creation of a specific mood the constancy and intensity of which become a religious devotee's primary concern (1972: 201). This matches Geertz's general formulation that religion "acts to establish powerful, pervasive, and long-lasting moods and motivations" (1973: 90), where moods are kinds of disposition "which lend a chronic character to the flow of . . . activity and the quality of . . . experience" (1973: 95). Thus cultural performances are primary arenas not only for representation but also for the active constitution of religious forms of life.

In contrast to performances as events, the sociolinguistic approach formulates performance as a specific kind of action carried out within a distinct genre.

There is *behavior,* as simply anything and everything that happens; there is *conduct,* behavior under the aegis of social norms, cultural rules, shared principles of interpretability; there is *performance,* when one or more persons assumes responsibility for presentation. (Hymes 1975: 18)

It is necessary to assess the "degree of performance" in each instance, since texts from the same genre may in different situations take on greater or lesser degrees of performance (Hymes 1975). For example, the full performance of a myth cycle entails a greater degree of performance than the recitation out of context of a single myth from that cycle. William Hugh Jansen (1975) notes that different genres customarily involve different degrees of performance, as for example the difference in force between uttering a maxim like "Rain before seven, clear by eleven" on a morning stroll and uttering a sermon in a church. For Jansen, the degree of performance is contingent on the function of a text in a particular situation, on whether the form or content of the text necessarily implies performance, and on whether the performer is recognized as such by the audience.

The concept of genre in this approach is a modification of the concept as used in literary criticism. In particular, Northrop Frye argues that any analysis of the rhetorical functions of language is contingent on a theory of genres.

The basis of generic distinctions in literature appears to be the radical of presentation. Words may be acted in front of a spectator; they may be spoken in front of a listener; they may be sung or chanted; or they may be written for a reader. . . . The purpose of criticism by genres is not so much to classify as to clarify . . . traditions and affinities, thereby bringing out a large number of literary relationships that would not be noticed as long as there were no context established for them. (1957: 246–248)

This approach may be even more essential to the cross-cultural study of oral performance than it is to comparative literature, for whereas literature typically deals with a limited number of more or less well-defined genres (epic, drama, lyric, novel), anthropologists have encountered a multiplicity of specialized speech varieties and oral performance forms. In these instances the "radical of presentation" looms large, and clarification of "traditions and affinities" is contingent on careful ethnographic analysis. Richard Bauman suggests that "performance sets up, or represents, an interpretive frame within which messages being communicated are to be understood, and that this frame contrasts with at least one other frame, the literal" (1975: 292). The frame defines a genre by use of special codes or formulas, figurative language and formal stylistic devices, distinct prosodic or paralinguistic patterns, and appeals to tradition or disclaimers of performance.

The critical aspect of performance for our argument is its emergent quality that "resides in the interplay between communicative resources, individual competence, and the goals of participants, within the context of particular situations" (Bauman 1975: 302; see also Abrahams 1968: 148–149). The act of performance can create new forms of social relations.

It is part of the essence of performance that it offers to the participants a special enhancement of experience, bringing with it a heightened intensity of communicative interaction which binds the audience to the performer in a way that is specific to performance as a mode of communication. Through his performance, the performer elicits the participative attention and energy of his audience, and to the extent that they value his performance, they will allow themselves to be caught up in it. When this happens, the performer gains a measure of prestige and control over the audience—prestige because of the demonstrated competence he had displayed, control because the flow of interaction is in his hands. When the performer gains control in this way, the potential for transformation in the social structure may become available to him as well. (Bauman 1975: 305)

In this formulation what is created by performance, understood as a marked form of communicative behavior, is "social structure," understood by Bauman as the structure of relations between performer and audience. However, if our theory of ritual performance is not to revert to the idea of the individual performer as "charismatic leader," performance must also be understood to structure relations *among* members of the audience, some of whom may also at times have performative access to ritual genres. In other words, the conditions and processes of creativity must be identified in performance understood as a form of charismatic interaction among participants.

The third component of our theory of performance shifts analytic focus from the more general domains of event and genre to the specificity of the performative act. This approach originates with John L. Austin's (1975) and John Searle's (1969, 1979) notion of performative utterance. For Austin, not all utterances are "constative," or descriptive of states of affairs. Some are actually ways of *doing* things, so that in certain cases "saying something is doing something," and there is no simple distinction between spoken word and physical act. Austin also distinguishes the force of an utterance from its meaning. "I will come to the party" has a clear sense and reference but may have either the *force* of a promise or only that of a vague intention. In Austin's formulation, illocutionary force is effected in the act of saying itself, as in "I promise." In contrast, perlocutionary acts "produce certain consequential effects on the feelings, thoughts, or actions of the audience, or of the speaker, or of other persons" (Austin 1975: 101). For example, saying something can perform the perlocutionary act of "persuading" someone of something, but one cannot say, as with illocutionary acts, "I persuade you that . . . "

Anthropologists have applied the concept of performative acts cross-culturally to conventional forms of ordinary speech as well as to forms of ritual language, and have reinforced the theory's implicit blurring of the line between word and deed by including nonlinguistic ritual acts in their analyses. Tambiah (1979/1985) has proposed for the analysis of ritual language a distinction between the illocutionary frame, roughly that which establishes the force of an utterance, and the predicative frame, that in which qualities are attributed and transferred among persons and entities. This distinction can serve us as long as we recognize that the illocutionary act bears an aura of predication and that the performance of metaphors carries illocutionary force. It expands the notion of performative act to explicitly include the performance of metaphor. The power of metaphor to create form and movement in expressive culture has been decisively shown in the work of Fernandez (1986). Our adaptation of the notion of performative act incorporates both the Austinian emphasis on illocution and perlocution and a concern with the predicative force of metaphor.

In the subsequent discussion I will examine the structure of event, genre, and act in the performance of Catholic Charismatic ritual language.[2] I will adopt neither the functionalist perspective that performance acts primarily to reinforce behavioral patterns and belief systems nor the materialist perspective that religion mystifies language to create an illusion of its efficacy. Instead, I will adopt a hermeneutic approach to utterances and the way they make sense within a religious movement, such that a distinctive sacred reality is constituted in performance.

Events of Charismatic Ritual Performance

The prayer meeting is the central collective event for Catholic Charismatics, and as I have noted the organization of prayer groups and communities evolved directly from the organization of prayer meetings. You can best get a sense of a typical prayer meeting in a moderate-size group by imagining yourself one evening in the gymnasium of the parochial school in a suburban Catholic parish. About one hundred folding chairs are arranged in concentric circles with a small open space in the center, a physical representation of community in contrast to the typical arrangement of church pews in straight rows oriented toward an altar above and in front of the congregation (this physical arrangement on a larger scale appears in pl. 1). Against one wall is a long table that several women are filling with books, pamphlets, and cassette tapes. The people trickling into the room know one another and embrace in greeting. A young man greets you, the newcomer, with a handshake and a smile, asking if you have ever attended a Charismatic prayer meeting and if you know what to expect. He is a "greeter," a ritual office within the group, and is concerned that you are prepared for the potentially unsettling experience of hearing collective speaking (and eventually singing) in tongues for the first time. Someone at the center of the circle begins to play a guitar, and people drift toward the chairs, where they stand and join in singing "Alleluia, give thanks to the risen Lord." You are handed a book of Charismatic songs to help you participate.

After the song everyone sits, except for the head of the group's pastoral team, a man dressed in jacket and tie who stands at the center. He says, "The Lord be with you," and the assembly responds enthusiastically, "And with you too!" This is a greeting borrowed from the Catholic Mass, but endowed with an informal tone in the prayer meeting.

The man welcomes everyone, especially newcomers, reminding participants that they are gathered for the sole purpose of "giving praise and glory to God." He urges everyone to "worship the Lord" in a relaxed way and to "be open to what the Lord might have to say to the group in prophecy." He announces another song title, and the guitarist leads the singing. Afterward, participants sit quietly murmuring prayers to themselves, some with closed eyes. Some of these prayers are short phrases such as "Praise you, Jesus" or "Thank you for your love, Lord," while others utter a stream of glossolalic nonsense syllables, praying in tongues. The leader rises again, suggesting that everyone stand and praise God. Everyone does so, many raising their hands in front of themselves, palms open. The room is filled with a hubbub of voices and clapping, in the midst of which a voice begins intoning in tongues. Other voices join in, weaving a fabric of harmony around the original note, vaguely reminiscent of a Gregorian chant. Some contribute short melodic phrases that emerge from and then subside again into the collective chant. The singing in tongues swells and crests, subsiding after a minute or two back into a murmuring of voices. Everyone sits down.

Once again the leader stands, this time to introduce another member of the pastoral team who will deliver a "teaching" on the topic of "God's love." The man next to him stands and speaks for about ten minutes, quoting from the Bible and providing illustrations of how he has experienced divine love in his own life. The leader requests participants to "thank the Lord" for this teaching and to "be open to any word the Lord might have for them." The room is silent with anticipation, many sitting in the characteristic palms-open prayer posture. The silence is broken by a woman's voice speaking in an authoritative tone: "My children, I love you. I love you, for I am your God. Follow me and I will show you the glory of my love." No one watches her as she speaks; everyone looks ahead or sits with closed eyes. At the conclusion of the "prophecy," understood as the direct utterance of God through an inspired speaker, there are scattered, reverential murmurs of "Thank you, Jesus." Someone in the assembly begins a slow chant of "Alleluia, Alleluia," and the group joins in the simple, familiar melody.

When the chant subsides, a man rises and "shares" an incident from the past week in which he had an opportunity to show God's love to a fellow worker in his office. The theme of divine love is now well established as the focus of the prayer meeting, as a woman stands to narrate how the assurance of this love was helping her to deal with her husband, who was opposed to her participation in the prayer group.

Another woman announces that because of the group's love and concern—divine love incarnated in human caring—the sick relative for whom she had previously requested the group's prayers was now improved. A priest stands to publicly thank God for the love he has experienced since his ordination. The leader then asks if anyone has a prayer of petition for the group to collectively "lift up to the Lord." Several people speak up, following which all once again join in collective prayer, some speaking in English and others in tongues.

The leader now makes several announcements as the meeting comes to an end: the single people in the group are planning a weekend canoe trip, a men's prayer breakfast is planned for the next week, a couple is moving across town and needs help loading their furniture, a Life in the Spirit Seminar for the initiation of new members will begin in two weeks, an introductory talk for newcomers and a session of prayer for divine healing will be held in separate rooms immediately following tonight's prayer meeting. The group sings a final song, and people move from their seats, smiling and embracing one another. Some browse at the book table, others talk in groups, drinking coffee and nibbling cookies. The young man who greeted you earlier appears again, pointing out where the introductory talk is to be given. There with half a dozen others you listen to a group member describe the "Four Spiritual Laws," give some background about the history and organization of the prayer group, and narrate how his life has changed since joining the prayer group and being baptized in the Spirit. He answers questions about the group and about speaking in tongues, prophecy, and faith healing. The evening's activities have lasted a total of two to three hours.

Variations on the basic prayer meeting correspond to the features, described in earlier chapters, that distinguish types of charismatic groups and geographic regions within the movement. A small, casual prayer group is likely to gather around a lighted candle in the living room of a private home; a large group may meet in a gymnasium, with several instrumentalists to accompany group singing, a public address system for the speakers, and control by leaders over who may prophesy or share. In such a large group a second weekly prayer meeting may be held for more intimate communal prayer among core group members. Where groups have included communal households, there are small prayer meetings for the residents, and some covenant communities have adopted a weekly Sabbath ceremony. Where there is a more Catholic, as opposed to an ecumenical, orientation, the prayer meeting is often incorporated into a Charismatic mass, with segments of the liturgy expanded to include elements of the prayer meeting. Periodic conferences that last several days include multiple prayer meetings, along with workshops on various spiritual and pastoral topics. Finally, committed Catholic Charismatics typically spend a certain period every day in individual prayer, which may take the form of a prayer meeting for one.

The Pentecostal experience of Baptism in the Holy Spirit is understood as an infusion or release of divine, life-transforming power in a person. Initiation to this experience is closely tied to initiation into the Charismatic group (see also Harrison 1975). One need not have experienced the baptism to attend weekly prayer meetings, but even if one has undergone it in another setting or group, participation in the initiation rite is usually prerequisite to attendance at the more private core group meeting. Initiation typically occurs in a series of weekly seminars that meet for seven weeks. The first four sessions explain the "basic Christian message of salvation" and the meaning of Baptism in the Holy Spirit. The fifth week is devoted to prayer with laying on of hands for neophytes to receive the Baptism in the Holy Spirit. The final two weeks are "oriented toward further growth in the life of the Spirit." These Life in the Spirit Seminars are led by experienced group members following the format of a published manual.[3]

Each session consists of a carefully prepared talk, following which participants break into small "discussion groups" segregated by sex. The discussion group leader gives his or her own "testimony" of personal religious experience and encourages the participants to speak openly about, or share, their own spiritual background and personal lives. During the week preceding the special session of prayer for Baptism in the Holy Spirit, the discussion group leader has a private interview with each of his or her charges. The critical fifth session is a rite within a rite. Following an introductory explanation, participants make a formal "commitment to Christ," pray collectively for "deliverance" from evil spirits in a reiteration of Catholic vows made at sacramental baptism, receive individualized prayer with laying on of hands for Baptism in the Holy Spirit, pray collectively as a group in praise of God, and listen to a closing exhortation. Additional prayer group members are often enlisted to help the team members with laying on of hands, so that in the individualized prayer there are two men with each male initiate and two women with each female. At this point the neophytes are distributed about the room awaiting personal attention by the teams of two. The seminar leaders' manual advises the team to encourage a background noise of soft vocal prayer to create a sense of privacy for each initiate.

A good deal of excitement is generated on the seventh and final week of a Life in the Spirit Seminar, when the new members are introduced to the rest of the group at the weekly prayer meeting. They have assimilated a basic message that the world is in a state of sin and requires salvation, which can ultimately be obtained only by commitment to Christ. Thereupon the deity bestows the Holy Spirit and spiritual gifts on the faithful, initiating their spiritual growth into a life that can be most ideally and fully lived within a Christian community. The expected effects of the Holy Spirit are the desires to pray, to read the Bible, and to frequent mass and the sacraments; experience of gifts of the Spirit such as speaking in tongues and prophecy and fruits of the Spirit such as feelings of love, peace, and joy; and experience of the "presence of God" in daily life as well as in ritual settings.

The seminars expose neophytes to the repertoire of Charismatic ritual practices, to a specialized vocabulary and genres of ritual language, and to a mode of thinking about divine action in life that are expected to lead to transformation of personal consciousness and adoption of a distinctly "Christian" way of life.[4] As we have seen, the initiation process is considerably expanded in some covenant communities, where as many as two years of seminars may be required for full membership. In addition, in some groups rites of passage marking changes in state of life are used to mark new phases of commitment to the group. Charismatic weddings emphasize the new couple's place in the community, and some communities recognize a parallel state of celibacy called being single for the Lord. Finally, the initiation of new group leaders is typically marked with some degree of ritual observance. In all cases, the crucial gesture of confirmation of new status is the traditional Pentecostal laying on of hands.

Charismatic healers tend to specialize in one of several types of healing prayer (healing from physical illness, inner or emotional healing, and deliverance from evil spirits), and ritual healing may take place in four relatively distinct types of events: large public services with multiple patients, small services following prayer meetings, private services for the benefit of a single patient, and solitary healing prayer for oneself or absent others.[5] In large public healing services the principal healing minister, unless he or she is traveling as a guest in an unfamiliar region or country, is typically assisted by a staff. Members of this staff serve as ushers for those coming forward to receive prayer, "catchers" for those who may be overwhelmed by divine power and fall in a sacred swoon, musicians, and members of small prayer teams. Each patient receives at least a few moments of personal attention from either the principal healer or one of the prayer teams. Staff members of several well-organized "ministries" may be identified during services by a sash or jacket worn over their clothing, or by regular street clothing with a common color scheme.[6] In a typical scenario, the service begins with the leader walking up and down the aisles of the church, using a liturgical instrument called an aspergillum to sprinkle holy water on the assembly, and pausing periodically to lay hands on a person's head or shoulder. Returning to the front of the assembly, the leader delivers a sermon on divine healing, and a music emsemble composed of members of the staff leads the group in Charismatic songs. Several participants are solicited to share or "witness to" previous healings they have experienced. The body of the service consists in each participant coming forward for a minute or two of private prayer, much as they come forward for the Eucharist in a mass. Each is anointed with sacramental oil and "prayed over" with laying on of hands.

In prayer groups, healing prayers for self or others may occur in a segment of the weekly prayer meeting. Better-organized groups may have a selected team of "healing ministers" who, following the meeting, conduct prayer for individual supplicants in a separate prayer room or "healing room." Several pairs of team members dispersed through the room each see one patient at a time. They listen, talk, lay on hands, and pray for healing. Other patients wait outside the prayer room and are admitted one by one by another healing team member who acts as gatekeeper. The post–prayer meeting healing room session stands in contrast to the large service in its relative privacy, in the increased amount of time spent with each patient (10 to 20 minutes instead of 2 to 3), and in the greater likelihood of healers and supplicants having an ongoing relationship within the group.

Based on the recommendation of the healing room prayer team, on the recommendation of another prayer group member who senses that a person is troubled, or on one's own initiative, a person may arrange a private session with a more experienced healer or healing team, within or outside the group.[7] Private healing sessions typically take place in a home or counseling center but sometimes occur over the telephone or in hospital visits. Private sessions may last an hour or more and may be conducted by healers within the group or by those with broader reputations. Healers either stand over the seated supplicant with hands laid on head, shoulder, back, or chest; or they sit facing the supplicant, sometimes holding hands. Private sessions are informally structured into alternating segments of talk or "counseling" and of actual "healing prayer," though some healers regard the entire session as prayer. Multiple sessions over time on the model of psychotherapy are performed by more "psychological" healers who hold that healing can be a divine augmentation of gradual, natural processes, although more "fundamentalist" healers object that God's power or willingness to heal is slighted if lengthy, multiple sessions are held. Finally, healing prayer for oneself or others may be practiced in the solitude of private devotion. To my knowledge there is no formal procedure to such prayer, and it can obviously not be observed directly.

Along with prophecy and speaking in tongues, healing is regarded by Charismatics as one of the spiritual gifts, or charisms. However, the structure of healing events as cultural performances is essentially different from that of the prayer meeting and its variants. This is because the gift of healing is understood as the mediation of divine power through specific individuals, rather than as collective access to the divinity through worship and inspiration. Even though prophecy is also a mediation of divine power by an individual, and even though its message may be uniquely interpreted by each listener, anyone in a prayer meeting may be inspired with prophecy, and everyone hears the same prophetic utterance. The asymmetrical relationship among participants in healing, constituted by one person "ministering to" others, persists even when there is a group of healers working in teams. Only rarely is divine power given a collective locus, with the leader instructing all participants to lay hands on each other.[8] Thus, although movement leaders exhort participants to "focus on the gift, not the man," there is nevertheless a perception that some healing ministers are more gifted than others, and those in attendance at public healing services often show a preference to be "prayed over" by the service leader instead of by one of the teams of assistants.

The System of Ritual Genres

The major genres of Charismatic ritual language are named, formalized speech varieties used with regularity in ritual settings and frequently regarded as verbal manifestations of the sacred. There are four such major genres, including prophecy, teaching, prayer, and sharing. Several minor genres occur only in informal settings and are not formally named. These include maxims and slogans, jokes, and slang. Other minor genres integrate language with various forms of bodily movement and include liturgical dance, liturgical drama, and religious games. As *language,* these genres can be placed on a continuum defined by formality, sacredness, and distinctness from speech genres typical of the mainstream or background culture.[9] As *forms of social interaction* they are characterized by specific relations between performer and audience and relations among members of the audience. I will describe the genres of Catholic Pentecostal ritual language with respect to the place of each along the linguistic continuum, and with respect to the way they conventionalize social interaction. We begin with the major genres.

MAJOR GENRES OF RITUAL LANGUAGE

Prophecy. Prophecy is a first-person pronouncement in which the "I" is God; the human speaker is merely the divinity's mouthpiece. For Catholic Charismatics, prophecy is a kind of divine revelation, a means of access to the mind of God. In spite of this, prophecy is very rarely used to foretell the future. Instead, its primary functions are usually listed as exhortation, encouragement, conviction, admonition, inspiration, correction, guidance, consolation, and revelation. Prophecy can occur in a variety of settings and for a variety of audiences. One may be prophetically inspired while alone, while praying with another person, or in a prayer meeting. The prophecy may be intended for oneself, may be a "personal prophecy" for another individual, or may be intended for the group as a whole. The content of a prophecy may be standard and repetitive or innovative and unique and may be directive or nondirective in its implicit consequences for action. Acceptable or authentic prophecy may also be communicated in several modes: (1) a prophetic vision may be narrated in ordinary language; (2) a prophecy may in special cases be written down and read aloud later (even though it is a predominantly oral genre); (3) oral prophecy may be sung or spoken, either in the vernacular or in glossolalia.

Glossolalic prophecy must be "interpreted" into the vernacular, either by the original speaker or by another participant. In a prayer meeting, glossolalic oration will be followed by silent anticipation of its interpretation. The risk of exercising a charismatic gift in a group other than one's own, where one is initiated into the tacit local code of appropriateness, is illustrated by an incident in which a woman prophesied in tongues while visiting Charismatics in another city. The anxious silence was never broken by a vernacular interpretation, and the prophet's chagrin was relieved only when a group leader approached her after the prayer meeting with the reassurance that someone had "received" the inspiration to speak but either from timidity or for some other reason had not done so. The leader was in this case conforming to the precept that it is the responsibility of listeners to encourage or admonish the speaker according to the impact of the words.

Precisely because it lacks semantically intelligible meaning, prophecy in tongues is a compelling manifestation of the absolute other that constitutes the ultimate object of religion (van der Leeuw 1938). Its specialness is enhanced by its relative rarity in Charismatic ritual discourse. Nevertheless, a certain pragmatic attitude toward ritual language is illustrated in one prayer group leader who frequently prophesied in tongues. He regarded it not so much as a prophecy in itself but as a "prophecy facilitator." That is, since participants knew the ritual rule that a vernacular interpretation must be forthcoming following such an utterance, those who were hesitant, shy, or inexperienced would be encouraged to voice an inspiration of which they might be unsure.

As the literal word of God, vernacular prophecy is the most overtly sacred genre of Catholic Pentecostal ritual language. This status is highlighted in performance by distinctive features of prosody, and by the imposition of formal constraints on diction:

1) Prophecies are typically uttered in a strong, clear voice and a tone that can be declamatory, authoritative, imperative, or stern. Seldom will the tone be one of beseeching or imploring. Prophecy in guttural, harsh, strident, or whining tones is of questionable validity, for such tones are thought not to be adopted by the deity when speaking to his "people" and are often attributed to demonic inspiration.

2) Prophecies are usually prefaced by an opening formula, most often "My children, . . . " With increasing development and self-perceived maturity in a group, this formula tends to be replaced by "My people, . . . " In groups with extensive familiarity with prophecy, whose participants can recognize it by intonation and other conventional features, an opening formula is sometimes dispensed with altogether.[10]

3) There is a characteristic intonation pattern within each line of

prophecy, such that the voice rises in the middle and falls again at the end of the line, producing a kind of singsong effect. Several authors have suggested that such intonation patterns are typical of ritual language across cultural traditions (Goodman 1981; DuBois 1986).

4) Prophecy is usually recited in couplets such as the following taken from two separate utterances:

> This gathering is a great hope
> This meeting is both a hope and a promise

> I am doing a new kind of work of unity
> I am stirring you up to new dedication and new zeal in my service

This latter technique is common among varieties of oral poetry, such as the biblical Psalms and the Mayan Popol Vuh (Tedlock 1986), among Yugoslavian bards (Lord 1960), among the Rotinese (Fox 1974), and among the Weyewa (Kuipers 1990, 1993). For Charismatics, in juxtaposition to the less formalized genres of ritual language, the measured cadences of parallel structure add to the solemnity and sacrality of prophetic utterance.

Prophesying is not primarily a form of ecstatic speaking. What the prophet says is subject to an elaborate procedure of evaluation by himself and others, called "discernment." It is held that discernment is necessary because prophecy can be inspired not only by God but by the Devil (in which case it is "false prophecy"), or by the speaker's own human wants and needs (in which case it is "nonprophecy"). Prophetic words must be judged to agree with Christian teaching and Scripture, must be edifying, and must have a tone that is not frightening or condemning. The prophet's personal life must be "in order" if his words are to be trusted, and the prophecy must "bear fruit" in the lives of others. If the prophecy contains predictions, they must "come to pass."

An additional criterion of discernment is the degree of certainty a person feels regarding a particular inspiration. A continuum of certainty ranges from absolute conviction and powerful "anointing" to a weaker "sense of what the Lord might be saying" and finally to personal insight and opinion. Only when someone is fairly certain that an idea is "from the Lord" should it be cast in the verbal form of prophecy; otherwise it should be communicated in the more conversational genre of sharing, or not at all. Valid inspirations with didactic content should be communicated as "teachings." In some quarters of the movement, the "teaching prophecy" is regarded as an invalid and inappropriate mixture of genres. In all cases it is the responsibility of the listeners to admonish or encourage the speaker of prophecy according to the impact of his words.

The prophet must also discern or decide whether a particular divine message is appropriate to a particular setting: whether it is meant for a group or solely for his own inspiration, and whether it should be uttered immediately or at a later time. For example, given that the proceedings of a prayer meeting often coalesce around a distinct theme, an unrelated prophecy that is otherwise well formed may be regarded as inappropriate, or even disruptive. In one group a young woman was forbidden to prophesy for this reason; one of her last prophecies was an eloquent discourse on God's tears of sorrow at those who did not hear his word, but it was uttered during a meeting at which all the other prophecies had to do with "God's love." In this instance the group leadership was already convinced on other grounds that the person was "emotionally unstable," and the overt impropriety of her attempt at ritual discourse both confirmed that opinion and marked her as a potential threat to the order and continuity of the ritual event.

Teaching. Like prophecy, teaching is often performed by a class of cultural specialists. The chief requirement for teaching is "spiritual maturity," but at the same time the ability to teach is regarded as a spiritual gift from God and thus not entirely dependent on a person's native talents. Group leaders often deliver teachings, and in addition they recruit others whom they feel have attained the appropriate level of maturity. Teachers may be assigned topics or may be allowed to develop their own. The usual setting for teaching is the prayer meeting, where for many groups a prepared teaching is a regular weekly feature. Teaching is also given in initiation seminars, workshops, and conferences. Dozens of prerecorded cassette tapes are also available, with teachings by widely known and well-respected movement figures.

The principal generic criterion of teaching is that it clarify some spiritual truth and thus enable its hearers to lead better Christian lives. The teachings are often detailed elaborations of key terms and concepts that recur in less elaborated form in the other ritual genres. Teaching is distinguished from public "sharing" by the skill and rhetorical resources of the performer. The speaker draws on incidents from personal experience, standard anecdotes, and moral tales to illustrate his points and substantiates these points with citations from the Bible.

Teaching is expected to be relevant to actual situations and to be integrated by its hearers into their everyday lives. It is not just useful advice, but an articulation of the basic motives around which group life is supposed to coalesce. At the same time, the teaching itself is shaped in the context of collective experience and is enacted in a distinctive relationship between performer and audience. Teachers often ask listeners to pray with them before beginning, thus establishing a collaborative setting: the teacher becomes inspired, and the audience becomes prepared to receive and accept the message. The listeners are taught to evaluate the teaching not only on the speaker's clarity of expression and rhetorical skills but also insofar as they "can feel that the Holy Spirit is at work in it."

Teachers take their responsibility quite seriously, as is evident in the account of how a man, who had recently delivered a teaching accepted by his group as "inspired," had formulated his talk during the preceding week. It had evolved out of two thoughts shared by his wife and a Scripture passage shared by another woman. He was simultaneously influenced by a trip his sons were making to a conference for Catholic Charismatic youth and by news of a man in Atlanta who had quit his job and become a schoolteacher so as to have more time for religious activities. In addition, he knew that his teaching was to be given at the prayer meeting during the crucial fifth week of the Life in the Spirit Seminar, where neophytes would be present who had within hours received the Baptism in the Holy Spirit. As he prayed that week, the deity assured him that the teaching was in His hands. However, he became "upset with the Lord" because the synthesis of ideas, which for him usually comes early in the week before a teaching, was not occurring. He suffered the entire week with a "teaching bondage," which he described as "an urge to please people rather than to speak God's truth." The reason for this bondage was clear to him: Satan did not want the talk to be given. This example illustrates that the meaning of an utterance cannot be fully apprehended if performance is viewed solely in terms of interactions within the boundaries of isolated ritual events (see Bourdieu 1977).[11] For this informant, the total experience of teaching was interwoven in a universe of discourse. Emerging from the experience of everyday life, its message in performance became a normative commentary on that life and was experienced as "inspired" by its hearers.

Prayer. Prayer may be performed by an individual or a group, silently or audibly, in speech or in song, in glossolalia or in the vernacular, in a normal state of consciousness or "in the Spirit" (a mild ecstasy). As an everyday life activity, prayer need not be restricted to a particular setting, and indeed people may pray at any time or while engaged in any other activity. There are, however, specific settings, notably the prayer meeting, the main purpose of which is prayer. There are four basic types of Charismatic prayer: worship, which includes adoration, praise, and thanksgiving; petition or intercession on behalf of another for a special purpose such as healing; "seeking the Lord," or prayer for divine guidance; and "taking authority," or praying in the form of a command for evil to depart from a person or situation. Spontaneous expression is highly valued in Charismatic prayer, which very rarely requires the repetition of fixed texts. The notable exceptions are several formulaic invocations of the name "Jesus" (either in praise or in the casting out of evil spirits) and the texts of religious songs.

In prayer humans both speak and listen to the deity. The "Lord" should be "present" within a group or with an individual in prayer. Divine presence is experienced concretely in performance. One informant reported that sometimes it is "like He is right in the room." This is an "immediate thing," not a physical presence but yet more than "something in your head." She described a subtler instance of this experience as a moment in which, while reading a religious book, her apperception of the noise of trucks in the street contained God's presence. She felt that "God did it"—that he had the idea of that sound in his mind and she was perceiving the idea. The same informant also reported experience of the divine presence through mental images that arose during prayer. Typical for her were Christ's full body (as opposed to face alone), robed in white, wearing a gentle, peaceful expression, with arms opening in a gesture of welcome, and standing against a background of light. For Catholic Charismatics, some of these images appear spontaneously, and others are consciously invoked more or less as internal icons. Their importance varies with the individual; another informant reported "stumbling on them by accident" in the course of prayer and not experiencing them often or as very significant. When they do appear, their role is that of an internalized icon, an aid to prayer that is generated within the performance itself.[12] Such experiences in prayer of divine presence, vivid imagery, and shared subjectivity culturally thematized in terms of spontaneity have also been reported for Catholic Pentecostals by Neitz (1987).

Song is a highly elaborated form of prayer (worship) among Catholic Charismatics. Although participants sometimes sing spontaneously and sing in tongues, composed song is an aspect of nearly every gathering, and the song texts explicitly celebrate the themes of group life. As new themes emerge, new songs become popular, and where there is talent among members, new songs are written to express and celebrate "what the Lord has been saying to us" in the evolution of group life. Some groups have their own compilation of songs for use at prayer meetings, while centers of movement activity produce printed songbooks and albums of recorded songs.

By far the greatest amount of prayer is praise. Praise of the deity is the sole semantic load of that barrage of random vocalization called praying in tongues (glossolalia). Tongues are a divine spiritual gift (charism) that allow their user to praise him in a manner for which "mere man-made language" is regarded as inadequate. The most impressive public displays of glossolalic prayer are in the periodic conferences, during which the voices of thousands of people swell to a melodic crescendo as they collectively sing in tongues. At the same time, tongues can be used quietly and even subvocally while a person is engaged in other activities.

I will postpone discussion of the phenomenology of glossolalia and the semiotic contribution of unintelligibility to the structure of the sacred until the next chapter. For now, I will comment only on the generic criteria that allow speakers and hearers of Charismatic ritual language to distinguish between prophecy in tongues and prayer in tongues. With reference to the kinds of episodes that make up a prayer meeting, glossolalic prophecy is more likely to occur during periods when participants are called to "listen to the Lord" whereas glossolalic prayer tends to occur in periods of "worship and praise." Tonal qualities also distinguish these two forms of glossolalic utterance: prayer in tongues has a conversational or supplicative tone whereas prophecy in tongues has an authoritative or declamatory tone. Glossolalic prophecy must be "interpreted" into the vernacular for the edification of the participants; glossolalic prayer remains a mode of intimate communication between an individual and the deity that need not be intelligible to others. These features highlight the importance of Frye's radical of presentation in the differentiation of genres, even to the point of rendering the unintelligible utterance of tongues into meaningful generic performance.

Sharing. The formal criterion that distinguishes sharing from ordinary conversation is that its contents must have some spiritual value or edifying effect. These contents may be experiences, events, problems, or thoughts. To describe "how work went yesterday" is sharing if it has some religious significance. One might share about "what the Lord taught me this week" in the course of everyday life or through a crisis. The settings for sharing are various. People may arrange to get together to share in the process of becoming acquainted, or may have intimates with whom they share regularly. Sharing should be an aspect of a person's regular meeting with his head, or spiritual adviser. When sharing occurs publicly in a prayer meeting, it is referred to as "witnessing" or "testimony" (cf. Harding 1987 on Fundamental Baptist Witnessing). Nearly every person has a standardized account of "how I came to the Lord" and of the personal transformation undergone since Baptism in the Holy Spirit (cf. Stromberg 1993 on Evangelical Christian conversion narratives). Finally, as noted above, sharing occurs in the process of initiation, particularly in the "discussion groups" in which individuals reveal the spiritual state of their lives.

The manner in which Catholic Charismatics learn this genre in the initiatory discussion groups has been described by McGuire (1975) as a process in which the discussion leader "reframes" each member's contribution by translating it into the terms of the movement's ritual discourse. The leader adds comments that indicate the deity's action in the unfolding of everyday events, or alters the intended significance of a neophyte's statement. He or she subsequently reinforces appropriately formed utterances with a knowing look and a smile, or by sharing similar personal experiences (McGuire 1975: 8). The following exchange between a neophyte (N) and a discussion leader (L), recorded by me, supports McGuire's conclusion:

N: I want to change my mind.
L: Only God can change your mind. He will show you, you don't
    need to worry.

In expressing a desire for personal transformation, N's statement is already incorporated within Catholic Pentecostal discourse. The way L reframes the statement relieves N of personal responsibility for this transformation and directs her toward the project of discovering "the will of God" for her life. From this point on, she will learn to "seek the Lord in prayer" and to expect "leadings from the Lord." In this way, reframing restructures the neophyte's perceptions so that she will see the hand of the deity active in the world and will look to divinely inspired, rather than to personal, intuition as a source of knowledge about what to do and how to feel.[13]

The transformation of language and consciousness in sharing is complemented by a transformation of self and affect. An example is that of sharing in a headship relationship, as described by an unmarried covenant community man in his twenties and his married adviser, also in his twenties. The young man reported that when first baptized in the Spirit, he was "thrilled" by spiritual gifts, prayer meetings, and external elements of Charismatic life. Only through sharing with his head, he said, did he become aware of "internal deficiencies" in himself. When his head asked if he had ever been in love, he initially recoiled from the issue. Eventually, however, this exchange opened the way for sharing about the superficiality of his interpersonal relationships. Through sharing, the two linked his inability to open up to others with details of his relationship to his father and with the competitiveness that characterizes relationships among American men. He also reported being able to share about a "problem with masturbation" and about the "dating relationship" he was in with a woman in his covenant community; this woman also shared regularly with her head about the relationship. Performance of the genre of sharing within the headship relation in this way is thought to guide a person's life decisions and facilitate spiritual and personal growth.

Charismatics themselves would likely recognize each of these genres from the above description. However, also critical to our understanding of Charismatic ritual language as a performative apparatus for the creative transformation of self and habitus is analysis of the systematic cultural relations *among* the four major genres. Anthropologists studying language use in cultural context have described not only single genres but systems of genres (Gossen 1972, 1974; Fabian 1974; Stross 1974; Csordas 1987; Briggs 1988; Kuipers 1990; Bourdieu 1991; Leitch 1991). Synthesizing the descriptions presented above, such a systematic relation among the major genres of Charismatic ritual language can be outlined both in terms of structural features of the genres and in terms of performance.

There are two ways in which the four genres are structurally interrelated. First, they can be distributed along a hierarchical continuum such that, in comparison to what would be recognized as everyday conversation by middle-class speakers of North American English, proph-

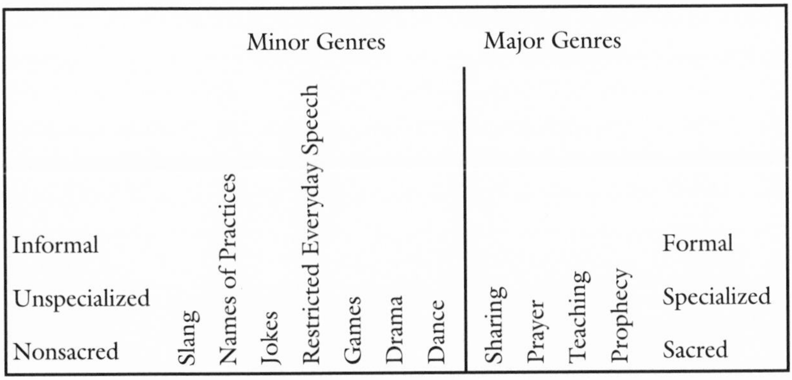

	Minor Genres							Major Genres				
Informal				Restricted Everyday Speech								Formal
Unspecialized		Names of Practices						Sharing	Prayer	Teaching	Prophecy	Specialized
Nonsacred	Slang		Jokes		Games	Drama	Dance					Sacred

Fig. 1. *Genres of Ritual Language among Catholic Charismatics*

ecy is the most formalized, sacred, and specialized, while sharing is the least formalized, sacred, and specialized. This is depicted in figure 1, which also shows the minor genres (to be discussed below), the performance of which shades into everyday speech. At the same time, variation of these three features occurs within each genre as a function of variation in relationships between performer and audience across different settings. In a public setting, for example, sharing becomes testimony and may even have a semistable narrative text if it is a person's account of "how I came to the Lord." Likewise, prayer can acquire a degree of formalization in public, collective worship or in songs with fixed texts. Prophecy, the genre that is most formalized and distinct from everyday conversation, loses some of these characteristics when it takes the form of a "personal prophecy," in which one individual delivers a message from God to another outside a ritual event. Finally, teaching can be uttered only in some kind of ritual setting, but it can either be a fixed part of the event or a spontaneous contribution, and its content can be more or less sacred depending on whether the speaker is perceived to be truly "inspired."

The relative places of the four major genres along the formal-specialized-sacred continuum corresponds to an even more compelling feature of their systematic relation, that is, their complementarity in outlining a paradigm or template for ideal communicative relationships among the participants in ritual performance. These are of two types: relationships among humans, and the relationship between humans and the divine Lord. Charismatic ritual language establishes each of these

Relation / Principle	Human–Human	God–Human
Intimacy/dialogue	Sharing	Prayer
Authority/monologue	Teaching	Prophecy
Mode		
Glossolalia	–	+
Song	–	+

Fig. 2. *Relations among the Major Genres of Catholic Charismatic Ritual Language*

relationships in two modes: that of dialogic intimacy or reciprocity between performer and audience and that of monologic authority or hierarchy between performer and audience. These relationships (fig. 2) are structured as follows:

1) Sharing is that form of ritual communication among humans that is most reciprocal and personal. In dialogue one shares one's inmost thoughts and feelings; one bares one's soul. Sharing constitutes a relation of intimacy between performer and audience, who ideally alternate roles, and gives that intimacy a specific religious meaning.

2) Teaching articulates human relations hierarchically. In the form of a monologue, the flow of information is unidirectional, from the spiritually mature teacher to the less mature participants or neophytes. Utterance constitutes a relationship of authority between performer and audience, although when the teacher asks his listeners to pray *with* him beforehand to assure the success of the teaching, it is emphasized that the authority is ultimately God's. The teacher is thus identified simultaneously with the audience and with the divine source of his authority.

3) Prayer is the reciprocal form of communication between the deity and humans. One can converse with the "Lord" as a friend, "go to the Lord" with a problem, or "give something to the Lord" in prayer, and he will respond with comfort, guidance, or inspiration. In the dialogue of prayer there emerges a relationship of intimacy between performer and (divine) audience that

emphasizes the deity's presence as an active participant in the speech event—someone who speaks back. Prayer is like sharing, but with a divine co-performer.

4) Prophecy is the hierarchical form of divine communication to humans. It is a pronouncement by the deity on his own initiative, and when uttered authentically it is his indisputable Word. As an authoritative monologue prophecy constitutes the relationship of authority between God and humans in a more immediate way than does teaching, and with an emphasis on the divine power immediately manifest in such an utterance. Because of this the role of performer (prophet) is ambiguous: in the abstract it is unimportant because the performer is but a mouthpiece; in practice it is very important because the prophet is responsible for discerning the validity and appropriateness of his inspiration and because his words bear powerful consequences for future action.

Within this system, the qualitative difference between relations among humans and relations with God is marked by another formal characteristic: the two genres in which God is a participant (prayer and prophecy) are sometimes performed in the specialized modes of song and glossolalia whereas the two others (sharing and teaching) are not (fig. 2). The option of expressing prayer and prophecy in these modes enriches their performance and enhances their sacredness vis-à-vis the genres of interhuman ritual communication. Song is regarded as an apt and edifying vehicle for prophecy or prayer, but would serve no purpose in sharing or teaching. Glossolalia in prayer is the highest form of praise to the deity, and in prophecy it is the sign of a specially charged message that must be "interpreted" into the vernacular, whereas sharing or teaching in glossolalia would contravene their essential purpose. In this way the most formal-specialized-sacred genres are precisely those that entextualize (Bauman and Briggs 1990) the relationship between human and divine rather than among humans. Thus if performance offers a "special enhancement of experience" (Bauman 1975), including experience of the sacred, the present case documents the existence of formal means through which the enhancement of experience can be systematically greater for some genres than for others.

Attention to relations among genres also has methodological consequences for the analysis of performance and its creative/transformative effects. Peter Stromberg (1993) presents a compelling analysis of

Evangelical Christian conversion narratives, a genre that corresponds to one form of what we have identified among Charismatics as sharing. Stromberg's analysis demonstrates how performance of such narratives effects self-transformation through an interplay between two types of what he calls constitutive language, namely, canonical and metaphoric language. In this formulation self is, reminiscent of Hallowell, "the ability of the human organism to be reflexively aware" (Stromberg 1993: 27), and self-transformation is, reminiscent of psychodynamic psychotherapy, "the result of changing embodied aims into articulable intentions" (Stromberg 1993: 29). These definitions are nicely suited to the genre of conversion narrative, for while it may be embedded in a dialogue (with an interviewer or with another believer or potential convert), such a narrative is at base a person talking about and generating insights about himself or herself, and therefore it is reflexive by genre convention. There are analytical implications, however. Since self is characterized by reflexivity, what would be the nature of self-transformation effected by less reflexive genres? Since in this view embodied aims are by definition outside the self, must we exclude the possibility that they could be ritually transformed precisely as bodily aims without being linguistically objectified? Are these definitions adequate to analytically deal with transformation of habitus as well as self-transformation? In sum, while Stromberg's concepts of self and self-transformation are well matched to the analysis of a particular genre, they might not be generalizable to the entire life-world of Evangelical Christians or Charismatics, and hence not generalizable to other cultural settings.

When we turn to the relation among genres in performance, rather than the hierarchical structure of performance or how it outlines a paradigm of ideal social relations, our analysis becomes one of multiple ways in which the speaking subject (Benveniste 1971) is constituted in relation to the apparatus of enunciation. Charles Briggs and Richard Bauman (1992) have called for studies of generic intertextuality, referring to the meaningful consequences of gaps and continuities between different utterances within the same genre. Such genre intertextuality is evident in Charismatic ritual language, and in the next chapter we will examine a particularly important instance in the genre of prophecy. Beyond intertextuality within genres, however, recognizing a system of genres requires attention to *inter*genre intertextuality. The importance of intergenre intertextuality is evident in the questionable mixed genre of the "teaching prophecy," questionable perhaps because it conflates a genre based on divine authority and one based on human intelligence, or perhaps because it confuses the prophetic function of "forthtelling" with that of exegesis. Again, the tendency of utterances in different genres within a prayer meeting to coalesce around a theme bespeaks the importance of intergenre intertextuality, as does the possibility of both prayer and prophecy to be performed in tongues. We have yet two steps to take to fully appreciate the scope of intertextuality and to complete our analysis of the system of Charismatic ritual performance. In the next section I will describe the minor genres of ritual language and then take up the act/motive complex that constitutes the formal means by which intergenre intertextuality is guaranteed in performance.

MINOR GENRES OF RITUAL LANGUAGE

The existence of what we are calling minor genres of Charismatic ritual language demonstrates the permeation of ritual form through everyday life and discourse. In some ways even more than our discussions of community life, ritual events, and major genres, the texts I will present offer an ethnographic window on the ethos of everyday Charismatic life. In the following order, I will treat maxims and slogans, pastoral slang, jokes, games, drama, and dance.

Maxims and Slogans. The genre of maxims and slogans is composed of texts at the sentence level of linguistic patterning, the content of which is widely shared among neo-Pentecostals and Charismatics. There are no specified settings for performance, and anyone may utter them as a commentary on a situation or for special emphasis. In the guise of practical advice or insight into the divine "plan," such maxims and slogans frequently encode either imperatives for action or inarguable statements of essential truths, what Rappaport (1979) has called "ultimate sacred postulates."

Text	*Gloss*
Jesus is Lord	Jesus' authority as God is absolute
God has a plan for your life	You are part of the divine will, and since Jesus is Lord you are required to discover and follow his plan for you
Praise the Lord in all things	God should be praised because he is all-worthy, even when things do not appear

Text	*Gloss*
	to be going right or when one does not understand his plan
Speak the truth in love	Do not hesitate to be blunt in confronting someone on matters of faith or morals, but do so in a manner that expresses love and concern
Man is sinful, but God wants us happy	This is an abdication of older Catholic views that justified self-mortification and self-abnegation in expectation of happiness in the afterlife
Ours is a religion of the heart, not of the head	This emphasizes affective over cognitive dimensions of religious practice and experience, with overtones of anti-intellectualism
The devil attacks those who are very weak and those who are very strong	Those who are unprotected by faith and support of a Christian community are targets of demonic harassment, but so are committed Christians, who Satan perceives as the greatest threat; increasing harassment and temptation are signs that a Christian is getting closer to his goal
Keep into the Incarnation	This is a reminder of the continuing presence or embodiment of Jesus in the human world; this "hip" slogan (compare "Keep the faith, baby") was collected only in one community
God has no grandsons, only sons	This refers to the spiritual development of children, who must eventually come into a personal relationship with God unmediated by their parents
A vision is caught, not taught	This refers to both adults and children; one must be oriented and open to the spontaneity of divine revelation; its reception is not a skill that can be taught

Pastoral Slang. What I call pastoral slang includes informal terms coined by movement leaders to denote practices or attitudes they regard as inappropriate or excessive. The terms indicate behavioral dispositions of rank-and-file Charismatics that persist despite the advisement of movement elite.

Cultural baggage—Styles of worship and ritual practice adopted from Protestant Pentecostalism but perceived as inappropriate to or incompatible with middle-class, Catholic styles.

Spiritual battery—Prayer meeting participants sometimes regard exhilarating and "uplifting" events as opportunities to "recharge their spiritual battery," which has become depleted by a week's activity in the mundane world. As opposed to this kind of spiritual materialism or utilitarianism, the appropriate attitude toward prayer meetings is that they are occasions to worship God.

Charismania—Overextensive use or attention to Charismatic gifts, to the detriment of serious worship and community building; a kind of enthusiastic sensationalism.

Hothouse spirituality—Overintensive cultivation of charismatic gifts, with the danger of being carried to potentially destructive excess by lack of "discernment" in using them. There is spiritual danger in becoming involved in situations where one is "over one's head" and beyond one's competence, or where one is exposed to more "spiritual power" than one can handle.

Superspirituality—Although the deity is thought to provide direction and concrete "leadings" for people in their lives, one can carry surrender/submission to the divine will to the extent that one becomes reduced to inactivity by waiting for inspiration in the most routine tasks and decisions.

Charismatic tourism—The practice of going from one prayer group to another without making a commitment to any, a practice felt to retard a person's "spiritual growth" as well as to hinder the process of building stable communities.

Charismatic density—Large, centralized groups are felt to be more likely to have all the charisms necessary for building community represented among their members; the expression bears the connotation of a "critical mass" necessary to generate a fully Charismatic environment.

Dry spells—Periods in which one's spiritual life or "prayer life" seems flat, uninspired, or distant from intimate contact with God.

Jokes. Charismatic jokes illustrate the "esoteric-exoteric" factor that affects oral genres when a group is relatively isolated, possesses a really or apparently peculiar knowledge or training, or is considered by others as particularly admirable or awesome (Jansen 1975: 49–50). The Charismatic Renewal has all three characteristics to some degree. Therefore, I will offer more explanatory comment on these texts than I did for the preceding two genres. First, a sanction against going through life with a "negative spirit" is typically extended to disapproval of "negative humor," a style of joking observable in varying degrees across regions and ethnic categories in North America. Negative humor generally includes sarcasm and any joke at the expense of another. This sanction, in conjunction with a degree of seriousness about pursuing a divinely bequeathed mission, at times lends an almost humorless cast to the demeanor of some Charismatics. One group leader commented that though he thought Charismatic jokes funny, others "did not fully approve." Thus as a genre they tend not to be widespread. One example is the following:

A man bought a horse, but when he tried to ride it, it wouldn't budge. "Giddyup," he shouted again and again, but the horse stood stock still. In a rage the man returned to the horse's seller. The latter apologized, saying, "I forgot to tell you that this is a Charismatic horse. To get it to go you say 'Praise the Lord' and to stop say 'Amen' [or "Alleluia" as a variant]." The purchaser was nonplussed, but consented to give it a try. He said "Praise the Lord," and the horse took off at a canter. He said "Praise the Lord" again and the horse broke into a gallop. He was having a great time when he realized he was heading straight for a cliff. "Whoa," he cried, but in vain. Then, just at the edge of the abyss, he remembered his instructions and shouted "Amen!" The horse stopped dead, inches from the edge. Leaning back in the saddle and wiping the sweat from his brow, the man sighed, "Praise the Lord."

An element of self-commentary is evident in the premise of the joke, namely, that the clearest behavioral marker identifying a Charismatic is punctuation of everyday speech with frequent exclamations of "Praise the Lord," "Amen," or "Alleluia." The power of praise to mobilize divine power is coded in the efficacy of repeated exclamations of praise to increase the velocity of the horse. The presumption of a generalized human tendency to abandon one's faith in moments of crisis, just when it is most needed, is vivid in the horseman's predicament. Finally, the danger of practice without thought, or of allowing religious practice to become mere habit, is brought home in the story's tragicomic ending.

Here is another example:

A young boy was riding his bicycle past the church when one of its wheels fell off. "Son of a bitch," he said. The Charismatic parish priest, on the church steps, overheard and reprimanded the boy, saying, "You should praise the Lord in all things." Shrugging his shoulders, the little boy obliged, praising and thanking Jesus. Suddenly the wheel reattached itself to the bicycle and the little boy rode off smiling. The priest looked up at the sky and said, "Son of a bitch."

This story also emphasizes the efficacy of praise in mobilizing divine power. It capitalizes on a perceived tendency of spiritual maxims such as "Praise the Lord in all things" to become matters more of habitual utterance than of experience, and gives a specifically Charismatic slant to a fairly common folkloric theme of the clergyman who does not fully believe what he preaches.

The following jokes, mostly in the form of riddles, are based on puns between conventional and Charismatic meanings of common words.

Q: What do you call a haircut by a barber who's been baptized in the Holy Spirit?
A: A hairismatic removal.

The pun is on Charismatic Renewal.

Q: What would you call a group that prohibits Charismatic gifts at their assemblies?
A: A nonprophet organization.

This pun is triple, referring first to prophecy, the most prominent charism, second to the understanding that prayer groups benefit or profit from the exercise of spiritual gifts, and third to the fact that many Charismatic groups are in fact incorporated as nonprofit organizations.

Q: What would you call a program to train preschool children in the exercise of pastoral authority in committed relationships of submission?
A: A Headstart program.

A degree of self-commentary on the evolution of an elaborate, esoteric jargon that hardly conforms to a Christian ideal of "childlike simplicity" is evident in the premise of the joke. The pun is between the popular U.S. government educational program for underprivileged children and the covenant community institution of personal headship. The implication is that children are underprivileged because they have not yet had the opportunity to enter a relationship of submission to a head, a relationship understood as a vehicle for achieving spiritual maturity.

Q: What did Lewis and Clark get when they prayed for guidance?

A: The Northwest Passage.

This pun is between the new route to the Pacific sought by the explorers Lewis and Clark and the Charismatic practice of exploring or "seeking" the divine will by opening the Bible at random. In this practice, frowned on as "magical" in some quarters of the movement, one expects spontaneously to receive or "get" a scriptural "passage" relevant to a current problem or situation.

Those who do not pay their exorcism fee within thirty days after deliverance will be repossessed.

The pun here is between commercial activities in which goods are delivered and can be repossessed if not paid for in time and the Charismatic practice of deliverance from the influence of evil spirits that can "repossess" a person who fails to lead a Christian life supported by a Christian community. An element of the ridiculous is added by the notion of a "deliverance fee," for Charismatics do not typically charge for a service that is understood to be a voluntary ministration of a spiritual gift originating with the deity.

Games, Drama, and Dance. Passing to genres that add a bodily dimension to that of language, I will briefly discuss games, drama, and dance. The game of "Bible charades" resembles secular charades, except that the subject must be a scriptural character or incident. Thorough familiarity with the sacred text is requisite for success in this pastime, which is engaged in by both adults and children. In the game of "Instant Theater" teams take turns pantomiming episodes from the Bible, while their opponents attempt to identify the scene. I took part in one such game during which a partner and I were required to climb beneath the cushions of a sofa and roll out, being born as the twins Jacob and Esau. Such games keep participants focused on religious topics even in settings in which pleasure and relaxation are in order. I am not aware how widespread this form of play is among Charismatics, though I would expect it to be observable among a variety of born-again Christians.

Drama and dance require a degree of participation and resources typically available only in covenant communities. In the late 1970s The Word of God had a troupe that performed original material such as the following skit presented as part of the community anniversary celebration.

A little girl asks her grandfather to read her a story. He looks on the shelf for *Winnie the Pooh* and sees some Charismatic books. The little girl asks for a Bible story instead. (Grandfather is a comic character; he takes a very long time to settle into his chair and repeatedly dozes off.) Grandfather asks the girl to use her imagination during the story.

"What's imagination?" she asks.

"Pictures in your head," he replies.

"I'm doing it!" she says excitedly.

"I haven't started reading yet," says Grandfather.

The old man reads a parable from the Book of Matthew about a tree that bears good fruit and one that bears bad fruit. The girl's mental image is portrayed onstage by actors garbed as trees. The bad tree is covered with streamers—"spinach" in the little girl's imagination—and the good one with lollipops. The actor and actress portraying the good tree speak with sugary sweet and blended voices. Their counterparts are gruff and shrill, and their comment to the good tree is "Yuck!" A woodsman enters, tastes the fruit of both trees, and chops down the bad one.

The girl asks Grandfather to interpret the parable. He replies that one is a good person and the other a bad one. She can fall asleep more easily now. Grandfather dozes again, and as the girl awakens him he is startled, thinking his deceased wife was there.

"Oh, she's in heaven, Grandpa," the girl reminds him.

"I *know*," he says, gulping with a bit of fear.

The little girl falls asleep under the Christmas tree and dreams. Angels are deciding to announce the birth of Jesus with a lullaby, which is rendered as a jazzy "Noel." Grandpa enters and reads her the story of baby Jesus.

"Remember to use your imagination when I read you a story. Remember what it is?" says the old man.

"Pictures in my head," she responds.

This time she sees shepherds frightened by the angels. The shepherds depart for Bethlehem, and the little girl goes off to bed.

"That little girl sure has quite an imagination," comments Grandfather, and he exits the stage humming "Noel" to himself.

Cultivation of the imagination as a medium through which the deity communicates with humans in ritual healing prayer, worship, and prophetic inspiration is a distinctive feature of the Charismatic world (see Csordas 1994). It is the theme of imagination that makes the skit explicitly Charismatic and not simply a generalized Christian setting for the enactment of Bible stories. The audience, many of whom were children, was expected to take away an understanding of imagination as

"pictures in your head," along with concrete examples of how imaginative scenes might unfold for them. Performance is thus an aid to in-
culcating a disposition for guided spontaneity and regulated improvisation in imaginative practice.

The embodied concreteness of ritual performance might be expected
to be most fully elaborated in the genre of dance as a self-conscious aesthetic fulfillment of habitus in a locale where habitus has been subject
to the greatest degree of cultivated transformation. This appeared to be
the case at The Word of God during the late 1970s, when the community had its own chief choreographer, a woman then in her twenties. Thus, though dance is in fact a rare genre of Charismatic performance, it is worth some time to examine the rhetorical principles that
guided its practice in that locale at that historical moment. The community choreographer stated that the discourse of the body in dance
guides the mind into a pattern of thought, whereas mere words allow
thoughts to wander. This is true, she said, because the form of abstract
modern dance captures essences, not ideas, so that, for example, the
message of an image such as "streams of living water" is more aptly
conveyed by dance. In comparison to Charismatic modern dance, however, secular modern dance "has little joy." It "works out of anxiety"
and regards the incorporation of joy into choreography as frivolous.
Secular dance also celebrates movement for movement's sake, whereas
Charismatic dance is intended to be communicative and spiritually edifying. The "non-Christian" would choreograph "what she felt like,"
cutting it up and putting it together any way, and her audience would
watch it as "art." In the Charismatic view, this fails to give life to the
dance, whereas by contrast community dancers attempt to produce
works that "share" and "speak." As the choreographer said, the "value
systems" of the two forms are opposed. "It is not useful to fill your
mind too much with those ideas if you are trying to grow in another
direction."

The community choreographer saw the development of dance in the
group toward expression of the "deeper aspects of experience." She
noted that her troupe formerly did a collective improvisation on "joy,"
with the sole preparation of a session of "sharing" among the dancers.
They subsequently discovered, she said, that emotions are the "shallow
version of an experience" and that joy is in fact a "deep experientially
founded affirmation." In recognizing this the troupe began "dancing
our convictions, not our emotions." Performing became a reverential,
"absolutely ground-level experience under God," and a "praise-oriented
activity." At the same time, the artist's personal relation to her art was

transformed in a double movement. First, creativity within the ritual attitude surpassed the boundaries of the performance event. Thus she had recently begun to dance spontaneously in the streets of town. Second, she began to perceive the practice of art as less closely bound to her own ego. Whereas before her conversion she had a compulsion to constant expressive activity (dancing, drawing, and writing), she reported having attained the comfortable feeling that "you can do it when you want."

The phenomenological integration of body and language, essence and word, representation and being-in-the-world, is evident in the orientation of dance toward major genres and key terms that repeatedly appear in all the genres as well as toward ritualized practices of everyday life. Sharing, prayer, "listening to the Lord" (for divine guidance), "giving something to the Lord" (surrendering a decision or situation to the divine will), or headship could receive choreographic treatment. "Fruits of the Spirit" such as "love, peace, and joy" may serve as themes for dance. The latter are key terms but also "essences," and the Charismatic choreographer trying to dance them "does not need to think much since you're experiencing them already." The group would also choreograph key terms such as "darkness," "growth," "freedom," "praise," "renewal," and "covenant." "Order" and "authority" would be portrayed literally by "nice-looking patterns" that would metamorphose as the dancers moved. "Power" is difficult to portray because it is difficult to "overwhelm an audience," and you immediately "sense your own weakness." The terministic pair "heart" and "head" (as in the maxim "Ours is a religion of the heart not the head") is also difficult in that the terms are "too conceptual" and would require more talented and trained dancers. The significance of these key terms as themes enacted in dance is that they motivate Charismatic discourse and through it, all of Charismatic life. We have encountered these motives in a variety of contexts, and we are now prepared more formally to examine their role as a structured component of ritual language.

Ritual Acts and the Vocabulary of Motives

Thus far I have fleshed out my threefold theory of performance by describing types of Charismatic ritual events and a system of Charismatic ritual genres. In turning to discussion of discrete ritual acts, several distinctions are necessary for the sake of clarity. First is a distinction between acts describable as named practices or techniques and any enactment of or utterance in one of the genres. In my study of Charismatic healing, I identified a series of named practices under the headings of empowerment, spiritual protection, revelation, deliverance, sacramental grace, and emotional release (Csordas 1994a: 45–49). These acts are often performed within one of the ritual genres. For example, the act of deliverance from evil spirits is achieved in a "prayer of command" to those spirits to depart, and the act of giving or lifting something up to the Lord (commending it to divine Providence) is done "in prayer." However, not all acts of performance in a genre include one of these practices. Second, we must distinguish between acts of utterance and gestures or bodily movements. Acts such as anointing with oil, laying on of hands, resting in the Spirit, or taking the Eucharist may be but are not necessarily accompanied by utterance in verbal genres. Blurring the verbal/nonverbal distinction, dance can be almost literally a form of "body language" when it is choreographed as the nonverbal enactment of verbal concepts. Third, it is necessary to distinguish between the formal performative of speech act theory and the illocutionary or predicative effect of discreet ritual acts. Thus while the illocutionary act must have a particular linguistic form, analysis of an utterance in the illocutionary frame has to do with the nature of its force and authority (the importance of this distinction will be evident in analysis of specific prophetic utterances in the next chapter).

In general, I am less concerned with the form of any of these acts than with their performative (illocutionary or predicative) effects. The goal is to understand ritual acts as part of the rhetorical apparatus by means of which participants are oriented and reoriented in the sense I have described as essential to a definition of self. To this end a final distinction is critical, that between act and motive, where motive has a precise cultural sense distinct from the psychological sense of motive or intention. Specifically, every utterance or gesture is oriented by a "motive," which is a term that defines its illocutionary or predicative effect. A principal component of the Charismatic system of ritual performance, then, is the movement's specialized *vocabulary of motives,* a phrase introduced in the work of C. Wright Mills (1940).[14]

Mills's concept of motive stems from Weber, in whose formulation "a motive is a complex of subjective meaning [*Sinnzusammenhang*] which seems to the actor himself or to the observer an adequate ground for the conduct in question" (1947: 98). The relationship between act and motive is reciprocal: motive orients act, and act articulates motive.

This notion of a motive as a complex of meaning that orients action is explicated by Mills.

Motives are words. Generally, to what do they refer? They do not denote elements "in" individuals. They stand for anticipated situational consequences of questioned conduct. Intention or purpose (stated as a "program") *is* awareness of anticipated consequences; motives are names for consequential situations, and surrogates for actions leading to them. (1940: 905)

Just as we have found the locus of charisma to be not in individuals but among them, so in Mills's conception the locus of motives is not within people.[15] The utterance of a motive is the declaration that a situation is consequential, and its rhetorical impact may be the impulse to charismatic action.

In this respect, a vocabulary of motives is not a random list but a self-referencing system of terms. In the dramatistic theory of Kenneth Burke (1966), what Mills calls motives are identified as terms (words) situated with respect to an act, scene, agent, agency, and purpose. In Burke's theory, a vocabulary of motives constitutes a "terministic screen" through which experience is filtered and organized. Terministic screens are essential aspects of human affairs.

We *must* use terministic screens, since we can't say anything without the use of terms; whatever terms we use, they necessarily constitute a corresponding kind of screen; and any such screen necessarily redirects the attention to one field rather than another. Within that field there can be different screens, each with its way of directing the attention and shaping the range of observations implicit in the given terminology. (Burke 1966: 50)

Burke's argument suggests that a vocabulary of motives is a basis for orientational process in that it directs the attention and shapes the range of observations in a cognitive sense. Returning to Mills, we can understand a second dimension of orientational process in that the deployment of motives in social life can direct action in a strategic sense.

When they appeal to others involved in one's act, motives are strategies for action. In many social actions, others must agree, either tacitly or explicitly. Thus, acts must often be abandoned if no reason can be found that others will accept. Diplomacy in choice of motive often controls the diplomat. Diplomatic choice of motive is part of the attempt to motivate acts for others in a situation. Such pronounced motives undo snarls and integrate social actions. Such diplomacy does not necessarily imply intentional lies. It merely indicates that an appropriate vocabulary of motives will be utilized—that they are conditions for certain lines of conduct. (Mills 1940: 907)

In this passage Mills refers not to affairs of state, for as terministic screens are essential to human affairs, so vocabularies of motives are fundamental to the diplomacy of everyday life. That "diplomacy controls the diplomat" suggests that there is a continuity between the motivation of everyday life and what the theorists we encountered in the preceding chapter referred to as the terror of the text, the terror of play, fatal logic, or swallowing of the charismatic figure by the myth-dream. The "charisma" of everyday life differs from that of a Charismatic movement primarily in the tightness of articulation between the vocabulary of motives and the system of performance in which those motives are circulated, such that motives are more easily not only strategies for action but also instigations to action.

The following definitions of terms that comprise the Charismatic vocabulary of motives are based on their use in the performance of ritual genres.[16] The categories I have imposed on them for purposes of analysis reflect the manner in which the motives shape and give content to the ideal relationships embedded in the system of genres, and thus how they orient action among participants. These categories include (1) forms of relationship among individuals or between individuals and God; (2) forms of collectivity or collective identity; (3) qualities or properties of individuals or relationships; (4) activities or forms of action essential to life within the movement; and (5) negativities or countermotives that refer to threats to the ideal constituted by the totality of positive motives.

FORMS OF RELATION

Authority—Stems from God's absolute authority. Group leaders have authority over members, and all Christians can invoke God's authority over Satan.

Word—Divine message, power, the Savior: "In the beginning was the Word." The Word is manifest especially in Scripture and in the utterances of prophecy.

Covenant—Solemn agreement between God and humans and among humans themselves in the founding of a community. "Covenant" also refers to the written document stating the terms of such an agreement among humans.

Gift—Charism or ability given by God for service to the community of believers. The "gifts of the Spirit" are enumerated in Saint Paul's epistles.

Promise—God promises salvation and healing to his followers.

Presence—God is in the world and can be concretely experienced as present. The term has a connotation of the Incarnation of God as man.

Sonship/brotherhood—God is a father god. All humans are his sons, as Jesus is his son. Therefore, all humans must treat one another as brothers. (In some quarters of the movement, women are explicitly included as "brothers" in this sense.)

FORMS OF COLLECTIVITY

Community—Ideal form of Christian collectivity, based on the intimacy of a life in common, guided by Christian principles; the term has connotations of the Mystical Body in Christ.

People—Christians, or a Christian community, conceived as a nation in analogy to biblical Israel.

Army—Christians engaged in struggle against the Devil and the world, in an effort to save and protect the Church, form an army of Christ.

Kingdom—The reign of God is destined to become universal. Christians are already living in his Kingdom.

QUALITIES

Lordship—Possessed by God in his attribute of Supreme Being with dominion over all creation.

Light—Enables one to see the truth clearly and follow without faltering.

Heart—Capacity for feeling, and for experiencing spiritual truth.

Head—Capacity for rational and analytic thought, sometimes interfering with the spiritual purpose of Heart.

Power—Efficacy of the Holy Spirit that can be felt either physically, in the utterance of ritual language, or in the events of everyday life.

Expectant faith—Belief that things will go according to God's plan and that God's power will manifest itself in Charismatic gifts (especially healing).

God's plan—An attribute to the mind of God that represents the destiny of the world and humanity. It is progressively revealed to believers, and they must participate in bringing it to fruition.

Love/peace/joy—Affective states that are essential "fruits of the Spirit" as listed in Saint Paul's epistles. Love can also be understood as an activity, bearing the connotation of "charity."

Maturity—Closeness to God as a result of "spiritual growth." Maturity is characterized by prayer, discernment, and sound relationships.

Freedom—From the Devil, for service to the community of believers, and to love others and praise God.

Order—The discipline necessary to promote growth, build the Kingdom, and protect against Satan's chaos.

ACTIVITIES

Service—Every Christian must take an active part in building the Christian community.

Praise—The ultimate form of prayer to an all-worthy God, and a natural response to the experience of Baptism in the Holy Spirit.

Spiritual warfare—Christians must ceaselessly combat the work of Satan until his ultimate and inevitable defeat.

Growth—The process of becoming closer to God, initiated for many at the moment of being baptized in the Holy Spirit.

Healing—The intervention by God in human affairs to correct illness, whether its cause is physical, spiritual, emotional, or demonic.

Renewal—The process of change and revitalization brought about by Catholic Pentecostalism, both in individuals and in the Church as a whole.

Commitment—The act by which one affirms one's status as a Christian, or one's membership in a Christian community.

Submission—The proper attitude to authority, also a synonym for "yielding" in that one submits or yields to gifts (i.e., accepts gifts) given by God.

Obedience—The proper response to the commands of God and those he places in authority.

NEGATIVITIES

World—Primary source of distraction from God's work. The materialism of the world is opposed to the spirituality of the Kingdom. Everyday cares and pleasures, as well as sinful pleasures, can be said to be "of the world."

Flesh—Primary source of sexual temptation and sin.

Devil—Evil spirit who is the primary source of subversion and active opposition to God's plan.

Darkness—Negative quality including blindness to truth, corruption, and loss of direction in life or in spiritual growth.

Motives play a distinctive role in Catholic Charismatic ritual performance. Across ritual events, discrete acts of utterance constantly circulate motives through the genres, whether as the topic for a teaching, as the theme of a prayer meeting, as constituent elements in a prophecy, or even as the subject of dance. In this way the vocabulary of motives constitutes the concrete basis for a specific kind of intertextuality within and across genres. We can best understand this by invoking Rappaport's (1979) observation that ritual performance communicates two kinds of messages to participants. The first are messages invariantly encoded in the ritual canon that correspond to enduring aspects of the social and cosmological order. The second are messages carried by variations in the performance that index current states of participants in relation to the invariant order encoded by the canon. Although Rappaport is concerned primarily with fixed, invariant rituals of a liturgical order, the distinction is quite relevant to Charismatic ritual communication and has its locus precisely in the vocabulary of motives.

To be precise, the Charismatic motives are terms common in many other Christian forms of religious discourse, derived directly from and referring directly to the Scriptures (see Burke 1970). Thus, on the one hand, the vocabulary of motives constitutes the Charismatic canonical language. On the other hand, as the motives are circulated in performance each genre endows them with a characteristic rhetorical function, indexical in that it addresses and reflects the immediate state of participants. Specifically, in prophecy motives are promulgated; for example, "My people, you are part of my *plan*." In prayer they are invoked; for example, "Lord, help me serve your purpose and your *plan*." In teaching they are expounded; for example, "It is part of God's *plan* that we should build strong Christian communities." In sharing they are negotiated; for example, "When I did that, I felt I was helping to bring about a small part of God's *plan*." Thus not only does performance circulate motives by formulating them into generically recognizable utterances. The key terms literally motivate the genres, giving them the specificity to redirect attention and instigate to action. Furthermore, through performance the motives are metaphorically predicated onto selves (Fernandez 1974). We have seen this process in the naming of communities, and it also occurs in deliverance from evil spirits, the names of which are derived from the vocabulary of motives (cf. Csordas 1987, 1994a).

Thus participants are persuaded to orient their attention to the world, and action in the world, in the direction indicated by the motives. Performance keeps the motives constantly in the purview of participants, so that they eventually come to be taken for granted as the standard vocabulary in terms of which people should interact. Moreover, the circulation of motives helps prevent them from becoming semantically static. As ideal forms of relation, collectivity, and so on, they undergo a shift and specialization in meaning as they are circulated by performance in the changing context of group life.[17] In this way, circulation of motives is the rhetorical condition for the radicalization of charisma and ritualization of practice we found in the evolving notions of covenant and commitment in The Word of God/Sword of the Spirit. In the next chapter we will see how, given the right conditions, the circulation accelerates into the processes of rhetorical involution.

Conclusion

In an important chapter on religious speaking and hearing among Catholic Charismatics, McGuire (1982) observes that insofar as ritual language is regarded as having a divine source (as an inspiration or spiritual gift), its performance alters the relationship of the speaker to his utterance by altering the sense of responsibility for what is said, the sense of freedom/spontaneity with which it is said, and the sense of its authoritativeness and expected consequences for others. Ritual performance also alters the hearing of language, both insofar as "hearers focus on the expressive intent of the speech, and actively impose metaphorical, allusory, and poetic expectations on the content" (McGuire 1982: 123) and insofar as ritual performance invites its own confirmation and validation by asserting its divine origin. These observations are not unlike those made by anthropologists studying ritual language across a wide range of cultural settings (see references in note 1 of this chapter). For our purposes the changed relationship to language on the part of both speakers and hearers can be conceptualized as an interpretive gap or rhetorical space among participants, and it is precisely on this interactive space that I would identify the locus of charisma. However, McGuire's discussion is restricted to the social setting of the prayer meeting, where she sees religious language as creating a Schutzian "alternate reality" distinct from that of everyday life. Essential to the present argument is that the performance of ritual genres and its transformative effects transcend the boundaries of ritual events like the prayer meeting, bleeding over into the sphere of everyday life and contributing to the transformation of habitus described in earlier chapters.

The discussion of religious experience among Catholic Charismatics by Neitz (1987) captures this everyday transformative dimension of ritual language. She describes rich imagery experiences in prayer, special signs in the form of visions, transformative moments, and talking with God as part of the "personal relationship with the Lord" that is a trademark of Charismatic and born-again spirituality. Focusing not so much on the relationship between speakers and hearers as on the relationship between the individual and the deity, she observes, "Rather than one leader having the religious experience and then offering a tradition to followers, each person has the separate-in-space-and-time experience of the sacred, and then uses that to create a new way of being in the world" (1987: 118). Here again we are outside the Weberian conceptualization of charisma, but once again a rhetorical space opens up, this time between the human speaker and an interlocutor who is none other than the sacred other.

Charismatics are people whose daily thoughts about their world become framed in terms of a conversation with the Lord. Nearly all conscious thought seems to be considered a form of prayer. . . . In terms of everyday language the phrase "I thought about this" becomes "I prayed about this" or, even more likely, "I talked to the Lord about this." Prayer, as conversation with God, is the framework within which reflection in general takes place. Again these conversations, like the image of God who is seen as participating in them, are highly personalized. They clearly reflect the problems, the language and the general style of the individual involved. (Neitz 1987: 119–120)

Both in the ritual performance of prayer as a form of everyday conversation and in a quotidian readiness for prophetic inspiration, the divine interlocutor can communicate not only in the words of a "still, small voice" but also in vivid multisensory imagery, and in a way that invests incidental features of everyday events and surroundings with personal meaning. All these ways "the Lord speaks to me" are profoundly implicated in the Charismatic transformation of habitus because communication with the deity provides answers to concrete questions of everyday life. The answers to such questions are everywhere, and as people come to inhabit the Charismatic habitus, "eventually, almost any experience can be interpreted as bearing a message from the Lord" (Neitz 1987: 120).

The systematic relationship among genres and the consequent criss-crossing, weblike structure of ritual language as motives are circulated through everyday life and ritual events bring about a transformation of linguistic habitus continuous with and thoroughly integrated into the transformations of habitus with respect to space and time that were described in chapter 2. As William Hanks has observed in a study of traditional Maya discourse, "genres become part of the organization of habitus. They are the relatively lasting, transposable resources according to which linguistic practice is constituted. At the same time, they are produced in the course of linguistic practice and subject to innovation, manipulation, and change" (1987: 677). However, this statement can be taken to preserve a distinction between everyday speech and more or less formal genres of performance. We must also consider the issue raised earlier regarding degree of performance, recognizing that there is a gradual shading between everyday speech and speech marked as performance. Certainly the genre of sharing shades off into everyday conversation, and it can be said that the more it does so, the greater is the transformation of linguistic habitus. Minor genres such as pastoral slang and maxims can be characterized by minimal degrees of performance insofar as they are incorporated into everyday speech in a taken-for-granted way. In this same light we must recall the rules introduced to regulate informal speech itself, such as those prohibiting "speaking against" others discussed in chapter 4 as part of the ritualization of personal conduct in The Word of God. Again, we must acknowledge those subtle subgeneric speech habits or characteristic turns of phrase sifted from ethnographic observation. An example is reference to "what usually happens" in contrast to "what we usually do" as a subtle celebration of spontaneity over agency or intention (see the anecdote about Martin and Clark in chapter 5). Another is the expression "to speak into" or to intervene by means of speech, as in the following remark regarding adult imposition of community authority on children: "Look, if you're not gonna get to know these kids, we've got no right to speak into their life the way we do." Finally with respect to transformation of linguistic habitus are hard-to-document sublinguistic speech dispositions such as what often appeared to me as a certain style of clearing one's throat characteristic of covenant community members.

Viewed across the entire performative apparatus, this transformative process can be summarized as a kind of triple dialectic. Corresponding to the understanding of performance as event, genre, and act, each component of this dialectic is embedded in one more comprehensive in scope. At the most general level, we can understand the organization of the movement and its distinctive habitus to have evolved in a dialectic with the system of ritual performance. The result of this dialectic between performance events and nonritual interaction is the progressive blending of the two that I have described as the ritualization of practice. The performative "transformation of context" (Kapferer 1979a) in this case transforms the very boundary between ritual event and everyday life. Within the system of ritual language, a second dialectic takes place between genres and motives. It guarantees the circulation of motives in performance such that they do not remain static, but remain attuned to the exigencies of daily life. As we have seen, the potentialities of the sacred self are immanent in the structure of this dialectic: the system of major genres constitutes an ideal template for social relations, while the vocabulary of motives orients and shapes social action. Finally, on the level of discrete acts, a third dialectic can be identified, this time between motives and the metaphors generated from them. In the following chapter, we will examine how this dialectic is played out in the performance of Charismatic prophecy.

7

Prophetic Utterance and Sacred Reality

I think a lot of times people would voice their opinions through prophecy, and it was their own beliefs and they were just saying it was prophecy and that was their way of . . . see, the thing was, I remember sitting at the prayer meetings and watching the people go down to the microphone if they wanted to speak, and they would tell the people sitting down front what they wanted to say, and those people would tell them if it was relevant or not. And if it wasn't, they'd be sent back to their seats, and that also struck me as kinda strange. Maybe these people have an opinion to voice, and it's a very strong opinion, and they're doing that through calling it a prophecy, and since it's not an opinion that these people wanted to hear, they basically rejected it and said go away because we don't want these people to hear this viewpoint.

—Man, age 22

Often prophecy is not foretelling the future as much as speaking about the person's identity in Christ, now. Which is kind of an immediate entering of the kingdom of God to the person. It's a sort of immediacy of God speaking to the person. It's not like an actor on the stage where an actor speaks in God's name. There's usually a spiritual sense about it. When you hear a prophecy you're really hearing something of God addressing you. It's not just this person. An example might be, you're listening to a sermon or a talk and you think, wow, that was a little deeper than usual, that really touched me, somehow you connected with God. Prophecy does that if it's real prophecy.

—Man, late forties

The Old Testament prophecy that's recorded in the Scripture is of a different nature or . . . not nature, but a different weight, or something, than what we experience or what we see among Christians today. On a couple of counts. One is, those that were preserved over time were those that had the stamp of God's spirit clearly enough on them, registered strongly enough with God's people, to be preserved through the ages, that Christians would say, "Yeah, those are true, we can be confident that that's really God's word." And also they have something of a universal application. Often they're predictive. The prophecy that we get now doesn't carry that same weight. That is, I wouldn't make a claim for any of it that it's 100 percent true, that we got it just right. It hasn't stood the test of hundreds of years, or thousands of years of confirmation by God's people. So instead what God is giving is encouragement, direction, that's much more temporal, much more immediate, and which, because we're pretty fallible human beings, is mixed.

—Man, late thirties

I know girls who made up prophecies. I know girls who made up prayers that they would pray out loud. Girls who would stand up and fake praying in tongues. And this one girl—this is really funny—she stood up and prayed in tongues and this other girl stood up and translated it, and the first girl was speaking jargon and the second girl was just making it up! It's just like, it was totally . . . we look back on that and go, I can't believe I did that, but that was what was expected, so we came through. And it got to the point where now, today, if God hit me with a sledgehammer I would wonder who dropped it. You really don't know when God's speaking to you and when he's not. Bolts of lightning, please! A roll of thunder! [laughs]

—Girl, age 16

Prophecy occupies a pivotal position in Charismatic ritual language, and to more fully understand performance as a collective self process we must deepen our analysis of this mode of inspired speech.[1] So far I have defined its formal properties and rules of use and determined its place in the system of ritual genres. In this chapter I will carry out two parallel analyses of prophecy's effect on self and habitus. First, at the level of act and motive in performance, I will examine a series of prophetic utterances to demonstrate the rhetorical conditions under which it is performed and recognized as authoritative, transformative discourse. This will include analysis of formal features of utterance, including reported speech, verb use, and pronoun use, as well as of the particular role of the vocabulary of motives and the manner in which motives are transformed and elaborated through metaphorical extension in performance. Second, we will examine Charismatics' experience of prophetic inspiration as well as that of being "spoken to" by prophecy. The discussion will include the manner in which prophecy emerges into consciousness as speech or sensory imagery, issues of responsibility, intentionality, and control of prophetic utterance, experience of the sacred, and the consequence for understanding prophecy of the manner in which speech is grounded in bodily experience and the habitus. This dual approach resumes the theoretical project of my earlier book (Csordas 1994a; see also Csordas 1994b) to reconcile semiotic and phenomenological understandings of culture, juxtaposing rhetorical analysis in terms of textuality with existential analysis in terms of embodiment.

Before entering these analyses, however, I want to outline what is at stake in prophecy from the standpoint of participants by commenting on the four epigraphs that begin this chapter. All are from members of The Word of God/Sword of the Spirit shortly after the community schism in the early 1990s. Together they offer a perspective on prophecy with respect to a series of closely interrelated issues: social control in the group as a whole, the listener's experience of the sacred, the divine authority of prophetic utterance, and the authenticity of the speaker's inspiration.

The first quote must be understood in light of the development of specialized word gifts groups the members of which were not only recognized as regularly gifted with the charisma of prophecy but who along with community coordinators also came to serve as gatekeepers who screened the occasional prophecies of the rank and file in large gatherings. Word gifts groups are not unique to covenant communities; some of the larger prayer groups have prophecy ministries, and in the late 1980s there was a transparochial word gifts group in the archdiocese of Boston. Such groups are based not only on an implicit distinction between people with occasional and enduring gifts of prophecy but also on the inclusive notion that prophetic inspiration will be more accurate and comprehensive if people "listen together to what the Lord is saying to us." The result in a community such as The Word of God was that those with occasional gifts of individual inspiration became subject to discipline by those with enduring gifts supported by group consensus. Although prophetic themes that guided the course of collective life continued to be experienced as spontaneous within the elite, within the rank and file they came to be experienced as dogmatically predetermined. The issue embedded in the young man's commentary is that of how strong an opinion or conviction must be before it can legitimately be cast as an authoritative utterance in the genre or prophecy. In sociological terms, this is the issue of how "delegated power" (Bourdieu 1991) to speak in authorized language is guaranteed; in linguistic terms it is the issue of whether the first-person pronoun, the "I of discourse" (Urban 1989), is the human or the deity. Critically at stake is the way the social control of prophecy went hand in hand with prophecy as social control.

Prophecy is also the linchpin between social authority and immediate experiential access to the deity. The second epigraph emphasizes immediacy of divine presence (the kingdom of God within) and connectedness with the deity from the perspective of a person listening to prophecy. Reference to the "person's identity in Christ" highlights the importance of prophecy as an orientational self process, albeit one in which the self cannot be understood in isolation from the collectivity. This stance notably introduces an element of intimacy with the deity that is not a conversational intimacy as in prayer but an experience of the sacred the vitality of which maximizes the authoritativeness of the utterance. At the same time it minimizes the agency of the prophet (who is only a mouthpiece and not "an actor who speaks out in God's name") and thereby preserves the listener's experience as the criterion for validating what counts as "real" prophecy.

The third quote emphasizes the connection between prophecy and scripture while taking care to avoid a potentially heretical equation of the two. Indeed, one of the consequences of experiencing prophecy as sacred in a scripturally based religion such as the Charismatic Renewal is that in some places it has come to occupy a pivotal position between oral and written genres. The logic would appear to be that prophecy is a direct experience of God insofar as god is his Word; and if prophecy is the holy word of God it should be preserved. Thus in some communities prophecies are tape recorded and transcribed. They may be archived and studied by coordinators to get a sense of the pattern of the divine plan over time, or the most recent prophecies may be circulated by inclusion in a group newsletter. Thus it would be inaccurate to hear prophecy merely as the authoritative reiteration of canonical language. Its indexical features—as communication about the current state of participants in ritual life—are evident in the process of both entextualization (Bauman and Briggs 1990) into generic form in oral performance and inscription into canonical form as written texts. Transcription decontextualizes only in the limited sense of abstracting the utterance from the circumscribed ritual event, for both in its performance and in its inscription prophecy is grafted onto the roots of sacred scripture, and ramifies like running sap through the branches constituted by the multiple events and situations of collective life.

The fourth quote is the bemused but sincere reflection of an adolescent on the implications of intentionally inauthentic ritual speech. She describes her classmates at the community school faking the complex dyadic interaction of prophecy in tongues and its interpretation, which in theory requires independent but coordinated inspirations in two separate individuals. One does not get the impression, however, that the girls were trying to pull the wool over anyone's eyes, but simply trying to "perform" to the expectations of their teachers. The error, to use a more phenomenological language, was their enactment of an intention to speak without the intentionality of taking up or engaging a divine project, and with a phenomenological horizon defined externally by expectation rather than internally by inspiration. The adolescent girl laments the weight of responsibility for discerning the authenticity of an inspiration perhaps as powerful as the blow of a sledgehammer but not as definitive as a bolt of lightning, precisely at an age when North American culture problematizes her own authenticity as an autonomous self. Her dilemma: there is a god, and god speaks, but how do I know if he's speaking to me?

The Bulwark Prophecies

We are due at this point for an extended examination of actual prophetic utterance, using examples recognized as authoritative and consequential. Much of Charismatic prophecy is highly redundant, literally a circulation of motives as guides for action and indexes of the current state of participants. Less common are prophecies in which motives or metaphorical extensions of motives lead to innovative courses of action; and prophecies that are named, recognized, and alluded to in subsequent discourse are relatively unique. Earlier I discussed the importance of the Rome prophecies and their warning of hard times for God's people. The texts of those prophecies were widely circulated through *New Covenant* magazine, but in their wake came a less widely known series of prophecies that were critical to subsequent relations within and among covenant communities. Informally referred to as the "bulwark prophecies," the first two texts were uttered by experienced prophets at the 1975 conference convened to establish a federation of Charismatic communities. The third was spoken a little over a year later at the anniversary gathering of The Word of God. Having transcribed them in the late 1970s, and faced with a tendency to downplay the importance of the divine mouthpiece in prophecy, I was unable to determine the identities of the prophets. However, it is probably safe to assume that they were leading members of the word gifts group of The Word of God.

These prophecies constitute an exhortation and a call for unity in service to a collective goal of protecting the Church against the onslaught of evil in the world. They emphasize the difficulty of achieving this goal and enumerate a variety of possible pitfalls along the way. Adherents saw in them the articulation of a vision and a mission in which the alliance of covenant communities would serve as a protective bulwark for the endangered Church. As ritual performance that is at the same time a manifestation of the sacred, however, I suggest that the utterance of these prophecies achieved more than this. In an experientially real sense, it *created* the bulwark as an enduring objectification of the collective self. In examining the process of this creation in the bulwark prophecies, we will find ourselves at the performative locus of charisma as a rhetorical self process.[2]

SUMMER 1975: PROPHECY 1

This gathering is a great hope   1
This meeting is both a hope and a promise.
I am raising up courageous, strong, gifted men and women who
    will join themselves to you.
As you hold fast to one another others will come and be
    joined to you.
Together you will labor with me to stem the tide of evil   5
    that is sweeping the earth.
I have brought you together for this purpose; go on with
    confidence, courage, and determination.

I will be with you, and in the days to come I will raise up
   men in communities
Who will bind themselves fast to you in my service.
Let yourselves be joined together;
Hold on to one another in faith and hope and see what I will   10
   do.

SUMMER 1975: PROPHECY 2

I am doing a new work of unity;
I am stirring you up to new dedication and new zeal in my
   service.
Those of you who have never seen one another will be drawn
   into unity
As you recognize your common bond of commitment to me and to
   my purpose.
I will stir you up;   15
I will rally you to new effectiveness in my service:
For I am forming a people to proclaim my Word anew.
The day is at hand when my Word will be proclaimed with
   new power.
When those who have never heard it before,
Whose ears have been closed, will begin to hear.   20
I have brought you here to the beginning of something very
   important in my Church;
I have brought you together here to join you together
And to give you a vision of what is to come:
I will make you a bulwark to defend against the onslaught
   of the Enemy.
Those of you who are not prepared,   25
Those of you who are not ready,
I will not have them swept away because they are not
   ready;
But I will protect them behind the bulwark that I form out
   of you.
I want you to be ready to join yourselves with others
And to stand together with them in the battle against the   30
   onslaught that's coming:
To defend the weak
And to defend those who are confused;
To protect those who are not prepared
Until I am able to fulfil my entire plan.
I tell you, you are a part and not the whole;   35
You are a part and not the whole.
There are many other things I am doing in this world today
And there are many other ways that I am at work to raise
   up my people in strength and in glory.

I want you, though, to take your part seriously,
And to lay your lives down for it.   40
But I want you to understand that only I see the entire
   plan;
Only I see every front of the battle.
I will raise you up with others,
And bind you together to make a bulwark.
But that is not all there is to be, because when you have   45
   stemmed the onslaught of the Enemy
Then I will reveal to you greater things.
In the unity you have with one another there is a
   prefigurement and foreshadowing of something much
   greater that I intend to do;
Something greater, much more vast, much more glorious I
   will unveil at that time.
You are a foreshadowing and a prefigurement
You are a bulwark I have set up to stem the onslaught of   50
   the Enemy.
You are a part and not the whole;
You are my servants and my people.
Lay down your lives now for the things I have revealed to
   you;
Commit yourselves to them, so that in the day of battle you can
   stand fast and prove victorious with me.

NOVEMBER 21, 1976: PROPHECY 3

I have spoken to you of a bulwark;   55
I have told you that I am raising a bulwark against the
   coming tide of darkness,
A bulwark to protect my people
And protect my Church.
And because your mind of man cannot comprehend the mind of
   God,
I've spoken to you in figures.   60
You might envision the bulwark as a wall of rock:
I speak to you now of that bulwark in the figure of an
   impenetrable hedge.
Yes, I have scattered my seed of truth widely across the
   surface of the earth;
And some of that seed has sprouted and begun to grow into
   the impenetrable hedge that will be my bulwark.
Yes, see how just four seeds have landed in your midst and   65
   sprung up;
And other seeds have been carried by the wind of my Spirit,
Other seeds have been windbroke at that first sprouting of
   the hedge,

And there they too have germinated and taken root and grown
    up,
And the hedge has grown,
And more seeds have been brought to it by the wind of my   70
    Spirit.
It continues to flourish, to rise in strength;
And I prune it vigorously.
Yet look about and see that other seeds have germinated away
    from the hedge;
They stand by themselves—they grow unpruned.
I say to you, you are the bulwark   75
You are the hedge,
And you are to see that the bulwark grows in strength:
You are to go to those outlying sprouts and call them in.
It is for you to see that they receive my Word, that they
    are gently uprooted and transplanted,
That they too may flourish and add strength to my bulwark   80
    that I am raising up.
And you are to be open to sending parts of that hedge out,
To seeing it transplanted to extend the bulwark across the
    face of the earth.
But are you ready;
Are you ready to believe in your hearts that you are that
    bulwark?
Do you have the conviction   85
Do you have the courage
To say to the world
To say to others,
"We are that bulwark,
We are God's work: Come stand with us"?   90
I tell you this,
That unless you have come to me
And become utterly destitute,
You will not have the courage to speak that truth.
If you say, "I am God's plan, we are God's bulwark"   95
And you cling to anything from the world,
You will not speak the truth, you cannot be believed.
You cannot be believed unless you are utterly destitute.
If you say to me,
"I have received your truth,"   100
And yet you have protected a corner of your heart to cling
    to the things of the world,
I cannot believe you.
If you say to yourself,
"I believe God's Word,"
And yet you treasure things of the world,   105

You cannot believe yourselves.
If you say to the world,
"We are God's bulwark, we know God's truth, we are God's
     plan for man,"
And the world sees that you treasure things that belong to
     them,
They will not believe you.   110
Only if you are utterly destitute,
Only if you give up all that you have
And come to me with empty hands,
Can you be believed.
The truth is too great, the truth is too profound   115
To be compromised by any attachment to things of this world.
Yes, you are free to receive from me a great abundance,
But you are not free to take it for your own purposes;
You can receive from me riches and power, lands and cities,
But you cannot use them for your own pleasure.   120
All that you have must be turned to my service,
And when you speak my word of truth
The world will be convicted,
And the world will believe.
Know this,   125
That no one who has given all to me,
No one who has entrusted himself completely to me,
Has ever perished.
Those who give themselves to me
Are they who endure and taste everlasting victory.   130

The best place to begin to understand the performance of prophecy
as a rhetorical self process in a semiotic/linguistic sense is with pronouns. Pronouns are simultaneously rhetorical and indexical, asserting both a claim about relationships and demonstrating those relationships in speech. Thus they may also belong to both the illocutionary
and predicative frames. The classic paper by Roger Brown and A. Gilman (1960) showed how the use of formal and familiar pronouns of
address determines relations of "power and solidarity." More recently,
Singer (1984, 1989) has elaborated Peirce's the pronominal "I-It-
Thou" triad in a semiotics of self. In the present instance, the "I" of
Charismatic prophecy must be considered both in its pragmatic relation to the person who utters the prophecy (an I-I relation) and in its
discourse-internal relation to the audience addressed by the prophecy
(an I-you relation).

What is at stake in the I-I relation is the authoritativeness of the speech and its self-evidence, as well as the nature of responsibility and control over that speech by the speaker. Two authors have recently proposed schemes by means of which linguistic analysis can identify a continuum of possible relations of speaker to speech in this sense. The continuum outlined by Greg Urban (1989: 43) refers specifically to the first-person pronoun and runs from everyday speech in which the "I" indexes an everyday self to speech characteristic of trance in which the I "projects" a nonordinary self. The continuum outlined by John Du Bois (1986: 328) refers to degree of speaker control and runs from sovereign speech ultimately controlled by the ego to speech in trance and beyond ego control. Both emphasize increasing reliance on formal features and contextual metapragmatic cues to distinguish stages of distance from everyday self or sovereign ego. The linchpin of both systems, however, is the role of indirect speech, or "reported speech" in the sense derived from Valentin Voloshinov (1986) and taken up in much current linguistic anthropology (Lucy 1993; Hill and Irvine 1993). In addition, Urban develops his analysis as an elaboration of Emile Benveniste (1971) and Milton Singer (1984) on personal pronouns. Thus the "I" of everyday speech is "indexical referential" in that its reference is not fixed but indexes or points to whoever the speaker might be in a particular situation. The "I" of direct quotation actually refers to a third person, but as speech moves along the continuum toward mimicry or the role-playing of theater the speaking first person (in Du Bois's terms the proximate speaker who produces the utterance) disappears, leaving an "I" in the form of an alter ego (the prime speaker to whom the speech is attributed) that can ultimately, in trance behavior, take on the autonomous character of an ancestor or a deity.[3]

The critical difference between the two accounts is that for Du Bois the end of the continuum with the least ego control suggests the possibility of apersonal, intentionless speech, while for Urban the continuum is folded back on itself in a way that suggests the possibility of a dual "I." We will take up this issue in greater detail both with respect to its theoretical implications and to its efficacy as a rhetorical self process when we treat the subjective conditions under which prophecy is produced and heard. For the present it is enough to emphasize that the "I" of prophecy is subjectively and formally distinguished from the indexical referential self of the proximate speaker but that *within the text* it functions as an indexical referential self in its own right, that is, as God.

Thus, to begin with, Charismatic prophecy is typically not reported speech. Whereas reported speech is quoted or paraphrased from what has previously been said, by definition prophecy is the deity speaking directly through the prophet in the present moment. Certainly in some instances the formal and archaic (and more typically Protestant) opening is "Thus saith the Lord . . . ," but in use this appears more to signal a change in present speaker than a report of another's (the deity's) previous speech. In addition, the formula is a form of emphasis, with a performative force equivalent to "I tell you . . ." (line 35), "I say to you . . ." (line 75), "I tell you this . . ." (line 91), and "Know this . . ." (line 125). We should note that in informal and more intimate settings the divine speaker may be paraphrased colloquially as in "I really feel the Lord wants you to know that . . . ," but here too it is also common for the deity to speak directly in the first person rather than through reported speech. Much more typical as an opening in group settings is a term of direct address, such as "My children," or "My people." In the bulwark prophecies even this formality is dispensed with, and God begins to speak straightaway in his own voice.

Furthermore, given the strength of the performative convention that the deity may speak continuously regardless of his mouthpiece, there is no opening formula in the second bulwark prophecy. Indeed the convention is so powerful that the first word of the second utterance is the pronoun "I," with no apparent need to preface this with any specification that the "I" is God and not the proximate human speaker. This tightly articulated transition merges the predicative and illocutionary frames, predicating intimacy between speakers insofar as they are participating in the same inspiration and bearing the force of authority insofar as it is recognized that the deity can choose his mouthpieces at will. Moreover, it is a concrete embodiment of the point (made explicitly in the third prophecy) that the divine plan is larger than any individual or even any community—"you are a part and not the whole" (lines 36, 51). The performative result is the virtual absence of an "intertextual gap" (Briggs and Bauman 1992) between the first and second utterance.

The only significant reported speech in these texts occurs in lines 55–60, and quite remarkably this passage consists of the deity reporting his own previous speech ("I have spoken to you . . . ," "I have told you . . . ," "I've spoken to you . . . "). Much more than a simple reminder, this is once again a rhetorical strategy for reducing the intertextual gap between utterances separated in time by more than a year. Thus following these prefatory remarks the very next line shifts into the present with "I speak to you now . . ." (line 62). These strategies of intertextuality that render prophecy independent of individual speakers and continuous across time are critical contributions to its authority. Taken together with the circulation of motives identified in the last chapter as another strategy of intertextuality (and that I will illustrate as our analysis of the bulwark prophecies continues) and the strategy of inscription in which prophecies are transcribed and kept as a community archive, these oral performative strategies implicitly seek to minimize the intertextual gaps between prophecy and sacred scripture. If scripture is the word of God, prophecy is its direct extension in the present—the living word of God among his people.

Another strategy of pronoun use occurs in the form of what we can call hypothetical reported speech in lines 89–90, 95, 100, 104, and 108 (e.g., line 95, "If you say, 'I am God's plan, we are God's bulwark'"). In these instances the divine speaker formulates possible articulations of collective identity that might be made by those listening to the prophecy. In a curiously hyperreflexive way, the "I" in these lines could be the indexical referential "I" of the prophet as well as that of any other participant, here as it were twice removed by being embedded as a hypothetical in divine speech, which is in turn embedded in the utterance of the prophet. What is particularly striking is that these hypotheticals are the only places in which the first-person plural "we" occurs—only four times in 130 lines, *and only within quotes* to instruct community members how they should articulate the relationships among themselves (lines 89, 90, 95, 108). Thus the "we"—the pronoun of intimacy—indexes participants' collective identity but not the relation between the divine speaker and the assembled audience. That this usage is not only indexical but also bears rhetorical force is brought home by the avoidance of "we" even where its use might be presumed obvious: in line 5, when God says "Together you will labor with me" instead of "Together we will labor." In sharp contrast, a relation of authority is asserted by the occurrence in twenty-two lines of the sequence I/you and in eleven lines of the inverse sequence you/I-me-my. The former sequence typically frames a statement of what God will do with or for his followers, while the latter frames a statement of reciprocal commitment and obligation to the divinity and his plan. The separation of divinity and humanity is further emphasized by the occurrence of pronouns of address (you-your-yourselves) alone in thirty-six lines and of pronouns of self-reference (I-me-my) alone in sixteen lines. The survey of pronoun use is rounded out by noting the occurrence in ten lines of them–they and in nine lines of who–whose–those who. The third-person pronouns refer either to people in the "world" opposed to the divine plan or to Christians outside the community who are threatened by the "world" and therefore must be protected from it. Their rhetorical function is therefore to serve as foils or coordinates against which the intimate "we" of the community can define its own identity.

Although there remains the possibility in other contexts of an intimate I-Thou "personal relationship with the Lord," this analysis shows the force of pronominal usage in constituting prophecy as an utterance affirming the authoritative dimension of an "I-you" human relation with the divine. There are several ways in which the absence of the pronoun of intimacy contributes to this end. Intimacy characterizes the "we" of the human community, and reciprocity among humans may be oriented by the egalitarian motive of "brotherhood," but in prophecy the relation between human and divine is oriented by the hierarchical motive of "Lordship." Thus in a rhetorical sense the pronominal separation between human and divine circumscribes the kind of self that ultimately gives and entrusts itself entirely to the deity (lines 126–130). That self does not in the process "merge" with the deity and thereby lose itself but "commits" a discrete self that thereby becomes a sacred one. In a pragmatic sense, to use the pronoun "we" is to speak on behalf of a group, and in so doing would compromise the sovereign nature and authority of the utterance (see also Duranti 1993a: 38). Finally, in a metapragmatic sense, too liberal use of "we" could compromise the carefully crafted separation of subjectivities between the proximate human speaker and the prime divine speaker, potentially leading to attributions of authorship to the prophet and God or the prophet with God's endorsement (i.e., we = God and I; see the first epigraph to this chapter).

I turn now to the role played by the vocabulary of motives in structuring ritual discourse in these texts. The repeated use of these motives and repeated judgments about the appropriateness of their use ensure that prophetic utterance expresses a consistent attitude toward the social world. Their prominence in the texts is evident, and I will only briefly list them in order of the frequency of their occurrence: world (9), word (5), service (5), people (4), plan (4), enemy (3), darkness/ evil (2), commitment (2), power (2), battle (2), promise (1), freedom (1). Once again, this terminological domain contributes to both the illocutionary and predicative frames of ritual language. First, motives reinforce the illocutionary effect by serving as aids in composition. Such elementary constituents of verbal formulas are, as Albert Lord (1960) has shown, an essential part of the linguistic repertoire of individuals fluent in spontaneous oral composition. Command of the vocabulary of motives and the ability to generate poetic formulas from them not only help a speaker utter prophecies that are likely to be "discerned" as appropriate. They also abet the spontaneity of composition, experienced by speakers and hearers as inspiration from a source outside the individual and as a manifestation of divine power. Second, motives guide the predication of qualities both in the manner in which they are elaborated and in that they suggest or "motivate" appropriate metaphors. Describing this process will lead us to the heart of the problem of creativity in ritual language.[4]

I have identified the divine "promise" as one of the key motives of Charismatic discourse, and although it appears only once at the beginning of the bulwark prophecies it will be valuable to trace its elaboration in the texts. It is also of interest because for speech act theory (Austin 1975; Searle 1969, 1979), in which illocutionary force typically is found to inhere in "performative verbs" (i.e., those verbs by use of which "to *say* something is to *do* something" [Austin 1975: 12]), promising is the prototypical "commissive" illocution. I suggest that the use of "promise" (line 2) as a motive in its noun form in fact fuses the predicative and illocutionary frames. First, both hope and promise are predicated onto the meeting, lending a particular quality to what otherwise would be a typical case of a Charismatic ritual gathering. Second, I would argue that, while in formal linguistic terms the illocutionary act of promising is not performed ("I promise that . . ."), to consider the utterance in the illocutionary frame suggests that it does indeed have the force of a promise ("This meeting is a promise"), especially since the speaking subject is God.

We must pay close attention to the subsequent use of verb tense to define the force of what we might call this "commissive predication." Lines 3 through 8 specify the contents of the promise as what the divinity "will" do in the indeterminate future. Yet a sense of immediacy for fulfillment of the promise is added by use of the present progressive tense in line 3. Lines 9 and 10 use verbs in the imperative mode— let, hold on, see—to define the requirements of reciprocity and open-ended anticipation that count as adequate responses to the promise. In prophecy 2, lines 11 through 28 continue to elaborate the divine promise, again seasoning future tense articulations (lines 13, 15, 16, 18, 20, 24, 27, 28) with those in the present progressive (lines 11–12, 17) and present perfect (lines 21–22) tenses. Line 35 marks a shift from the commissive predication to a declaration, with a corresponding shift in lines 35 through 52 to a preponderance of present tense over future tense verbs and a shift in reference from God's promise to God's intention (line 47). This shift is accompanied by the same call to openended commitment that we heard in the prophecy giving The Word of God its name (chap. 4). Thus the command to "lay your lives down" (line 40) for a plan that only God sees in its entirety (lines 41–42) is accompanied by a further promise to "reveal to you even greater things" (lines 46–48). Line 49 can be read as a climactic transformation of line 2 in which the earlier predicated qualities of hope and promise become foreshadowing and prefigurement and in which the entity onto which they are predicated shifts from the "meeting" to the more personal and immediate "you" of collective identity. Finally, as in the first prophecy, the pattern is completed in lines 53 and 54 with a return to the imperative verbs "lay down" and "commit."

The same pattern is repeated in the third prophecy, only this time the contents of the promise are reiterated in the present perfect (lines 55–74), indicating that its fulfillment is already under way. The break comes with another performative in line 75—"I say to you . . ." It is critical once again to observe the subsequent verb usage (lines 75–79), which shows that this act combines the force of two kinds of illocution identified by Searle (1979): declaration ("you are . . .") and directive ("you are to . . ."). Completion of the form is initiated by another performative in line 91 with "I tell you this . . ." Lines 91 through 116 are not simple imperatives but introduce a series of if/then propositions that elaborate the conditions of reciprocity under which the divine promise will be fulfilled. Reciprocity—the promise and the response to that promise—remains constrained by hierarchy, however. This is shown in lines 117 through 124, where the limits of freedom to receive and use the divine gifts are spelled out. Yet freedom there is, for in the end the divine plan requires consent. The final illocutionary act of line 125, "Know this," combines the force of a directive and a declaration and is followed by a capsule statement specifying that to give and entrust the self to the deity corresponds to an ultimate promise of imperishability and everlasting victory.

That these prophecies conclude with such an emphasis should remind us of Rosaldo's analysis of the cultural implications of the promise as a prominent and even privileged speech act in Euro-American society.

To think of promising is, I would claim, to focus on the sincerity and integrity of the one who speaks. . . . It is a public testimony to commitments we sincerely undertake, born of a genuine human need to "contract" social bonds, an altruism that makes us want to publicize our plans. Thus the promise leads us to think of meaning as a thing derived from inner life. A world of promises appears as one where privacy, not community, is what gives rise to talk. (1982: 211)

For Rosaldo the possibility, and perhaps even the necessity, of the promise presumes a prior lack of connection among discrete, private selves that have inner lives characterized by capacities for orientation to the world such as sincerity and commitment. In contrast she posed the example of the Ilongots. For them the self is not at all an "inner" one, continuous through time, such that its actions can be judged in terms of sincerity, integrity, and commitment. "Because Ilongots do not see their inmost 'hearts' as constant causes, independent of their acts, they have no reason to 'commit' themselves to future deeds" (Rosaldo 1982: 218). Rosaldo is here distinguishing a self culturally constituted as constant and interiorized from one constituted in the consequences of acts for relationships in a community. We will shortly have occasion to warn against drawing such a distinction too sharply. Nevertheless, Rosaldo's observation helps refine our understanding of the rhetorical conditions under which the sacred self struggles to come into being. That is, as the condition of possibility for promise and commitment, the individuated self characteristic of both the deity and his followers is at the same time that which makes community problematic. We thus begin to understand the internal connection among motives such as promise, commitment, and community.

Having demonstrated the elaboration of a key motive in prophetic utterance, let us now consider the transformation of motive into metaphor. Recall that the setting for the first two prophecies was a conference convened to form an alliance among covenant communities. The perceived need for this alliance evolved through the elaboration of motives including community, commitment, and the negativities of world, flesh, and devil. Given its pivotal role in group life, and culminating with the words spoken at the Rome conference, prophecy was a principal medium for articulating these motives. In the utterances recorded here, the alliance was taken up into this body of discourse not in terms of motives as a "community of communities" but as a metaphorical "bulwark," the purpose of which is to stem the onslaught of evil and protect the Church. The establishment of the alliance as a sacred reality is achieved by the creation of the bulwark through performance of a complex illocution/predication by God, the ultimate speaker in prophetic utterance. We will examine the bulwark image in the illocutionary frame by returning to the use of verb tense, and in the predicative frame in its relation to motives, "inchoate pronouns" (Fernandez 1974), and to itself as it is transformed in discourse.

In line 24 the divine speaker first says, "I will make you a bulwark," and continues to describe the function of the bulwark in his plan. Again in lines 43–46 the deity states this promise/intention, adding that there will be more to come afterward. The critical act occurs in line 50: the tense changes to simple present, and God says, "You are a bulwark that I have set up." In Searle's (1979) terminology, the "commissive" act marked by the future tense is replaced by a "declaration" in the present tense. In the act of utterance the bulwark has been created, and this creation is rhetorically effected by a simple change in verb tense from future to present. There is yet more, however, for the tense immediately changes again to the present perfect "have set up." This enhances illocutionary force by, in Austin's (1975) terms, referring to the bulwark in a constative or simply descriptive mode, thus marking the creation of the bulwark as already a fait accompli.[5]

Cultural reality is not created once and for all, however; to be sustained, it must be continually re-created. Thus we find that more than a year later, in prophecy 3, the creative act is repeated. In line 56 it is stated "I have told you that I am raising a bulwark," but by line 75 this has become "I say to you, you are the bulwark." The temporal continuity between the prophecies is evident not only in the affirmation by repetition of the performative act but also in the difference in choice of verb tenses. The later prophecy acknowledges the prior creation of the bulwark by initiating the performative sequence with the present perfect (I am raising) rather than the future (I will raise). The illocutionary force of the act is emphasized by inclusion of the formula "I say to you . . . ," leaving no doubt that the utterance is declarative and not constative. Again, however, the temporal continuity of prophetic discourse suggests that the declaration is not only a re-creation of the bulwark. It maintains a locutionary or constative element insofar as it is a reminder of an act already performed, a description of an already extant state of affairs. It can also be construed to have the force of an assertive insofar as it can be read as taking for granted that God is in fact creating the bulwark and then asserting that the listeners "are that bulwark." In either case, once more the bulwark appears as a fait accompli.

From this analysis we can see that the efficacy of the bulwark metaphor is dependent on Frye's radical of presentation (see chap. 6) within conventions of prophecy as a genre. This radical of presentation is constituted by the use of performative speech acts, the force of which derives from their combination in performative sequences within each utterance *and* across a temporally continuous body of utterances. This sequence can be summarized as progressing from commissive to declarative to constative (assertive) speech acts. To the extent that prophetic utterance is heard as the definitive word of the deity and to the extent that the deity is omnipotent, the conditions for their effect on the audience are self-contained in the utterance: prophecy encodes what we might call a "presumptive perlocution" and therefore carries its own "guarantee" of performative felicity and predicative success.[6]

Let us be more precise regarding this claim about presumptive perlocution. Searle points out that in both commissive and directive utterances, which form the bulk of these texts, the relation of "world" and "word" is that the world "fits" the words: I promise things will be a certain way, and that state of affairs is expected to come to pass. On the other hand, the assertive/constative presupposes the inverse, that the words fit the world: such and such is the case, and I am saying so. As the middle term, a declarative act achieves its mediation by means of what Searle understands as a "very peculiar relation" between world and words that "the performance of a declaration brings about by its very successful performance" (1979: 18). To explain how this is possible he appeals to the necessity of an "extra-linguistic institution" that determines constitutive rules in addition to those of language, and within which the speaker and hearer must occupy specific places. Among Charismatics these conditions are met, respectively, in the constitutive rules that define prophecy as a genre and in the organization of the covenant community.

Searle carries us even further, however, in observing that the only two exceptions to the requirement that an extralinguistic institution underlie every declaration are declarations that concern language itself and "supernatural declarations. When, e.g., God says 'Let there be light' that is a declaration" (1979: 18). The remarkable state of affairs is that in this instance the constitution of the extralinguistic institution erases the requirement of its own existence as assurance of a declaration's efficacy. In our case, insofar as the declaration must be understood to be made by God even to count as prophecy, we can say there is a presumptive perlocution already embedded in the utterance.

Scholars such as Michelle Rosaldo (1975) and James Fernandez (1986, 1991) have observed that the performance of metaphors effects a qualitative transformation in participants, a movement either from one state to another or from formlessness and lack of identity to definiteness and specificity. I will take this argument a step further and show how metaphors can then themselves be cycled back into performance with fresh implications for the understanding of basic motives, creating the possibility for generations of still other metaphors. The circulation of motives is thus a self-sustaining dialectical process: motives generate metaphors, metaphors move people, people are reoriented by motives, motives generate new metaphors, and so on.

I would argue that this process has a transformative effect in part because metaphors such as that of the bulwark constitute a critical link between prophecy as an arbiter of social practice (intersubjectivity) and as an ongoing body of discourse (intertextuality). In the first instance, the metaphor supplies a concrete identity to an inchoate "we" that is in search of a new pattern of relationships motivated by religiously prescribed goals (see Fernandez 1974). Indeed, as we have seen, the texts give explicit instructions on how to use the pronoun "we." Second, the metaphor contributes to the temporal continuity and coherence of discourse as it is repeated in successive utterances and applied in new situations. This pivotal role of metaphor goes beyond the possibility for repetition of the constitutive act documented above, in which the bulwark is created and re-created in prophetic utterance. Once it has entered into ritual discourse, the metaphor can be transformed or amplified, as occurs in the third prophecy. In line 60 the deity specifically acknowledges speaking in figures, and the figure introduced to transform the bulwark is that of a hedge, as opposed to a wall of solid rock. The semantic transformation is from inorganic to organic, and from monolithic unity to the plural unity of intertwining shoots. This allows an amplification of meaning through the incorporation of aspects of group life into the web of sacred discourse. Thus, the "four seeds" from which the hedge has grown is simultaneously an allusion to the "good seed" of Matthew's gospel and to the four founders of the community, a doubling that not incidentally contributes to the mythologization of their role. The image of separate shoots intertwining to form the hedge is an idealization of interpersonal relationships among members of the community. The notion of "pruning" the hedge refers both to the loss of members who cannot maintain their commitment to the group and to the complex of self-discipline and group authority by means of which individuals are disburdened of their "worldly" attachments. Incorporating wayward shoots into the hedge refers to the necessity of recruiting new members, and transplanting parts of the hedge refers to the community's plan to send out small groups of members who would establish outposts in other localities.

This dialectic of motive and metaphor in performance is a locus for the radicalization of charisma and ritualization of practice documented above in Part Two. Let us make one final pass through the bulwark texts with an eye to how this dialectic in the performance of prophecy contributes to the dual processes of involution in Charismatic ritual life. Recall that I have already identified, in the earlier brief consideration of the prophecy by which The Word of God was named, a rhetoric of open-ended commitment that called listeners toward a phenomenological horizon where plans and actions that once seemed "crazy" became accepted and incorporated into collective life. Returning to the bulwark prophecies, we find a similar dynamic at work. The "hold on and see" at the end of the first prophecy (line 10) is not the deity teasing his people, or a sign that people do not know what to do next, but discourse awaiting inspiration and leaving its hearers expectantly on the edges of their seats. It is a formulaic elaboration of the ritual motive of the promise. The second prophecy begins (line 11) with the statement that something new is being done, describes that something, and promises that once it is accomplished something much more grand and glorious will be revealed (lines 46–48). Here is an elaboration of the ritual motive of a plan that invites hearers of the prophecy to "seek the will of the Lord" for ever-deeper, profound, and open-ended meanings and goals. The call to "lay down one's life for the Lord" (lines 40, 53) is a frequently occurring formula of Charismatic oral composition based on the motive of commitment. In the radicalization of charisma the formula's ambiguity has allowed it to remain unchanged—but not stable (see Bloch 1986)—as its meaning has expanded from the horizon of "commit your life" to that of "give up your life," and finally to the possibility of physical martyrdom promulgated in the Sword of the Spirit Training Course.

In this light, the statement "You are a part and not the whole," redoubled in lines 35 and 36 and stated a third time following the promise of greater things to come (line 51), takes on a dual rhetorical function. On one level it is an exhortation to resist an inflated sense of self-importance over being called to play a role in the divine plan. On another level it emphasizes the immensity of the plan that will be revealed gradually as each stage is completed. It thus keeps listeners on the hither side of the phenomenological horizon of divine revelation. Finally, the entire second half of the third prophecy (lines 83–130) is an open-ended statement of what is required of listeners in order that they be effective participants in fulfillment of the divine plan. It is, in effect, an extended elaboration of the ritual motive of commitment.

If ambiguity and open-endedness are textual conditions for the rhetoric of radicalization, so also is the source domain from which metaphors are drawn (Sapir and Crocker 1977). It is critical to observe that the dialectic between motive and metaphor is not hermetic. Motives "motivate" and therefore constrain metaphors, and metaphors amplify the meaning of motives, but motives do not definitively determine which metaphors from the available repertoire will be applied in particular situations. The Word of God has consistently drawn on the military as its preferred self-predicative domain, cultivating images of battle against the forces of evil. In contrast, the transformation of bulwark into hedge can be compared with a parallel transformation from tree into house in the prophecies of its former sister community, the People of Praise. Their prophecy described a tree full of life being cut down and sawed into lumber, and the wood being built into a house. At the time, members were unable to interpret its meaning. However, several years later a reorganization of the community was initiated, and those charged with planning recalled the earlier prophecy. The planners had the "sense" that their reorganization was "what was in God's mind when that prophecy was uttered." They interpreted this "sense" as "God [re]calling it to mind," and thus as a "confirmation that we were in [i.e., within the scope of] God's will."

The People of Praise prophecy began with the same motive of "community," and as in the bulwark prophecies, this motive was transformed by performance of a metaphor whose salience persisted over time. Note that the transformation in both cases is predicated on a structural opposition between an inanimate cultural edifice (bulwark, house) and an animate natural entity (hedge, tree). The vector of transformation across this opposition does not appear particularly salient, for in the first case it is from culture to nature and in the second, from nature to culture. However, both imply a process of development, advance, internal elaboration, and sophistication, and both create images of shelter and protection.

It is also of little consequence that the two metaphors draw on the different *technical domains* of horticulture and construction. The critical difference is that the *metaphorical source domain* for the tree/house is that of domesticity, whereas for the bulwark/hedge it is that of defense. The salience of this difference was aptly summarized by a People of Praise coordinator who, following the split with The Word of God, had observed ritual discourse in his community gradually shift away from the rhetoric of conflict.

The rhetoric of war, siege is very effective at eliciting commitment and dedication from your followers. We against them, they against us, the hostile forces of evil surrounding us, survival is at stake—these are very powerful rhetorical terms and images that get people to dedicate everything they have and put up with all sorts of hardships. They pump up the adrenaline. In fact, we found that after the separation, to the degree that we had talked like The Word of God talked, and to the degree to which that began disappearing, our members could tell, and for a while there was a lack of rhetorical effect. So we could see the advantage to using that kind of language. I don't mean to imply anything cynical that they use that language only to pump up, but just from the sociological or linguistic point of view, you can see that certain languages have certain effects on mass movements, because when that language ceases to be used, the effect, in the corresponding fashion, disappears.

People in the community "felt their energy level going down" and found themselves in search of vision and direction. Eventually they "felt the energy and focus come back," as the vocabulary of motives continued to circulate and orient collective life, but with different emphases and enriched by different metaphors.

These considerations lead to a critical series of questions about the performance of ritual language. To what extent is the calling into play of different metaphoric domains a function of intentionality? Does a vocabulary of motives allow for conscious choice in performance, or for partial choice among a restricted set of domains? To what extent does it demand thematic consistency across successive utterances? Does it generate its own rhetorical dynamic that, once activated, drives it toward ever more radical and symbolically charged formulations? Does the choice of militaristic rhetoric initiate the dynamic, or does the dynamic invite expression in military images?

I would argue that the Charismatic vocabulary of motives is indeed structured in such a way that it invites radicalization, and this in two senses. First is an unresolvable tension created by two cosmological oppositions embedded in the vocabulary: one between the world and the Kingdom of God and the other between God and Satan (the Enemy). Both sources of tension are evident in the texts examined above and readily lead to preoccupation with the topics of "getting free from the world," "building the Kingdom of God," and "spiritual warfare" between the forces of God and those aligned with Satan. The second element is suggested by the work of Burke (1970) on the relations of key terms in the writings of Saint Augustine and in the Book of Genesis. Burke shows that the rhetorical power of these texts is grounded in the way that each key term implies the next so as to form a neatly closed system—a tautological cycle of terms. That is, discourse constitutes a circular argument on a grand scale. The cycle is seamless, absolute, incontrovertible, and eternal; in short, it is sacred (cf. Rappaport 1979). Not coincidentally, Burke's focus is precisely those key motives of covenant and order from which the radicalization of charisma in the communitarian ideal took its departure. While in the preceding chapter I organized the contents of the vocabulary of motives into topical domains, what I am now suggesting is that in performance, the vocabulary is structured as a tautological cycle of terms. To recapitulate the tautological cycle within the Charismatic vocabulary of motives, the notion of *commitment* to a *community* can lead to the adoption of a written document, or *covenant,* that specifies forms of *order,* instituting structures of group *authority* that command *obedience,* and so on. We could expand this discourse to include the entire vocabulary, ending where we started.

The vocabulary of motives is thus a closed system in which the terms imply one another and require one another to complete their meaning. Burke's analysis adds to the idea that speech circulates motives throughout ritual and social life the further suggestion that in speech the entire tautological cycle in a sense "revolves" in a systematic way. Although this would likely also be the case if we were to extend Burke's analysis through the written texts of biblical scholars, under the social conditions of ritual speech we can expect a lively interplay between creativity and constraint in the elaboration and transformation of motives critical to entextualization and intertextuality. As motives are inserted into discourse at ever new moments of implication, the structure of the tautology remains, but the canonical terms no longer refer solely to one another within fixed texts. Concretely experienced as sacred words, they become indexical to social relations and motivate those who speak and hear them. Motivated actions instantiate sacred discourse in social life, and thus social life becomes a sacred reality.

This leads us to postulate a final rhetorical condition for the radicalization of charisma. Where, as in covenant communities, motives are structured as a tautological cycle of terms, those terms may be driven around that cycle at increasing velocity as performance amplifies oppositional tensions (e.g., world/kingdom, God/Satan) embedded in the vocabulary. As the cycle revolves it spins off new metaphors and compositional formulas with a kind of centrifugal force. Closed upon itself, the velocity of the cycle results in a rhetorical spiral as the meaning of motives such as covenant and formulas such as "to lay down one's life for the Lord" become amplified in the direction of traditional authority or apocalypsis. Like Blake's depiction of Jacob's Ladder, the straight and narrow path is a spiral staircase of charisma upon which the sacred self ascends toward a destiny perceived as glory.

In this way the dialectic between ritual and social life may be endowed with a directionality that is to some extent independent of events external to discourse. However, there is nothing internal to discourse that renders such a result necessary or inevitable. We have observed that Charismatics outside covenant communities are not typically involved in the radicalization process. Neither are all covenant communities, and as I have shown, it is quite possible, as in the case of the People of Praise, to become extricated from the rhetorical dynamic. In summary, we can suggest several social conditions that may facilitate the processes of rhetorical involution:

(1) the degree to which life situation permits experimentation with lifestyle among the people who become involved in a particular locale, such as young married couples, the unmarried, or college students;

(2) the degree of radical religious vision and rhetorical skill possessed by individual leaders, given the reservations already expressed about the "charismatic figure" in Weber's sense;

(3) the degree to which relief from boredom is needed in a settled religious life, as, for example, when Charismatics motivated by the desire for "spiritual growth" undergo periods of stagnation or "dry spells";

(4) the degree to which it is necessary to intensify commitment in order to maintain it, requiring the mission of a movement to become ever more urgent, its correctness ever more certain, its scope ever wider.

It is unlikely that any particular combination of these factors or others—whether they be personality characteristics of participants or preoccupation with psychocultural themes such as intimacy, spontaneity, and control—can predict the initiation of a rhetorical spiral based on a tautological cycle of terms. It might be suggested, however, that such a process, with an incremental change in what ceases to "seem crazy" and what begins to "make sense," can be identified in retrospect in those movements in which the radicalization process is carried to extreme or even fatal lengths. Such a process likely occurred in the case of the unfortunate Savonarola, as well as in the contemporary aberrations of David Koresh, Jeffrey Lundgren, Charles Manson, Jim Jones's People's Temple, the Solar Temple, and Aum Shinrikyo[7]—all of which lacked the constraints on radicalization that moderate even the most radical among Catholic Charismatics.

With this analysis of the elaboration and transformation of motives, I have completed the description of the triple dialectic of ritual performance on the levels of event, genre, and act. In sum, the dialectic between motive and metaphor appears when motives like community, commitment, and world generate metaphors such as that of the bulwark, which in turn reorients the motives themselves such that in subsequent utterances the bulwark itself becomes transformed into the impenetrable hedge. This textual, illocutionary-predicative process is embedded in the pragmatic, action-behavior process that characterizes the dialectic between the system of genres and the vocabulary of motives. The global rhetorical apparatus for "speaking the Kingdom" keeps motives in circulation as the verbal lubricant of ritual life. This dialectic is in turn embedded in the habitus-based, event-situation process that characterizes the dialectic between ritual and social life, where we have observed the ritualization of practice and radicalization of charisma.

Prophecy and the Cultural Phenomenology of Revelation

We have one task yet ahead, for the semiotic/symbolic analysis of prophetic texts does not complete an understanding of prophecy as a self process. The "extrinsic theory" of thought and meaning (Geertz 1973) takes us a considerable distance in showing how rhetorical processes circumscribe the boundaries of the sacred self, outline the motivational space of everyday social interaction, and shape the contours of collective identity. If we are serious about defining self as a capacity for orientation in the world that is integrated into a habitus, the necessary complement of a semiotics of performance is a cultural phenomenology of performance. When we make the methodological move from representation to being-in-the-world (see Csordas 1994b), it becomes evident that the phenomenology of prophecy is about the experience of revelation. This is the phenomenon that can allow us to understand how prophecy "works" and thereby approach a conclusion about the problem of creativity in ritual language. The ground here is largely uncharted, perhaps because of the difficulty of obtaining data about revelatory experience in languages in which the anthropologist may be not entirely fluent and in cultures in which the appropriate questions are difficult to pose or respond to. We must therefore take advantage of a ritual system and ritual practitioners that operate in English to describe ritual language not only as utterance but also as experience.

Prophecy is regarded as a spiritual gift, in the use of which one can "grow" or become increasingly experienced. More precisely, it is one among a class of "word gifts," all of which are understood to be forms of divine revelation.[8] The capacity to experience revelation is an orientational capacity of the culturally constituted self in the sense we have defined it. Its phenomenological criterion is spontaneous insight or inspiration, often in the form of sensory imagery. We have already witnessed the cultivation of imagination as a self process in the children's drama described in the preceding chapter and alluded to its central role in ritual healing (see Csordas 1994a). For the present, we will note that a prophecy emerges into consciousness in one of several ways. A person may simply feel impelled or "anointed" to speak without a clear sense of what should be said. Even though there are implicit guides to utterance (in the themes of ongoing group life, in a theme implied by previous speakers or stated by leaders of the assembly, or in the vocabulary of motives), the prophet in this ambiguous circumstance feels that to speak is a test of faith and responsiveness to the divine call. There is a collective acknowledgment that such faithfulness can be rewarded by a special message. One experienced covenant community prophet stated that the most frightening inspiration is one that just says "Speak." When he goes to the front of the assembly and the leaders who screen prophecies ask what it's about and he says "I don't know," they say "Oh, one of *those*," implicitly acknowledging their own experience of inspiration as a test of nerve.

The prophet may also have a "sense" of the entire message, leaving to "faith" only its articulate utterance. Again, the prophet may "receive" a verbatim text of the initial line or two of the prophecy, leaving to "faith" only its spontaneous elaboration once she or he begins to speak. Such a text may suggest itself in a way that is not only spontaneous but immediate as well—much, I imagine, as a statement one might make during a group conversation suggests itself prior to one's saying it. In such a case there are several criteria by means of which the inspiration can be distinguished from "one's own" thoughts. These are, if it is directly addressed to the themes at hand, if it is obviously of "spiritual" content, if it occurs precast in the vocabulary of motives and formulas of ritual composition, or if it *feels* like it is not one's own thought or is something one "wouldn't have thought of on one's own." Prophecy may also be presented—not represented—in consciousness as the audition of an internal voice, as the visualization of a written text, or as a visualization either already accompanied by words or which must be described/expressed in words by the prophet. These experiences appear to have nothing of the character of hallucination and require instead an understanding of the cultural elaboration of imagination. Through these variations, we begin to see the central issue of a phenomenology of revelation when revelation is culturally supposed to occur in a completely wide-awake state: it is much less fruitful to invoke dissociation or trance as explanatory concepts than to outline a capacity of self constituted as the "recognition" of revelation.

Let us make our analysis more concrete with a brief portrait of what Singer (1958, 1972) would call a "cultural specialist" in prophecy at The Word of God. In his mid-thirties, during a difficult period in his marriage, G received the Baptism in the Holy Spirit and the gift of tongues at a religious conference after reading an inspirational book. Shortly thereafter, while driving on an errand, he "felt thoughts" in his mind that were "different from prayer, like someone else thinking in my mind telling me 'I've loved you, I've been waiting for you a long time.'" He spoke the words aloud in the first person, though he had never yet heard of prophecy. Attending his first prayer meeting at The Word of God several days later, he heard prophecy for the first time. His wife was baptized in the Holy Spirit at home during the following week, and he began experiencing prophecy nearly every night. At the summer's end he prophesied publicly for the first time, and continued to do so at every community prayer meeting afterward. In two years he was asked to join the community's word gifts group.

The new prophet faces a dilemma in observing that the content of an utterance is an outgrowth of personal experience. The concern arises that he or she is speaking to everyone a message intended only for his or her own edification, or that he or she is not being truly inspired but is "making it up." With experience one learns to focus and "listen" according to context. G explained that he makes himself ready and available for inspiration at times when it is clear that "the Lord wants a general word [to be spoken in prophecy], while other times it just pops into my head." As in the formulation of a "teaching" described in the preceding chapter, a prophecy may also evolve over a period of time. G recounted his experience of formulating a prophecy that elaborated his revelatory image of a "multitude clothed in white receiving the mark of God." The prophecy came at a critical moment, when the community was in the process of its controversial recommitment and adoption of ritual clothing. The core visual image is of an already mantle-and-veil-clad membership amplified into a multitude and marked or chosen by the deity. G's experience of inspiration begins in the week preceding the prayer meeting, during which he "had trouble coming before the Lord" (i.e., praying with a sense of divine presence) and felt "unacceptable about his own attitudes to the community, life, etc." He came to the meeting still feeling that the "Lord was inaccessible" to him, though he later realized that the divinity "was preparing him for that word" (of prophecy). God "began talking" to him during the preparatory meeting of community prophets (the word gifts group) that precedes every prayer meeting. At that time, G said,

I saw God on a throne in a white/yellow burst of light, almost silhouetted. I felt something is wrong with me, I shouldn't be here Lord, but He touched my lips with two fingers to stop the protest, then made a mark on my forehead like they do in [the Catholic sacrament of] Confirmation. I asked myself was I supposed to be home, am I being harassed by Satan. Then as I was praying I got [i.e., was inspired to open the Bible to] a passage from Revelations about sealing of the multitude, which was exactly what was going on [at the time in the community]. I received the actual prophecy in the early praise period of the meeting [the opening period of collective prayer in tongues], and at first thought it was [a message meant] just for me. Then [a head coordinator] gave a [teaching] talk using the same imagery—"before the Lamb we will, etc.," and as I sat down I got the feeling I should share it, the strongest anointing [i.e., experience of divine inspiration and empowerment] I've had in a while. As I was deciding whether to share it, testing it, the confirmation [from God] was "I want you to share and also speak" [indicating that part of his utterance should be in the genre of sharing and part "spoken" as prophecy]. Under the usual procedure I shared it with [two coordinators who were screening prophecies], and as I walked up and was waiting to speak I got the words [to the prophecy], adding later. Sometimes there's an air of unreality, but this time I didn't even have to get back to my seat and ask my wife if it was right—I *knew* it this time. Since

then a lot of people have felt a change of heart to the community, accepting
themselves in their attitude toward being there. Like the prophecy said, "The
seal can never be erased, face the future with less fear."

This text shows that the phenomenology of revelation is constituted
as a gestalt of spontaneity and reflection, self-questioning and confirmation, multisensory imagery, mixed genres of ritual language, coordinated sequences of motives and metaphors, personal circumstance,
and collective concern. Insofar as this gestalt describes his orientation
to the world and to others, we can understand the sense in which the
performance of prophecy is a linguistic and imaginal self process for the
prophet. In the context of what we know about Charismatic life, we
can say that the *ability to prophesy* is a spontaneous disposition of the
habitus grounded in a configuration of capacities for orientation in the
world.

If there is a distinct cultural phenomenology of revelation for the
prophet, no less is there one for the hearer of prophecy. As with its utterance, then, we must understand the hearing of prophecy in a manner
that is experience based and not simply rule based. To be sure, there
are no explicit "teachings" on how to listen to prophecy, since one is expected to have a distinct "personal response" to each utterance. It is
generally said that it is easier to "receive" a prophecy from another than
it is to be confident in one you utter yourself. This is doubtless in part
because the speaker is more preoccupied with the speaking and with
doubts about the inspiration's validity than with incorporating its meaning. It is said that most people "try to make a conscious effort to decide
it is the Lord speaking," and that this gets easier with time as one "sees
them fulfilled." The language in which the incorporation of prophecy is
described includes an "emotional feeling" or a "physiological quickening" similar and parallel to the "anointing" that indicates one should
utter a prophecy. People may say "It felt right," "It spoke to my needs,"
"I felt the Lord was in it," "It answered a question I was having," "I
was really convicted by that prophecy" (i.e., I was grasped by its truth
and aptness), or "That prophecy really spoke to my heart" (i.e., I heard
it and was moved by it). For some, "the words make more sense and
[one] hears them more clearly than talking plainly, and [one's] understanding seems sharpened."

The obvious but critical observation that experience transcends the
text is only a truism if it is assumed that experience does not matter.
Hints at what really constitutes the efficacy of ritual language are given

in the response of two people present during the prophecy in which the bulwark was transformed into the hedge. From a man who recalled that he pictured the big square hedge along with other hedges and got the feeling of runners going out to attach them together, we learn that imagery may accompany the hearing of prophecy as well as its utterance. The "big square" shape of the hedge is probably a formal feature retained from its precursor the bulwark, suggesting that we are accurate in describing the phenomenological process as a transformation instead of a substitution of metaphors. Whereas the text describes transplanting sprouts that germinate from separate seeds into the bulwark, and transplanting parts of the hedge to extend the bulwark, the hearer's image elaborates, specifies, and interprets by evoking a scene that includes multiple hedges linked by runners. Another hearer stated that the image of the bulwark in prophecy brought to mind "all the other things the Lord has told us about our mission as a community," a datum that is a tribute to Victor Turner's (1967) insight that key symbols are multivocal and polysemic. This woman described her original notion of the bulwark as a kind of seawall. The seawall represented "an idea she could understand," but the transformed hedge made it much clearer for her, "since the hedge is both penetrable and impenetrable." I do not believe that there is anything necessarily "feminine" about her valuation of this particular enhancement of the metaphor. Instead, it appears to reconcile a felt contradiction between the broader understandings of the community as an inclusive space of intimacy and as an exclusive barrier to aggression. Here we are at the phenomenological core of ritual language as self process.

I have shown that thematic consistency and intertextuality in Charismatic ritual language are grounded in the circulation of motives through genres in performance, but a few more words are in order about how that consistency is experienced as divine power. Charismatics observe that when everyone is "open to the movement of the Spirit" there is a kind of prophetic "fallout." Participants, especially members of the word gifts group, claim at times to be aware of precisely when the deity is "giving" prophecy, and even of who is "getting" it. The deity might say to one, "X is distracted, tell her I want to speak through her." Everyone is "picking up the general sense of what the Lord is saying," and no one can be sure he or she is the one receiving the "word" that is actually to be uttered. It is not uncommon for prayer meeting participants to report with awe that they "received" exactly the same message moments before it was uttered by another. In this situation the person who did not speak can "confirm" the validity of the prophecy, verifying the speaker's accurate rendering of the inspiration on the ground that both were, so to speak, tuned into the same divine transmission. Major prophecies are also "confirmed" by minor prophecies that follow, or synthesize minor prophecies that come before. As with the first two bulwark prophecies, it sometimes happens that a single speaker "receives" only part of a prophecy and its continuation is "received" by someone else. In "discerning" whether or not to speak, the inexperienced prophet may hesitate because his inspiration seems incomplete. The experienced prophet may in contrast "step out in faith" and speak, on the assumption that the sense of his utterance will be completed by a subsequent speaker—again as in the bulwark prophecies, where the second prophecy (beginning at line 11) is a nearly seamless continuation of the first. Finally, when the prophet has discerned that he (or she) should speak, he may begin the utterance with only a vague sense of the content or with a clear idea of only the first line or two of the prophecy. As in the above example from the cultural specialist, spontaneous oral composition is then experienced as a manifestation of divine power.

Those who listen attentively often report that prophecy moves them in ways they would not expect from utterance that had a "human source." It is not expected that every prophecy will have such a profound effect on every hearer, but the miraculous nature of sacred discourse is confirmed for listeners by the experience that the same lines of prophecy may carry different messages for different individuals. But precisely the opposite is also the case: apparently unrelated prophecies may be interpreted as bearing the same message or addressing the same issue. During the late 1970s it was said that the head prophet of The Word of God received about a hundred prophecies per week. In addition, he was sent a steady flow of prophecy mail from the general membership. Whenever over a period of time he was "praying about" a particular topic, the contents of prophecy mail were said to skew toward that topic, even tough "people do not necessarily know that the coordinators are discussing that topic." This experience of spontaneous, apparently unprompted thematic consistency is an experience of the sacred produced and sustained by the dialectic between ritual and social life. That is, given the intense cultivation of habitus, it is not surprising that the membership and the administrative staff express similar concerns at any one time. Given the tightly articulated system of genres and motives, neither is it surprising that the body of prophetic discourse can at any one time be searched and interpreted for messages relevant to a given theme—certainly no more surprising than that the Bible can be used in this manner.

Given these elements of experience it is also the case that, just as the prophet must discern when and whether to speak, those who hear prophecy must discern or test its validity and relevance. A woman in her early forties put it as follows:

Predictive prophecy, or directive prophecy, is always treated with a certain amount of caution. You're not supposed to do anything solely based on a prophetic word unless it's something so innocuous you would do it anyway. A prophetic word that says "little children love one another," there's no problem with something like that. But if the prophetic words says, "Behold hard times are coming, you must sell your house and live together in clusters"—and we had prophetic words that said more or less that (they didn't get quite that explicit)—that sort of thing needs to be judged and tested. The category of things that's tested most extensively is personal prophecy—"Behold, John, you should marry Mary."

Here the hearer's interpretive intentions are as much at issue as are the communicative intentions of the human/divine speaker. At least for the ideally "mature" hearer, being experientially moved and spiritually tuned in to a divine wavelength are not the sole sources of validation. The relative need for external validation is determined based on criteria distinguishing innocuousness/momentousness, generality/specificity, and collective/personal target of the divine message.

These observations are directly relevant to theoretical discussions of creativity in ritual language. Despite attestations of the importance of the audience in performance, such discussions typically overprivilege the flexibility or constraint allowed by rules for the *production* of utterances, to the neglect of conventions for the *interpretation* of those utterances and their *incorporation* into practice (see Duranti and Brenneis 1986 for a major exception). I will address the problem of creativity directly in the concluding chapter. For now, my point is that the phenomenology of language allows us to grasp both how the validity of utterances is confirmed and, insofar as discourse is concretely experienced as originating outside its speakers and as conveying a special message to each listener, how it creates a sense of sacred otherness. The kind of account I have provided suggests that we not conceive the efficacy of ritual language as a function only of its texts, or conceive of performance as merely the generation of texts. In the extrinsic analysis of textuality and representation, prophecies are metaphorical extensions of the linked motives of community-people-covenant. We must now take another step toward embodiment and being-in-the-world, picking up with respect to prophecy in particular the thread of analysis of the transformation of habitus woven into the argument in chapters 2 and 6.

We can describe how prophecy extends into the habitus in several directions through a metaphorical social space. First, it diffuses "downward" from ritual event into everyday domestic life. As authoritative utterance invades the space of intimacy and through the ritualization of practice becomes an additional tool of patriarchal social control, it also adapts to that space by losing the prosodic features that characterize it as a formal genre. One covenant community man noted that for several years, when uttering prophecy in the domestic context to his wife and children, he maintained genre conventions such as prefacing his words with an opening such as "Thus saith the Lord." Eventually he came to feel that formal speech was somewhat stilted and distance creating and that the divine message could be conveyed just as effectively with an opening such as "N, I really feel the Lord wants you to know that . . ." followed by a message framed in colloquial speech. The problem of how one recognizes such an utterance as a prophecy in the absence of prosodic conventions disappears when we realize that this change accompanies the incorporation of prophecy into a habitus. That is, one has an ongoing relationship of intimacy with the speaker, knows whether that speaker is endowed with the gift of prophecy, recognizes the kinds of things that are customarily said in prophecy, knows how seriously one should weigh words heard in prophecy especially if they are directed unequivocally at oneself, and recognizes the kind of response that an apt prophecy typically evokes in oneself.

The linguistic self process also diffuses "upward" insofar as covenant community coordinators appropriate increasing authority to both utter and interpret ritual language. In The Word of God this was marked by a relative shift in the locus of efficacy away from the genre of prophecy, customarily accessible to all, to the genre of teaching, based on the authoritative "discernment" of the coordinators. Some of those who objected to the teachings of the Training Course in the mid-1980s also perceived that community prophecies were no longer the source of direction for the group, but appeared increasingly to mirror "preconceived" ideas promulgated by the community elite. From the coordinators' point of view, utterance delivered as teaching was no less a product of divine inspiration than that delivered as prophecy. This ambiguity about the social role of prophecy is predicated on its dual property, observed above, wherein the same utterance may have different meaning for different hearers (preserving elements of intimacy with the divine even in the most authoritative of utterances and reciprocity among participants who search for an egalitarian consensus of interpretation) while separate utterances can have the same meaning for all (reflecting unequivocal authority in the divine word and hierarchical separation between the rank and file and the gatekeepers of divine will). Once again the tension was between intimacy and authority, reciprocity and hierarchy.

We have already examined how the force of ritual utterance diffuses "inward" as one makes the "decision" that it constitutes the divine word and experientially incorporates its meaning. Finally, it diffuses "outward" beyond the bounds of the verbal genre into the body. In certain instances it comes to be performed as prophetic gesture, transforming the motives of ritual life in what Laurence Kirmayer (1992) has called "enactive metaphor." An example comes from a meeting between The Word of God leaders Martin and Clark, accompanied by their chief prophet, and Cardinal Suenens, accompanied by his prophet. The Word of God prophet was divinely prompted to "get a rope" and bring it to the meeting, where he was to bind together the hands of Martin and Suenens. In this instance not only did the prophet perform or enact a metaphor indicating the divine ordination of the alliance, he also enacted a wordless performative act (see Tambiah 1973/1985: 80) of binding, and thus establishing, that alliance. A second example from the same prophet is a gesture that accompanied a verbal prophecy at one of the community's anniversary celebrations. While the deity described how he had "lifted up" the community and given it broad influence within the Charismatic movement, the prophet lifted his white mantle above his head. Suddenly he announced that this influence and respect would be sorely tested in the future, flinging the mantle to the floor and trampling on it. The reported effect was to bring about a profound transformation in the mood of the assembly from that of jubilant celebration to sober apprehension.[9] A final example comes from a lesser prophet in the same community who once, while meeting privately with a group of district heads, felt inspired to perform the prophetic gesture of laying on of hands while prophesying verbally. The gesture's prophetic meaning was to encourage and exhort the leaders not to be overwhelmed by the pastoral responsibility they bore. That such em-

bodied performances of prophecy are relatively rare, apparently elaborated only in the covenant community setting, reinforces my earlier conclusion that the radicalization of charisma is accompanied by its progressive embodiment.

Let us pursue the significance of the observation that the performance of ritual language exceeds the bounds of textuality and over-
flows into embodiment. My discussion suggests that the experience of
divine power in Charismatic discourse is more than a function of attributing utterances to the deity by the rhetorical use of the first-person
pronoun. Instead, power is grounded in the phenomenology of prophetic inspiration, composition, speaking, and hearing. What, then, is the
relation between the phenomenology of religious experience and the
phenomenology of discourse, between divine power and the power of
language? What is the relation between the "I" of prophecy and the
"I" that is a sacred self? Tambiah offers a provocative suggestion.

There is a sense in which it is true to say that language is outside of us and
given to us as a part of our cultural and historical heritage; at the same time language is within us, it moves us and we generate it as active agents. Since words
exist and are in a sense agents in themselves which establish connections and
relations between both man and man, and man and the world, and are capable
of "acting" upon them, they are one of the most realistic representations we
have of the concept of force which is either not directly observable or is a metaphysical notion which we find it necessary to use. (1968: 184)

The two critical features of language that Tambiah's argument highlights are its "inwardly otherness" and its realistic "representation of
force." These features, however, are not distinctive of language per se,
but of language insofar as it participates in the generality of our embodied existence. And it is the error of an overly textualized approach
that leads Tambiah to write that the aspect of language he is tapping is
a *representation*, rather than an *instance*, of force.

Merleau-Ponty (1962) captures this embodied nature of language
by suggesting that at its root speech is not a representation of thought
but a verbal gesture with immanent meaning. For Merleau-Ponty, speech
is coterminous with thought, and we possess words in terms of their ar-
ticulatory and acoustic style as one of the possible uses of our bodies.
Strictly speaking, speech cannot be said to express or represent thought,
since thought is for the most part inchoate until it is spoken (or written). Instead, speech is an act or phonetic gesture in which one takes up
an existential position in the world. The clearest example I can think of
to illustrate this position is that of Charismatic glossolalia.[10] The two

relevant facts about Charismatic glossolalia are that it takes the form of nonsense or gibberish and that its speakers regard vernacular language as inadequate for communication with the divine.[11] It thus seems to challenge taken for granted canons of vernacular expressivity and intelligibility, and in so doing calls into question conventions of truth, logic, and authority.

A semiotic account might accordingly hold that glossolalia ruptures the world of human meaning, like a wedge forcing an opening in discourse and creating the possibility of creative cultural change, dissolving structures to facilitate the emergence of new ones. This interpretation is not incorrect, but a different light is thrown on the problem when glossolalia is viewed as a phenomenon of embodiment. Note that I am not saying that glossolalia is *only* a gesture, for we must grant its phenomenological reality *as language* for its users. What I would argue, along with Merleau-Ponty, is that *all* language has this gestural or existential meaning. Glossolalia, by its formal characteristic of eliminating the semantic level of linguistic structure, highlights precisely the existential reality of intelligent bodies inhabiting a meaningful world. In playing on the gestural characteristic of linguisticality, speaking in tongues is a ritual statement that the speakers inhabit a sacred world, since the gift of ritual language is defined as a gift from the deity. The stripping away of the semantic dimension in glossolalia is not an absence but the drawing back of a discursive curtain to reveal the grounding of language in natural life, as a bodily act. At the same time, "speech is the surplus of our existence over natural being" (Merleau-Ponty 1962: 197), that is to say, of our *existence as persons* over mere *being as things* or objects. Glossolalia thus reveals language as incarnate, and this existential fact is homologous with the religious significance of the "Word made Flesh," the unity of human and divine.

Once we acknowledge the embodied nature of language, we have a new basis for understanding the significance of Tambiah's observation that it is both outside and within us, both other and self. In the words of the phenomenological philosopher Richard M. Zaner, our bodies are alien presences to us at the same time as they are compellingly ours, both "intimately alien" and "strangely mine," such that "the otherness of my own body thus suffuses its sense of intimacy" (1981: 55). To the extent that our experience of language is also an experience of our bodies, it partakes of this ambiguous embodied otherness. It thus contributes to the conditions for our senses of the uncanny and of the sacred. My argument, then, is that the *existential* otherness of language is not grounded in the abstract otherness that allows us to consider it as *langue* instead of as *parole* but in the concrete otherness it shares as a feature of embodiment.

The second feature of language singled out by Tambiah is its realistic representation of the abstract notion of force. In later writing Tambiah (1973/1985), taking up Austin's theory of performative speech acts, observes, as did Bronislaw Malinowski, that speech can be considered "part of action." Also like Malinowski, however, he does not take the next step to an embodied theory of language. Hence while in the later work he makes the shift from language as a representation of force to language as an instance of force, and never forgets the importance of "actions other than speech," his analysis remains within the mode of textuality and with philosophers of language (1968/1985: 32–34; 1973/1985: 78–80). More recent work from philosophers of the body suggest a somatic origin for the experience of force. These arguments are all the more persuasive in that they are formulated from the divergent standpoints of cognitive science and phenomenology.

Consider first the argument of the cognitive philosopher Mark Johnson:

The meaning of "physical force" depends on publicly shared meaning structures that emerge from our *bodily experience* of force. We begin to grasp the meaning of physical force from the day we are born (or even before). We have bodies that are acted upon by "external" and "internal" forces such as gravity, light, heat, wind, bodily processes, and the obtrusion of other physical objects. Such interactions constitute our first encounters with forces, and they reveal patterned recurring relations between ourselves and our environment. Such patterns develop as meaning structures through which our world begins to exhibit a measure of coherence, regularity, and intelligibility. . . . These patterns are embodied and give coherent, meaningful structure to our physical experience at a *preconceptual* level, though we are eventually taught names for at least some of these patterns, and can discuss them in the abstract. (1987: 13)

For Johnson, these developmentally primordial experiences of force are the nonpropositional basis of fundamental metaphors and image schemas. Thus it makes sense that the force we experience in language, insofar as we agree that language is a form of action and is embodied, is not an abstraction from the primordial sense of force but an example of it.

From a more explicitly phenomenological standpoint, Zaner, drawing on the work of Hans Jonas, carries us further in this direction by observing that causality itself is not an a priori of experience but an extrapolation from "propriobodily prime experience" that constitutes the ground of our very "idea of force and action in the world" (1981: 36). Every execution of a movement involves the feeling of kinesthetic "flow" that "most fundamentally constitutes this body as my embodiment," concretely enacting rudimentary strivings or efforts and doing so in such a way that it is strictly correlated with whatever appears to our senses. The important point for the genesis of a sense of force is that the kinesthetic feelings exhibit an if/then pattern:

"If" I move my arm in specific ways, "then" the glass is knocked off the table. Thus *bodily experience at its roots, and not only in relation to resistant or impacting objects, has this "causal" style.* Indeed, the experience of force and effort Jonas describes turns out to be far more basic and complex than even he indicates. This "force" is first and foremost an enacting by kinaesthetic patterns of elemental strivings—whether they are initiated by the organism towards the world, or whether they are reactions by it to impacting things. (Zaner 1981: 42; emphasis in original)

Causality is not first a logical relation, but an embodied one. Likewise, force is not first invisible or metaphysical, but a concrete experience of effort. Once again, to the extent that utterance partakes of embodiment and effort, speech is a real instance of force.

Including phenomenology alongside semiotic/symbolic interpretation thus gives us additional purchase on the ritual consequences of the inherent "otherness" and "force" of language. More precisely, it gives us a way to grasp the possibility that discourse, insofar as it can be understood to be "outside us," can be experienced as continuing independently of us—as "speaking itself." If the presumed unobservable and metaphysical force is in fact an embodied property of discourse, we can grasp the religious experience of that force—perceived principally in terms of its essential otherness—as a manifestation of divine power.

How this feature of language, this "embodied otherness," participates in the phenomenology of a sacred reality can be no more aptly summarized than by the following passage from Foucault:

I would have preferred to be enveloped in words, borne way beyond all possible beginnings. At the moment of speaking, I would like to have perceived a nameless voice, long preceding me, leaving me merely to enmesh myself in it, taking up its cadence, and to lodge myself when no one was looking, in its interstices as if it had paused an instant, in suspense, to beckon me. There would have been no beginnings: instead, speech would proceed from me, while I stood in its path—a slender gap—the point of its possible disappearance. . . . A good many people, I imagine, harbour a similar desire to be freed from the obligation to begin, a similar desire to find themselves, right from the outside,[*] on the other side of discourse, without having to stand outside it, pondering its particular, fearsome, and even devilish features. To this all too common feeling, institutions have an ironic reply, for they solemnize beginnings, surrounding them with a circle of silent attention; in order that they can be distinguished from far off, they impose ritual forms upon them. (1972: 215)

Foucault here taps the embodied otherness of language. The mystification of this otherness is the final rhetorical condition for the efficacy of Charismatic prophecy,[12] the source of both its spiritual meaning and its persuasive power. It is a paradoxical situation in which the speaker is at the moment of speaking enmeshed in a voice long preceding itself, in which the speaker stands in the path of the speech that proceeds from him, and in which because the speaking "I" is not the self, one is already on the other side of discourse—its charismatic side—safe from its fearsome, devilish, or uncanny features.

The institution of Charismatic prophecy ritualizes this paradox, precisely, I would suggest, because of its salience to the critical psychocultural themes of control, intimacy, and spontaneity. The beginning that it distinguishes "from far off" is a beginning of the self, the circumstance that the prophet is not "really" speaking but yet bears responsibility for what he says. It thus constitutes the compromise of the culturally constituted North American self that strives for control but incessantly feels it slipping away. Moreover, all utterances are attributed to the same "real" divine speaker, while anyone can serve as a font of discourse. The shared participation in the mind of God, the mutual tuning in to the divine will, is thus a concrete experience of intimacy as well as of authority. Finally, this decentering of intentionality exposes the semiautonomy of language from its speakers. This is, once again, not because langue is independent from parole, but because the body has an "autonomous" existence, and speaking is a feature of embodiment. The ritual act raises the possibility of a speakerless discourse, of language "speaking itself," and in this embodied otherness manifests the presence of the sacred as spontaneity.

This discussion suggests that we pursue the issue of intentionality, and by extension that of subjectivity, as a preliminary to our concluding discussion of creativity in the next chapter. The kind of embodied otherness we have uncovered in language is related to the understanding of intentionality as a general structure of embodied existence in phenomenological philosophy (Merleau-Ponty 1962; Kelkel 1988). Intentionality has also been analyzed as a specific characteristic of utterances

*Foucault clearly means "outset," not "outside."

in the philosophy of language (Searle 1983; Lepore and Van Gulick 1991). For the most part, anthropologists have taken up the problem of intentionality in the domain of sociolinguistics, particularly with respect to the relations among intention, responsibility, and control in speech and to the critique of the role ascribed to intentions in speech act theory (Rosaldo 1982; Duranti 1993a, 1993b; Du Bois 1986, 1993; Kuipers 1993).

The critique mounted by these authors has been an important corrective to accounts that place the intention of individual speakers universally at the center of the meaning-making process in language. Thus Alessandro Duranti (1993a: 26, 42, 44) gives ethnographic examples of how the audience rather than a speaker's intent determines the force of an utterance.[13] Kuipers (1993: 101) highlights examples of when responsibility is not a personality trait but an act of exchange between persons. Du Bois (1986: 328; 1993) points to examples of speech characterized by the absence of ego control instead of sovereign ego control. Despite its powerful contribution, however, in its strongest version this "antipersonalist critique" of meaning (Duranti 1993a) and the elaboration of "intentionless meaning" (Du Bois 1993) could easily be interpreted to draw an irreconcilable distinction between the Western speaker characterized by subjective intention and the non-Western speaker characterized by collective determination. Indeed, the linguistic argument closely parallels the distinction drawn in psychological anthropology between an entified Western egocentric self and a permeable non-Western sociocentric self, an implicitly orientalist distinction that has recently come increasingly to be modified and attenuated (see the literature cited in Csordas 1994c: 336–337).

To their credit some of these authors grant speech act theory and the speaker's intention a degree of value, rejecting only its universal claims (Duranti 1993a: 44; Du Bois 1993: 69). Duranti in particular calls for a balanced approach, not denying that there may be occasions in Samoa where individual intention can be invoked in understanding meaning, while Du Bois acknowledges the advances made by speech act theory even in pointing to the occurrence of intentionless meaning in Euro-American societies. Charismatic prophecy, and Charismatic ritual language in general, adds a vivid ethnographic example of the intersubjective constitution of meaning in a Euro-American setting, but one that at the same time remains permeated with intention. As in Samoa, there is a much more obvious concern on the part of hearers of prophecy with the "public, displayed, performative aspect of language" than with the "actors' alleged subjective states" (Duranti 1993a: 44). Yet prophecy is far from the intentionless meaning in the version of the critique formulated by Du Bois using the example of divination, for it displays control, responsibility, and intention at the same time as spontaneity, collectivity, and intersubjectivity.

Our corrective to the antipersonalist corrective requires recognition of two points: the kind of genre typically presented as an example and the kind of assumption typically made about subjective states of the speakers. The kind of genre is often one characterized by substantial structure and rigidity allowing for diminished spontaneity in the enactment of more or less fixed texts. Duranti's (1993a) example of Samoan political oratory perhaps offers the most flexibility in allowing the speaker to strategically switch between adopting a dramatis persona representing a group and a personal identity, but his version of the critique is based more on the co-construction of meaning by performer and audience. Du Bois, however, argues that the need in ritual language for self-evidence and authority not subject to critical scrutiny dictates a fixed source of meaning "which stands outside the chain of human fallibility" (1986: 333), and he makes the strongest case for this position with respect to the extreme example of the highly overdetermined language of divination (1993). Even in traditional narrative genres such as the Shokleng origin myth (Urban 1989) or the Weyewa words of the ancestors (Kuipers 1993) the vector of intentionality is in the direction of approximating a timeless and fixed mythic account. By contrast, in prophecy the vector of intentionality is reversed, and utterance is an elaboration rather than an approximation of the timeless word of God fixed in scripture. This is the case for both the proximate and prime speakers: the intentionality in prophecy is toward the mind of God, ultimately toward the revelation of the divine plan. The intentional horizon is defined by the extent to which that plan is perceived already to have been revealed; the intentionality of the prophet becomes concordant with divine intentionality as an act of "forthtelling" in the way a surfer catches a wave.

The subjective state that corresponds in an ideal typical way to the speech of intentionless meaning is trance, which as we observed above is placed at the opposite end of a continuum with the wide-awake awareness of everyday speech (Du Bois 1986; Urban 1989). Once again, I would argue, implicit in such continua is that the everyday self is modeled on the sovereign, egocentric Western self while the nonordinary self is modeled on the trance-prone sociocentric non-Western self. I think Urban becomes snared in this distinction while at the same time offering a way out. He offers the intriguing suggestion that the far right of the continuum is connected back up with the left, such that projective "I" merges with the indexical referential "I" of everyday speech (Urban 1989: 42, 47). This analysis leads him to a conception of "embodied iconic otherness" (1989: 47–48) that from a semiotic standpoint parallels the phenomenological account elaborated above. In Urban's account the projective "I" operates just like an everyday "I" and constitutes an alternate self. If there is truly a merging, however, then the alternate self does not supplant the everyday self but is superimposed on it. This appears to create the paradox that there must be *both* an ordinary and a nonordinary self present, both sovereign speech and trance at the same time. Moreover, if the projective "I" is really behaving like the referential indexical "I" of everyday speech, then it *won't* be speaking in a fixed or rigid text as the model of trance speech would predict. Indeed, this is where Urban becomes entangled, stating at one point that the projective "I" tells an emergent story with no script or story accessible to the audience apart from its manifestation in present speech (1989: 42) and later that where the projective "I" is involved, texts display an extreme rigidity (1989: 47).

The ethnographic example of Charismatic prophecy offers a way to get beyond this theoretical impasse, while at the same time Urban's analysis offers additional insight into how prophecy contributes to the creation of a sacred self. Urban suggests that it is the interplay between the imaginary "I" and the everyday "I" in discourse that makes possible a truly cultural self. More important, he suggests that metapragmatic awareness of this interplay is the "motor of cultural change in the discourse constitution of self" insofar as it creates the ground for apprehension of possible discrepancy between superego and id, self and ideal, cultural constraint and creativity, and "consequently for representable internal affective processes that might otherwise never exist" (Urban 1989: 50). Charismatic prophecy is neither a fixed-text genre like the origin myth narrative nor a genre that presupposes an everyday self supplanted in trance by a nonordinary self, but one characterized by a remarkable degree of metapragmatic awareness. In prophecy, the "I" of discourse is intentionally and subjectively doubled insofar as the speaker is aware that "I am speaking responsibly, but the I of my speech is not me." There is in addition a second doubling for the hearers of prophecy because "God is speaking to us but may have a special mes-

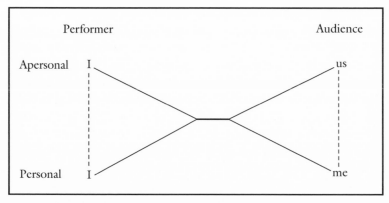

Fig. 3. *Structure of Intentionality and Subjectivity in Charismatic Prophecy*

sage for me." Finally, these doubled subjectivities carry out the constitution of meaning in the intersubjective dialogue of ritual performance.

These relationships result in the metapragmatic structure of intentionality and subjectivity presented in figure 3. The double doubling of
embodied otherness is the condition for the coexistence of intentional
and intentionless meaning in the sense adopted by the antipersonalist
critics (note that the term "apersonal" could easily be replaced by "trans-
personal"). At the same time, in another sense each pole is riddled with
intention: the speaker's conscious act of prophecy that includes not just
the intention to speak but the recognition of inspiration and frequently
its pragmatic content (compare Du Bois 1993: 67), the deity's authoritative expression of intention often in the form of performative speech
acts, and the hearers' decision to understand the utterance as prophecy that yet remains subject to a further act of judgment and testing.
Furthermore, this structure not only characterizes the social relation
among participants but is also incorporated within each participant:
every hearer is in theory inculcated with the disposition to assume the
prophetic role and continue the open-ended discourse of the divine
word, and every prophet could in fact say "Insofar as God is speaking
to the group of which I am a part, he is speaking to me through me."

Charismatic prophecy thus offers an ethnographic example that allows us to decenter the authority of the sovereign intentional ego in
precisely the way insisted on by the anthropological critics. It also allows us to connect the issues of intention and control with those of

creativity and constraint in language use. To the extent that the speaker is absorbed in the utterance, language speaks itself and the rhetorical dynamic of discourse reigns autonomous; to the extent that the speaker retains metapragmatic awareness of the dual "I" of discourse, there is a self process defined by the possibility for internal dialogical creativity. Likewise, to the extent that the utterance is granted ultimate authority as sacred discourse by the audience, it is the unassailable voice of divine will; to the extent that it is dialogically constituted by the way it "speaks to" or is taken up by every hearer, there is necessarily space for multiplicity and creativity in meaning. Here the argument rejoins our earlier observations on the implicit paradox of a premodern patriarchal movement in a postmodern condition of culture. We can now understand that the centering of authority in the divine voice takes place from the standpoint of discourse whereas a postmodern fragmentation of intentionality takes place from the standpoint of subjectivities. Finally, it completes our account of the dual subjectivity of individual humans as speaking and hearing agents in performance and of charisma as an autonomous discursive force with its locus not in the person but in the self-sustaining rhetoric of performance grounded in the social conditions of its production and reception. Such speech "concentrates within it the accumulated symbolic capital of the group" (Bourdieu 1991: 109) and thereby "provides words with 'connotations' that are tied to a particular context, introducing into discourse that surplus of meaning that gives it its 'illocutionary force'" (Bourdieu 1991: 107).

If it is true, as Foucault suggests in the remark quoted above, that a good many people harbor the desire for submergence in discourse, then it is true that in comparison to most others Catholic Charismatics have gone quite a distance toward realizing this desire. If prophecy, as we might extrapolate from Foucault, can be seen as a model or miniature of discourse in general, one can consider the possibility that all discourse has a sacred substrate—that it is essentially a religious form of action and structure—or at least that discourse can be approached via its metaphysical implications. This in turn opens the category of communication a bit further, with implications for the relation of language to culture, reality, and the sacred. The "I" of prophecy is authentically "other" at the same time as it is authentically the self precisely because language is an embodied otherness, that is, because it is existentially grounded in the body.

Epilogue

8

Creativity, Constraint, and the Sacred

A central theme throughout this book has been human creativity, specifically, the transformation of self and habitus by practice and performance in a Charismatic world. In the concluding discussion I will explicitly problematize the notion of creativity, which with few exceptions is often either taken for granted or ignored in anthropological discussions of ritual and social life. A survey of how the term has been used since Weber shows that neither a definition of creativity nor a systematic account of how it is achieved and what is created is typically offered. Looking only at the question of what is created in ritual and social action leads to the following somewhat unwieldy list: new obligations, a new community, order, form for inchoate experience, a new religious culture, changes in traditional customs, new meaning for events, the conditions for the efficacy of ritual, re-creation of the rhythms of the natural world, new perspectives, the logical dimensions of thought, the semantic conditions for dealing with reality, new categories of meanings, an infinite number of novel and well-formed sentences, relevant features of the context of social interaction (see Csordas 1980a for citations). This state of affairs suggests that we devote some effort to clearing the conceptual path for future analyses, at the same time placing the present argument in the context of debate about creativity.

Let us first observe that creativity is not the same as liberation: not only does cultural form typically circumscribe the limits of creativity, as the poet William Blake was fond of demonstrating, it is always possible become bound by what one creates. The limits of cultural relativism are certainly tested by the Charismatic definition of liberation from "the world, the flesh, and the devil" in terms of patriarchal gender discipline and the authoritarian regulation of personal conduct (see Csordas 1996). Tension between creativity and constraint was a constant feature of the struggle of The Word of God/Sword of the Spirit to enact the psychocultural themes of intimacy, spontaneity, and control in domains such as personal behavior and gender discipline. In opting for a permanent space of intimacy as a hedge against alienation, they initiated the cultural restrictions on behavior that I have labeled the ritualization of practice. In opting for the spontaneity of spiritual renewal as a hedge against spiritual malaise, they initiated the increasing sense of apocalyptic urgency I have labeled the radicalization of charisma. In opting for authoritative control as a hedge against anomie, they generated a struggle between intimacy and authority, reciprocity and hierarchy.

If creativity and liberation cannot be considered to be identical, we must also distinguish creativity from efficacy in ritual performance. Emily Ahern (1979) has shown the methodological difficulty of defining efficacy, distinguishing intended effects like curing from unintended effects like the Durkheimian promotion of social solidarity, and distinguishing strong illocutionary acts that intend an effect from weak ones that only "wish for" something. It would appear that ritual can have conventional effects without being creative, since creativity bears the connotation of something unique or de novo. No one would argue that the performance of a rite of passage is efficacious, but is it creative? It does not create a new social status, but it does create a new member or occupant of a social status. The claim for creativity is thus stronger and more complex than the claim for efficacy. Theoretically unelaborated as it is, however, it is the conceptual engine that pulls the train of adjectives like "constituted, constructed, emergent, transformed" frequently encountered in discussions of the effects of ritual on self and world.

Let us place the problem in critical perspective by examining an argument that is strongly for efficacy while strongly denying the possibility of creativity.[1] In his work toward a theory of formalized language, Bloch (1974) argues that ritual language is typical of traditional authority in Weber's sense. He describes it as restricted with respect to vocabulary, repertoire of illustrations permissible within discourse, and variety of appropriate grammatical sequences. In consequence, utterances become predictable to such an extent that the speaker becomes anonymous by not having a choice of what to say—or, as suggested above, language begins to "speak itself." At the same time, the restriction of syntactic possibilities reduces the capacity of language to carry propositional force, instead creating series of fused utterances with expanded illocutionary force. The expanded illocutionary force is due to the fact that as its ability to carry truth value diminishes, statements become impossible to contradict. At first glance, this might seem to be an adequate description of Charismatic ritual language, especially the highly formalized genre of prophecy with its measured articulation of motives and formulaic style of oral composition. However, this formulation fails to account for the dialectic between ritual and social life wherein motives evolve, metaphors are generated, and the nature of social relationships is altered.

In more recent writing Bloch (1986: 181–187) refines and clarifies his position, arguing that ritual communication is essentially different from nonritual communication because the former "combines the properties of statements and actions." In addition, there is a "changed balance between the propositional and performative aspects of language," characterized by a relative shift away from propositional toward illocutionary force. The result of this shift of balance is that "the fact of using language becomes what matters, rather than what is said." My analysis concurs with Bloch's insofar as the fact of using language does come to matter. Indeed, it is the fact of using language that brings to the fore its embodied nature, allowing the "I" of prophecy to be recognized as a manifestation of the divine other. The vast majority of prophetic utterances are redundant messages of encouragement and exhortation, the main effect of which is to impress on the audience that the deity is in fact speaking to them.

Even though they occur much less frequently, however, a theory of ritual language, in particular a theory of charisma as the rhetorical force of ritual language in performance, must be able to account for prophecies with a more specific, directive content and especially for those prominent enough to be recognized by name—the Shining White Cross prophecy, the bulwark prophecies, and the Trampled Mantle prophecy of The Word of God; the Tree and House prophecy of the People of Praise; or the Rome prophecies. Bloch's argument must deny creativity even here, insofar as it never construes the "action" side of ritual communication as creative action (never even as the creation of authority), but only as the exercise of a traditional authority that by definition connotes the stifling of creativity. Creativity lies entirely on the propositional side of the equation, and part of the reason they lack creativity is that "rituals cannot form a true argument, because they imply no alternative." This again is true to an extent, as was implicitly understood by those members of The Word of God who objected to the use of prophecy to institute the wearing of mantles and veils—because it was divine utterance, there was no alternative. It is only true to an extent, however, for again it cannot account for the generation of significant metaphors and their rhetorical effect. Moreover, a theory of ritual language must also be able to account for the choice of metaphorical domains in ritual utterance. For example, as we saw in the evolution of relations between The Word of God and the People of Praise, whether or not divine inspiration is expressed in military terms does constitute a true alternative with definitive consequences.

Part of the difficulty is the problematic nature of the term "proposition" itself, which Bloch appears to take in the strictly logical sense of a statement that can be shown to be true or false.[2] Yet ritual language retains a certain sense of propositionality, not in a weak sense as Bloch would have it, but in the strong sense of "predicativity" that I have demonstrated throughout this analysis. This is the sense in which "a proposition exists as a continuous, analog pattern of experience or understanding, with sufficient internal structure to permit inferences" (Johnson 1987: 3).

The larger question behind this issue is the place granted to symbol and metaphor in theories of thought and rationality. Bloch (1986) favorably cites Dan Sperber's (1974, 1979) argument that symbolism is an essentially unique form of knowledge that operates "when the rational device is overloaded." This suggests a fundamental discontinuity between propositional and metaphorical modes of thought, knowledge, and discourse. The analyses of theorists such as Johnson (1987), however, indicate that metaphor, the sine qua non of symbolism, is an essential structure of all thought. Paul Ricoeur (1977) argues that the critical question of reference is not irrelevant to metaphor but is shifted from the semantic (sentence) or propositional to the hermeneutic level, that is, from the level of the *object* to that of an entire *state of affairs*. Moreover, he argues "that the possibility of speculative discourse lies in the semantic dynamism of metaphorical expression, and yet that speculative discourse can respond to the semantic potentialities of metaphor only by providing it with the semantic resources of a domain of articulation that properly belongs to speculative discourse by reason of its very constitution" (Ricoeur 1977: 259). Thus, while retaining a difference between "poetic" (symbolic, metaphoric) and "speculative" (propositional, philosophical) modes of discourse, he points to a level at which that difference is transcended. He thus opens the possibility that creativity lies not only in propositions but in predications, especially in the mutual grounding they provide for each other.

In sum, to posit discontinuity among modes of discourse leads to the position that metaphor and symbol are essentially different from— or encode radically different forms of knowledge than—rational, speculative, propositional thought. To posit continuity among modes of discourse leads to the position that metaphor and symbol can create the conditions of possibility for knowledge that can subsequently be cast in propositional form.[3] The methodological choice in favor of discontinuity has a definitive consequence for Bloch's account. This becomes evident when we note that Ricoeur's "speculative" discourse refers explicitly to the language of philosophy, while Bloch's category of "nonritual communication" includes ordinary language as well. The latter thus presumes that ordinary language partakes more of the character of formally rational propositional discourse than of the symbolic and metaphoric discourse of ritual and poetry.

Let us juxtapose Bloch's approach to that of Tambiah (1973, 1979), who takes the opposite tack. Tambiah argues against distinction both between magical and religious language and between ritual language in general and ordinary language. For him, all are still language and so conform to the principles of how language operates. Tambiah would likely take issue with Bloch's assertion that ritual communication is distinct because it combines properties of statements and actions, pointing out that all language does so. In contrast to Bloch's description of a shift away from propositional toward illocutionary force, Tambiah emphasizes the mutual importance of both the predicative and illocutionary frames within ritual language. This is in part congenial with our own account, as indeed we have not been required to go beyond principles of ordinary language to understand the workings of Charismatic ritual language. We have been able to understand the rhetorical force of the "I" of prophecy in terms of properties attributed to the speaker within specific speech genre conventions. We have examined the role of metaphor in relation to everyday social life, on the one hand, and to the motives of ritual language, on the other. Finally, we have come to an understanding of the embodied character of all language as the ground for the experience of divine power in ritual utterance.

Let us, however, take a closer look at the issues that separate Bloch and Tambiah, based on their divergent perceptions of creativity and of whether there is an essential difference between ritual and ordinary language. We begin with an example that is symptomatic, involving not only whether ritual creates anything but also the possibility for flexibility or creative evolution of ritual form itself. Tambiah cites the historical instance in which a nineteenth-century Thai king broke ritual precedent, replacing his traditional stand-in and personally taking the role of the god Shiva in the tonsure rite that marked the investiture of his son as heir. For Tambiah, this was an "innovative step" that bore "emergent meanings" and had the effect of "enlarging the institution of kingship" prior to being once again "incorporated into the preexisting framework of conventions" (1979/1985: 160–161). Bloch cites a different nineteenth-century example of a cutting rite, the circumcision ceremony as it was used to legitimate the power of Merina rulers in Madagascar. However, unlike Tambiah, he insists that the "kings did not see themselves as creators, but users" of the ritual[4] and that these uses served only to bring about "a few minor transformations that remained within the general logic of the symbolism as it had existed before" (Bloch 1986: 190).

Both authors note the persistence of convention, but with quite different attitudes toward creativity. For creativity to occur, Bloch requires the conscious intention to create, and refers utlimately not to what ritual may create but only to whether ritual form itself can be created. Tambiah allows both that ritual innovation is a kind of creativity and that the effect produced by performance of that innovation is creative, even though (as with the example of the bulwark metaphor) it is eventually reincorporated into the framework of cultural meanings. This difference is evident in how Bloch addresses Tambiah's (1979/1985: 166) query about the conditions under which rituals may turn "right" toward conservatism and loss of semantic meaning, or "left" toward the effervescence of revival and reform.[5] Bloch sees this query not as one about conditions for creativity but as one about the "adaptation" of rituals to changed conditions, or about "matching the particular ritual expression to a particular event" (1986: 184). Moreover, for Bloch, the obverse process, matching the event to the expression, cannot be considered creative because it must be inscribed on the illocutionary side of the equation. The methodological difference can be summarized as the perception by Bloch of a gap between a ritual form and its "use" and the perception by Tambiah of an integral connection between a ritual form and its "performance."

Bloch adopts his position on ritual not only because of what he sees as its "fixity" and lack of "plasticity," but also because it is "impoverished," "arthritic," "frozen," "non-creative," and "disconnected from reality." His use of these adjectives stems from a Chomskyan equation of creativity with the generativity of an infinitely large number of possible utterances. He holds this view both for ritual discourse and for "art" in general. Thus it is everyday speech that is most creative, while verbal art is an "inferior form of communication." In his earlier paper he suggests why art is "mistakenly" thought to be otherwise.

The reason for this view probably lies in the fact that the generative processes of language are normally unconscious and that they are so complicated that they cannot usually be raised to a conscious level. However, when nearly all this generative potential of language (or bodily movement) has been forbidden, removed, the remaining choices are so simple that they can suddenly be apprehended consciously. Creativity has suddenly become controllable, enjoyable. This, however, is an illusion of creativity, in fact this is the sphere where it occurs least. (Bloch 1974: 73)

My analysis of ritual language has shown quite the opposite for the skillful Charismatic prophet: instead of being raised to a conscious, controllable level, the simplified choices of ritual language can be experienced as spontaneous, as language speaking itself. More at issue is that Bloch's argument confounds creativity as an act of imagination with generativity as an algorithm of recombination. He further restricts the possibility of creativity by noting the existence of constraints on what can be said even in ordinary conversation and arguing that once a speaker has actually said something he has lost some creativity by committing himself to a particular form. In this view a brilliant conversationalist would be considered less creative than a boorish blabbermouth because his speech is "impoverished" by adherence to codes of wit and analogy.

One can argue that a hammer is more constrained than a stone in the way it is shaped and the way it must be gripped but that it is still a better tool for building and pounding things. One can show that a sonnet bears more linguistic constraint than everyday speech but argue that in the work of a skillful poet its lines can be moving and creative because of processes that are not simply masked by everyday speech, but are unavailable to everyday speech. Likewise, one can argue that ritual language, precisely because of its formalization, can be a tool of creative persuasion. In short, Bloch's conception of art comes from regarding formalization as an interdiction or removal of generative potential, missing the fact that creativity does not "suddenly become controllable," but is a result of skill in a performance that may or may not be consciously controlled.

As Bloch reaffirms in his later writing, what remains as characteristic of ritual language is its "redundancy" and "repetitiveness" (1986: 184), characteristics we have observed in the couplet structure and the circulation of a limited vocabulary of motives in Charismatic prophecy. For Bloch, these features are sure symptoms of the absence of creativity. Tambiah (1979: 137–146) again differs, pointing out two distinct creative possibilities within redundancy itself. The first requires recognition that "meaning" can refer to pattern recognition and configurational awareness, rather than to explicit propositional content or the unpredictability and low probability of occurrence that are criterial for meaning in information theory. The second depends on the capacity of redundancy to heighten, intensify, and fuse the meaning of ritual communication. In both respects, attention is on the subtle variation within redundant utterance rather than on the element of repetitiousness per se. The perception of creativity would thus seem in part to depend on the aspect of ritual utterance that falls under the analytic gaze.

For both authors, however, redundancy has not only a textual but a psychological aspect as well, and here both fall back on speculative arguments that sidestep phenomenological data. Bloch suggests that the frequent occurrence of repetition in the rituals of various cultures makes it "reasonable to ask if this type of activity does not cause an automatic physiological response. . . . This repetition of every kind is indicative that we are not dealing with a statement with a clear proposition but, rather, with something that shares attributes of a semi-hypnotic spell" (1986: 184). His gratuitous conclusion that speakers "must be in trance" is based on no more data than the observation that redundancy and repetition are cross-culturally common in ritual language. If one adds to this conclusion Bloch's above-cited position that creativity requires the conscious intention to create, it appears that for Bloch creativity must be precluded a priori on psychological grounds, even before any of the textual arguments he offers.

Tambiah is more subtle, suggesting that the psychological effects of redundancy and conventionality may be "focusing" or "distancing" as well as trance-inducing (1979/1985: 146). Although distancing is not dissociation, it is predicated on the notion that ritual language does not express "the intentions, emotions, and states of mind of individuals in a direct, spontaneous, and 'natural' way. Cultural elaboration of codes consists in the *distancing* from such spontaneous and intentional expressions because spontaneity and intentionality are, or can be, contingent, labile, circumstantial, even incoherent or disordered" (1979: 132).[6] What Tambiah means by spontaneous is problematic, for, as we have seen, spontaneity is typical of North American ethnopsychological predications on the self—a problem that Tambiah only implicitly acknowledges by setting off "natural" in scare quotes. Intentionality is also problematic, for as we saw in chapter 7, whether the analysis of a meaning's utterance depends on what a speaker "intended" to mean is a subject of considerable debate.

Consider once more the relation of the Charismatic prophet to his utterance, in which the "I" of prophecy is not the speaker himself. This certainly constitutes a distancing, but does it exclude spontaneity and intentionality? Spontaneity is in fact a requisite of felicitous prophecy, insofar as the sense of sudden inspiration out of the blue assures the prophet "I am not making this up." The prophet's utterance also requires intentionality, in the sense that one does not simply blurt out the spontaneous inspiration but must "discern" its relevance and appropriateness to the situation at hand. Our readiness to attribute states of dissociation to speakers of ritual language may be related to inadequate inquiry into the phenomenology of utterance. One of the typical criteria is that speakers do not remember what they said after they say it. Indeed, the cultural specialist we encountered in chapter 6 made precisely such a statement—but when questioned concerning a particular utterance was fully able to discuss what it was *about* and the process by which the content of his inspiration was built up in consciousness. Given the sacredness of the divine word, could it not be that by saying he never remembered his prophecies he was merely saying he could not recall verbatim exactly what the deity was saying? How much have anthropologists missed by stopping with the question, Do you remember what you said? and neglecting to follow up with, Can you tell me what it was about? Likewise, the description of physiological correlates to ritual language typically presumes that these are signs of trance and hence of some degree of obliteration of the contents of consciousness. While at first this might also be concluded of the Charismatic prophet's "anointing," could it not be that the "physiological quickening" described may not be more akin to what we would recognize as stage fright than trance?

On another level, to what degree can the relationship of speaker to utterance be said to be one of "sincerity"? Here we find a substantial range in the possible relations between the speaker and the "I" of utterance, none of which require a notion of trance or dissociation. At one end of the continuum Rosaldo (1973) describes Ilongot oratory, in which it is accepted that the "tongue" can be separate from the speaker, and one can "lend his tongue" or rhetorical skills to a cause he does not support—much, incidentally, as a lawyer among ourselves can represent a client for whom she has no real sympathy. At the other end of the continuum, M. Foster (1974) describes Iroquois longhouse speeches of thanking and beseeching, in which "sincerity counts more than correct procedure," and "the important thing is to have one's mind on the Creator" with no great concern for "variations in the content and length of speeches." If one follows Lionel Trilling's (1972) argument that in our own society sincerity has been superseded by authenticity as an essentially valued capacity of self, it is not surprising that the Charismatic criterion of "discernment" does not determine sincerity but authenticity of utterance and experience. Not only do questions of trance or dissociation become moot in defining the relation between speaker and discourse, the same criterion of self is applied to the speaker of ritual language as might be applied to the speaker of ordinary, everyday language. Insofar as the speaker is distanced from a sacred discourse that "speaks itself," the distancing is not psychological but existential.

Bloch's conception of language leads him to conclude that ritual language "hides reality" and is "disconnected from" reality. This not only implies that such language is not really about anything but also reduces its illocutionary force to the functionalist status of reinforcing traditional authority—"keeping the natives mystified." There is no question that ritual language can do this in some cases. Among Catholic Charismatics there are tendencies both to place ritual language in service to authority and to use it in more liberating ways. These tendencies can be described as rhetorical strategies, but not as inevitable consequences of formalized language as such; and even where traditional authority is affirmed, ritual language is less static than Bloch's theory would allow. I would suggest that Bloch's own method ensures that he is unable to tap this dimension. That is, he reinforces the assumption that what ritual "statement/actions" mean to actors is inaccessible to analysis by pitching his analysis at the level of macrohistory, where such meaning is inaccessible from methodological necessity. In contrast, by adopting a microhistorical approach covering twenty-five rather than two hundred years, we have been able to provide a detailed account of how, in Geertz's phrase, "as life moves, persuasion moves with it."

While I agree with Bloch that there is a fundamental misapprehension involved in ritual language, it is, if anything, misapprehension not of its imputed "arthritic" character but of the source of its creativity in human action. When two Catholic Charismatics simultaneously "receive" the same prophetic inspiration, their conclusion that the message must have come from a divine source outside both of them is not a misapprehension of the poverty of their own language but of their own creativity. Interestingly, Bloch makes a similar point, but outside the domain of ritual language. He acknowledges that the Merina identification of the ancestors and the tomb as the true source of creativity, like the attribution of economic creativity to capital in capitalism, "depends on a negation of the creativity of human beings" (1986: 176). My inclusion of ritual language as an arena of human creativity is based on my demonstration throughout this discussion of continuity between practice and performance and on the argument in this final chapter for continuity between ritual language and ordinary language. The misapprehension of the human source of creativity in any of these domains has the same origin. This has been precisely stated by Bourdieu in his study of the Kabyle: "The illusion of mutual election or predestination arises from ignorance of the social conditions for the harmony of aesthetic tastes or ethical leanings, which is thereby perceived as evidence for the ineffable affinities which spring from it" (1977: 82). Our discussion has shown that participants in ritual language remain ignorant precisely of the social conditions for creativity, such that what they necessarily misapprehend is that, through performance, they have themselves created the sacred self and the Charismatic world it inhabits.

I am convinced that the only way the problem of creativity can be resolved is with an adequate theory of performance, in conjunction with a precise definition of what counts as creativity. A theory of performance must attend to all three levels of analysis I have identified: that of *event* in its relation to situation and social life; that of *genre* not only with respect to individual genres but also with respect to systems of genres; and that of *act* in which motives are circulated in both illocutionary and predicative frames. Creativity may be found to occur at any of these levels or in the interaction between levels but in any case must be identified in terms of the following essential components: its social and rhetorical conditions of possibility, the media and processes whereby it is achieved, the specific contribution of creative agents, and the products of the creative process. Only in this way will we be able confidently to distinguish the properties of, for example, the oratory of elders in a circumcision ceremony of the Merina kingdom and the prophecy of participants in a prayer meeting of the Charismatic Renewal.[7] Only in this way can we determine whether the perception of creativity in a "Charismatic movement" is illusory because of our preconceptions about innovation in social movements,[8] or whether the perception of creativity's absence in a "traditional kingship" is illusory because of our preconceptions about traditional authority. By the same token, only methodological rigor can resolve conflicting perceptions of creativity by analysts working with similar examples, such as the kingly cutting rituals examined by Bloch and Tambiah.

Lacking such a concept of performance, Bloch sees only constraints in ritual language, and neither the rhetorical skill of the performers nor variations in degree of formalization, specialization, sacredness, or the performer/audience relationship. Given the identity of the speakers (elders) and the nature of the events (circumcision rites), it is hardly surprising that the genre (oratory) with which Bloch is principally concerned can be analyzed as an affirmation of traditional authority. A generalization from this instance across all genres of formalized language skips the step of empirically defining the conditions under which particular genres might serve traditional authority or liberation, exist as static or creative cultural forms, and constitute impoverished forms of ordinary language or collective mobilizations of the imagination. The same genre may be relatively redundant in one instance and creative in another, and this variation may correlate with the significance of the utterance, the scope of the audience addressed, and the duration of its impact. Charismatic prophecy exhibits the range from redundant spiritual encouragement in a small prayer group to named prophecies like that of the Bulwark which orient group action over a long period to those such as the Rome prophecies addressed in theory to the public at large even beyond the Charismatic Renewal. Likewise, the Thai tonsure ceremony discussed by Tambiah (1979) bears different properties and addresses a different audience when performed for commoners than for royalty. Finally, across cultures, even given the same degree of formalization, a genre that is accessible to all members of a community will likely have different rhetorical properties than one that can be performed only by elders (Schieffelin 1985).

Tambiah, in collapsing magic into ritual and then collapsing ritual into ordinary speech, runs the opposite risk of having to work with an undifferentiated theory of performance that gives inadequate weight to distinctions among event, genre, and act. Moreover, distinction among genres may lead to recognition of distinctive *kinds* of creativity. The creativity of "spells," for example, may have to do with uses of redundancy. Rosaldo (1975) documents a metaphoric redundancy that reorders experience by forging "new relationships among the sensuous things of the world" in Ilongot spells. Tambiah himself (1968, 1979) examines the redundant combination of metaphors from different sensory domains with metonymic enumeration of an object's parts and shows how this combination "intensifies meaning" in Trobriand spells. However, Tambiah too operates with an imprecise definition of creativity. His defense of creativity devotes considerable attention to the possibility for variation within standardized ritual performances and to the performative freedom of oral composition. While thereby showing the possibility within ritual language for creation of a relatively unique text, this is not the same as demonstrating the creation of meaning. Although meaning may be created in this manner, following Bourdieu we have seen that such "regulated improvisation" as is found in formulaic oral composition, or in the ritual experimentation with living situations in covenant communities, may be quite highly constrained. However, we have seen in chapter 6 that meaning can be created through catachresis, that is, "the use of a word in some new sense in order to remedy a gap in the vocabulary" (Max Black, quoted in Sapir 1977: 8), even when the structure of ritual appears relatively static. Ultimately there can be no agreement about the creativity of performance until we decide on the relative importance of creating meaning, creating a text, creating a rite, or creating a ritual system.

Again, we must also consider the performative relation among genres *within* a system of ritual language such as I have described, or such as has been described by Johannes Fabian (1974), Gary Gossen (1972), Gilbert Lewis (1980), Corinne A. Kratz (1989), and Joel C. Kuipers (1990). Investigating the creative function of language here extends beyond the discrete act or genre to the circulation of motives among genres with varying rhetorical properties. The possibility of creativity then becomes a question not of prosodic features and fixity of form but, as Lewis (1980) has noted, of the thematic "openness" of motives.[9] Ideally the analysis must encompass ordinary speech, for independent of the argument over the formal continuity between ritual and everyday language there is a pragmatic continuity insofar as ritual language never *replaces* ordinary language, but in any speech community is available *in addition to* it, as something extra and often extraordinary. If the circulation of ritual motives in everyday speech impoverishes that speech, it may also elaborate those motives and even enrich the way they are used in formal settings. Such an analysis is precluded by a purely textual notion of formalization as a *mechanical* removal of generative potential that allows formerly masked processes to "suddenly be apprehended consciously." My examination of the relation between performer and audience suggests that the formalization of language in performance acts as a phenomenological cue for the audience to *attend to* the utterance in a manner unique to each genre. Different genres open the possibility for different rhetorical movements, some of which may or may not be available in everyday speech.

The comparison of Bloch and Tambiah has demonstrated that the perception of creativity depends on methodological predisposition as much as on differences among empirical cases. One methodological predisposition that both authors appear to share is that while much of their discussion is explicitly about ritual *language,* there is no distinct boundary between verbal and bodily acts in ritual. Just as I have shown the extension of Charismatic prophetic utterance into prophetic gesture and the intimate connection in glossolalia between linguistic utterance and bodily gesture, both Bloch and Tambiah acknowledge a continuity between ritual language and ritual gestures, including the manipulation of objects. Both are forms of representation, but both—including language itself—are forms of action and performance as well. I have argued that language is not only a form of action but also an embodied one, and I have emphasized the role of embodiment as the inclusive context of self, creativity, and being in the world. Creativity cannot be understood as a function of representation without being in the world, or of textuality without embodiment. Imagination is not a matter of mental representation but a multisensory engagement of the world best understood as a transformative, imaginal self process. Ritual language takes its place among techniques of the body (Mauss 1950) as a tool for reordering the behavioral environment, cultivating the dispositions of the habitus, and creating a sacred self.

My own discussion must be judged in the context of these issues. I have tried to understand Charismatic ritual performance as a rhetorical apparatus by means of which the attention of participants toward their own experience is redirected in such a way that their very capacities for orientation in the world are altered, thus creating a sacred self in a Charismatic world. I have been careful to specify the creative conditions, media, agents, and products of ritual performance. Furthermore, I have argued that creativity is to be found not only in one instance or moment but also in the dialectical relations between ritual and social life, between a system of genres and a vocabulary of motives, and between motives and the metaphors generated from them. On the first level, performance, in taking up existential problems formulated in terms of basic psychocultural themes, creates an idealized template for relationships subsequently enacted in situations of everyday life beyond the boundaries of ritual events, and by metaphorical predication creates collective identities for groups and personal identities for individuals. On the second level, insofar as ritual utterances are seldom mere repetitions of fixed tests, each performance is a creative product that draws on the speaker's individual experience as well as his knowledge of genres and motives. Finally, performance creates new meaning within the discursive system as new metaphors are created, extending the meaning of motives and thereby increasing the symbolic repertoire and rhetorical resources of the ritual language.

The interplay of creativity and constraint in this process can best be summarized in terms of what we have learned about the psychocultural themes of spontaneity, intimacy, and control. In the broadest sense, these themes are constraints in that they are given as preexistent cultural preoccupations, the raw material upon which, to borrow Obeyesekere's (1990) phrase, the "work of culture" must be carried out. It is creative only in a weak sense for the movement to have selected these particular themes among others. It is creative in a stronger sense for the movement to have synthesized them into a thematic complex or gestalt. The strongest sense of creativity, however, becomes evident only when we can specify the ways in which the psychocultural themes have been phenomenologically "thematized" in practice. For Charismatics, spontaneity is thematized not only as a capacity of self that can be threatened by various types of interpersonal and spiritual "bondages" but also as the phenomenological criterion of a sacred that is manifest "suddenly" or "out of the blue." Intimacy is thematized as an ideal characteristic of personal relationships with the deity, with one's spouse, and with other members of one's Charismatic group or community. Finally, both control and lack of control are thematized in positive and negative ways. One must be in control of one's behavior, but surrender control of one's affairs to the divine will; conversely, one may be out of control if control is surrendered to the deity, as in the sacred swoon, but may not be out of control if it means being under demonic influence. The language that thematizes control is ubiquitous in Charismatic discourse, as bondage, possession, oppression, letting go, giving problems to the Lord, release from burdens, the lifting of heaviness, surrender, submission, and being overwhelmed by divine power. Perhaps most striking from a cultural standpoint is that the Charismatic sacred self appears to be engaged, not in a struggle for control, but in a struggle to "let go."

We have seen how the North American psychocultural themes of spontaneity, intimacy, and control, all virtual capacities of the self, have been taken up in cultural practice and elaborated in specific ways in the Charismatic world. Likewise, we have touched on the cultural elaboration of imagination beyond its minimal role in the cultural psychology of North America. The Charismatic imagination is put into action in everyday life, in prayer, in revelatory gifts such as prophecy, and in ritual healing. Whether the specific images produced are conventional or original, the cultivation of this capacity is a moment of creativity in the Charismatic world, and its use in specific settings constitutes moments of creativity for a sacred self.

If these are specific modulations of self as the capacity for orientation and engagement, their existential coherence can be summarized by the word *sacred*. We must finally understand the sacred, not as a characteristic of the cultural objectifications and representations in a ritual system, but as a characteristic of how they are produced from our being in the world. Especially insofar as what is being created is a sacred self, sacredness cannot be understood to inhere in symbols or utterances alone. It inheres as well in the existential precondition of both self and the sacred, that preobjective sense of otherness identified by the phenomenologists of religion as defining the sacred (see Bettis 1969), and which we identified in the preceding chapter as grounded in embodiment (see also Csordas 1994a).

Bynum (1989) has pointed out that the spirituality of the Middle Ages, especially that of women, was much more explicitly bodily than that with which we are familiar. It is thus perhaps only an artifact of history that to identify the body as the existential ground of the sacred should appear to be a discovery. We have seen how the sense of embodied otherness is cultivated and objectified in the Charismatic world by playing out psychocultural themes characteristic of the North American cultural context. Spontaneity is not only an ego-ideal but also a phenomenological criterion of the sacred. Intimacy is not only an interpersonal ideal for relationship to the social other but also one that defines the moment of relationship to the divine other. Control is not only an issue of the affairs of everyday life but also something that may be surrendered to the deity or usurped by the demonic. Imagination is not only the vehicle of fantasy and daydream but also the (experientially "im-mediate") medium in which divine presence appears in its most phenomenologically concrete form.

Like the phenomenologists of religion, Emile Durkheim ([1915] 1965) observed the importance of otherness as a feature of the sacred. However, by restricting the human experience of otherness to the category of the social, he committed a major error of reductionism. To show that the social was a methodological category sui generis, he argued that society creates the sacred by appearing as something radically other and outside the individual, and in the massiveness and mystery of this otherness establishing an absolute moral authority. Subsequent generations have followed him in this sociological reductionism, in large part precluding an authentically phenomenological and psychocultural theory of religion in anthropology. The phenomenologists, for their part, were ignored, either for making what appeared to be arbitrary claims about human nature or because it was assumed that to accept the sui generis definition of the sacred was to adopt a theological position. I suggest that we are now in a position to formulate the sacred as a modulation of being in the world, operationalized by the criterion of otherness that we have found to be grounded in the socially informed body. Since otherness is a characteristic of embodied human consciousness, defining the sacred is not a theological but an ethnological task.

Appendix:
Performance and Practice
as Domains of Social Action

Schematizing conceptual relationships is often risky, but it strikes me as potentially valuable to offer a tentative synthesis of the critical conceptual distinctions that underlie the basic distinction I have drawn between performance and practice. In figures 4 and 5 I present the structures of performance and practice as I understand them, not as a model I have applied (in which case they would have appeared in the introductory chapter), but as a hypothesis about the relations among concepts that have been central to the analysis in this book. Note that what is portrayed is explicitly the conceptual structure of two interacting and interpenetrating domains of action. The issue of context is inevitably raised by such an exercise, and here it is safest to invoke the broadest understanding of "a relationship between two orders of phenomena that mutually inform each other to comprise a larger whole" (Goodwin and Duranti 1992: 4). The diagrams would need a third dimension in order to portray the sense of context given in the body of our analysis by the telescoping focus on increasingly wider spheres of act, genre, event, and social life (see Duranti and Goodwin 1992 for a variety of conceptualizations of context from the standpoint of language use).

My limited intent here is threefold: to suggest that these domains have a parallel structure that is the condition for them to be mutually transformative; to sort out the different levels of analysis (identified by the terms in the left-hand column of each diagram) in these parallel domains; and to locate the contributions of several leading scholars with

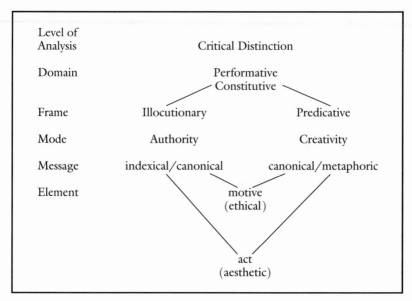

Fig. 4. *The Structure of Performance*

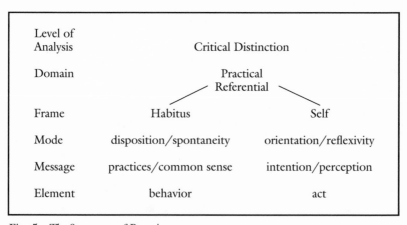

Fig. 5. *The Structure of Practice*

reference to these levels of analysis. To begin, what I have referred to as the performative and practical domains correspond in large part to what Peter Stromberg (1993) has labeled the constitutive and referential domains. The fundamental difference is between language or other action that sets the conditions for social life and language or action that forms the connective tissue of mundane social life.

Within the performative domain (fig. 4) social action can occur within either an illocutionary or a predicative frame, a distinction we have adopted from Tambiah (1979/1985) that allows us to frame analysis of the relationship between force and meaning in ritual. In the diagram I have glossed the mode of social interaction associated with illocutionary force as authority and that associated with predicative meaning as creativity, precisely the relation made problematic by the ethnographic case we have been dealing with. Performative interaction in each of these modes is characterized by two options for encoding messages. In the authoritative mode these two options are elaborated by Rappaport (1979) as indexical messages that point to the immediate state of participants and canonical messages that articulate cosmological truth. Stromberg's (1993) analysis demonstrates that messages in the creative mode can be encoded either in canonical language (in Rappaport's sense) or metaphoric language. In both modes it is the relation between the two types of messages (indexical/canonical or canonical/metaphoric) in performance that is critical in the performative efficacy of authority or creativity. Finally, the elementary form of performance is characterized by the relation between motive and act. Motives are terms in the sense we have borrowed from Mills (1940) and Burke (1966, 1970). They condense and summarize canonical language and its ethical import. The acts by means of which those motives are circulated are the instances of utterance or gesture that always, insofar as they are characterized by a style of performance, have aesthetic import. In the diagram I have drawn a link through act between the metaphoric and indexical to draw out the aesthetic predication of metaphors onto the immediate state of participants, a relationship elaborated by Fernandez (1974) in his account of how "inchoate pronouns" are given identity and form by performance.

In the practical or referential domain (fig. 5) we have pursued an account of the transformation of self and habitus, and the diagram schematizes these as equivalent frames of analysis. As was the case with the illocutionary and predicative frames in the performative domain, I would argue that the same data of social action can often be understood simultaneously in terms of both frames. Although habitus has more of a collective and self more of an individual connotation, I would continue to insist that both are grounded in embodiment, and that this fact is what requires us to consider them to occupy the same level of analysis/abstraction. My understanding of habitus follows Bourdieu (1977, 1984) insofar as the mode of social interaction is given by a structured and structuring structure of bodily dispositions inculcated in people such that social life has an aura of spontaneous improvisation and that the essential messages of interaction are inscribed in practices and have to do with issues of common sense. Correspondingly, the characteristic mode of interaction in the frame of self is orientation in the sense I elaborated in the introduction to this book (see also Hallowell 1955; Csordas 1994a) in which self is constituted by processes of bodily/sensory engagement with features of the social world. This is not only necessarily reflexive and therefore constitutive of subjectivity (see Merleau-Ponty's [1962] reworking of the Cartesian cogito), it also implies a mutual orientation when the object is another person and is therefore constitutive of intersubjectivity (e.g., "I am aware that she is aware that I am aware . . ."). Messages are thus imbued with intention and have to do with the manner in which the perceptual reality impinges on and is taken up by persons in the immediacy of being-in-the-world. Finally, each element of social action in the practical domain can be understood as a behavior insofar as it is characterized by anonymity or as act insofar as it is characterized by intentionality.

Notes

Preface

1. Spiro (1990) offers a thoughtful analysis of the vicissitudes of these complementary methodological operations in the recent history of anthropology.

2. The results of this study are to appear in a separate publication.

3. For a rare example of this type of interactional immediacy and intimate access to group activities in a contemporary religious group, see Warner (1988).

Chapter 1

1. In the American religious landscape, Pentecostal-Charismatic religion is placed by the historian Martin Marty (1976) alongside mainline denominational Christianity, evangelical-fundamentalist Christianity, ethnic religions, new religions (including North American variants of Hinduism, Islam, and Buddhism), and civil religion (see Bellah 1970 on the latter). Pentecostalism originated in the United States at the turn of the twentieth century as a predominantly working-class, fundamentalist movement based on the immediate experience of divine power (Bloch-Hoell 1964; Hollenweger 1972) and in its several variants is considered to be the fastest-growing form of Christianity in the world (Marty 1976: 124). In the United States these variants are summarized by Vinson Synan (1975: 2–3): (1) the holiness-pentecostal movement that began with Charles Parham in Topeka (1901) and James Seymour in Los Angeles (1906), with the later split between the two leaders marking the division of an originally racially integrated movement into white and black segments; (2) the "Finished Work" Pentecostal movement that began with

Charles Durham in Chicago (1910) and includes the Assemblies of God, the largest among Pentecostal denominations; (3) the "oneness" or unitarian Pentecostal movement that began in a schism from the Assemblies of God (1913–1916); (4) the Protestant neo-Pentecostal movement with one branch that began with Demos Shakarian's Full Gospel Business Men's Fellowship International in Los Angeles (1951) and developed into a nondenominational form of Pentecostalism and a second branch that began with the Episcopalian pastor Dennis Bennet in Van Nuys, California (1960), and established a trend of Charismatic movements within the major individual Protestant denominations, especially Episcopalian, Lutheran, and Presbyterian; (5) the Catholic Charismatic movement that began in Pittsburgh and South Bend (1967). From the Catholic side, one precursor to the Charismatic Renewal was the Cursillo movement (*New Catholic Encyclopedia* 1967), and apologists attempt to ground its legitimacy in a variety of theological trends seen as culminating in the Second Vatican Council.

Major works on "classical" Pentecostal denominations have been produced by Bloch-Hoell (1964), Hollenweger (1972), Synan (1975), and Cox (1995). "Neo-Pentecostal" and "Charismatic" movements and congregations have been treated by Gerlach and Hine (1970), Quebedoux (1976), McGuire (1982), Neitz (1987), and Warner (1988). In the 1980s a group of evangelicals and pentecostals identifying themselves as a "third wave" in the "modern outpouring of the Spirit" emerged under the banner of "spiritual warfare" against demonic forces said to be on the rise in contemporary society (Cox 1995: 281–285). Characterizing the difference in ethos between classical and neo-Pentecostalism in terms of popular culture icons, the theologian Harvey Cox writes, "If Jimmy Swaggart is the Mick Jagger of Pentecostalism, the charismatic movement is its Guy Lombardo" (1995: 152). There is no doubt that some of the more forceful phenomena of Pentecostalism have been "domesticated" by Charismatics (Neitz 1987; Csordas 1994a; Cox 1995). For example, the experience of being overcome by divine power is called being "slain in the Spirit" by classical pentecostals and "resting in the Spirit" by Charismatics; and whereas the expulsion of evil spirits from an afflicted person is likely to be manifested by vomiting among classical pentecostals, it is just as likely to be manifested by a burp or a cough among Charismatics. By the same token, in keeping with Cox's mode of characterization, the third wave's musical totem would have to be Screamin' Jay Hawkins or perhaps the Rev. Billy C. Wirtz.

2. The split came about formally at the movement's 1977 national conference in Kansas City. Notably, this was the first national conference held on neutral ground, as all previous ones had taken place in South Bend under the sponsorship of the People of Praise covenant community.

3. These efforts were epitomized in a series of mass events called FIRE (Faith, Intercession, Repentance, Evangelization) rallies. At the same time the leadership of the parochial wing under the aegis of the National Service Committee established an office of Traveling Timothy, in which experienced Charismatics were sent to localities to aid and encourage prayer groups that were not interested in becoming covenant communities.

4. The move was designed in part to give added autonomy to the National

Service Committee as a national body independent of the People of Praise community in South Bend, as well as distance from the split among covenant communities that occurred earlier in the 1980s and is described below.

5. While The Word of God was at first instrumental in the migration of the international office to Brussels under the auspices of their ally Cardinal Suenens, once in Rome that community's influence progressively declined, and it turned its attention to the international expansion of its own network of communities, the Sword of the Spirit. The International Communications Office (ICO) later became known as the International Catholic Charismatic Renewal Office (ICCRO), and in 1994 it was again rechristened International Catholic Charismatic Renewal Services (ICCRS).

6. Cardinal Suenens has published a series of influential manifestos known as "Malines Documents" on the movement's theology, pastoral issues, ecumenism, social activism, casting out of evil spirits, and the ritual technique of the body known as resting in the Spirit.

7. Indeed, although the movement is overtly apolitical in its public stance, it is not without political implications. In the United States, some movement leaders have belonged to the conservative Intercessors for America, a group dominated by Protestant evangelicals, the express purpose of which is to pray for the well-being of the nation. At least two Latin American movement leaders were formerly well-placed government officials in their respective countries, one an ambassador to Washington and the other a president of the Senate. In Nicaragua, a leader of the Managua branch of the Sword of the Spirit covenant community is a prominent anti-Sandinista. The attraction of such people in Latin America suggests that the Charismatic Renewal provides a new overtly apolitical arena for reformulating older ideas of Christian Democracy and Catholic Action and counteracting the influence of liberation theology. Thus Pentecostalism, usually described as a "third force" in Christianity after Catholicism and Protestantism, may appear in its Catholic form as a "third force" between political Left and Right, appealing to communitarian sentiments while advancing conservative values.

8. Regional diversity among Charismatics is likely to reflect that among Catholics at large. An interesting if impressionistic summary of regional variants of Catholicism is given in True (1977): eastern coastal Catholicism is strongly based in neighborhoods, with many children in parochial schools, is linked to the eastern intellectual establishment, and has a powerful hierarchy conservative with respect to the reforms of the Second Vatican Council; midwestern and West Coast Catholicism is characterized by provincialism, clericalism, and anti-intellectualism, with less powerful bishops than in the East, and with a history of initiatives in favor of liturgical reform, social action, ecumenical reform, and lay leadership. Southern Catholicism is a largely missionary church in which a person "chooses to be Catholic as an act of will," and which unlike the other two regions lacks a Catholic university system and has few religious periodicals; ethnic Catholicism based on nationality is relatively insular but is the source of movements such as the United Farmworkers' Union. My observations of diversity among Charismatics support this picture of regional variation, including the existence of a largely distinct Catholic Charismatic

Renewal among Hispanics in the United States. In spite of diversity, the ritual language and practice of the movement are remarkably uniform in North America, largely due to circulation of vast amounts of written and audiotaped material and to frequent conferences and workshops of local, regional, and national scope.

9. Westley (1977) documents the social dynamics of a case in which a Catholic Charismatic prayer group's attempt to incorporate speaking in tongues into its ritual life was unsuccessful.

10. Community members regard this as reintroduction of the "double monastery" that existed in previous periods of Benedictine history, a structure whose recognition was formalized in 1985 with the reaffiliation of the community within the Benedictine order from the Swiss-American Federation to the Olivetan Congregation.

11. The emergence of this model in New England, under the leadership of priests and with an integration of Catholic liturgy into Charismatic ritual, conforms to the prominence of Catholics in the region's demographics and to the more traditional style of New England Catholicism.

12. Prophecy is one of the spiritual gifts by means of which the divinity is understood to directly address the faithful through the speech of humans (see chapters 6 and 7).

13. Most affiliated with one or the other network, though in the covenant community in Minneapolis divided loyalties led to a split. Part of the community went with the federation and part with the fellowship and as of the late 1980s maintained no ongoing interaction between them.

14. The remainder were in Canada, Costa Rica, Nicaragua, Mexico, Honduras, the Philippines, Lebanon, Hong Kong, South Africa, Northern Ireland, Ireland, Scotland, England, Belgium, France, Spain, Austria, and India. Twelve were full branches, and the rest were categorized as either affiliated or associated groups, the latter differentiated both by the degree to which a community has committed to the Sword of the Spirit covenant and by its potential for such commitment as seen by the Sword of the Spirit governing council and assembly, headed, respectively, by Ralph Martin and Steven Clark of The Word of God.

15. The six original communities of the fellowship subsequently went through a process of regional consolidation, with the merger of three midwestern members and two western members, the southeastern group remaining discrete.

16. The channeling of increasing energy by The Word of God into formation of the Sword of the Spirit as an international covenant community, as well as a degree of disappointment in the decline of communitarian development by the Charismatic Renewal at large, led to its withdrawal in the 1980s from active participation in Charismatic conferences sponsored by the National Service Committee (NSC), still based in South Bend. While the NSC instituted a new outreach to Charismatic prayer groups and communities in which Traveling Timothys visited localities, the Sword of the Spirit initiated its aforementioned outreach of large FIRE rallies (see note 3, above) to recruit and evangelize rank-and-file Charismatics to the communitarian vision derived from the 1975

Rome prophecies. The Sword of the Spirit also largely withdrew from activities of the International Catholic Charismatic Renewal Office, which it had founded a decade earlier. Covenant communities in general were not active in this body through the 1980s, and only in 1990 were representatives of the Fellowship of Communities and the International Brotherhood of Communities once again elected to its council at the encouragement of Bishop Paul Cordes of Rome's Pontifical Council for the Laity, acting in his new capacity as Episcopal adviser to the Catholic Charismatic Renewal.

17. The Alleluia community in Augusta, Georgia, also has such denominational fellowships, but as a member of the Catholic Fraternity its Catholic fellowship is under the sole authority of the local bishop, while The Word of God Fellowship also came under the translocal authority of the Sword of the Spirit community network.

18. A true comparison is quite impossible, as it would require access to the privileged communication between head and advisee, recording the strength and frequency of advice and guidance, the range of issues that are actually submitted to this relationship, and the frequency with which the words of the head are presented as advice or as divine guidance. Moreover, the advisee's subjective expectation of guidance would have to be taken into account, since if both parties share the same expectation, regardless of its comprehensiveness it is unlikely to be perceived as "heavy-handedness."

19. Nevertheless, a People of Praise coordinator acknowledged that "were a feminist to look at both of us they would say we were both inflexible." This acknowledgment may be somewhat more significant than it appears, for it implies a legitimacy for the feminist position that leaders of The Word of God would likely be reluctant to grant.

20. The difference between the groups is exemplified by the comment of a People of Praise coordinator on a talk given at a presplit meeting of leaders from both groups:

One of their [Word of God] guys was talking about the possibility of fathers helping mothers with changing diapers. With great disdain he virtually eliminated the possibility of any man with a decent degree of male hormones doing that sort of thing. For us that was a matter of charity as opposed to hormones—if the wife needs some help, you help her. . . . We would say that's more of the wife's and mother's responsibility than the father's. On the other hand, when charity demands, don't let your image of masculinity stand in the way.

21. A coordinator of the People of Praise summarizes the disagreement as follows:

With historical perspective you can see that there have been very bad times throughout for the Church but somehow God in his love proved superior to evil, and he pulls it out of the fire. We take that kind of perspective without minimizing sin and the evil that's around us; we might emphasize more God's redeeming work that is going on. . . . Kevin Ranaghan [Principal Branch Coordinator, People of Praise, South Bend] talked at a conference three or four years ago entitled "Renewing the Face of the Earth," painting a picture of different worldviews using the example of if the *Titanic* is sinking, you don't waste time rearranging deck chairs but get lifeboats and take emergency precautions to save lives. That was the example they [The Word of God] liked to use a lot in the old days [before the split]. Depending on your reading of the signs of the times you see the *Titanic* sinking or not, and if it's sinking your agenda is different—we don't see it as sinking, and our agenda is different.

22. In part through this group, the Korean Protestant Charismatic evangelist Yonggi Cho has had a broad influence on Catholic Charismatics throughout the United States as well as Asia.

23. For a comparison of Cuban-American Catholic Charismatic and *santeria* healers, see Espin 1988.

24. The exact quote is as follows: "Toujours, l'experience religieuse charismatique vient refaire le moi, le reconstituter en profondeur" (1979: 91).

25. Doutreloux and Degive (1978) offer a critical account of a prayer meeting and Charismatic language use in French-speaking Belgium, probably based on observation of a group affiliated with Cardinal Suenens and The Word of God community in the United States.

26. Lanternari (1994: 48–50) offers a comparison, albeit somewhat artificial, between a branch of the French Lion of Judah covenant community in Rome and a healing ministry led by one Brother Cosimo in the southern region of Calabria.

27. In an analogous vein, in the same year a Zairean priest named Abbé Pius Kasongo, who had also had a Charismatic healing ministry and led a prayer group since the early 1970s, was suspended by his bishop from his rights and duties as a priest. Kasongo, however, remained in Zaire, living at a Catholic parish and continuing his healing services (Fabian 1994: 273).

Chapter 2

1. The interpretation of glossolalia as a phenomenon of trance or altered state of consciousness is prominent in Goodman 1972, while Samarin (1972) approaches it as a ritual speech act within a religious speech community and Gerlach and Hine (1970) see it as a mechanism of commitment to a fringe religious movement. For more on psychological interpretations of glossolalia, see Richardson 1973.

2. Danforth (1989) attempts to apply a postmodern paradigm to his analysis of the American firewalking movement and the Greek Anastenari. While his analysis of each independently is excellent, their juxtaposition is an artifact of his ethnography rather than of any cultural process in which incongruous symbols or social forms appear as unaccustomed bedfellows. Hence, as an exercise in postmodernism, his discussion appears strained and ultimately unconvincing.

3. An informant who had converted to Catholic Pentecostalism after being raised by Protestant missionary parents in the Southwest stated that in his youth Catholics and Pentecostals had been considered "the two kinds of weird people" and that his initial reaction to the new movement was that "they deserve each other."

4. "Charism" is the theological term for an extraordinary spiritual power

given to a Christian by the Holy Spirit for the good of the Church. The common charisms, including speaking in tongues, prophecy, and healing, are enumerated in Paul's second letter to the Corinthians.

5. McGuire (1974) presents an early comparison of the Charismatic Renewal and the "underground church," suggesting that while participants' sociological profile was quite similar, Charismatics exhibited a relatively greater "crisis mentality" about the state of religion in the contemporary world and a correspondingly greater degree of escapism in place of activism.

6. In the first decade of the movement Mawn (1975: 123) received the following responses from 455 respondents about their participation:

1) experienced "faith crisis" when joining: 47.3% yes, 51.9% no;
2) "happy with life" before joining: 54.9% yes, 43.4% no;
3) lives lacked meaning and purpose: 34.3% of men and 65.7% of women yes;
4) uncertain about values to pursue: 41.4% of men and 58.6% of women yes;
5) no clear answers about how to conduct life: 37.2% of men and 62.8% of women yes.

Based on biographical case studies, Harper (1974) suggested that a typical profile of a Catholic Charismatic included strong early religious socialization in conjunction with significant later alienation from the Church. McGuire's (1975) early work took a social psychological functionalist approach, suggesting that the movement's appeal to stable, educated, middle-class, active Catholics was based on a series of factors centering on a need for security. Harrison (1974b) emphasized the role of preexisting social networks in recruiting members of The Word of God in its early days, though notably many of its early members were drawn from a university student population.

After two decades of the movement, our 1987 survey of 587 participants in Charismatic healing services showed the following response to why people enjoyed attending these services:

1) It gives meaning and purpose to my life: 64%
2) It relieves me of stress and tension: 59%
3) It is one of the few quiet times I have: 24%
4) It is one of the few things I can rely on: 24%

Within the subset of respondents who were active participants in other Charismatic activities, the proportion of those to whom the services contributed meaning and purpose rose to 74%.

7. It is also possible using Erikson's framework to distinguish the Charismatic Renewal from the contemporaneous "Jesus people" and new religions such as Moon's Unification Church. While early Charismatics were dominated by young adults engaged in the crisis of intimacy versus isolation, many of the new cults appealed to teenagers looking for a basic sense of orientation in life, the adolescent crisis defined by Erikson as between identity and role confusion (1963: 261–263).

8. In 1990 representatives from all Catholic orientations participated in a massive conference in conjunction with Charismatics from the United Church

of Christ, American Baptist, Presbyterian, Messianic Jewish, Episcopalian, Elim Fellowship, Lutheran, United Methodist, Wesleyan Holiness, nondenominational, and classical Pentecostal orientations.

9. Charismatic leaders of such services often explicitly refrain from inclusion of speaking in tongues so as not to shock or alienate participants who may be unfamiliar with the practice.

10. Resting in the Spirit is a characteristic Charismatic and Pentecostal experience of motor dissociation and falling in a sacred swoon, thought to be caused by exposure to the overwhelming force of divine power, presence, and love.

11. Based on the analysis identifying Charismatics by degree of ritual participation shown in table 5, 86% of those who attended prayer meetings weekly and spoke in tongues often reported having been healed at some time, whereas 64% of those who attended less than weekly and never spoke in tongues reported having been healed. The relatively large proportion of non-Charismatics who have been healed might be accounted for by the attraction of large public healing services for a clientele that transcends active movement participation. Nevertheless, the analysis had a chi-square value with three degrees of freedom of 11.58 and was significant at a .009 level of probability. Charismatics also reported a significantly greater tendency to have rested in the Spirit on multiple occasions. Only 10% reported never having rested in the Spirit, 31% reported having the experience between one and five times, and 59% reported having it six or more times. For non-Charismatics the corresponding results were flat, with 34% never having rested in the Spirit, 38% between one and five times, and 28% six or more times. This result had a chi-square at six degrees of freedom of 32.8, with a .00 level of probability. Unfortunately, the robustness of these results is compromised because on top of the fact that the original determination of Charismatic/non-Charismatic was based on 82% of total respondents, each of the secondary analyses required that there be no missing values on three separate items. This compounded the problem of missing data such that each secondary analysis was based on only 65% of the 587 total respondents.

12. Fabian (1991) observes that preexisting Catholic prayer groups in Zaire became Charismatic by subsequent exposure to movement activities and ritual forms.

13. As for whether Charismatic identity includes identity as a "fundamentalist," in addition to individual variation and variation among communities, there is a clearly discernible dynamic within the Catholic movement between a theologically sophisticated and highly organized leadership and a tendency among grassroots participants toward biblical literalism and enthusiastic spirituality.

14. A good sense of the postmodern mélange of meanings in North American ritual healing is conveyed by McGuire (1988), who found 130 different healing groups of four broad types in a single suburban New Jersey county.

15. For an analysis of Charismatic speaking in tongues from the standpoint of embodiment, see Csordas (1990a).

16. Baudrillard's (1983) notion of simulacra in American culture is most clearly applicable to a phenomenon in the Protestant neo-Pentecostal born-

again movement, the now-defunct Heritage USA theme park created by televangelist Jim Bakker, an installation that imitated the Kingdom of Heaven imitating Disney World imitating an idealized America. For a description and cultural analysis of Heritage USA, see Harding (1988).

17. Zaner (1981: 112) has done us the service of defining this terminological set, including both colloquial and technical terms: self, spirit, soul, psyche, subjectivity, subject, inner man, person, mind, consciousness, mental substance, ego, monad, transcendental unity of apperception, *Da-sein, pour-soi, etre-au-monde,* agent, transcendental ego. In addition, one should not forget identity and the individual.

18. I will not follow the strategy of analyzing the self into its components as has been done fruitfully by a number of theorists (Mead 1934; Bailey 1983; James 1983; Singer 1989). Each of those analyses in its way specifies critical functional aspects of self, serving as aids to thought much as do theories of multiple souls among peoples typically described by anthropologists. Neither is my aim primarily to apply concepts of self developed in the contemporary discussion among psychologists, ranging from M. Brewster Smith's (1985) attempts to define the conditions necessary to the ideal of an "integral selfhood" to Robert Jay Lifton's (1976) analysis of the fragmentation and mutability of a "protean self." Each of these analyses is a cultural critique with an implicitly prescriptive and therapeutic purpose and as such must be excluded as conceptual starting points for an interpretive ethnography such as this one, although they may appropriately be applied to its results. Finally, we must be cautious about the principal characteristics we attribute to the self, for these bear methodological consequences. Such consequences are evident in Descartes's understanding of the self as a substance, or the early Christian understanding of self as a kind of entity, the soul. No less consequential are contemporary theories of self that define it as consciousness (DeVos, Marsella, and Hsu 1985), self-awareness (Hallowell 1955), states of mind (Johnson 1985), systems of signs and bundles of habits (Singer 1984), or a locus of experience composed of intrapsychic structures and processes (Harris 1989).

19. This hypothesis could be empirically tested by examining the role assumed by each of the divine persons in prayerful interaction, the texts of prophecies, and in healing imagery.

20. In earlier work I have addressed these themes in the domain of ritual healing (Csordas 1994a); in the present discussion the focus is on Charismatic collective life and ritual language. Note that McGuire (1982: chap. 4) explicitly characterizes the Charismatic prayer meeting by its "controlled spontaneity." Clow (1976) identified the theme of control among classical Pentecostals, and Sequeira (1994) highlights intimacy among Episcopalian Charismatics.

21. For a more complete analysis of laying on of hands as a technique of the body, see Csordas (1983: 351–353).

22. This dictum does not explicitly extend to homoerotic stirrings, perhaps because in the exceedingly conservative sexual morality of Charismatics their possibility is too culturally threatening to be acknowledged.

23. Identifying the ethos of localities according to their characteristic demons is a "third wave" practice associated with leaders like C. Peter Wagner, Timothy Warner, and Dick Bernal, who has declared that "San Francisco is

ruled by the Spirit of Perversion, Oakland by the Spirit of Murder, San Jose by the Spirit of Greed," and the whole of Marin County by the "New Age Spirit" (Cox 1995: 285).

24. The speaker was Francis MacNutt, a leading Charismatic healer.

Chapter 3

1. Steven Clark, the most influential ideologist of the covenant community movement, counts the Charismatic Renewal alongside these developments as "renewal movements" within the Church. In his view such movements so nearly inevitably produce "renewal communities" that it "seems to be almost a sociological law" (1976: 4).

2. The former is in essence a withdrawal from all conventional ties and "creaturely interests," whereas the latter entails the responsibility to participate in conventional institutions in order to transform them.

3. The form of covenant community headship apparently is an adaptation of the "shepherding" relationship practiced earlier in Derek Prince and Robert Mumford's neo-Pentecostal Christian Growth Ministries, now defunct.

4. Such a move is not unheard of, however, since in 1977 a community of roughly the same size moved from the San Francisco Bay area en masse to join the People of Praise (see Lane 1976, 1978).

5. In the short term, the questions before the Pontifical Council for the Laity are significant not only for the general status of Catholics within the covenant community but also for the long-standing desire of Steven Clark for himself and other members of his celibate brotherhood for ordination to Catholic priesthood. Since the Charismatic covenant community is neither formal religious order nor diocese, and has training distinct from that of the conventional seminary, Clark's goal has to date not achieved legitimacy. The ultimate resolution of these issues will doubtless affect the degree to which the covenant community comes to be regarded as a contribution of the Charismatic Renewal to the Church on the level of a predominantly lay charismatic religious order, or whether it will be regarded as the source of protoschismatic tension.

6. Wimber's emphasis on signs and wonders qualifies him as a representative of the so-called third wave of spiritual outpouring identified in the preceding chapter.

7. This was done under the auspices of a newly formed outreach organization called the Michigan Christian Association. The traditional vehicle of initiation, the Life in the Spirit Seminar, was updated and renamed A New Way of Living in anticipation of new recruitment from these prayer meetings.

8. Several other communities also opted for an allied status in the Sword of the Spirit. To neutralize the split between its paramount leaders Martin and Clark, the relatively unaligned leader of the Managua, Nicaragua, branch was appointed head of the community's governing council.

9. Somewhat ironically, this coincided with the time described above when several Sword of the Spirit branches were coming under increasing critical scrutiny by local Catholic bishops.

10. While at the rank-and-file level Wimber's appeal was predominantly in terms of signs and wonders, there may be another dimension of this appeal to the elite of Martin's faction. It will be recalled that great emphasis in community direction is given to prophetic utterance. However, prophecy in the Sword of the Spirit is dominated by Bruce Yocum, the community-confirmed head prophet who is Clark's lieutenant in the Servants of the Word. It is conceivable that the independent voice of Wimberite prophecy provided Martin with an alternative reading of "divine will" that supported a retreat from the Sword of the Spirit vision.

11. Here is an example where a trend in contemporary society (and one that is particularly lively in a university city like Ann Arbor) not only diffuses across the cultural boundary between "world" and "kingdom" but becomes amplified within the cultural configuration of the Charismatic world. It appears that as many as half of the presplit community membership were involved in twelve-step or codependency groups.

Chapter 4

1. A similar rhetorical dynamic is apparently at work in Lane's (1978: 28) observation that the first person to broach the subject of moving the St. John the Baptist community to Ann Arbor or South Bend in 1977 prefaced his remarks with "You may think this is off the wall, but . . ."

2. Catholic student centers on American university campuses are typically called Newman Centers after a churchman prominent for pastoral and educational work with youth.

3. A sociological analysis parallel to this cultural analysis can be formulated in terms of "transactional" method (Kapferer 1976), the main concern of which is how people organize and regulate relationships that involve some kind of exchange or give-and-take. In naming The Word of God, performance would appear as the means by which participants negotiated a definition of their collective life: various names were suggested, some were eliminated by prophecy and sharing, and the result was "confirmed" by prophecy. In this view the role of the prophet in the "management of meaning" is similar to that of the political broker or the persons responsible for arranging the terms of a marriage exchange in traditional societies (see Cohen and Comaroff 1976).

4. The text is cited in a version from the late 1970s.

5. Another occasion in which the mythic history is recited is the "community weekend," a retreat that is part of the initiation process attended by prospective members prior to their public commitment to the covenant.

6. Based on a study of eight nineteenth-century American communal groups,

Sue Marie Wright (1992) presents a hypothesis that gender roles and proportion of female members change over the course of four typical stages of development including core group, communal venture, expansion, and isolation. A
study of whether this model would hold true across Catholic Charismatic covenant communities would be of considerable sociological interest.

7. It may in fact be that foot washing was adopted from Reba Place Fellowship, a Mennonite Charismatic community with which The Word of God was
in contact.

8. A Wimberite healing service conducted by Sword of the Spirit leaders is
described in Csordas (1990a). The collective signs and wonders appear to ex-
emplify what Blacking identifies as

a universal biological model that might be called proto-ritual, a shared somatic state of
the social body that generates special kinds of feelings and apparently spontaneous
movements and interactions between bodies in space and time. . . . Observations of the
cultural *forms* of such states shows transformations of individual facial expression and
body movement, and of the corporate movements in space and time of the bodies involved. "Waves" of feeling are generated in the body and between bodies, not unlike fits
of sneezing or hiccoughs, and discrete sequences of tempo and patterns of movement
can be discerned, analogous to the ebb and flow of a piece of music. (1977: 14)

The experiential primordiality of this experience appears also to be evolutionar-
ily primeval for Blacking, as elsewhere he emphasizes the species-specific emergence of "proto-dance" and "proto-music" for the originary moments of human sharing of patterns of movement and sound (1976: 11). Unfortunately,
Blacking never offers concrete examples of protoritual that could be useful for
comparative purposes.

9. Following the appropriation of living situation assignments by the coordinators in 1972, members were transferred quite frequently, resulting in some
rank-and-file dissatisfaction over the consequent instability of household life. It
is uncertain whether this juggling of residents was intended to make more people more broadly acquainted with other members, to prevent the development
of deep personal attachments that would compete with commitment to the
community, or simply to experiment until the most compatible groupings were
found.

10. The contextual specificity of this use of the polysemic potential of gender symbolism as a strategy for subsuming female under male is highlighted by
contrast with the attribution in the Middle Ages of a female body to Christ and
"his" representation as divine mother (Bynum 1986b).

11. Feminist theory has rendered problematic a simple correspondence between public/private and civic/domestic, but for the limited purpose of the
present argument the correspondence retains some usefulness.

12. If Karl Marx was upset about the fetishization of commodities, he
would doubtless be appalled by the contemporary commodification of money.

13. An analysis of Charismatic Christianity as a global ideology in competition with that of world socialism and corporate multinationalism is formulated
in terms of world systems theory in Csordas (1992).

14. Holloway (1966) describes similar courtship and marriage practices
among other communitarian societies in North American history.

15. Examination of child development in The Word of God/Sword of the Spirit should yield significant insight into phenomenological characteristics of the covenant community behavioral environment and into how successfully its habitus has been reproduced in the first generation to receive it as the cultural status quo. Data from the community school, children's prayer meetings, observation of play, and interviews on cultural and religious themes were collected under my supervision by Sue Wasserkrug in 1991 and 1992 and will form the basis of subsequent publications on moral development and the role of child-rearing issues in the community schism.

Chapter 5

1. The separability of charisma from a person is, generally speaking, more easily recognized with respect to religious than political charisma. This is already true in the work of Weber (1963: 2) where religious charisma is assimilated to notions of impersonal spiritual power such as *mana, orenda,* and *maga*; see also Tambiah's (1984) study of Thai Buddhist amulets as charisma-bearing objects. Nevertheless, the distinction remains blurry even for some political scientists (Willner 1984: 2), and a rhetorical theory of charisma need not bestow too great an emphasis on it, particularly since it incorporates a popular Western cultural assumption that the relation between religion and politics corresponds to the ideological distinction between church and state.

2. Warner's (1988) work identifies the Mendocino Presbyterian church he studies as an institution and identifies the charismatic Antioch Fellowship influential in that church during the 1970s as a movement. Insofar as it was a distinct entity, the fellowship became more associated with nondenominational neo-Pentecostalism especially as promulgated by the now-defunct Christian Growth Ministries, while others in the church could be described as participants in the Presbyterian Charismatic Renewal. Insofar as this latter group were also Charismatics, the movement/institution distinction could be applied within the church itself, independently of the Antioch Fellowship, as is often the case in the Catholic movement where a prayer group attempts to revitalize or take over a parish.

3. In recent writing Fabian (1991) rejects out of hand that the Catholic Charismatic Renewal is a charismatic movement in the Weberian sense, in part because it lacks a charismatic leader. My strategy of separating sociological charisma from the person of the leader and identifying its rhetorical basis is in fact more compatible with Fabian's (1979a) earlier formulations about movements as discourse.

4. The four founders were along with Martin and Clark, Gerry Rauch and Jim Cavnar, who became community coordinators.

5. An excellent analysis of the relation between leaders' personal characteristics and how those are rhetorically transformed is presented by Willner (1984: 128–150).

6. Good (1994) has recently revived Wilfred Cantwell Smith's observation

that the original meaning of "belief," etymologically related to "beloved," had a great deal to do with commitment.

7. Schiffer (1973) also sees charismatic appeal as addressed to the adolescent fear of being a loser. He argues that in the fight between charismatic Father and Son, we the people want both to lose so that we can be reunited with Mom. This is clearly an inadequate account of the virtual elimination of the feminine ideal in covenant community life and the corresponding aggrandizement of Father and Son. Neither can it account for the attempt to overcome the adolescent feeling of being a loser by a tobacco-chewing identification with an ostensibly Bible-based masculine ideal.

Chapter 6

1. Although much anthropological discussion of ritual has focused on symbolic objects and actions, specific concern with the linguistic dimension of ritual can be traced back at least as far as Malinowski's *Coral Gardens and Their Magic* (1935). Lienhardt's (1961) work on Dinka religion encouraged this concern by offering, in addition to a chapter on ritual action, a separate chapter on religious language. Since then, a substantial body of literature has emerged. These studies can be summarized under the following general headings: specialized religious vocabularies (Fabian 1971; Zaretsky 1974; Wheelock 1981); genres of religious language (Bauman 1974; Fabian 1974; Gossen 1972, 1974; McDowell 1983; Briggs 1993); religious speaking as illocutionary act (Austin 1975; Ahern 1979, 1982; Finnegan 1969; Gardner 1983; Gill 1977; Ray 1973; Rosaldo 1982; Tambiah 1968, 1973, 1979; Wheelock 1982); religious language as discourse (Fabian 1979a; Jules-Rosette 1978; Samarin 1976); religious language as power or authority (Andelson 1980; Bloch 1974; Field 1982; McGuire 1983; Kratz 1989; Kuipers 1990); ecstatic language and glossolalia (Eliade 1964; Goodman 1972; Jennings 1968; May 1956; Motley 1981; Pattison 1968; Samarin 1972); evidence of authoritativeness and speaker responsibility for utterance (Du Bois 1986, 1993; Duranti 1993; Chafe 1993; Kuipers 1993).

2. Performance in the domain of Charismatic ritual healing is treated separately in Csordas (1994a).

3. To my knowledge, three versions of the rite are extant. One was developed by The Word of God covenant community in Ann Arbor, Michigan, a second by the Franciscan-oriented Children of Joy community in Allentown, Pennsylvania (since disbanded), and a third by the Charismatic community centered around the Benedictine monastery of Pecos, New Mexico. My discussion draws primarily on the first of these variants. The minor doctrinal and theological differences among them is beyond the scope of this work.

4. McGuire (1975, 1982) gives a detailed account of linguistic and rhetorical techniques by which Charismatic "testimony" achieves these results in Life in the Spirit Seminars.

5. A more comprehensive analysis of Charismatic healing can be found in *The Sacred Self* (Csordas 1994a). See also Csordas (1983, 1988, 1990a, 1990b, 1996); McGuire (1982, 1983); Ackerman (1980); and Charuty (1987).

6. This is the only instance of ritual clothing among Charismatics aside from the mantles and veils of the Sword of the Spirit communities. I am not aware of any ceremony in which members of a healing ministry are formally invested with this ritual garb.

7. Healing practice in covenant communities takes on a different complexion, partly because of the existence of ongoing everyday relationships and partly because the significantly younger membership is not afflicted with as great a proportion of physical illnesses. In the early 1970s some covenant communities made the deliverance from evil spirits a mandatory part of becoming a community member, institutionalizing the premise that everyone is in need of healing. Later, the directive, ongoing relationship of pastoral leadership ("headship") counseling tended to replace formal healing sessions as the preferred setting for healing and spiritual growth. This system is felt to be consistent with the relatively masculinized ethos of covenant communities that regards much of Charismatic emotional healing, with its imagery processes and biographical review (see below), as too "feminine." Covenant community leaders, or coordinators, have the responsibility to pray for those in their charge, and there are informal opportunities for persons to ask one another for prayer for a variety of issues in addition to healing, but private sessions for individual supplicants take place infrequently.

8. The latter practice is associated primarily with the Protestant healing evangelist John Wimber. A Catholic Charismatic healing service in the Wimberite style is described in Csordas (1990a).

9. The concept of genres is as relevant to everyday speech as it is to the domains of performance in ritual, literature, or verbal art. As Bakhtin (1986: 60) observed, "The wealth and diversity of speech genres are boundless because the various possibilities of human activity are inexhaustible, and because each sphere of activity contains an entire repertoire of speech genres that differentiate and grow as the particular sphere develops and becomes more complex." Indeed, Bakhtin captured the relationship between everyday speech and the kind of speech we are analyzing with his distinction between primary (simple products of "unmediated speech communion") and secondary (complex and ideological) speech genres (1986: 62).

10. It is worthy of note that Protestant charismatics use different opening formulas in their prophecies, such as "Thus saith the Lord." This difference is largely one of diction that reflects the influence of different Bible translations preferred by different strains of Pentecostals and neo-Pentecostals. However, it also serves as a kind of cultural diacritic that distinguishes these strains from one another.

11. Bourdieu warns "against all forms of the occasionalist illusion which consists in directly relating practices to properties inscribed in the situation" and argues "that the truth of the interaction is never contained in the interaction" (1977: 81–82). The critique is aimed specifically at social psychology, interactionism, and ethnomethodology; analysis of ritual performance can be

exempt only insofar as it recognizes (1) that creative transformation is in part a function of preexisting dispositions embedded in a world of commonsense reality and a particular social structure; (2) that the rhetorical elements in use (e.g., demonology, prophecy), as well as the individuals who use them, have histories that in part determine the interaction; (3) that social practice generates motives as much as it is guided by them; (4) that transformative intent expressed within a situation or interaction cannot in itself be taken as evidence either of nature of transformation or even of the fact that some kind of transformation has been achieved. It must be left for the reader to decide if the present analysis meets these criteria.

12. Imagery plays an even greater role in some forms of Charismatic healing (Csordas 1994a).

13. McGuire (1975) emphasizes the central role of sharing in the resocialization of neophytes, and argues contra Gerlach and Hine (1970) that public witnessing is a more significant overt act of commitment and "bridge-burning" than is the public utterance of glossolalia.

14. The relation of performance and motive as form and content should be compared to the relation between the notion of "discourse" developed by Fabian et al. (1979a) and the notion of "metaphor" elaborated by contributors to Sapir and Crocker (1977). The former discuss the metaphorical content of discourse, whereas the latter point out that metaphors not only reveal logical structure but also are performed or enacted in discourse.

15. The familiar notion of a motive in psychological terms is that of a reason for action somehow rooted in an individual's personality. This "subterranean" conception of motivation is influenced by psychoanalytic theory and by the legal concept of a motive as a hidden factor that must be uncovered by the skillful criminal prosecutor. The concept of motive elaborated here is, through Burke (1966), influenced by the literary notion of motive as orienting theme and, through Weber (1947) and Mills (1940), by a sociological interest in action. It is compatible with the "extrinsic theory" of thought as propounded in anthropology by Geertz: "Thinking, conceptualization, formulation, comprehension, understanding, or what have you consists not of ghostly happenings in the head but of a matching of the states and processes of symbolic models against the states and processes of a wider world. . . . This view does not, of course, deny consciousness: it defines it" (1973: 214–215).

16. Definitions even from context do not give the whole picture, however. Connotations of the terms can vary slightly from setting to setting, and from one community or branch of the movement to another. Also, despite their coherence as a vocabulary of motives, the terms differ among themselves in a variety of ways. A Catholic Pentecostal theologian who reviewed the list identified the following factors relevant from the movement point of view. The terms differ in generality, in relative importance, in the precision of their concept, in the availability of alternative expressions, and in their individual development over time in the movement. Formal analysis taking all this into account is beyond the scope of the present work.

17. The rhetoricians' technical term for such shifts in meaning is "catachresis," which Max Black defines as "the use of a word in some new sense in order

to remedy a gap in the vocabulary" (quoted in Sapir 1977: 8). The process of catachresis is an important one in the history of any language, for, as Sapir points out, it is these shifts in meaning that "through time, provide a language with its abstract vocabularies" (1977: 8).

Chapter 7

1. The present analysis should be compared with that of McGuire (1977), which centers on what we have called the motive of "power" in Catholic Charismatic prophecy.

2. Although Charismatics typically transcribe prophecy in paragraph form, I have versified the texts both to facilitate analysis and to highlight the couplet form of Charismatic prophecy. While I feel quite comfortable doing so, the question is raised as to whether prophecy is more accurately referred to as a genre of prose or poetry.

In an earlier discussion (Csordas 1979), I described Charismatic prophecy as a kind of "inspired oral poetry." Although Charismatics recognize the occurrence of metaphor and poetic language in their prophecy, they do not regard it as a kind of poetry but as a kind of sacred speech the relevant characteristic of which is that it is a message from the divinity to the faithful. The question of whether poetry must be so labeled by its producers to count as such—whether poetry is an emic or etic category—is complicated by certain shared features of these genres. One recalls Blake's argument that "the Religions of all Nations are derived from each Nation's different reception of the Poetic Genius which is everywhere called the Spirit of Prophecy" (1965). His reference to poetic "Genius" as against a "Spirit" of prophecy suggests that although the two are in essence identical, poetry resides in the aesthetic pole (appreciation of structure and form) and prophecy in the ethical pole (demand for action in the world) of creative discourse. In less cryptic form, Chadwick argues that

Poetry and Prophecy are the expressions of human thought at its most intense and concentrated moments, stimulated by excitement, and expressed in artistic form. Prophecy is the expression of thought, whether subjective or objective, and of knowledge, whether of the present, the future, or the past, which has been acquired by inspiration, and which is uttered in a condition of exaltation or trance, or couched in the traditional form of such utterances. Poetry, it has been said, is the record of the happiest and best moments of the best and happiest lives. (1955)

To the continuum between ethics and aesthetics, Chadwick thus adds for prophecy the element of enthusiasm, invoking trance, exaltation, and excitement. Her distinction between poetry and prophecy, however, seems grounded in one between natural and supernatural, as prophecy is exalted and inspired while poetry has to do with the mundane world of happy lives. As we see in the case of Charismatics, at least some prophecy can be applied to the course of mundane affairs, and it goes without saying that the poetry of "happy lives" unduly neglects the role of inspiration, exaltation, and melancholy in literary history.

3. The distinction drawn by these authors appears to be implicit in both a linguistic and phenomenological sense in Benveniste's (1971) distinction between the speaking subject (*sujet parlant*) and the enunciating subject (*sujet de l'enonciation*).

4. Some of the motives are themselves metaphors, and some are metaphors of metaphors. Using the forms of collectivity as an example, if the continuous term (tenor) is, following Fernandez (1974, 1979), the pronoun "we," then the discontinuous term is either Kingdom, Army, People, or Community (e.g., "We are a People of God"). Second-degree metaphors, or metaphors of metaphors, can be constructed by using one of the discontinuous terms as the tenor (e.g., "The Community is the Kingdom of God"). Note: For this use of "continuous" and "discontinuous" terms in the structure of metaphor, see Sapir (1977: 7).

5. The nature of this creation can be placed in ethnological perspective by comparison with a similar rhetorical device in the Navajo Holy Way prayer as analyzed by Gill (1977). The act achieved is that of being healed, as the supplicant addresses one of the Navajo sacred beings, or Holy People. As in the texts presented above, the rhetorical change in verb tense is the basis for a presumptive perlocution:

> The Navajo verbal modes of the constituent reveal a shift from the imperative—"you must take it [the illness] out of me . . ."—to the perfective mode—"you have taken it out of me . . ." and "you have taken it away . . ." Beginning with an imperative, "you must take it out of me," the prayer constituent concludes in the perfective indicating the completion of the act of removal. (Gill 1977: 150)

In addition, the Navajo prayer ends with the statement "I am walking about," using a "verb in the progressive mode with a continuative aspect. In other words, the form of the verb indicates that the action is in progress and will continue or endure" (Gill 1977: 151).

Tambiah implies a similar role of verb tense in Trobriand "spells," the third and final segment of which is typically a "statement that the intended effect has been achieved" (1968: 38). Taken together, the examples of Catholic Pentecostal prophecy and Navajo healing prayer and Trobriand spells suggest the cross-cultural generalization of tense change as a rhetorical strategy for achieving presumptive perlocution in ritual language. Yet in spite of this essential similarity, it must be borne in mind that these linguistic practices exhibit only a family resemblance as instances of ritual language. They differ with respect to genre—prayer, prophecy, and spell; with respect to textuality in that they span a continuum from fixed text intended for verbatim recitation to spontaneous oral composition; and with respect to purpose in that the Navajo prayer is meant to restore a previous state of health, the Trobriand spell to accompany and render efficacious a technical activity, and the Charismatic prophecy to create a new state of personal and communal identity.

6. Thus prophecy bears what Ahern (1979), in pointing out that regardless of the speaker's forcefulness or enthusiasm different types of illocution are rhetorically endowed with different degrees of force, calls "strong" illocutionary force.

7. For a discussion of Manson and Jones, as well as Adolf Hitler, see Lindholm (1990).

8. The "word of knowledge" and the "word of wisdom" are word gifts predominantly found in situations of ritual healing (see Csordas 1994a).

9. It might appear that this prophecy has come to pass—at least as a self-fulfilling one—in the events surrounding the community schism of the early 1990s.

10. For a more complete elaboration of the analysis that follows, see Csordas (1990a).

11. Schwartz (n.d.) challenges the notion that glossolalia necessarily lacks a semantic component with the example of the African Legio Maria movement. Her argument should be taken up in any comparative examination of glossolalia.

12. The same mystification, some might say, is also the condition of Foucault's own theory of discursive formations.

13. Thus in Samoa, "one does not say 'you mean x?' but 'is the meaning of your words x?'" (Duranti 1993a: 42); "people cannot really know whether they have done wrong until someone else says so" (1993a: 42); and people "display an obvious dispreference for explicit guessing" about the intentions and motives of others (1993a: 44).

Chapter 8

1. More specifically, Bloch acknowledges the possibility of change and therefore the value of identifying "principles of transformation," but creativity in ritual appears to be restricted to the "initial creation" of rituals themselves, the analysis of which Bloch recognizes as a virtual historical impossibility (1986: 10).

2. Not incidentally, Rappaport (1979) ran up against this problem and was led to change his term for the constitutive statements of a religion from "ultimate sacred propositions" to "ultimate sacred postulates."

3. Ricoeur (1977) in fact works out a compromise between these positions, analyzing the "interanimation" of philosophical and poetic discourse.

4. How Bloch could know how the nineteenth-century Merina kings saw themselves in this respect is not specified in his text.

5. Not incidentally, both "turns" have occurred among Charismatics, the former in the ossified redundancy of "everyday" prophecy and the latter in the radicalization of charisma in The Word of God/Sword of the Spirit. Other examples of the turn toward conservativism are the decline in vitality of ritual language described by Andelson (1980) in the American Amana community and by Fabian (1979b) in the African Jamaa movement.

6. Such distancing is also an essential aspect of Scheff's (1979) theory of catharsis, in which its dual aesthetic and affective character is emphasized.

7. Within a system of ritual language it would be important to distinguish

between, for example, Charismatic sharing and prophecy in a prayer meeting, or between prophecy in a prayer meeting and in a domestic setting. Irvine (1979) has made a similar point about the necessity to distinguish between properties of formalized language per se and properties of formalized settings in which language is used. Her account leads to four types based on the distinction between formalized code and formalized situation. This two-dimensional scheme roughly corresponds to the performance-centered approach's concern with genre and the cultural performance concern with event that frames our own discussion, excluding explicit consideration of the third dimension constituted by the performative act.

8. In religious movements the ritual language may itself presume creativity in evoking the "new man" as in cargo cults or the person who is "born again" as in Charismatic Christianity, while what is actually being created is itself a form of authority that aspires to become traditional authority.

9. Lewis uses the term "motif" in the literary or musical sense of a recurrent theme in ritual, but his point is equally applicable to our notion of "motive" as a complex of meaning that orients action. Thinking at the performative level of event (rite) rather than of genre, he writes, "Certain motifs in the [Gnau] puberty rites recur in other rites. By recurring they point to connections between the rites. Responses to the motifs change with experience of them. The understanding of why they are done and what they mean is revised, changed, and expanded in the light of later knowledge and experience" (1980: 134). "If, as with the Gnau, the meaning of certain motifs is left relatively open and unstated, we may see variety in their responses to them . . . , and the way in which motifs may be used within rites to impose pattern, and by repetition may link different rites, provoking new responses with changed experience of them" (1980: 223). Here is a distinct parallel to the process we have described in the circulation of motives in Charismatic ritual.

References

Abrahams, Roger
  1968   "Introductory Remarks to a Rhetorical Theory of Folklore." *Journal of American Folklore* 81: 143–148.
  1972   "Folklore and Literature as Performance." *Journal of the Folklore Institute* 8: 75–94.
Ackerman, S. E.
  1981   "Language of Religious Innovation: Spirit Possession and Exorcism in a Malaysian Catholic Pentecostal Movement." *Journal of Anthropological Research* 37: 90–100.
Ahern, Emily
  1979   "The Problem of Efficacy: Strong and Weak Illocutionary Acts." *Man* 14: 1–17.
  1982   "Rules in Oracles and Games." *Man* 17: 302–312.
Aldunate, Carlos
  1975   "Chile." *ICO Newsletter* 1(5): 3.
Andelson, Jonathan
  1980   "Routinization of Behavior in a Charismatic Leader." *American Ethnologist* 7: 716–733.
Associated Press
  1995   "At Evangelical Colleges, A Revival of Repentance." *New York Times,* May 25.
Austin, John L.
  1975   *How to Do Things with Words.* 2d ed. Cambridge: Harvard University Press.
Bailey, F. G.
  1983   *The Tactical Uses of Passion: An Essay on Power, Reason, and Reality.* Ithaca: Cornell University Press.
Bakhtin, M. M.
  1986   *Speech Genres and Other Late Essays.* Trans. Vern W. McGee. Austin: University of Texas Press.

Barrett, David B., ed.
   1982   *World Christian Encyclopedia: A Comparative Study of Churches and Religions in the Modern World*, A.D. *1900–2000*. Oxford: Oxford University Press.
Baudrillard, Jean
   1983   *Simulations*. Trans. Paul Foss, Paul Patton, and Philip Beitchman. New York: Semiotext(e).
Bauman, Richard
   1974   "Verbal Art as Performance." *American Anthropologist* 77: 290–310.
   1975   "Quaker Folk Linguistics and Folklore." In Dan Ben-Amos and Kenneth Goldstein, eds., *Folklore, Communication, and Performance*. The Hague: Mouton. Pp. 117–139.
Bauman, Richard, and Charles L. Briggs
   1990   "Poetics and Performance as Critical Perspectives on Language and Social Life." *Annual Review of Anthropology* 19: 59–88.
Bax, Mart
   1987   "Marian Apparitions in Medjugorje: Rivaling Religious Regimes and State-Formation in Yugoslavia." *Sociologisch-Tijdschrift* 14: 195–223.
   1990   "The Madonna of Medjugorje: Religious Rivalry and the Formation of a Devotional Movement in Yugoslavia." *Anthropological Quarterly* 63–75.
   1992   "Female Suffering, Local Power Relations, and Religious Tourism: A Case Study from Yugoslavia." *Medical Anthropology Quarterly* 6(2): 114–127.
Bellah, Robert
   1970   *Beyond Belief*. New York: Harper and Row.
Bellah, Robert N., and Phillip E. Hammond
   1980   *Varieties of Civil Religion*. San Francisco: Harper and Row.
Bellah, Robert, R. Madsen, W. Sullivan, A. Swidler, and S. Tipton
   1985   *Habits of the Heart: Individualism and Commitment in American Life*. New York: Harper and Row.
Benveniste, Emile
   1971   *Problems in General Linguistics*. Coral Gables, Fla.: University of Miami Press.
Bettis, Joseph Dabney, ed.
   1969   *Phenomenology of Religion*. New York: Harper and Row.
Blacking, John
   1976   "Dance, Conceptual Thought and Production in the Archaeological Record." In G. de G. Sieveking, I. H. Longworth, and K. E. Wilson, eds., *Problems in Economic and Social Archaeology*. Boulder: Westview Press. Pp. 3–13.
   1977   "Towards an Anthropology of the Body." In John Blacking, ed., *The Anthropology of the Body*. New York: Academic Press. Pp. 1–28.

Blake, William
1965   *The Poetry and Prose of William Blake.* Ed. D. Erdman. Garden City: Doubleday.

Bloch, Maurice
1974   "Symbols, Song, Dance, and Features of Articulation: Is Religion an Extreme Form of Traditional Authority?" *Archives Europeen de Sociologie* 15(1): 55–84.
1986   *From Blessing to Violence: History and Ideology in the Circumcision Ritual of the Merina of Madagascar.* Cambridge: Cambridge University Press.

Bloch-Hoell, Nils
1964   *The Pentecostal Movement.* Halden: Scandinavian University Books.

Bord, Richard J., and Joseph E. Faulkner
1975   "Religiosity and Secular Attitudes: The Case of Catholic Pentecostals." *Journal for the Scientific Study of Religion* 14: 257–270.
1983   *The Catholic Charismatics: The Anatomy of a Modern Religious Movement.* University Park: Pennsylvania State University Press.

Bourdieu, Pierre
1977   *Outline of a Theory of Practice.* Trans. Richard Nice. London: Cambridge University Press.
1984   *Distinction.* Trans. Richard Nice. Cambridge: Harvard University Press.
1991   "Authorized Language: The Social Conditions for the Effectiveness of Ritual Discourse." In Bourdieu, *Language and Symbolic Power.* Cambridge, Mass.: Harvard University Press. Pp. 107–116.

Briggs, Charles L.
1993   "Generic versus Metapragmatic Dimensions of Warao Narrative: Who Regiments Performance?" In John Lucy, ed., *Reflexive Language: Reported Speech and Metapragmatics.* Cambridge: Cambridge University Press. Pp. 179–212.

Briggs, Charles, and Richard Bauman
1992   "Genre, Intertexuality, and Social Power." *Journal of Linguistic Anthropology* 2: 131–172.

Brown, Roger W., and A. Gilman
1960   "The Pronouns of Power and Solidarity." In T. Sebeok, ed., *Style in Language.* Cambridge: MIT Press. Pp. 253–276.

Burke, Kenneth
1966   *Language as Symbolic Action.* Berkeley, Los Angeles, and London: University of California Press.
1970   *The Rhetoric of Religion.* Berkeley, Los Angeles, and London: University of California Press.

Burridge, Kenelm
1960   *Mambu: A Melanesian Millennium.* London: Methuen.

Bynum, Caroline W.
1986   "Introduction: The Complexity of Symbols." In C. W. Bynum, S. Harrell, and P. Richman, eds., *Gender and Religion: On the Complexity of Symbols.* Boston: Beacon Press. Pp. 1–20.

1989   *The Female Body and Religious Practice in the Later Middle Ages in Fragments for a History of the Human Body, Part I.* Ed. Michael Feher, with Ramona Naddaff and Nadia Tazi. New York: Urzone. Pp. 160–219.

1991   " ' . . . And Woman His Humanity' ": Female Imagery in the Religious Writing of the Later Middle Ages." In *Fragmentation and Redemption: Essays on Gender and the Human Body in Medieval Religion.* New York: Zone. Pp. 32–57.

Carter, Lewis F.
1990   *Charisma and Control in Rajneeshpuram: The Role of Shared Values in the Creation of a Community.* Cambridge: Cambridge University Press.

Chadwick, Nora Kershaw
1955   *Poetry and Prophecy.* London: Bowes and Bowes.

Chafe, Wallace
1993   "Seneca Speaking Styles and the Location of Authority." In Jane Hill and Judith Irvine, eds., *Responsibility and Evidence in Oral Discourse.* Cambridge: Cambridge University Press. Pp. 72–87.

Chagnon, Roland
1979   *Les Charismatiques au Quebec.* Montreal: Editions Quebec/Amerique.

Charuty, Giordana
1987   "Guerir la memoire: L'Intervention rituelle du Catholicisme Penetotiste Français et Italien." *Social Compass* 34: 437–463.

Chirot, Daniel, and Thomas D. Hall
1982   "World-System Theory." *Annual Review of Sociology* 8: 81–106.

Clark, Steven
1976   *Unordained Elders and Renewal Communities.* New York: Paulist Press.

1980   *Man and Woman in Christ: An Examination of the Roles of Men and Women in Light of Scripture and the Social Sciences.* Ann Arbor: Servant Books.

1984   *Patterns of Christian Community: A Statement of Community Order.* Ann Arbor: Servant Publications.

Clow, Kenneth
1976   "Social Organization of the American Pentecostal Church." Ph.D. dissertation, Duke University.

Cohen, A. P., and J. L. Comaroff
1976   "The Management of Meaning: On the Phenomenology of Political Transactions." In Bruce Kapferer, ed., *Transaction and Meaning.* Philadelphia: Institute for the Study of Human Issues. Pp. 132–157.

Cohen, Martine
1986   "Vers de nouveaux rapports avec l'institution ecclesiastique: L'Exemple du renouveau charismatique en France." *Archives Sciences Sociales des Religions* 62: 61–79.

1993   "Ethique charismatique et esprit de capitalisme avance: Essai sur le mouvement Charismatique Catholique Français." *Social Compass* 40: 55–63.

Cornelius, Wayne

1973   *Political Learning among the Migrant Poor: The Impact of Residential Context.* Beverly Hills: Sage Publications.

Coser, Lewis

1974   *Greedy Institutions.* New York: Free Press.

Cox, Harvey

1995   *Fire from Heaven: The Rise of Pentecostal Spirituality and the Reshaping of Religion in the Twenty-first Century.* Reading, Mass.: Addison-Wesley.

Crawford, Robert

1984   "A Cultural Account of 'Health': Control, Release, and the Social Body." In John McKinlay, ed., *Issues in the Political Economy of Health Care.* New York: Tavistock. Pp. 60–103.

Csordas, Thomas J.

1979   "Inspired Oral Poetry and Sacred Reality." Paper delivered at the Symposium on Communication, Duke University.

1980a   "Building the Kingdom: The Creativity of Ritual Performance in Catholic Pentecostalism." Ph.D. dissertation, Duke University.

1980b   "Catholic Pentecostalism: A New Word in the New World." In S. D. Glazier, ed., *Perspectives on Pentecostalism: Case Studies from the Caribbean and Latin America.* Washington, D.C.: University Press of America. Pp. 143–175.

1983   "The Rhetoric of Transformation in Ritual Healing." *Culture, Medicine, and Psychiatry* 7: 333–375.

1987   "Genre, Motive, and Metaphor: Conditions for Creativity in Ritual Language." *Cultural Anthropology* 2: 445–469.

1988   "Elements of Charismatic Persuasion and Healing." *Medical Anthropology Quarterly* 2: 121–142.

1990a   "Embodiment as a Paradigm for Anthropology." *Ethos* 18: 5–47.

1990b   "The Psychotherapy Analogy and Charismatic Healing." *Psychotherapy* 27: 79–90. Reprinted in Walter Andritzky, ed., *Yearbook of Cross-Cultural Medicine and Psychotherapy.* Berlin: Verlag für Wissenschaft und Bildung, 1992. Pp. 277–292.

1992   "Religion and the World System: The Pentecostal Ethic and the Spirit of Monopoly Capital." *Dialectical Anthropology* 17: 3–24.

1993   "Somatic Modes of Attention." *Cultural Anthropology* 8: 135–156.

1994a   *The Sacred Self: A Cultural Phenomenology of Charismatic Healing.* Berkeley, Los Angeles, and London: University of California Press.

1994b   "The Body as Representation and Being in the World." In T. Csordas, ed., *Embodiment and Experience: The Existential Ground of Culture and Self.* London: Cambridge University Press. Pp. 1–23.

1994c   "Self and Person." In Philip K. Bock, ed., *Handbook of Psychological Anthropology.* New York: Greenwood Press. Pp. 331–350.

1996   "A Handmaid's Tale: The Rhetoric of Personhood in American and Japanese Healing of Abortions." In Carolyn Sargent and Caroline Brettell, eds., *Gender and Health: An International Perspective*. Englewood Cliffs, N.J.: Prentice Hall. Pp. 227–241.

Danforth, Loring M.
1989   *Firewalking and Religious Healing: The Anastenaria of Greece and the American Firewalking Movement*. Princeton: Princeton University Press.

DeVos, George, A. Marsella, and F. Hsu
1985   "Introduction: Approaches to Culture and Self." In A. Marsella, George DeVos, and F. Hsu, eds., *Culture and Self*. London: Tavistock. Pp. 2–23.

Douglas, Mary
1973   *Natural Symbols*. New York: Vintage.

Doutreloux, Albert, and Colette Degive
1978   "Perspective anthropologique sur un mouvement religieux actuel." *Social Compass* 25: 43–54.

Dow, Thomas E., Jr.
1978   "An Analysis of Weber's Work on Charisma." *British Journal of Sociology* 29: 83–93.

Driver, Harold
1969   *Indians of North America*. 2d ed. Chicago: University of Chicago Press.

Du Bois, John W.
1986   "Self-Evidence and Ritual Speech." In Wallace Chafe and Johanna Nichols, eds., *Evidentiality: The Linguistic Coding of Epistemology*. Norwood, N.J.: Ablex. Pp. 313–336.
1993   "Meaning without Intention: Lessons from Divination." In Jane Hill and Judith Irvine, eds., *Responsibility and Evidence in Oral Discourse*. Cambridge: Cambridge University Press. Pp. 48–71.

Duranti, Alessandro
1993a   "Intentions, Self, and Responsibility: An Essay in Samoan Ethnopragmatics." In Jane Hill and Judith Irvine, eds., *Responsibility and Evidence in Oral Discourse*. Cambridge: Cambridge University Press. Pp. 24–47.
1993b   "Truth and Intentionality: An Ethnographic Critique." *Cultural Anthropology* 8: 214–245.

Duranti, Alessandro, and Donald Brenneis, eds.
1986   "The Audience as Co-Author" (Special issue). *Text* 6.

Duranti, Alessandro, and Charles Goodwin, eds.
1992   *Rethinking Context: Language as an Interactive Phenomenon*. Cambridge: Cambridge University Press.

Durkheim, Emile
[1915]   *The Elementary Forms of the Religious Life*. New York: Free Press.
1965

Eliade, Mircea
1958   *Patterns in Comparative Religion*. Trans. Rosemary Sheed. Cleveland: World Publishing.

1964   *Shamanism: Archaic Techniques of Ecstasy.* Trans. W. R. Trask. Princeton: Princeton University Press.

Erikson, Erik H.
1963   *Childhood and Society.* 2d ed. New York: W. W. Norton.

Espin, Oliva
1988   "Spiritual Power and the Mundane World: Hispanic Female Healers in Urban U.S. Communities." *Women's Studies Quarterly* 16: 33–47.

Evans-Pritchard, Edward
1976   *Witchcraft, Oracles, and Magic among the Azande.* Oxford: Clarendon Press.

Fabian, Johannes
1966   "Dream and Charisma: Theories of Dreams in the Jamaa Movement." *Anthropos* 61: 544–560.

1971   *Jamaa: A Charismatic Movement in Katanga.* Evanston: Northwestern University Press.

1974   "Genres in an Emerging Tradition: An Anthropological Approach to Religious Communication." In A. Eister, ed., *Changing Perspectives in the Study of Religion.* New York: John Wiley and Sons. Pp. 249–272.

1979a   "The Anthropology of Religious Movements: From Explanation to Interpretation." *Social Research* 46: 4–35.

1979b   "Text as Terror: Second Thoughts about Charisma." *Social Research* 46: 166–203.

1983   *Time and the Other: How Anthropology Makes Its Object.* New York: Columbia University Press.

1991   "Charisma: Global Movement and Local Survival." Paper presented at conference on Global Culture: Pentecostal/Charismatic Movements Worldwide, Calgary Institute of the Humanities.

1994   "Jamaa: A Charismatic Movement Revisited." In Thomas D. Blakely, Walter E. A. van Beek, and Dennis Thompson, eds., *Religion in Africa: Experience and Expression.* London: James Currey. Pp. 257–274.

Fabian, Johannes, ed.
1979   "Beyond Charisma: Religious Movements as Discourse" (Special issue). *Social Research* 46.

Faron, Louis
1964   *Hawks of the Sun: Mapuche Morality and Its Ritual Attributes.* Pittsburgh: University of Pittsburgh Press.

Featherstone, Mike
1991   *Consumer Culture and Postmodernism.* London: Sage.

Fernandez, James
1972   "Persuasions and Performances: Of the Beast in Every Body . . . and the Metaphors of Every Man." *Daedalus* 101: 39–60. Reprinted in Fernandez, *Persuasions and Performances: The Play of Tropes in Culture.* Bloomington: Indiana University Press, 1986. Pp. 3–27.

1974   "The Mission of Metaphor in Expressive Culture." *Current Anthropology* 15: 119–145. Reprinted in Fernandez, *Persuasions and Performances: The Play of Tropes in Culture.* Bloomington: Indiana University Press, 1986. Pp. 28–70.

1977   "The Performance of Ritual Metaphors." In J. D. Sapir and C. Crocker, eds., *The Social Use of Metaphor.* Philadelphia: University of Pennsylvania Press.

1979   "On the Notion of Religious Movement." In J. Fabian, ed., "Beyond Charisma: Religious Movements as Discourse" (Special issue). *Social Research* 46: 36–62.

1982   "The Dark at the Bottom of the Stairs: The Inchoate in Symbolic Inquiry and Some Strategies for Coping with It." In Jaques Macquet, ed., *On Symbols in Anthropology: Essays in Honor of Harry Hoijer.* Malibu: Udena. Reprinted in Fernandez, *Persuasions and Performances: The Play of Tropes in Culture.* Bloomington: Indiana University Press, 1986. Pp. 214–238.

1986   *Persuasions and Performances: The Play of Tropes in Culture.* Bloomington: Indiana University Press.

Fernandez, James, ed.
1991   *Beyond Metaphor: The Theory of Tropes in Anthropology.* Stanford: Stanford University Press.

Fichter, Joseph
1975   *The Catholic Cult of Paraclete.* New York: Sheed and Ward.

Field, Karen
1982   "Charismatic Religion as Popular Protest." *Theory and Society* 11: 305–320.

Finnegan, Ruth
1969   "How to Do Things with Words: Performative Utterances among the Limba of Sierra Leone." *Man* 4: 537–552.

Fitzgerald, Frances
1986   *Cities on a Hill: A Journey through Contemporary American Cultures.* New York: Simon and Schuster.

Fogelson, Raymond D., and Richard N. Adams, eds.
1977   *The Anthropology of Power: Ethnographic Studies from Asia, Oceania, and the New World.* New York: Academic Press.

Ford, J. Massyngberde
1976   *Which Way for Catholic Pentecostals?* New York: Harper and Row.

Foster, George, T. Scudder, E. Colson, and R. V. Kemper
1979   *Long-Term Field Research in Social Anthropology.* New York: Academic Press.

Foster, M.
1974   "When Words Become Deeds: An Analysis of Three Iroquois Longhouse Speech Events." In R. Bauman and J. Sherzer, eds., *Explorations in the Ethnography of Speaking.* Cambridge: Cambridge University Press.

Foucault, Michel
1972   *The Discourse on Language.* In Foucault, *Archaeology of Knowledge.* New York: Harper and Row.

Fox, James
    1974   "Our Ancestors Spoke in Pairs." In R. Bauman and J. Sherzer,
            eds., *Explorations in the Ethnography of Speaking.* London: Cam-
            bridge University Press.
Friedman, Jonathan
    1994   *Cultural Identity and Global Process.* London: Sage.
Frye, Northrop
    1957   *Anatomy of Criticism: Four Essays.* Princeton: Princeton University
            Press.
Gallup, George, Jr., and Jim Castelli
    1989   *The People's Religion: American Faith in the Nineties.* New York:
            Macmillan.
Gardner, D. S.
    1983   "Performativity in Ritual: The Mianmin Case." *Man* 18: 346–
            360.
Garrison, Vivian
    1977   "Doctor, Espiritista, or Psychiatrist? Health-seeking Behavior in a
            Puerto Rican Community of New York City." *Medical Anthropol-
            ogy* 1: 66–180.
Geertz, Clifford
    1973   *The Interpretation of Cultures.* New York: Basic Books.
    1977   "Centers, Kings, and Charisma: Reflections of the Symbolics of
            Power." In Joseph Ben-David and Terry Nichols Clark, eds., *Cul-
            ture and Its Creators: Essays in Honor of Edward Shils.* Chicago:
            University of Chicago Press. Pp. 132–157.
Gerlach, Luther, and Virginia Hine
    1970   *People, Power, and Chance.* Indianapolis: Bobbs-Merrill.
Gill, Sam D.
    1977   "Prayer as Person: The Performative Force in Navaho Prayer
            Acts." *History of Religions* 17: 143–157.
Glock, Charles Y., and Rodney Stark
    1965   *Religion and Society in Tension.* Chicago: Rand McNally.
Goldstein, Kenneth, and Dan Ben-Amos, eds.
    1975   *Folklore: Communication and Performance.* The Hague: Mouton.
Good, Byron
    1994   *Medicine, Rationality, and Experience: An Anthropological Per-
            spective.* Cambridge: Cambridge University Press.
Goodman, Felicitas
    1972   *Speaking in Tongues.* Chicago: University of Chicago Press.
    1981   *The Exorcism of Anneliese Michel.* New York: Doubleday.
Goodwin, Charles, and Alessandro Duranti
    1992   "Rethinking Context: An Introduction." In Alessandro Duranti
            and Charles Goodwin, eds., *Rethinking Context: Language as an
            Interactive Phenomenon.* Cambridge: Cambridge University Press.
            Pp. 1–42.
Gossen, Gary
    1972   "Chamula Genres of Verbal Behavior." In A. Paredes and R. Bau-
            man, eds., *Toward New Perspectives in Folklore.* Austin: University
            of Texas Press. Pp. 145–167.

1974   *Chamulas in the World of the Sun: Time and Space in a Maya Community.* Cambridge, Mass.: Harvard University Press.

1976   "Language as Ritual Substance." In William Samarin, ed., *Language in Religious Practice.* Rowley: Newbury House.

Greenberg, J. R., and Stephen A. Mitchell
1983   *Object Relations in Psychoanalytic Theory.* Cambridge: Harvard University Press.

Grimes, Ronald
1976   *Symbol and Conquest: Public Ritual and Drama in Santa Fe, New Mexico.* Ithaca: Cornell University Press.

ter Haar, Gerrie
1987   "Religion and Healing: The Case of Milingo." *Social Compass* 34: 475–493.

Hallowell, A. Irving
1955   "The Self in Its Behavioral Environment." In Hallowell, *Culture and Experience.* Philadelphia: University of Pennsylvania Press.

1960   *Ojibwa Ontology, Behavior and World View.* Reprinted in *Contributions to Anthropology.* Chicago: University of Chicago Press, 1976. Pp. 357–390.

Handelman, Don
1985   "Charisma, Liminality, and Symbol Types." In Eric Cohen, Moshe Lissak, and Uri Almagor, eds., *Comparative Social Dynamics: Essays in Honor of S. N. Eisenstadt.* Boulder, Colo.: Westview Press. Pp. 346–359.

Hanks, William
1987   "Discourse Genres in a Theory of Practice." *American Ethnologist* 14: 668–692.

Harding, Susan
1987   "Convicted by the Holy Spirit: The Rhetoric of Fundamental Baptist Conversion." *American Ethnologist* 14: 167–181.

1988   "The World of the Born-Again Telescandals." *Michigan Quarterly Review* 27: 525–540.

Harper, Charles L.
1974   "Spirit-filled Catholics: Some Biographical Comparisons." *Social Compass* 21: 311–324.

Harris, Grace G.
1989   "Concepts of Individual, Self, and Person in Description and Analysis." *American Anthropologist* 91: 599–612.

Harrison, Michael
1974a   "Sources of Recruitment to Catholic Pentecostalism." *Journal for the Scientific Study of Religion* 13: 49–64.

1974b   "Preparation for Life in the Spirit: The Process of Initial Commitment to a Religious Movement." *Urban Life and Culture* 2: 387–414.

1975   "The Maintenance of Enthusiasm: Involvement in a New Religious Movement." *Sociological Analysis* 36: 150–160.

Harwood, Alan
    1977   *Rx, Spiritist as Needed: A Study of a Puerto Rican Community Mental Health Resource.* New York: Wiley.

Hébrard, Monique
    1987   *Les Nouveaux Disciples Dix Ans Apres.* Paris: Editions de Centurion.

Hegy, Pierre
    1978   "Images of God and Man in a Catholic Charismatic Renewal Community." *Social Compass* 25: 7–21.

Hollenweger, Walter
    1972   *The Pentecostals.* London: SCM Press.

Holloway, Mark
    1966   *Heavens on Earth: Utopian Communities in America, 1680–1880.* New York: Dover.

Horton, Robin
    1970   "African Traditional Thought and Western Science." In B. R. Wilson, ed., *Rationality.* Oxford: Blackwell Publications. Pp. 131–171.

Hymes, Dell
    1975   "Breakthrough into Performance." In Kenneth Goldstein and Dan Ben-Amos, eds., *Folklore, Communication, and Performance.* The Hague: Mouton.

ICCRO
    1987   *ICCRO International Newsletter* 13: 4–5.

Irvine, Judith T.
    1979   "Formality and Informality in Communicative Events." *American Anthropologist* 81: 773–790.

James, William
    1983   *Principles of Psychology.* Cambridge: Harvard University Press.

Jansen, William Hugh
    1975   "The Esoteric-Exoteric Factor in Folklore." In A. Dundes, ed., *The Study of Folklore.* Englewood Cliffs, N.J.: Prentice Hall. Pp. 43–51.

Jenkins, Janis H.
    1991   "Anthropology, Expressed Emotion and Schizophrenia." *Ethos* 19: 387–431.

Jennings, George
    1968   "An Ethnological Study of Glossolalia." *Journal of the American Scientific Affiliation* 20: 5–16.

Johnson, Frank
    1985   "The Western Conception of Self." In A. Marsella, George DeVos, and F. Hsu, eds., *Culture and Self.* London: Tavistock. Pp. 91–138.

Johnson, Mark
    1987   *The Body in the Mind.* Chicago: University of Chicago Press.

Jules-Rosette, Benetta
    1978   "The Veil of Objectivity: Prophecy, Divination, and Social Inquiry." *American Anthropologist* 80: 570–594.

Kanter, Rosabeth Moss
  1972   *Commitment and Community*. Cambridge, Mass.: Harvard University Press.
Kapferer, Bruce
  1976   *Transaction and Meaning: Directions in the Anthropology of Exchange and Symbolic Behavior*. Philadelphia: Institute for the Study of Human Issues.
  1979a   "Ritual Process and the Transformation of Context." *Social Analysis* 1: 3–19.
  1979b   "Entertaining Demons: Comedy, Interaction and Meaning in a Sinhalese Healing Ritual." *Social Analysis* 1: 108–176.
  1979c   "Mind, Self, and Other in Demonic Illness: The Negation and Reconstruction of Self." *American Ethnologist* 6: 110–133.
  1983   *A Celebration of Demons: Exorcism and the Aesthetics of Healing in Sri Lanka*. Bloomington: University of Indiana Press.
Keane, Roberta
  1974   "The Word of God Community." Ph.D. dissertation, University of Michigan.
Kelkel, A. L.
  1988   "Le probleme de l'intentionnalite corporelle." In Anna-Teresa Tymieniecka, ed., *Maurice Merleau-Ponty: Le psychique et le corporel*. Paris: Aubier. Pp. 15–38.
Kirmayer, Laurence J.
  1992   "The Body's Insistence on Meaning: Metaphor as Presentation and Representation in Illness Experience." *Medical Anthropology Quarterly* 6: 323–346.
Knauft, Bruce
  1979   "On Percussion and Metaphor." *Current Anthropology* 20: 189–191.
Koss-Chioino, Joan
  1992   *Women as Healers, Women as Patients: Mental Health Care and Traditional Healing in Puerto Rico*. Boulder: Westview Press.
Kratz, Corinne A.
  1989   "Genres of Power: A Comparative Analysis of Okiek Blessings, Curses, and Oats." *Man* 24: 636–656.
Kuipers, Joel C.
  1990   *Power in Performance: The Creation of Textual Authority in Weyewa Ritual Speech*. Philadelphia: University of Pennsylvania Press.
  1993   "Obligations to the Word: Ritual Speech, Performance, and Responsibility among the Weyewa." In Jane Hill and Judith Irvine, eds., *Responsibility and Evidence in Oral Discourse*. Cambridge: Cambridge University Press. Pp. 88–104.
La Barre, Weston
  1970   *The Ghost Dance: Origins of Religion*. Garden City: Doubleday.
Laderman, Carol
  1991   *Taming the Wind of Desire*. Berkeley, Los Angeles, and Oxford: University of California Press.

Laderman, Carol, and Marina Roseman, eds.
1996   *The Performance of Healing.* New York: Routledge.

Lalive d'Epinay, Christian
1969   *Haven of the Masses.* London: Lutterworth.

Lane, Ralph
1976   "Catholic Charismatic Renewal." In Charles Y. Glock and Robert N. Bellah, eds., *The New Religious Consciousness.* Berkeley: University of California Press.
1978   "The Catholic Charismatic Renewal in the United States: A Reconsideration." *Social Compass* 25: 23–35.

Lange, Joseph, and Anthony Cushing
1974   *Friendship with Jesus.* Vol. 1 of *Living Christian Community.* Pecos, N.Mex.: Dove Publications.

Lanternari, Vittorio
1987   "Un Corto-circuito religioso tra Africa e Italia: La Terapia Afro-Catolica del Rev. Milingo." In Lanternari, *Medicina, Magia, Religione: Dalla Culture Populare alle Societa traditionali.* Rome: Libreria Internazionale Esedra. Pp. 165–182.
1994   *Medicina, Magia, Religione, Valori.* Naples: Liguori.

Laurentin, René, and Henri Joyeux
1987   *Scientific and Medical Studies on the Apparitions at Medjugorje.* Dublin: Veritas Publications.

Lepore, Ernest, and Robert Van Gulick, eds.
1991   *John Searle and His Critics.* Cambridge, Mass.: Blackwell.

Levine, Stephen B.
1991   "Psychological Intimacy." Paper presented at Grand Rounds, Case Western Reserve Medical School, Department of Psychiatry, Spring.

Lewis, Gilbert
1980   *Day of Shining Red.* Cambridge Studies in Social Anthropology no. 27. Cambridge: Cambridge University Press.

Lewis, Jeanne
1995   "Headship and Hierarchy: Authority and Control in a Catholic Charismatic Community." Ph.D. dissertation, University of Michigan.

Lhamon, W. T., Jr.
1976   "Pentecost, Promiscuity, and Pychon's V.: From the Scaffold to the Impulsive." In George Levine and David Leverenz, eds., *Mindful Pleasures: Essays on Thomas Pynchon.* Boston: Little, Brown. Pp. 69–86.

Lienhardt, Godfrey
1961   *Divinity and Experience: The Religion of the Dinka.* Oxford: Clarendon Press.

Lifton, Robert Jay
1976   *The Life of the Self.* New York: Simon and Schuster.

Lindholm, Charles
1990   *Charisma.* London: Basil Blackwell.

Lord, Albert
    1960   *The Singer of Tales.* Cambridge: Harvard University Press.
Lucy, John, ed.
    1993   *Reflexive Language: Reported Speech and Metapragmatics.* Cambridge: Cambridge University Press.
Lyotard, Jean-François
    1984   *The Postmodern Condition: A Report on Knowledge.* Minneapolis: University of Minnesota Press.
McAvoy, Thomas
    1969   *A History of the Catholic Church in the United States.* Notre Dame: University of Notre Dame Press.
McDowell, John H.
    1983   "The Semiotic Constitution of Kamsa Ritual Language." *Language in Society* 12: 23–46.
McGuire, Kenneth
    1976   "People, Prayer, and Promise: An Anthropological Analysis of a Catholic Charismatic Covenant Community." Ph.D. dissertation, Ohio State University.
McGuire, Meredith
    1974   "An Interpretive Comparison of Elements of the Pentecostal and Underground Church Movements in American Catholicism." *Sociological Analysis* 35: 57–65.
    1975a   "Sharing Life in the Spirit: The Function of Testimony in Catholic Pentecostal Commitment and Conversion." Paper delivered at the annual meeting of the Society for the Scientific Study of Religion.
    1975b   "Toward a Sociological Interpretation of the 'Catholic Pentecostal' Movement." *Review of Religious Research* 16: 94–104.
    1977   "The Social Context of Prophecy: Word Gifts of the Spirit among Catholic Pentecostals." *Review of Religious Research* 18: 134–147.
    1982   *Pentecostal Catholics: Power, Charisma, and Order in a Religious Movement.* Philadelphia: Temple University Press.
    1983   "Words of Power: Personal Empowerment and Healing." *Culture, Medicine, and Psychiatry* 7: 221–240.
    1988   *Ritual Healing in Suburban America.* New Brunswick: Rutgers University Press.
MacNutt, Francis
    1975   "Report from Nigeria." *New Covenant* 4: 8–12.
Malinowski, Bronislaw
    1935   *Coral Gardens and Their Magic.* London: Allen and Unwin.
Manning, Frank
    1983   *Celebration of Society: Perspective on Contemporary Cultural Performance.* Bowling Green: Bowling Green University Press.
Marcus, George E., and Michael M. J. Fischer
    1986   *Anthropology as Cultural Critique: An Experimental Moment in the Human Sciences.* Chicago: University of Chicago Press.
Martin, Ralph, ed.
    1976   *The Spirit and the Church.* New York: Paulist Press.

Marty, Martin
1976   *A Nation of Behavers.* Chicago: University of Chicago Press.
Mathy, Francis, S.J.
1992   "Charismatic Renewal Comes of Age." *Japan Missionary Bulletin* 46: 199–205.
Mauss, Marcel
1950   "Les Techniques du Corps." *Sociologie et Anthropologie.* Paris: Presses Universitares de France.
Mawn, Benedict
1975   "Testing the Spirits." Ph.D. dissertation, Boston University.
May, L. Carlisle
1956   "A Survey of Glossolalia and Related Phenomenon in Non-Christian Religions." *American Anthropologist* 58: 75–96.
Mead, George Herbert
1934   *Mind, Self, and Society.* Ed. Charles W. Morris. Chicago: University of Chicago Press.
Merleau-Ponty, Maurice
1962   *Phenomenology of Perception.* Trans. James Edie. Evanston: Northwestern University Press.
Milingo, Emmanuel
1984   *The World in Between: Christian Healing and Struggle for Spiritual Survival.* Maryknoll, N.Y.: Orbis Books.
Mills, C. Wright
1940   "Situated Actions and Vocabularies of Motives." *American Sociological Review* 5: 904–913.
Motley, M.
1981   "Linguistic Analysis of Glossolalia: Evidence of Unique Psycholinguistic Processing." *Communication Quarterly* 30: 18–27.
Needham, Rodney
1972   "Percussion and Transition." In William Lessa and Evon Vogt, eds., *Reader in Comparative Religion: An Anthropological Approach.* 3d ed. New York: Harper and Row.
Neitz, Mary Jo
1987   *Charisma and Community: A Study of Religion in American Culture.* New Brunswick: Transaction Publications.
New Catholic Encyclopedia
1967   S. V. Cursillo. Vol. 4. New York: McGraw-Hill.
Nicholas, R.
1973   "Social and Political Movements." *Annual Review of Anthropology* 2: 63–83.
Obeyesekere, Gananath
1981   *Medusa's Hair: An Essay on Personal Symbols and Religious Experience.* Chicago: University of Chicago Press.
1990   *The Work of Culture.* Chicago: University of Chicago Press.
O'Connor, Edward
1971   *The Pentecostal Movement in the Catholic Church.* Notre Dame: Ave Maria Press.

O'Dea, Thomas
 1968   *The Catholic Crisis.* Boston: Beacon.
Ojo, Matthews A.
 1988   "The Contextual Significance of the Charismatic Movements in Independent Nigeria." *Africa* 58: 175–192.
O'Neill, John
 1985   *Five Bodies: The Shape of Modern Society.* Ithaca: Cornell University Press.
Opler, Morris
 1945   "Themes as Dynamic Forces in Culture." *American Journal of Sociology* 51: 198–206.
Ortner, Sherry
 1984   "Theory in Anthropology Since the Sixties." *Comparative Studies of Society and History* 26: 105–145.
Otto, Rudolf
 1927   *The Idea of the Holy.* Trans. J. W. Harvey. New York: Oxford University Press.
Pace, Enzo
 1978   "Charismatics and the Political Presence of Catholics." *Social Compass* 25: 85–99.
Pattison, E. Mansell
 1968   "Behavioral Science Research on the Nature of Glossolalia." *Journal of the American Scientific Affiliation* 20: 73–86.
Peacock, James
 1968   *Rites of Modernization.* Chicago: University of Chicago Press.
Poewe, Karla
 1989   "On the Metonymic Structure of Religious Experiences: The Example of Charismatic Christianity." *Cultural Dynamics* 2: 361–380.
Poewe, Karla, ed.
 1994   *Charismatic Christianity as a Global Culture.* Columbia: University of South Carolina Press.
Poloma, Margaret
 1982   *The Charismatic Movement: Is There a New Pentecost?* Boston: Twayne.
Quebedoux, Richard
 1976   *The New Charismatics: The Origins, Development, and Significance of Neo-Pentecostalism.* Garden City: Doubleday.
 1983   *The New Charismatics II.* San Francisco: Harper and Row.
Rappaport, Roy A.
 1979   *Ecology, Meaning, and Religion.* Richmond: North Atlantic Books.
 1992   "Ritual, Time, and Eternity." *Zygon* 27: 5–30.
Ray, Benjamin
 1973   "Performative Utterances in African Ritual." *History of Religions* 13: 16–35.
Reny, Paul, and Jean Paul Rouleau
 1978   "Charismatiques et socio-politiques dans l'Eglise Catholique du Quebec." *Social Compass* 25: 125–169.

Ribeiro de Oliveira, Pedro A.
  1978   "Le Renouveau Charismatique au Bresil." *Social Compass* 25:
          37–42.
Richardson, James T.
  1973   "Psychological Interpretations of Glossolalia: A Reexamination of
          Research." *Journal for the Scientific Study of Religion* 12: 199–
          207.
Ricoeur, Paul
  1977   *The Rule of Metaphor.* Toronto: University of Toronto Press.
Robertson, Roland
  1992   *Globalization: Social Theory and Global Culture.* London: Sage.
Robertson, Roland, and JoAnn Chirico
  1985   "Humanity, Globalization, and Worldwide Religious Resurgence:
          A Theoretical Exploration." *Sociological Analysis* 46: 219–242.
Roelofs, Gerard
  1994   "Charismatic Christian Thought: Experience, Metonymy, and
          Routinization." In K. Poewe, ed., *Charismatic Christianity as a
          Global Culture.* Columbia: University of South Carolina Press. Pp.
          217–233.
Rosaldo, Michelle
  1973   "I Have Nothing to Hide: The Language of Ilongot Oratory."
          Language in Society 2: 193–223.
  1975   "It's All Uphill: The Creative Metaphors of Ilongot Magical
          Spells." In Mary Sanches and Ben Blount, eds., *Sociocultural Di-
          mensions of Language Use.* New York: Seminar Press. Pp. 177–
          203.
  1982   "The Things We Do with Words: Ilongot Speech Acts and Speech
          Acts Theory in Philosophy." *Language in Society* 11: 203–237.
Rose, Susan D.
  1987   "Women Warriors: The Negotiation of Gender in a Charismatic
          Community." *Social Analysis* 48: 245–258.
Roseman, Marina
  1990   "Head, Heart, Odor, and Shadow: The Structure of the Self, the
          Emotional World, and Ritual Performance among Senoi Temiar."
          Ethos 18: 227–250.
  1991   *Healing Sounds from the Malaysian Rainforest: Temiar Music and
          Medicine.* Berkeley, Los Angeles, and Oxford: University of Cali-
          fornia Press.
Samarin, William
  1972   *Tongues of Men and Angels: The Religious Language of Pentecostal-
          ism.* New York: Macmillan.
  1979   "Making Sense of Glossolalic Non-sense." In J. Fabian, ed., "Be-
          yond Charisma: Religious Movements as Discourse" (Special is-
          sue). *Social Research* 46: 88–105.
Samarin, William, ed.
  1976   *Language in Religious Practice.* Rowley: Newbury House.

Sangren, P. Steven
　1988　"Rhetoric and the Authority of Ethnography: 'Postmodernism' and the Social Reproduction of Texts." *Current Anthropology* 29: 405–435.

Sapir, Edward
　1961　"Anthropology and Psychiatry." In David G. Mandelbaum, ed., *Edward Sapir: Culture, Language, and Personality, Selected Essays.* Berkeley and Los Angeles: University of California Press.

Sapir, J. David
　1977　"The Anatomy of Metaphor." In J. David Sapir and J. C. Crocker, eds., *The Social Uses of Metaphor.* Philadelphia: University of Pennsylvania Press.

Sapir, J. David, and J. C. Crocker, eds.
　1977　*The Social Uses of Metaphor.* Philadelphia: University of Pennsylvania Press.

Scheff, Thomas
　1979　*Catharsis in Healing, Ritual, and Drama.* Berkeley, Los Angeles, and London: University of California Press.

Schieffelin, Edward L.
　1985　"Performance and the Cultural Construction of Reality." *American Ethnologist* 12: 707–724.

Schiffer, Irvine
　1973　*Charisma: A Psychoanalytic Look at Mass Society.* Toronto: University of Toronto Press.

Schutz, Alfred
　1970　*On Phenomenology and Social Relations.* Chicago: University of Chicago Press.

Schwartz, Nancy
　n.d.　"Inscribing a Whirlwind: Making Meanings in Legio Maria, an Independent African Church." Unpublished MS.

Searle, John
　1969　*Speech Acts.* Cambridge: Cambridge University Press.
　1979　*Expression and Meaning: Studies in the Theory of Speech Acts.* New York: Cambridge University Press.
　1983　*Intentionality: An Essay in the Philosophy of Mind.* Cambridge: Cambridge University Press.

Sennett, Richard
　1975　"Charismatic De-Legitimation: A Case Study." *Theory and Society* 2: 171–181.

Sequeira, Debra L.
　1994　"Gifts of Tongues and Healing: The Performance of Charismatic Renewal." *Text and Performance Quarterly* 14: 126–143.

Shils, Edward
　1975　*Center and Periphery: Essays in Macrosociology.* Chicago: University of Chicago Press.

Singer, Milton
  1958   "From the Guest Editor." *Journal of American Folklore* 71: 191–204.
  1972   *When a Great Tradition Modernizes.* New York: Praeger.
  1984   *Man's Glassy Essence: Explorations in Semiotic Anthropology.* Bloomington: Indiana University Press.
  1989   "Pronouns, Persons, and the Semiotic Self." In B. Lee and G. Urban, eds., *Signs, Self, and Society.* Berlin: Mouton de Gruyter. Pp. 229–296.

Smidt, Corwin
  1988   "Praise the Lord Politics: A Comparative Analysis of the Social Characteristics and Political Views of American Evangelical and Charismatic Christians." *Sociological Analysis* 50: 53–72.

Smith, M. Brewster
  1985   "The Metaphorical Basis of Selfhood." In A. Marsella, George DeVos, and F. Hsu, eds., *Culture and Self.* London: Tavistock. Pp. 56–88.

Sperber, Dan
  1974   *Le Symbolisme en General.* Paris: Hermann.
  1979   "La Pensee Symbolique est-elle pre-rationelle?" In M. Izard and P. Smith, *La Fonction Symbolique.* Paris: Gallimard.

Spiro, Melford
  1990   "On the Strange and the Familiar in Recent Anthropological Thought." In J. W. Stigler, R. A. Shweder, and G. Herdt, eds., *Cultural Psychology.* Cambridge: Cambridge University Press.

Strathern, Marilyn
  1987   "Out of Context: The Persuasive Fictions of Anthropology." *Current Anthropology* 28: 251–281.

Stromberg, Peter
  1993   *Language and Self-Transformation: A Study of the Christian Conversion Narrative.* Cambridge: Cambridge University Press.

Synan, Vinson
  1975   *Aspects of Pentecostal-Charismatic Origins.* Bridge Publications.
  1987   *Twentieth-Century Pentecostal Explosion.* Strang Communications Co.

Talavera, Carlos
  1976   "The Charismatic Renewal and Christian Social Commitment in Latin America." *New Covenant* 6: 2–3.

Tambiah, Stanley
  1968   "The Magical Power of Words." *Man* 3: 175–208. Reprinted in Tambiah, *Culture, Thought, and Social Action.* Cambridge: Harvard University Press, 1985. Pp. 17–59.
  1973   "Form and Meaning of Magical Acts." In R. Horton and R. Finnegan, eds., *Modes of Thought.* London: Faber and Faber. Pp. 199–229. Reprinted in Tambiah, *Culture, Thought, and Social Action.* Cambridge: Harvard University Press, 1985. Pp. 60–86.

1979   "A Performative Approach to Ritual." *Proceedings of the British Academy* 65: 113–169. Reprinted in Tambiah, *Culture, Thought, and Social Action*. Cambridge: Harvard University Press, 1985. Pp. 123–166.

1984   *The Buddhist Saints of the Forest and the Cult of Amulets: A Study in Charisma, Hagiography, Sectarianism, and Millennial Buddhism*. Cambridge: Cambridge University Press.

1985   *Culture, Thought, and Social Action: An Anthropological Perspective*. Cambridge: Harvard University Press.

Tedlock, Dennis, trans.

1986   *Popul Vuh: The Mayan Book of the Dawn of Life*. New York: Simon and Schuster.

Tiryakian, Edward A.

1995   "Collective Effervescence, Social Change and Charisma: Durkheim, Weber, and 1989." *International Sociology* 10: 269–281.

Trilling, Lionel

1972   *Sincerity and Authenticity*. Cambridge: Harvard University Press.

True, Michael

1977   "Four U.S. Catholic Churches." *National Catholic Reporter*, 27 May, 7–9.

Turner, Bryan S.

1984   *The Body and Society*. New York: Basil Blackwood.

Turner, Victor

1967   *The Forest of Symbols: Aspects of Ndembu Ritual*. Ithaca: Cornell University Press.

1969   *The Ritual Process: Structure and Anti-Structure*. Chicago: Aldine.

1974   *Dramas, Fields, and Metaphors: Symbolic Action in Human Society*. Ithaca: Cornell University Press.

Tyler, Stephen A.

1987   *The Unspeakable: Discourse, Dialogue, and Rhetoric in the Postmodern World*. Madison: University of Wisconsin Press.

Ugalde, Antonio

1974   *The Urbanization Process of a Poor Mexican Neighborhood*. Austin: Institute of Latin American Studies.

Urban, Greg

1989   "The 'I' of Discourse." In Benjamin Lee and Greg Urban, eds., *Signs, Self, and Society*. Berlin: Mouton de Gruyter. Pp. 27–51.

van der Leeuw, Gerardus

1938   *Religion in Essence and Manifestation*. Trans. J. E. Turner. London: Allen and Unwin.

Varenne, Herve

1986   "'Drop in Anytime': Community and Authenticity in American Everyday Life." In H. Varenne, ed., *Symbolizing America*. Lincoln: University of Nebraska Press. Pp. 209–228.

Vukonic, Boris

1992   "Medjugorje's Religion and Tourism Connection." *Annals of Tourism Research* 19: 79–91.

Wallace, Anthony F. C.
1957   "Revitalization Movements." *American Anthropologist* 58: 264–281.
Wallerstein, Immanuel
1977   *The Modern World-System*. New York: Academic Press.
Warner, R. Stephen
1988   *New Wine in Old Wineskins: Evangelicals and Liberals in a Small-Town Church*. Berkeley, Los Angeles, and London: University of California Press.
Weber, Max
1947   *The Theory of Social and Economic Organization*. Trans. A. M. Henderson and Talcott Parsons. New York: Free Press.
1958   *From Max Weber: Essays in Sociology*. Ed. H. Gerth and C. W. Mills. New York: Oxford University Press.
1963   *The Sociology of Religion*. Trans. Ephraim Fischoff. Boston: Beacon Press.
Westley, Frances R.
1977   "Searching for Surrender: A Catholic Charismatic Renewal Group's Attempt to Become Glossolalic." *American Behavioral Scientist* 20: 925–940.
Wheelock, Wade
1981   "A Taxonomy of Mantras in the New and Full-Moon Sacrifice." *History of Religions* 19: 349–369.
1982   "The Problem of Ritual Language: From Information to Situation." *Journal of the American Academy of Religion* 50: 49–71.
Willner, Ann Ruth
1968   *Charismatic Political Leadership: A Theory*. Research monograph no. 32. Princeton: Center of International Studies.
1984   *The Spellbinders: Charismatic Political Leadership*. New Haven: Yale University Press.
Wright, Sue Marie
1992   "Women and the Charismatic Community: Defining the Attraction." *Sociological Analysis* 53: S35–S49.
Wuthnow, Robert
1980   "World Order and Religious Movements." In A. Bergesen, ed., *Studies of the Modern World-System*. New York: Academic Press. Chap. 4.
Yoshimasa, Ikegami
1993   "Okinawan Shamanism and Charismatic Christianity." *Japan Christian Review* 59: 69–78.
Zablocki, Benjamin
1971   *The Joyful Community*. Baltimore: Penguin.
1980   *Alienation and Charisma: A Study of Contemporary American Communes*. New York: Free Press.
Zaner, Richard M.
1981   *The Context of Self: A Phenomenological Inquiry Using Medicine as a Clue*. Athens: Ohio University Press.

Zaretsky, Irving
   1974   "In the Beginning Was the Word: The Relationship of Language
           to Social Organization in Spiritualist Churches." In Irving Zaret-
           sky and Mark Leone, *Religious Movements in Contemporary
           America*. Princeton: Princeton University Press. Pp. 166–219.
Zylberberg, Jacques, and Jean-Paul Montminy
   1980   "Reproduction socio-politique et production symbolique: En-
           gagement et disengagement des Catholiques Charismatiques Que-
           becois." *Annual Review of Social Sciences of Religion* 4: 121–148.

Index

Designer: U.C. Press
Compositor: Prestige Ty
Text: 10/13 Galli
Display: Galliard
Printer & Binder: Braun-Brum